P9-CFX-012

Diagnostic and Remedial Reading

for Classroom and Clinic

Diagnostic and Remedial Reading

for Classroom and Clinic

Fifth Edition

Robert M. Wilson
University of Maryland

Craig J. Cleland
Mansfield University

Charles E. Merrill Publishing Company
A Bell & Howell Company
Columbus Toronto London Sydney

Published by
Charles E. Merrill Publishing Company
A Bell & Howell Company
Columbus, Ohio 43216

This book was set in Clarendon.
Production editor: Pamela D. Hedrick
Text designers: Cynthia Brunk and Tracey Dils
Cover designer: Cathy Watterson
Cover photograph: Jean Greenwald

Library of Congress Catalog Card Number: 84–42850
International Standard Book Number: 0–675–20285–X
Printed in the United States of America.
1 2 3 4 5 6 7 8 9 10—90 89 88 87 86 85

All photographs in the text by Jean Greenwald
except the following:

Photos by Irma McNeila: pages 15, 160, 188, 286,
307, 350, and 383.
Photo courtesy of Keystone View Company: page 66.
Photo from "The Voyage of Mimi," PBS,
copyright © 1984, Bank Street College of
Education: page 56.
Photo by Jerry Harvey: page 73.
Photo by Jan Smyth: page 247.
Photo by Strix Pix: page 324.
Photo copyright © C. Quinlan: page 388.
Photo courtesy Med-Tech Photographic Service,
Miami, Florida: page 395.

To my parents, Jack and Mary Cleland,
with love and appreciation.

C.J.C.

To my wife Marcia
for her years of support and
understanding that "sometimes" the
book comes first.

R.M.W.

Foreword

The authors of this text are cognizant of the fact that in any classroom where efficient approaches have been employed, the range of differences between good and poor readers will widen. Yet, they have endowed the reader with all they know about children experiencing difficulty in reaching their potential as readers. The better the teaching, the greater the differential between the two groups. While this book is primarily designed for the remedial and resource teacher, the classroom teacher will find tenets which, if employed efficiently, will serve to minimize the emergence of those children who might in an inappropriate learning climate experience difficulty in learning to read.

I found reading this text both enjoyable and rewarding. My only regret is that I am not in a classroom where I could employ the techniques and materials suggested, which assuredly would preclude the emergence of some children who might otherwise experience difficulty learning to read.

This is a revision of the fourth edition, which was a *hallmark* text. This fifth edition is a reflection of the authors' maturity as scholars, and their concern for the children who, through no fault of their own, have not advanced in reading skills according to their innate abilities. The fact that we see a number of children who experience difficulty in learning to read should not be construed as an indictment against the teaching profession. The authors have identified those factors which may contribute to the lack of adequate growth in reading skills. However, beyond this identification, they have suggested therapeutic measures which, if appropriately followed, will get the child on the proper developmental mainstream to successful growth in reading skills.

As I read this text, features of reorganization, change, and amplification became evident. The chapter on the handicapped reader has been moved from chapter 6 to 10, thereby giving the reader the full benefit of the contents of previous chapters; it is educationally sound that the reader benefit from the techniques presented on word identification and comprehension before reading this expanded chapter.

Scattered throughout the chapters are excellent photos with pithy captions readers can keep in mind as they grasp the obvious and subtle meanings presented by the authors. For instance: "Teachers should remember that different does not mean deficient." This gives an excellent backdrop for the first chapter, as well as "The classroom teacher is in the best position to notice potential problems." Others most worthy of note are "Skill instruction should always end with silent reading time"; "Next to the classroom teacher, parents can do more to prevent difficulties from arising than anyone else"; and "The interview between the parent and the specialist should start with information from the parent." These and others serve as condiments as readers ingest this text's scholarly material.

As with the fourth edition, most chapters have been amplified and extended to a significant degree, thereby giving the reader new insights into tests and techniques tried and validated in the reading clinic at the University of Maryland. Even a hurried perusal of the book will testify to the timeliness of the content of this book. The reorganization and expansion of the chapter on the handicapped child is of special interest.

As with other editions, the main emphasis is on *diagnostic* teaching. Viable suggestions are presented for refining the learning climate for all children, thus enabling them to reach their potentials in reading and language Arts. Comprehension, its nature, and ways of creating an optimal learning climate for students to master comprehension skills have been perplexing problems for years. Thus, a thoughtful reading of chapter 9 on comprehension development will enable readers to abstract relative data, thus enabling them to acquire a more sophisticated understanding of the reading process, resulting in improved means by which the teacher, whether novice or seasoned, can provide a learning environment conducive to the development and refinement of comprehension skills.

As has been implied throughout this foreword, the fifth edition is a marked improvement over other editions. It is a statement of the authors' scholarship and their understanding of the reading process. The authors submit proven methods by which optimal learning climates may be provided for the mature, reluctant, and handicapped reader. Perhaps these methods pose, by implication, more questions than they answer. But isn't a text such as this one designed to do that very thing? If, by reading this edition, readers are stimulated to test the doctrines and measures presented herein, they will have grown in professional stature, and such growth is the end result the authors intended.

I invite your purposeful and reflective reading of this text with the sincere hope that it will be as rewarding for you as it was for me.

Donald L. Cleland
University of Pittsburgh
Pittsburgh, PA
September 1, 1984

Preface

POINT OF VIEW

In many areas of scientific inquiry, authors exercise extraordinary care attempting to keep personal beliefs and biases from being reflected in their manuscripts. The field of education, however, requires that teachers blend knowledge, skill, compassion, intuition, and beliefs in making hundreds of informed professional judgments each day. It would be impossible (and undesirable) for teachers to divorce themselves from their personal beliefs. Likewise, our beliefs and biases have played a major part in writing this book, and we wish to state them at the outset in order to aid the reader in evaluating the ideas which will follow.

We believe that good teaching is necessarily diagnostic and prescriptive. It requires that teachers evaluate student strengths and needs and adapt instruction accordingly. In both diagnosis and remediation, we recognize the importance of focusing on student strengths in attempting to correct areas of weakness. This is particularly important for students who have experienced prolonged failure in reading, since reading failure breeds lower self-concepts, feelings of inadequacy, and avoidance behaviors. Throughout this text, ways of addressing skill deficits without slighting affective concerns have been presented.

Reading comprehension is emphasized in all chapters because we believe reading *is* comprehension. Because no single approach will be successful with every student, many different approaches, strategies, and techniques have been suggested. Finally, we believe that diagnostic and prescriptive teaching properly falls within the domain of the classroom teacher. We are inspired by the many fine teachers with whom we work.

AUDIENCE AND PURPOSE

This text has been written for pre-service and in-service teachers who wish to gain a fundamental knowledge of diagnostic and remedial reading. We have assumed that readers have some basic knowledge and experience in teaching developmental reading and a firm grounding in educational psychology. We have tried to present ideas in enough detail to equip teachers adequately, but have sought to avoid becoming overly technical or theoretical. In the final analysis, we hope that the reader will find this book practical.

ORGANIZATION AND FEATURES

Although selected chapters of the text may be read out of sequence, the book follows a logical progression to develop an understanding of the diagnostic and prescriptive process. In chapter one the reader is introduced to the difficulties encountered by poor readers, and the personal and societal consequences of those difficulties. This opening chapter also discusses two different approaches to diagnosis: attempting to identify causes or seeking to treat the symptoms of reading difficulties. Chapter two overviews the diagnostic sequence and presents several important principles for guiding diagnosis. Intellectual, physical, and emotional correlates to reading success are discussed in chapter three. Classroom and clinical diagnosis are examined in chapters four and five, respectively. In each case, diagnosis is presented as a decision-making process that will be altered to fit the needs of the individual student. Chapters six through nine examine the various aspects of reading remediation. These chapters contain many valuable approaches, strategies, techniques, and materials for working with students experiencing reading difficulties. The diagnostic and remedial reading needs of handicapped students are discussed in chapter ten. Working with these students often requires a multidisciplinary approach, and it is important that both classroom teachers and reading specialists be knowledgeable in ways of adapting instruction to meet the unique learning needs of handicapped students. Chapters eleven, twelve, and thirteen discuss ways of organizing the total school reading program in order to deliver needed services to students effectively. Once again, the emphasis is on a cooperative effort, combining teachers, resource people, administrators, and parents, to plan the best possible diagnostic and remedial reading program.

To aid readers in gaining a thorough understanding of the material, we have begun each chapter with a "Chapter Emphases" section. These sections introduce the featured topics and distill the major ideas into several succinct statements. Readers are encouraged to use these statements to gain an overview of each chapter prior to reading, and to use them after reading in reflecting on the ideas presented. Chapter summaries have been included to bring closure to the chapters; however, these summaries are not intended to take the place of a thoughtful and careful reading of the text. The glossary, which is found at the back of the text, has been revised and substantially expanded to aid the reader's understanding of unfamiliar and technical vocabulary.

The editorials, which were first introduced in the fourth edition, were well received. These short essays recount ways in which individual teachers and administrators have adapted some of the ideas contained in each chapter in working with their students. We view such a process as being at the heart of this text. Effective diagnostic teaching is not a single regimen of instruction; rather it is a dynamic process that evolves in the hands of skillful and caring teachers who expand on ideas and make them their own.

NEW IN THIS EDITION

Many sections of this book have been updated and expanded to keep pace with rapid change within the field of education. The chapters on intellectual, physical, and emotional diagnosis and on reading needs of handicapped students have been thoroughly rewritten and expanded. New information on a variety of topics has been added including child abuse, learning disabilities, English as a second language, single subject research, multidisciplinary teaming, sign language, and story grammars. High technology has commanded considerable attention from our schools, so up-to-date discussions of instructional uses of microcomputers and closed-captioned television are new to this edition. Descriptions of testing materials have been updated to include new tests on the market and current editions of familiar tests.

ADDITIONAL RESOURCES

Readers wishing to further research some of the topics contained in this text are directed to the "Suggested Readings" sections at the end of each chapter. These readings both expand on chapter topics and offer alternate points of view.

The appendices contain updated listings of commercial tests and remedial materials. Teachers should familiarize themselves with a wide variety of materials (both commercial and teacher made), so that students may be matched to appropriate materials.

We trust that this fifth edition will provide a strong foundation in the study of diagnostic and remedial reading. It is our sincere hope that this text will provide incentive for further study in this important and fascinating field.

Acknowledgments

We are grateful for the opportunities of working with a wonderful group of colleagues, both at our universities and in the local schools. These fine teachers contributed to this book through countless interactions, but most especially by the spirit in which they teach their students. We would also like to thank our students, both present and former, who themselves taught us much.

Several persons deserve special thanks for their work on this fifth edition. They are Sandy Kalavritino for her help in updating the appendices; Jan Hafer for helping us understand the values of signing with hearing students; Patricia Koskinen for introducing us to closed-captioned television; University of Maryland Reading Center staff members Bruce Brigham, Beth Davey, Jean Dreher, Linda Gambrell, and Ruth Garner for being stimulating colleagues who contributed ideas reflected throughout this book.

The work of many others who contributed to past editions of this text remain in this edition. They are Margery Berman, Robert Duffey, William Druckmiller, Ward Ewalt, Donald McFeeley, Louise Waynant, and Marcia Wilson.

Charles E. Merrill submitted this text's manuscript to many reviewers. Our thanks go to Richard Chambers, Boston University; Laveria F. Hutchison, University of Houston, central campus; Patricia Knoll, Slippery Rock University; Shirley Merlin, James Madison University; Maxine Perine, University of Michigan-Flint; William R. Powell, University of Florida; Victoria Risko, George Peabody College of Education, Vanderbilt University; Leo Schell, Kansas State University; and Barbara Walker, Eastern Montana College.

We also wish to thank Pamela Hedrick for her careful copy editing, and the many fine photographers who contributed to this edition.

Craig Cleland wishes to thank his wife Karen and daughter Allison for the loving support and patient understanding which they so selflessly gave.

Robert Wilson thanks his wife Marcia, and the rest of his family, Rick, Judy, and Rebecca; Jim, Nancy, Jennifer, and Andrea; and Sharon, Russell, and Matthew for their total support.

R.M.W.
College Park, Md.

C.J.C.
Mansfield, Pa.

Contents

4

5

1

When Students Encounter Difficulties

CHAPTER OUTLINE

CHAPTER EMPHASES

- ☐ Most low-achieving readers face problems that are largely out of their control.
- ☐ Many teachers face problems that are largely out of their control.
- ☐ By focusing on readers' strengths, reading skills are most effectively developed and refined.
- ☐ The effects of low achievement in reading are borne by some students throughout life.
- ☐ In diagnosis, both symptoms and causes of reading difficulties should be assessed.

Educators often refer to low-achieving readers as *problem readers, dyslexic, learning disabled,* or *language disabled.* Such labels give the impression that something is wrong with the reader. In most cases of low achievement in reading, however, the problem is not *within* the reader; it is *encountered by* the reader. The educator's responsibility is to help the reader overcome the problem. In this chapter, some of these problems will be examined, along with their implications for teaching students with reading difficulties.

PROBLEMS READERS ENCOUNTER

Prejudice

Some readers encounter discrimination because of race, sex, social status, appearance, or some other perceived difference. Readers of any age, but most certainly beginning readers, can quickly feel that something is wrong with them when they encounter prejudiced treatment. When a reader encounters prejudice and receives discriminatory treatment, the motivation to make the effort needed to learn to read is dampened.

Instruction

When instruction is geared to the achieving readers, those who are achieving slowly or not at all can be quickly left behind. Catching up can be difficult even when the spirit is there, and is almost impossible when the reader gets so far behind that the desire to try is gone.

Materials

When the materials used for instruction are too difficult, reading can be frustrating. Readers can quickly develop the attitude that reading is difficult and unrewarding.

Grouping

Readers who are assigned to a group in which all students are experiencing difficulty with reading can easily become discouraged. They all know that their group is proceeding at a slower pace than the others and may start to believe that they are, in fact, slow.

Labels

When another person labels a low-achieving reader, it is difficult for that reader to maintain a positive self-concept. Furthermore, such labels are difficult to remove.

Labeling can cause low self-esteem.

Humiliation

Public displays of the readers' progress are humiliating to the low-achieving readers. No amount of encouragement can motivate those readers who must sit in a classroom and see their names on a chart that indicates that they are not doing well.

Indeed, the list of problems students encounter seems endless. Others include uninterested parents, problems at home, difficulties with peer acceptance, and inappropriate instructional materials. The point is that some readers encounter serious problems that are not of their doing. When this happens, they are likely to get the message that something is wrong with them and become so discouraged that they stop trying. The labels, special groupings, and special instructional materials that result only confirm this message.

PROBLEMS TEACHERS ENCOUNTER

Teachers cannot be blamed for all the problems of low-achieving readers. Many teachers do not have the resources that would enable them to provide the type of instruction necessary for all readers to be successful.

Class Size

For no good reason, classrooms have been constructed to accommodate thirty or more students. To provide efficient instruction to over thirty students at one time is an extremely difficult task.

Pressure

Parents, administrators, supervisors, and many others can apply great amounts of pressure on teachers. One of the worst pressures is to satisfy others that all readers are reading up to grade level. This expectation is unreasonable, but the pressure does exist; consequently, many readers are placed in materials far too difficult for them to use successfully.

Nonteaching Duties

In some schools teachers must spend too much time making reports, managing lunch counts, supervising hall behavior, and other such nonteaching duties. While necessary, these duties often interfere with time that should be allotted for instruction.

Materials

Many teachers face teaching their students with inadequate or insufficient materials. Learning suffers in those cases in which the teacher cannot make adjustments to overcome the inadequacy of the materials provided.

Preparation

Some teachers enter their teaching careers with extremely poor preparation. Colleges and universities that do not provide prospective teachers with adequate instruction and experience in reading, language, measurements, and psychology must bear part of the responsibility for poor teaching. A desire to teach well will not make up for poor teacher preparation.

Testing

In some schools testing has reached an unbelievable level. Tests for intelligence, readiness, phonics, spelling, reading achievement, reading subskills, and arithmetic are often required at the beginning, midpoint, and end of the year. Some students spend most of the first month of the school year in testing situations. Not only does this cut into instructional time, but it can well lead to a series of frustrating experiences, especially for the low-achieving readers who do not test well.

PROBLEMS READERS TAKE WITH THEM TO SCHOOL

Some students have personal problems that cause them difficulty learning to read. These types of problems cause low achievement far less often than those just discussed. Illness, physical or emotional handicaps, and limited intellectual ability cause some readers great difficulty with the reading process. Public laws have pinpointed the need for placing such students in the most advantageous learning environment to enhance the development of their academic and social skills. Chapter 3 will provide more detailed information about the problems that some readers take with them to school.

RAMIFICATIONS OF LOW ACHIEVEMENT IN READING

Low achievers not only face obstacles that interfere with achievement, but they must also face the task of overcoming the difficulties that low achievement creates. These difficulties occur in school, with peers, and at home with their parents.

In School

In school, where students often are pressured to achieve grade level performance, low achievers are a source of never-ending disappointments. Whether the pressure is subtle or direct, the readers themselves and the teachers sense failure. Teachers may react by giving up on them or by feeling that they are indifferent, lazy, or troublesome. These reactions may be followed by punishment that usually fosters a hostile attitude between the teacher and these students who are ill-equipped to accept hostility. Frustrated by the rejection and the labels, these readers either cannot or will not work independently. As more and more frustrating materials are heaped on them, they are likely to busy themselves with noneducational activities and finally decide that learning is just not worth the effort. As they fall behind in their classroom work, they may be faced with the continual threat of repeating a grade. Excessive absenteeism and complete rejection of the school program are inevitable as they proceed through school, being promoted on the basis of age alone. The reading level of high school dropouts tells the rest of the story. Penty says, "More than three times as many poor readers as good readers dropped out of school before graduation."[1]

Not all low achievers become dropouts; however, the strained school-pupil relationship raises dropout probabilities. Furthermore, some students will drop out emotionally although they continue to attend class. Psychological dropouts can be found in every school; they generally create problems for both the teacher and their success-oriented peers. In either case, the situation is critical.

With Peers

Although peers often treat them kindly, it is not uncommon for low achievers to be teased and taunted. They are not with the "in" group and are often found alone at play as well as in the classroom. Other children are not likely to seek their ideas for committee work since their contributions are limited. Rejection encourages them to seek companionship with others in the "out" group. A further complication occurs with the repetition of a grade, which places them one year behind their peers. They clearly recognize that they do not "belong" either in the group with which they are placed or with their peers. If they continue to meet peer group disapproval, they become highly susceptible to undesirable influences, the consequence of which can be seen in the reports of police authorities who handle juvenile delinquents. Summarizing a study from the Children's Court in New York, Harris reports, "Among those tested . . . 76 percent were found to be two or more years retarded in reading, and more than half of those were disabled five or more years."[2] Of course, all low achievers do not turn to delinquent behavior, but continued rejection from peers makes these students more susceptible to undesirable influences.

With Parents

Parents become anxious when their children are not succeeding in school. They may try to solve the problem by pressuring their children to make greater efforts. This often means piling on more of the same type of frustrating work that makes them reject school. When such children balk, they are often compared to siblings or playmates. Seemingly ashamed of their children's behavior, parents often will look for someone to blame. Students are not blind to this shame and rejection, and they too will look for someone to blame. Even more important, they are likely to look elsewhere for that acceptance that all children need from their parents.

By observing these readers, it can be concluded that the ramifications of their difficulties are felt not only by them, but also by the school, peers, and family. Their inability to solve their own problem causes the future to look incurably bleak.

Into Adulthood

Further problems emerge as low achievers reach adulthood. Post high school educational options are usually limited, and job opportunities restricted to unskilled labor that requires little reading skill. The problem is a huge one. Right to Read reports that "an estimated 1.4 million adults report that they cannot read or write in any language. More than 20 million are functionally illiterate."[3] *Functional literacy* is defined as having sufficient reading skills for surviving in a reading-based society. Right to Read once funded sixty-seven literacy projects in thirty-five states at a cost of $5.2 million.[4] So, the problem is not just the reader's; our society must face it as a serious gap in the development of human potential and correct it where it is first encountered—in the schools.

From one point of view, it appears that the reading and writing skills of adults have improved over the years. Weber points out, on the other hand, that the reading demands of our society have increased more rapidly than have improvements in literacy.[5]

In 1969, Allen reported that 25 percent of the students in school are likely to experience frustration in reading.[6] By adjusting instructional programs so as to minimize problems that readers face, that percentage could be reduced drastically.

Not all of those who experience difficulty in learning to read follow the patterns discussed here. Many are capable of making reasonable adjustments, usually with the help of understanding teachers and parents. The problem facing these teachers and parents becomes determining a way to help students maintain self-esteem while adjustments are made to allow for successful learning.

TYPES OF READING DIFFICULTIES

Students experience difficulty with learning to read for various reasons. For purposes of categorization, these can be classified into three types of difficulties.

First, students may be experiencing difficulty with reading because for some reason they do not read as well as their abilities indicate they should. They should not be judged by their reading skills in relation to their grade levels in school, but, rather, in relation to their potentials. Slow students reading below their grade levels in school may experience learning difficulties, but this does not necessarily imply that they are retarded in the development of their reading skills. On the other hand, more able students, although reading well above their grade levels, may be considered low achievers when their reading levels fall short of their intellectual potentials. Accurate assessment of the reading levels and abilities of students lets the teacher determine whether readers are operating below their potentials. For example, in table 1–1 Ruth is operating consistently with her ability; Beth is not.

TABLE 1–1
Ability compared to reading

Student	Grade Placement	Ability Level	Reading Level
Ruth	4	3	3
Beth	4	6	3

Second, students may have difficulty when, with the exception of a specific skill deficiency, all measures of their reading are up to their levels of potential. They read satisfactorily in most situations, but they have a specific weakness. Although their deficiencies are difficult to locate because most of these students' reading skills appear normal, once located, they are readily corrected through the precise nature of the remediation necessary. For example, since many adults read slowly, they have a specific skill deficiency. They can perform on tests and seem to read very well, but their slow speeds make reading tiresome and reduce their inclinations to read. Students, while appearing to read well, also may have specific skill deficiencies with speed, oral reading fluency, word attack, comprehension, and study skills.

The third type of reading difficulty occurs when, in spite of reading skills consistent with their potential, students lack the desire to read. LeGrand-Brodsky reports that 6 percent of the American population over the age of sixteen do not read anything at all and that 30 percent are non-book readers.[7] Strang points to this problem when she says, "If the book is interesting they read it eagerly and with enjoyment. . . . Students confronted with drab, uninteresting reading material show the opposite pattern. They read reluctantly, they skip and skim so that they can get it over with more quickly."[8] These factors discourage students from using available skills and tend to dampen the desire to read. Lack of desire to read should be considered an important reading problem because often there is no other apparent difficulty. Clinic reports for such students show that they are frequently subject to ridicule and disciplinary action, since it is often assumed that there is no excuse for their poor reading habits. An understanding of the students' reaction to reading, however, will indicate the need for adjustment of the school situation to help develop a better attitude toward reading.

DIAGNOSE FOR SYMPTOMS OR CAUSES?

When it becomes apparent that a student has difficulty learning to read, a basic decision must be made. Should the diagnosis be based on a survey of the symptoms, or should it attempt to determine causation? Or should both be considered?

If the cause of the problem can be determined, it would certainly help in diagnosis. However, causation is often difficult (and many times impossible) to determine. For example, if the reader cannot organize information read for speedy recall, then strategies are available to correct that cause of the difficulty. If, however, the cause is some type of minimal brain dysfunction, it may never be diagnosed—not even in the best medical facility. To continue diagnosis and withhold instruction in such a case would be foolish. A look at the following examples may be helpful for understanding assessment of reading difficulties for symptoms and causes.

Example 1: Tony

Tony is not alone. He is one of many students across the country who, day after day, sits in an elementary school classroom in which he encounters reading situations well beyond his ability. Tony, however, may be ranked among the fortunate; his teacher, Mr. Coley, realizes that Tony cannot read well enough to do fifth-grade work. He quickly discovered that Tony could read accurately at the third-grade level and that he could read only with frustration at the fourth-grade level. He noticed that Tony refuses to attack unknown words, and, on the rare occasions when he does, his pronunciation is inaccurate.

He also noticed that Tony's reading is characterized by word pronunciation without fluency, that he is uncomfortable in the reading situation, and that he seems hindered by what the teacher calls "word reading." A quick check of the school records indicates that Tony is average in ability but that each year he seems less responsive to reading instruction.

After carefully considering the information available to him and his own analysis of Tony's reading performance in the classroom, Mr. Coley implemented a two-pronged program to supplement Tony's regular reading. First, he encouraged Tony to read for meaning by providing highly interesting reading material at a low level of difficulty; second, he taught essential phonic skills from the sight words that Tony knew. Realizing that Tony's problem might be deeply rooted, he asked for an evaluation by a reading specialist. This approach to the situation reflects an interested, informed classroom teacher analyzing a student's problem and attempting to correct it, while waiting for the services of the reading specialist.

When the reading specialist, Mrs. Ruark, saw Tony, she knew that a careful diagnosis would be essential. She realized that, among other things, she needed to have complete information concerning Tony's ability, his knowledge of word attack, his comprehension skills, and his emotional stability. Therefore, the specialist began thorough diagnosis to establish the cause of the problem; without such diagnosis she could not properly recommend a corrective program.

This example illustrates two different reactions to Tony's symptoms. The classroom teacher used a pattern of symptoms to implement a program of correction. The specialist realized that the problem could best be understood by a more careful study of the student. Both the classroom teacher and the reading specialist reacted appropriately. The teacher instituted a corrective program as quickly as possible after carefully considering the symptoms, his basic concern being the continuation of Tony's educational program. The specialist initiated a diagnostic program, attempting to determine the cause of Tony's difficulty in order to recommend the most appropriate program of remediation.

To clarify further the difference between symptoms and causes of reading difficulty, we define *symptoms* as those observable characteristics of a case that lead to an educated guess about a reader's difficulties. Teachers must look for reliable patterns of symptoms so that an intelligent program of correction can be initiated with minimal delay to the student's educational progress. Harris states that "many of the simpler difficulties in reading can be corrected by direct teaching of the missing skills, without an intensive search for reasons why the skills were not learned before."[9] Average classroom teachers lack the time, training, and materials to conduct thorough diagnoses. Instead they must observe students to find a reliable pattern of behavior on which to base correctional instruction. The procedure involves these three steps:

1. Examining observable symptoms, combined with available school data.
2. Forming a hypothesis based on the observed pattern.
3. Beginning instruction.

With the possibility of referral in mind, teachers must formulate and conduct the most effective corrective programs possible within the limitations of the classroom. Reference may be made to chapter 2 for patterns of symptoms applicable to the classroom diagnosis of readers.

Causation may be defined as those factors that, as a result of careful diagnosis, might be accurately identified as being responsible for the reading difficulty. Robinson presents data to support the multiple nature of causation in reading difficulties.[10] The reading specialist is acutely aware that, since there is rarely just one cause for a given problem, a careful examination for causation is necessary. Poor home environment, poor physical health, inadequate instruction, lack of instructional materials, personality disorders, and many other factors have been identified as interfering to some degree with the development of reading skills.

The reading specialist realizes that if causes can be determined, programs of prevention are possible; Robinson states, "Preventive measures can be planned intelligently only if causes of difficulty are understood."[11] For example, the cause in Tony's case could have been a lack of auditory discrimination skills for learning phonics or an overemphasis on isolated word drill in earlier grades. The reading specialist, after a diagnosis designed to determine causes, sets the groundwork for a program of correction. For Tony's teachers, this could involve revision of portions of the reading curriculum for all grades or establishment of a more thorough readiness program in the early grades. Thus, a careful diagnosis is the first step toward the implementation of a preventive program.

The reading specialist may also emphasize causation to find the most effective program of correction, especially with the more seriously retarded reader. Strang states, however, that diagnosis is complex and that causes are difficult to uncover.[12] If Tony's classroom teacher's program of correction is not effective, a more thorough diagnosis will be essential. This is the other function of the reading specialist. By her diagnosis she will be able to assist the classroom teacher with recommendations to implement the most effective program.

Just because specialists look for causation and classroom teachers for patterns of symptoms in no way prevents classroom teachers from being aware of possible implications and complications concerning the causes of reading problems; nor does it excuse them from gathering as much diagnostic information as possible. The more informed they become about causation, the more effective they will become in analyzing patterns of symptoms. As Harris states, they should be "able to carry out the simpler parts of a diagnostic study."[13] At the same time, teachers must instruct all students in their care, and this obligation generally precludes thorough diagnosis in any one case. It is also possible that after careful diagnosis the reading specialist will not yet be able to identify the causes of the student's reading difficulty. However, if causative factors can be determined, they can serve as an excellent springboard for corrective instruction.

Example 2: Bill

"Bill, how many times have I told you not to hold your book so close to your face?" Despite repeated efforts to have him hold his book at the proper distance, his teacher, Ms. Beath, noticed that Bill insisted on this type of visual adjustment. Recognizing this as a symptom of a visual disorder, she began to observe him more closely. She noticed unusual watering of the eyes and an unusual amount of blinking, especially after long sessions of seat work. In response she adjusted the classroom situation to allow Bill maximum visual comfort (i.e., regulating visual activities to shorter time periods and assuring Bill the most favorable lighting conditions). Realizing that he might have a serious problem, the teacher referred him to a vision specialist.

The teacher's job was to recognize the symptoms and react: first, by adjusting Bill's physical setting to enable him to perform as comfortably as possible; second, to refer him to a specialist for necessary visual correction.

Mr. Nash, the reading specialist, reacted to Bill differently. He saw the symptoms of the difficulty and realized that referral was a possibility. However, in this case, a visual screening test involving near-point vision[14] was administered first to determine whether Bill's problem was a visual disability or a bad habit.

In all physical problems, referral to the proper specialist is the appropriate action for personnel in education; therefore, the reading specialist and the classroom teacher considered referral of Bill for visual analysis. However, their approaches differed. Ms. Beath observed a pattern of symptoms that told her that there was a good possibility that impaired vision was interfering with Bill's educational progress. Since education is her first responsibility, the teacher's proper reaction was to adjust the educational climate so that Bill could operate as effectively as possible. She also was obligated to make a referral for visual analysis. The reading specialist, however, was not immediately confronted with Bill's day-to-day instruction; rather, he was obligated to determine as accurately as possible whether vision was the factor interfering with Bill's education. Thus, he attempted to screen Bill thoroughly before making recommendations for visual referral or for adjustment of the educational climate.

Example 3: Craig

Craig was known as a daydreamer. His present teacher, Ms. Wilhoyte, confirmed that his attention seemed to drift off, but also noticed that he did not participate in discussions and was unable to respond to questions about material he had just read. One day she called Craig to her desk and asked him to read orally for her. Craig did so with ease and fluency. She then asked him a series of questions and found that he disliked reading the stories in the reading book. He became very interested in discussing crabbing, his favorite activity. She found that his father took him crabbing every possible weekend on Chesapeake Bay.

Armed with the information that he had the necessary reading skills and was interested in crabbing, Ms. Wilhoyte conferred with the media specialist to find some books that might interest Craig. The media specialist had two books about crabbing, *Chesapeake* and *Beautiful Swimmers.* She also had several editions of a high school publication named *Skip Jack.* Craig was delighted with these books. He studied them carefully, without daydreaming. He still seemed bored by the other reading he was expected to do, so Ms. Wilhoyte referred him to a reading specialist, Mr. Fowler.

Mr. Fowler was impressed with Ms. Wilhoyte's efforts. Craig seemed open and eager to talk about crabbing. Mr. Fowler found that Craig was in command of his reading skills and could read almost anything he wanted. He also confirmed that Craig seemed to be interested only in crabbing. After giving Craig an interest survey, however, he found that Craig was also interested in boating, soccer, photography, and swimming. This information provided numerous opportunities to select materials that would interest him. Ms. Wilhoyte arranged with the media specialist for Craig to always have available at least one book on a topic of his interest. Once he found reading personally enjoyable and meaningful, Craig's general interest in learning improved.

Again the teacher and the reading specialist assisted each other to determine how to best help Craig. The reading specialist, with instruments available and time to use them, was able to find Craig's areas of interest. His recommendations to Ms. Wilhoyte helped her to get Craig on task. Once involved in interesting material, Craig found school stimulating and informative.

These three examples illustrate the roles of teachers and reading specialists in diagnosis. The relationship between causes and symptoms is a delicate and sometimes confusing one. Educators, however, must deal with both symptoms and causes as they work to provide the best educational climate for their students.

SCHOOL SCREENING COMMITTEES

Many schools have organized all resource personnel into screening committees to handle teacher referrals. These committees meet regularly with the principal to make decisions based on all diagnostic information available. A committee is likely to include specialists in reading, special education, language disabilities, and speech, as well as the school nurse, psychologist, and guidance counselor. Multiple input helps prevent diagnostic errors. The referring teacher usually attends. When determined that the child is handicapped, the parent is represented and actively participates in decision making.

When all available information has been considered, an educational plan is developed and responsibilities assigned to the most appropriate persons for instruction. Periodic reports of progress are reviewed by the committee. When the child is handicapped, the parent must approve the program by signing the plan. In these cases the plan is called an Individualized Education Program (IEP) and is mandated by federal legislation, Public Law 94–142.

Several advantages of screening committees have been noted:

1. The principal is informed of the specialists' work.
2. Principals maintain records so that parents can be informed of progress.
3. Specialists, working together, find less conflict of interest among themselves.
4. Overlapping of responsibilities diminishes.
5. The school's complete resources can be used to aid students in becoming successful learners.

In each case described on the preceding pages, screening committee action would have been appropriate and helpful.

SPECIAL CONSIDERATIONS

Two groups of students need special consideration as teachers plan for their instruction: those who come from cultures different from those of their teachers and those who have been identified as handicapped.

Cultural Differences

Much has been written about students who come from different cultural environments. Some claim these students come to school with a cultural handicap and thus label them *disadvantaged.* Others attribute their difficulty in school to their cultural background, implying not only differences but undesirable influence as well. Labels such as "disadvantaged" and "undesirable" hold no value for diagnosis and create assumptions that hurt students. Numerous children from poor families or minority groups *do* have difficulty in school. Students from restricted

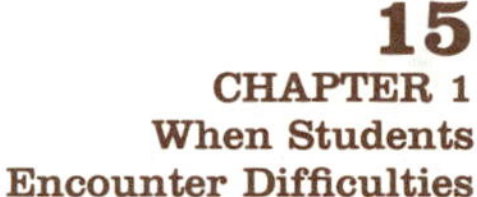

Teachers should remember that different does not mean deficient.

urban environments and isolated rural environments may be far below their peers in reading skills.

However, the environment alone cannot be blamed for the reading difficulty. Indeed, evidence also points to a lack of equal educational opportunity.[15] Yet culturally different children usually come to school with fully developed language and with wide backgrounds of experiences. Teachers must recognize culturally different students as having distinct and good cultures. They can be taught if their strengths are evaluated and their programs adjusted to those strengths. For example, since they can talk, they can be taught through the language-experience approach. Therefore, variations in technique are recommended on the basis of diagnosis. Alan Cohen claims, "Learning disability patterns as measured on clinic tests of disadvantaged retarded readers do not differ markedly from the learning disability patterns of middle-class children who are retarded readers."[16]

In research with low-income black students in inner-city schools, it has been found that almost all students produced larger portions of standard English than divergent English.[17] One or two divergent usages may attract teacher attention even when the student uses as many as twenty standard usages. Concentration on these uses may cause students to feel inadequate. Very low correlations exist between divergent usage and ability to listen to standard English. Apparently the user of divergent English has ample opportunities to listen to and comprehend standard English.

When working with these students, teachers should remember that *different* does not mean *deficient*. If we can accept a different dialect as a natural and effective means of communication, the students can develop positive self-concepts. Teaching with the dialect is not advocated; but teachers should accept dialect when communicating with students.

Teachers should be mindful of how the values of a divergent culture differ from their own. McDermott cites numerous instances of low achievement when ". . . a group in power educates the children of a minority group." He cites such factors as communication interferences, lack of understanding about motivation stimuli, and failure to understand cultural values.[18] If teacher-student relations are strained by a lack of understanding, then learning to read can become very difficult. Smith refers to it as *risk taking*.[19] If the readers do not believe that a given reading situation is worth the risk of embarrassment or humiliation, they will not try. One obvious solution is to make risk taking worthwhile: that is, no penalty or punishment for the risk taker who fails. Another solution is to study the different culture to enhance the possibilities of effective teacher-student relationships.

The third problem with teaching students from different cultures occurs when English is not the student's native language. The difficulty may involve a student completely unfamiliar with English and a teacher completely unfamiliar with the student's language, or a student skilled in, but not completely comfortable with, English. Unfortunately, the students in both situations respond to English slowly and create the false impression that they lack intelligence. Teachers in these situations need help, and volunteers or other teachers who know the child's native language must be used to bridge the gap until the student learns to communicate comfortably in English.

Students' strengths should always serve as the focus for instruction. Teachers must adopt strategies that involve acceptance of the student and that encourage risk taking.

Handicaps

Public Law 94–142 has mandated specific eduational processes for handicapped students. The mentally retarded, hearing impaired, deaf, speech impaired, visually impaired, seriously emotionally disturbed, deaf-blind, learning disabled, and multiple handicapped are all included in this provision.

As teachers diagnose and instruct the handicapped, they should give attention to the interpretation of the laws as they appear in the *Federal Register.*[20] Basically they call for full educational opportunities for all handicapped children. Individualized education programs must be written for each handicapped child. These programs are to be implemented in as normal a schooling situation as possible, and should be evaluated periodically.

Low achievers in reading may or may not be classified as handicapped. Reading is included under the term *specific reading disability,* when it can be determined that the low achievement in reading is due to some type of disorder in the psychological processes.

Teachers and reading specialists need to be familiar with all school policies that concern the handicapped—who makes the decisions, where everyone's responsibilities lie, and the established procedures for developing IEPs must be understood.

INSTRUCTING LOW-ACHIEVING READERS

Reading is a skill. Like all skills, it is developed and refined through practice. Practice activities must be planned so that the readers can complete them with speed, fluency, and accuracy. If they are designed to fit the readers' strengths, then the readers can refine their reading skills. If they are designed to their weaknesses, then it is likely that they will be practicing slow, nonfluent, inaccurate reading, and will be learning to read in that manner. Specifically teachers should:

1. Select reading material so that the readers encounter little difficulty understanding the material and are highly accurate. (See chapter 4 for details on acceptable word pronunciation criteria.)
2. Plan skill activities so that the student can achieve success with them. Low achievers have often had plenty of failures and need no more.
3. Plan alternative strategies for all activities. When the readers stall on an activity, help should be provided immediately or other activities initiated. Continued frustration with too difficult an activity leads to negative self-concept.
4. Encourage student decision making whenever possible. Students are likely to pick those activities that are of most interest to them and those that they can complete successfully.

Suggestions for activities designed to focus upon strengths will be provided in the various chapters that deal with instructional strategies.

The following selected authorities provide additional insight into the necessity of focusing on readers' strengths:

- ☐ Waetjen stresses that "if a person is accepted and valued and esteemed, he becomes an inquiring person and he actualizes himself."[21]
- ☐ Raths claims that "if our meanings gained from our experiences are frowned upon, are devalued—it constitutes a rejection of our life, and that is intolerable to everyone of us so treated. . . ."[22]
- ☐ Bowers and Soar say that "the more supportive the climate, the more the student is willing to share, the more learning will take place. . . ."[23]
- ☐ Cohen asserts, "tolerance for failure is best taught through providing a background of success that compensates for experienced failure. . . ."[24]
- ☐ Prescott stresses, "the unloved child who fails is in double jeopardy . . . to his insecurity is added the feeling of inadequacy, and he becomes more and more reluctant to try again with each failure."[25]
- ☐ Smith notes, ". . . attention is likely to be focused on what each child finds incomprehensible in order to 'challenge' them [*sic*] to further learning. Anything a child knows already is likely to be set aside as 'too easy.' Paradoxically, many reading materials are made intentionally meaningless. Obviously, in such cases there is no way in which children will be able to develop their ability to seek and identify meaning in text."[26]

While planning work for students experiencing reading difficulty, some time should be spent developing techniques that will help them develop a desire to learn. For example, the Institute for Research on Teaching reports that low achievers' major strategy for working independently at their seats is to get finished as quickly as possible.[27] They see that their teachers are pleased when they get finished with their work within a specified time period. These students do not monitor their efforts to determine if the activities make sense. They need techniques for self-monitoring their activities. For example, the teachers might ask these low achievers questions such as, "What did you learn from that activity?" "How will this type of work help you with your reading?" "Do you know why you were asked to do this work?" This procedure not only focuses on making sense of the work, but also forces the teachers to make sure seat work activities are meaningful.

If activities focus on strengths, school can be a happy, funfilled environment for all learners. As Margaret Mead put it, "If learning to read were seen as a path to individual triumphant success . . . each child's mastery of reading could, in its own way, be celebrated."[28]

SUMMARY

When students encounter difficulty learning to read, the reactions of teachers and parents are crucial. Attempts to apply more pressure, to label, and to focus on weaknesses can complicate the difficulty. Careful diagnosis followed by instruction that focuses on strengths can enable many low achievers to succeed and develop an "I can do it" self-concept.

NOTES

1. Ruth C. Penty, "Reading Ability and High School Dropouts," *Journal of the National Association of Women Deans and Counselors* (October 1959), 14.
2. Albert J. Harris, *How To Increase Reading Ability* (New York: David McKay Co., 1970), 3.
3. Albert J. Harris, "Adult Illiteracy: Changing the Statistics," *Reporting On Reading* 5, no. 3 (1979): 6.
4. Ibid.
5. R. Weber, "Adult Illiteracy in the United States," in *Toward a Literate Society*, ed. Carroll and Chall (New York: McGraw-Hill Book Co., 1975).
6. James Allen, "The Right to Read—Target for the Seventies" (Address given to the National Association of State Boards of Education, 23 Sept. 1969.)
7. Katherine LeGrand-Brodsky, "Hope for Reading in America: Practically Everyone Reads," *The Reading Teacher* 32, no. 8 (May 1979): 947.
8. Ruth Strang, *Diagnostic Teaching of Reading* (New York: McGraw-Hill Book Co., 1969), 106.
9. Harris, *How To Increase Reading Ability*, 201.
10. Helen M. Robinson, *Why Pupils Fail in Reading* (Chicago: The University of Chicago Press, 1946), 219.
11. Robinson, *Why Pupils Fail in Reading*, 219.
12. Strang, *Diagnostic Teaching of Reading*, 26.
13. Harris, *How To Increase Reading Ability*, 201.
14. Distance of eyes from print—twelve to fifteen inches.

15. James S. Coleman et al., *Equality of Educational Opportunity* (Washington, D.C.: U.S. Department of Health, Education, and Welfare, 1966).
16. S. Alan Cohen, "Cause vs. Treatment in Reading Achievement," *Journal of Learning Disabilities* (March 1970), 43.
17. Walter N. Gantt, Robert M. Wilson, and C. Mitchell Dayton, "An Initial Investigation of the Relationship Between Syntactical Divergency and the Listening Comprehension of Black Children," *Reading Research Quarterly* 10, no. 2 (1974–75): 193–208.
18. Ray P. McDermott, "The Ethnography of Speaking and Reading," in *Linguistic Theory,* ed. Roger Shuy (Newark, Del.: IRA, 1977), 153–85.
19. Frank Smith, *Understanding Reading,* 2d ed. (New York: Holt, Rinehart & Winston, 1978), 20.
20. *Federal Register* 42, no. 163 (Tuesday, August 23, 1977).
21. Walter B. Waetjen, "Facts about Learning," in *Readings in Curriculum,* ed. Glen Hass and Kimball Wiles (Boston: Allyn and Bacon, 1965), 243.
22. Louis E. Raths, "How Children Build Meaning," *Childhood Education* 31 (1954): 159–60.
23. Norman D. Bowers and Robert S. Soar, "Studies in Human Relations in the Teaching-Learning Process," *Evaluation of Laboratory Human Relations Training for Classroom Teachers* (Chapel Hill, N.C.: University of North Carolina Press, 1961), 111.
24. S. Alan Cohen, *Teach Them All To Read* (New York: Random House, 1969), 231.
25. Daniel A Prescott, *The Child in the Educative Process* (New York: McGraw-Hill Book Co., 1957), 359.
26. Frank Smith, *Understanding Reading,* 2d ed., 166.
27. Linda M. Anderson, "Student Responses to Seatwork," *Research Series no. 102,* Institute for Research on Teaching, Michigan State University, July 1981.
28. Margaret Mead, Editorial inside front cover, *The Reading Teacher* 28 (October 1974).

SUGGESTED READINGS

Bond, Guy L., Tinker, Miles A., Wasson, Barbara B., and Wasson, John B. *Reading Difficulties: Their Diagnosis and Correction,* 5th ed. Englewood Cliffs: Prentice-Hall, 1984. For another viewpoint of the disabled reader's characteristics, see chapter 3 of this text.

Denham, Carolyn and Lieberman, Ann, eds. *Time to Learn.* National Institute of Education, U.S. Dept. of Education, 1980. Reports the findings of a National Institute of Education funded study which examined the learning behaviors of students in the areas of reading and mathematics. Time spent on successful academic learning tasks resulted in superior student achievement, while time spent on unsuccessful activities interfered with student achievement.

Smith, Frank, *Understanding Reading,* 2d ed. New York: Holt, Rinehart & Winston, 1978. Essential text for those interested in understanding the processes in reading. Smith brings theory from a psycholinguistic base and applies it to various activities involved in learning to read.

Waetjen, Walter R., and Leeper, Robert R., eds. *Learning and Mental Health in the School.* Washington, D.C.: Association for Supervision and Curriculum Development, 1966. Several chapters by different authors illustrate the necessity for consideration of a theory behind instructional strategies. The writings of Syngg are especially valuable in regard to the necessity to focus on student strengths.

Editorial

Joseph G. Czarnecki
is a reading supervisor for the Arundle Public Schools, Arundle County, Maryland.

Mrs. Howell, a fourth grade teacher, entered the principal's office for the first School Screening Committee meeting of the year. She brought up John, an alert, but shy, boy from a school outside the county. No records from the previous school had arrived, but already Mrs. Howell was worried.

John functioned best in a basal with a stated readability of 2.5; his math and other subject work were on grade level; he was having considerable difficulty with both manuscript and cursive handwriting; he couldn't work independently and had a poor self-concept. John was being tutored at home three times a week in reading and handwriting. Mrs. Howell was pleased with John's progress in the basal, but would like to be able to pinpoint specific strengths and weaknesses in his reading and improve his weak self-concept.

After discussion, the group made these recommendations: (1) Expedite the transfer of records from John's previous school; (2) Obtain results from speech screening; (3) Proceed with an in-school assessment (Slosson Intelligence Test and Metropolitan Reading Achievement Test); (4) Ascertain the objectives of the after-school tutoring program; (5) Continue to gather information on strengths and weaknesses through the teacher's daily interactions with the student; (6) Try to have all information available at the next committee meeting.

The next meeting included the principal, the special education teacher, the school psychologist, the pupil personnel worker, and the nurse. They heard the following assessment results: Slosson Intelligence Test = 115, Metropolitan Achievement Test = 2.2. They then hypothesized that John had above average ability; was functioning at least two years below grade level in reading only; and demonstrated a low interest level and success in school tasks.

The group made the following recommendations: (1) Obtain permission to administer the WISC–R; (2) Administer an informal inventory to provide a more specific listing of reading strengths and weaknesses; (3) Invite parents in to obtain more information about John's perceptions of himself and school, his home situation, and his tutoring program; and (4) Be prepared to review all data and make final recommendations to school team and parents at the next meeting.

At the next meeting, both of John's parents were present. The school gave them all the assessment data: (1) WISC–R results indicated slightly above-average intelligence with a wide scatter in verbal and performance sections. Strengths were visual discrimination, visual sequencing, and common-sense reasoning. Weaknesses were in auditory and visual memory and spatial visualization; (2) The informal reading inventory detected strengths in using syntax clues and decoding both long vowels and vowel digraphs. Weaknesses were detected in using semantic clues, decoding blends and short vowels, and reading intact units of meaning (phrases, short sentences).

His parents said John's learning and attitude problems began when a younger brother was born. His mother said she had been working with John one hour per night (in addition to tutorial help) in reading and handwriting. She said these sessions were frustrating and often ended with John in tears.

The group concluded: (1) John's assessment information indicated a disability in one or more basic psychological processes. According to county and federal guidelines, this would qualify him for reading assistance from the special education teacher; (2) Since John felt incompetent and frustrated in reading tasks and because he would now be receiving specialized help in school, the home tutoring program should be terminated. Further the parent should replace mutually frustrating nightly work sessions with opportunities to go to a library or bookstore to select high-interest, low-readability material, followed by brief positive (10 to 15 minute) sessions to share what had been read or to have silent reading sessions. The parents were also involved in a discussion of factors and practices that contributed to feelings of self-worth, including opportunities to point out successes and strengths to John in both academic and non-academic situations; (3) The Individual Education Plan should include diagnostic lessons to supplement the existing information on strengths and weaknesses in both comprehension and word attack skills; assignment of tasks that reduced the amount of writing and provided high probability of success; close coordination with classroom teacher and parent; and scheduled review of program and progress in sixty days.

In the ensuing months, the teacher and parents detected gradual improvements in John's self-esteem, reading skills, and task completion. His parents reported a more positive home environment and growing interest in school.

Introduction to Diagnosis

CHAPTER OUTLINE

SOME MYTHS ABOUT DIAGNOSIS
TYPES OF DIAGNOSIS
STEPS IN DIAGNOSIS
DIAGNOSTIC PROCEDURES
SOURCES OF DATA
GUIDELINES FOR DIAGNOSIS
DIAGNOSIS FOR STRENGTHS

CHAPTER EMPHASES

- ☐ Three types of diagnosis are recommended for reading assessment.
- ☐ Assessment of the educational environment is as important as the assessment of the reader's behavior.
- ☐ Diagnosis for reader's strengths has many positive features.

If one views diagnosis from the medical viewpoint, an inaccurate perception of educational diagnosis will result. Medical diagnosis is the examination of the nature and circumstances of a diseased condition. However, the notion that a diseased condition causes educational achievement problems is misleading since such conditions are seldom the cause of low achievement. Educational diagnosis involves external factors such as the assessment of the home and school environments, the personal health and attitude of the learner, the learner's skills, and the self-report of the learner.

In the classroom, when first signs of difficulty appear, the readers' educational environment should first be examined. Is that environment a favorable one for the readers? Can easy-to-make changes remedy the situation so that learning efforts can become successful? If so, it is not necessary to involve the readers in testing activities; rather, teachers should make the changes and continue with instruction. For example, several readers may have had difficulty responding to instruction in a comprehension lesson. By evaluating the instructional procedures in the lesson, the teacher may find that several new terms were used in the text and that they were the key to understanding the material. While planning the lesson, the teacher may have missed the importance of these key terms and made no plans to introduce them. By going back and introducing the new terms, the teacher may note that the difficulty originally noticed has disappeared.

Teachers need to develop the habit of keeping careful notes about adjustments that prove effective. These notes can lead to a pattern of observed student behavior. When such patterns are observed again and again a reliable assessment of student behavior becomes possible. Occasional observations of a particular type of behavior create unreliable impressions.

SOME MYTHS ABOUT DIAGNOSIS

All teachers use diagnostic strategies as they teach. Teacher-made tests, observations of student behavior, and notations in student records are used by all teachers to assist in effectively understanding students. Some myths persist, however, that keep teachers from being as effective as they might be.

Myth 1 *Diagnosis requires the use of specially designed tests.* To the contrary, effective diagnosis is usually best achieved by using teacher observation and informal evaluations. The testing situation creates unnatural behavior with some students, and the results are often misleading.

Myth 2 *Group standardized tests provide useful information regarding individual students.* Not true. Group standardized test results provide very little useful information on individual students. (See discussion in chapter 4.)

Myth 3 *Diagnosis requires highly trained personnel.* As in all other areas of education, there are levels of competence in diagnosis. All teachers use diagnostic procedures every day. Those with more preparation are probably more efficient, but teaching requires continual assessment.

Myth 4 *Diagnosis calls for a case-study report.* Notes from diagnostic observations should be maintained, but in a very simple format. Case-study approaches are generally used when the reading difficulty is severe and a reading specialist has been asked to assist.

TYPES OF DIAGNOSIS

The preceding clarification of the myths often associated with diagnosis will aid in discussing the types of diagnostic procedures. Three types of diagnosis prove useful at various times.

Informal on-the-Spot Diagnosis

Teachers constantly assess student performances during instruction. Student responses to questions, writing activities, and general class participation provide teachers with informal input about student progress. When difficulties arise, adjustments are made on-the-spot to help students achieve success.

Classroom Diagnosis

If, after informal adjustments have been made, students continue to have difficulty, more structured diagnostic efforts may be initiated. Here the teacher sets some time aside to work individually with a student to determine what is causing the difficulty. Testing might be involved in an attempt to determine the degree of skill development in a given area. Those findings are checked against data in school records. Classroom instruction is adjusted to see if the student can then respond successfully.

Clinical Diagnosis

When instructional adjustments prove unsuccessful and reading difficulty increases, a reading specialist may be called in. Generally, clinical diagnosis will take place outside the classroom and involve specific skills testing and diagnostic lessons with the student. Recommendations for instructional adjustments will be made and the teacher and reading specialist can

Teachers should constantly assess student performance during instruction.

evaluate the success of those adjustments together. Clinical diagnosis may also involve specialists in speech therapy or special education, or involve the referral of the student to an outside diagnostic agency such as a college reading clinic.

STEPS IN DIAGNOSIS

The following steps will provide a better understanding of the relationships among the types of diagnosis.

The classroom teacher first makes an informal on-the-spot diagnosis and adjusts instruction accordingly. If this fails, the teacher conducts a classroom diagnosis and individualizes instruction. Should this step prove unsuccessful, the teacher can refer the student to a reading specialist for a more thorough analysis via clinical diagnosis. Instruction is then adjusted according to the recommendations of the specialist. If this entire sequence cannot produce the desired results, the necessity for other referrals is likely. A single failure will not likely cause the teacher to move immediately to the next type of diagnosis; rather, the teacher will use each diagnostic step thoroughly and repeatedly, if necessary, before moving to the next. Further, teachers should keep in mind that referral is possible at each step in diagnosis (see figure 2–1).

Since all effective learning relies on informal on-the-spot diagnosis and its subsequent follow-up, one might assume that this type of diagnosis will occur in good teaching. Further, the

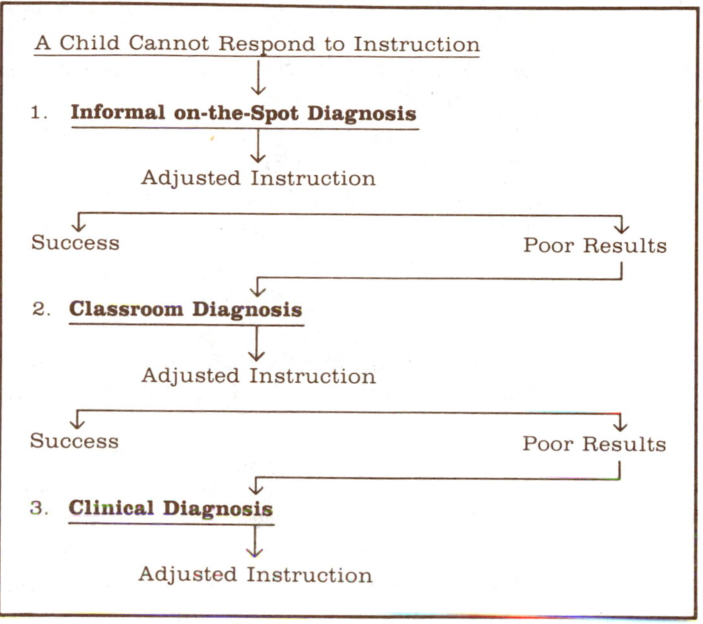

FIGURE 2–1
Steps in Diagnosis

types of diagnosis are not clearly separated; classroom teachers may use the reading specialists' clinical diagnostic tools when appropriate. All types of diagnosis include observation of the student to determine the effectiveness of the adjusted instruction.

DIAGNOSTIC PROCEDURES

Specific procedures will vary with the diagnosis of the difficulty and type of treatment initiated. The following treatment procedures for each type of diagnosis should be considered flexible.

Informal on-the-Spot Diagnosis

The procedures used with informal on-the-spot diagnosis are related to the instructional procedures used. When the teacher notices that students are experiencing difficulty, an immediate instructional adjustment is made in order to facilitate learning. Some examples may be helpful.

- ☐ Margi was not responding well to her teacher's questions on the material she had just read. When the teacher changed the type of question from literal to interpretive, Margi responded very well. Her teacher noted that Margi could deal better with the literal questions after she was successful with the interpretive ones.

- ☐ Roy read orally in a slow, choppy manner, only mispronouncing about one word out of fifteen. Roy was encouraged to practice reading orally to himself, and he soon became fluent and accurate.
- ☐ Catherine was the lowest achiever in her reading group. She knew it and so did the other students. Her self-concept as a reader was poor. Her teacher made arrangements for Catherine to tutor a young child in a lower grade for fifteen minutes each morning. This tutoring caused an instant change in Catherine's attitude because she felt worthwhile helping someone else.
- ☐ Joe was reading well in reading class but he seemed to encounter great difficulty doing assignments in his science text. His teacher noticed that the science text introduced a large number of new words at the beginning of each chapter. By using those new words in contexts that Joe could understand, his teacher could help him with those words before he encountered them on his own. His science assignments improved immediately.

Of course, informal on-the-spot diagnosis and its subsequent follow-up do not always work this nicely. At times, attempted adjustments miss their purpose, and the difficulty continues. If repeated informal on-the-spot adjustments do not have the desired effect, then a classroom diagnosis, allowing for a more careful look into the factors causing the difficulty, becomes necessary.

Classroom Diagnosis

Classroom diagnosis entails a more formal assessment than does informal on-the-spot diagnosis. When students are in a failure pattern and informal adjustments do not help, carefully planned classroom observation and testing become necessary.

Procedures for classroom diagnosis include the following.

Identification. The classroom teacher is in the best position to notice potential problem areas. In this way, classroom diagnosis is actually underway by the time the student's problems have been identified; informal on-the-spot diagnosis has previously established certain diagnostic information that the teacher will use in classroom diagnosis.

The tendency for educators to wait until a problem is well developed before acting on it can be avoided by increased atten-

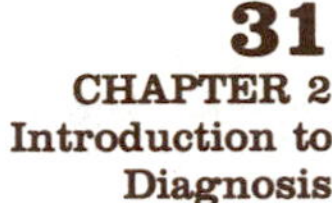

The classroom teacher is in the best position to notice potential problem areas.

tion to classroom diagnosis at all age levels, including first grade. Through immediate attention to the first symptoms of reading difficulty the number of low-achieving readers can be reduced.

Assessment of the Educational Environment. The classroom teacher should make notes on such factors as the instructional strategies, grouping and seating arrangements, and materials used in the classroom. These factors should then be carefully examined to determine if modifying any of them would create a more successful learning environment.

Gathering Available Data. The classroom teacher next searches for information about the student and organizes it for consideration during the diagnosis. School records, interviews with past teachers, health reports, and other sources provide considerable data concerning the student's past development, successes, and failures. Notes made during informal on-the-spot diagnosis can prove extremely useful, particularly if the teacher making the classroom diagnosis did not conduct the previous one. Other sources of data include:

- ☐ *Limited testing.* When necessary, classroom teachers may administer and interpret tests designed to provide information in the difficulty area. Testing, of course, is limited by the time that teachers have for individual testing as well as their skill in using the instruments.

- *Direct observations.* Using the information available at this stage of classroom diagnosis, teachers should observe students in various reading situations with particular attention to verifying other diagnostic information. When observations and other data complement previous findings, the next step can be taken. When they do not support each other, there is a need for reevaluation, more observation, possible testing, and new conclusions.

Formulation of Hypotheses. From the patterns observed, the teacher will form hypotheses about adjusting instruction for the group or individual and about the possibility of referral. By looking for patterns, one reduces the chances of error often caused by relying on one observation or test score.

Adjusting Instruction. Once instructional hypotheses have been formed, teachers adjust instruction and test each hypothesis. For example, if the diagnostic hypothesis is "Jack will read more fluently if I reduce the level of difficulty by one grade level," then the teacher finds materials at the level indicated and places Jack in a learning situation. If, in fact, Jack can read fluently in these new materials, then the hypothesis is accepted. If he cannot, then it is back to the diagnostic procedures to develop another hypothesis.

Classroom diagnosis *is* time-consuming. However, teachers can minimize the amount of time needed if they use existing records, conduct the diagnosis during times other students are occupied, and collect diagnostic data daily over a period of time. As teachers gain proficiency with diagnostic procedures, they will find them less time-consuming. Figure 2–2 summarizes the steps in classroom diagnosis.

Clinical Diagnosis

Clinical procedures may be implemented through individual study of the student outside of the classroom. These procedures are listed here and described in figure 2–3.

Referral. The reading specialist has the advantage of starting to work with a student who has been referred. The classroom teacher has either attempted classroom diagnosis or determined that the student needs clinical diagnosis. All available infor-

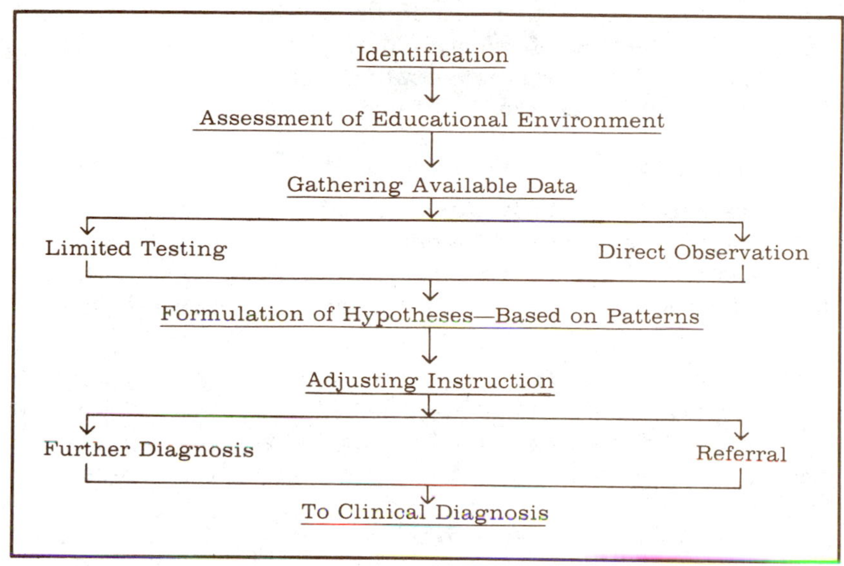

FIGURE 2–2
Procedures for Classroom Diagnosis

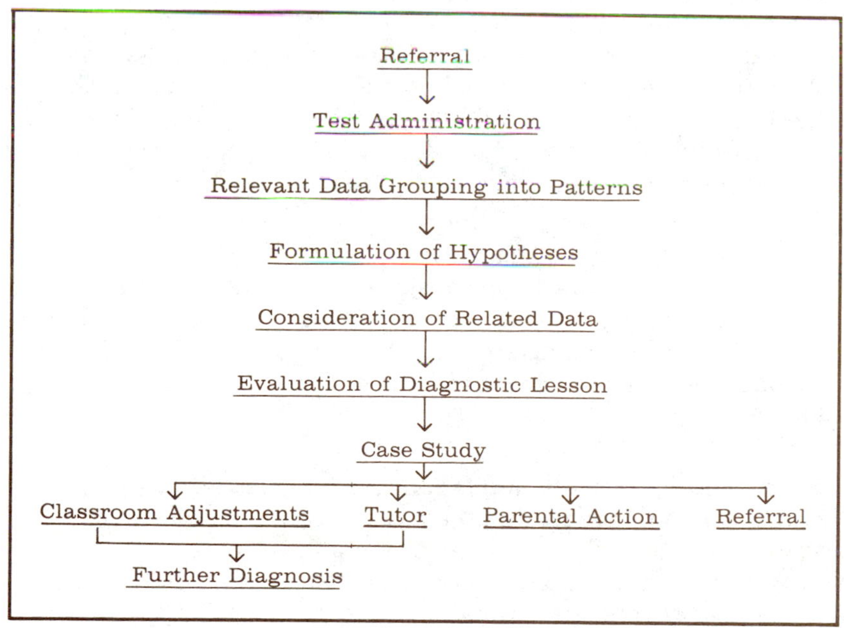

FIGURE 2–3
Procedures for Clinical Diagnosis

mation about the student should be forwarded to the reading specialist at the time of referral. Many times the referral comes from parents. The specialist should consult with the classroom teacher to obtain as much information as possible in these cases.

Administration of a Battery of Tests. Using a tentative evaluation of a student and that student's needs, the reading specialist proceeds with the administration and analysis of a battery of tests to gather objective data on the student's reading skills.

Observation of Patterns. The reading specialist carefully observes behavior patterns during the testing. Combined with test scores and the specialist's analysis of the reading responses on tests administered, these observations will be useful in grouping relevant data into meaningful patterns.

Formulation of Hypotheses. From the observable patterns, the reading specialist then forms tentative hypotheses concerning the causes of the problem.

Consideration of Related Data. Once the hypotheses have been formed, the specialist weighs related data from parent and teacher conferences, school records, and previous diagnostic results. When the specialist finds that the related data supports the hypotheses, the diagnosis gains validity; at other times conflicting information forces reconsideration of the original hypotheses. In many cases, further testing or reexamination of test results is needed for clearer insights into the difficulty.

Evaluation through Diagnostic Lessons. The lessons conducted during a clinical diagnosis are brief and specifically related to the diagnostic hypotheses. Parts of the lessons should be directed to the student's strengths and parts to the student's weaknesses. Short-term diagnostic sessions provide further validation of the diagnosis.

Formulation of Recommendations and Referrals. After consideration of all relevant data, the reading specialist develops a case study that includes recommendations for adjustments of school programs, remedial treatment, parental action, further testing, or necessary referral.

The time needed for effective clinical diagnosis will vary with the age of the student, the effectiveness of classroom diagnosis, and practical matters such as clinician load. Normally, a clinical diagnosis should take one to two hours. In some cases, however, much more time is needed due to the involved nature of the case.

While clinical diagnosis has the advantage of highly individualized study and the use of precise instruments for evaluation by a carefully trained person, it has the following limitations:

- ☐ The clinic situation involves one-to-one interaction, while the classroom situation necessitates working with others. Thus, the behaviors of students in the two situations will probably differ.
- ☐ Since the teacher and the reading specialist are two different people, students will naturally react to each in a different way.
- ☐ After the reading specialist checks diagnosis with the diagnostic teaching lessons, the teacher may be unable to make necessary instructional adjustments.

For these reasons, the specialist should discuss the results of the diagnosis with the teacher, in addition to providing a written report. To illustrate the techniques recommended in the report, the reading specialist should offer to work with the student in the classroom for one or two lessons.

Clinical diagnosis often establishes a need for further action for the reading specialist, such as the following:

- ☐ Reporting the results of the clinical diagnosis and their interpretation to a screening committee.
- ☐ Reporting and interpreting the results of the diagnosis to parents.
- ☐ Preparing teachers to use special instructional techniques through in-service sessions.
- ☐ Consulting with medical or psychological personnel when referrals are made.
- ☐ Instructing the student for a period of time when individual or small-group attention is needed.

SOURCES OF DATA

While conducting any type of diagnosis, teachers should be aware of the available sources of data. At times one can become so involved with testing that other sources of data are overlooked. Some of the other sources, however, are much more useful than test results.

Informal on-the-spot diagnosis relies heavily on observed student behavior, school records, and reports from others. Since most of this diagnosis takes place during instructional time, the only test results available are from teacher-made tests, which are normally used to assess the effectiveness of the instruction.

Classroom diagnosis relies on school records, observations of teachers, reports from past teachers, interviews with students and parents, records from home visits, and test results. In classroom diagnosis, the teacher also obtains important data from the assessment of the educational environment.

Data for clinical diagnosis include reports from psychologists, medical personnel, or speech therapists. Other useful data come from interviews and questionnaires, diagnostic lessons, and tests. In clinical diagnosis heavy reliance is placed on a variety of testing instruments. Physical screening tests, intelligence tests, attitude surveys, and a host of reading tests are available for use in clinical diagnosis.

In each type of diagnosis, information from the student can be very useful, though it is often overlooked. How does the reader see the difficulty? What are the reader's perceived strengths? What is his or her perception of the learning environment? These types of data from readers are useful for planning instructional programs.

GUIDELINES FOR DIAGNOSIS

Several guidelines should be kept in mind when entering into diagnostic activities. While they may not be applicable in every instance, failure to use them when indicated can drastically interfere with student performance.

Establish Rapport

Students will perform best in a relaxed environment where a good rapport with the supervisor present encourages a cooperative attitude. The classroom teacher, through daily contact with students, has a better opportunity for establishing this kind of situation than a reading specialist, who meets with students outside of the normal classroom setting. Both, however, should strive to make students comfortable so that inhibitions do not affect performance, thus resulting in inaccurate assessment.

Provide Individual Study

Since many group testing situations produce unreliable results, individual study is essential. Individual sessions with students reduce those competitive activities that are frustrating to low-achieving readers.

Provide Group Study

Evaluation of students as they interact can offer useful diagnostic insights. Diagnostic results that come from data collected during individual study only are often difficult to apply. Students' reactions in groups may be quite different from their performances during individual study. Both types of data are needed for a thorough diagnosis.

Test, Don't Teach

By resisting the urge to help students when they experience difficulty during testing, the tester can assure more accurate data. Comments such as "That was almost correct—try again" can serve to encourage some students and discourage others. This guideline applies most directly to clinical diagnosis and test administration. Of course, diagnostic teaching activities involve normal student-teacher interactions.

Maintain Efficiency

An efficient diagnosis includes only tests and observations likely to help the examiner determine the difficulty. There is a tendency to rely on a systematic diagnostic procedure regardless of the needs of the student, creating pointless testing situations which are often frustrating experiences. An efficient diagnosis, then, includes those measures needed by the educator to arrive at a solution; it eliminates those of questionable value to the objectives of the diagnosis.

Search for Patterns of Performance

Single observations of a reader's performance can lead to unreliable conclusions. A consistent pattern of performance over time, or over different testing situations, increases the probability that the results are a true indication of the reader's skills. For example, it would be best to check the student's reading comprehension skills with several passages at the same level. If a student scores well on one and poorly on another, it is difficult to determine whether the difficulty lies in the passage or the reader's comprehension. By checking on a few more passages, the teacher could confirm or reject that suspicion with more confidence.

DIAGNOSIS FOR STRENGTHS

Diagnostic reports of students experiencing reading difficulties usually focus on areas of weakness, with no mention of strengths. However, since instructional adjustments must start with areas of strengths, deliberate effort should be given to uncovering them in diagnosis. What students know is important. What they do not know can be assumed from what they do know. As the University of Maryland reading clinic moved toward strengths diagnosis, educators receiving the positive report felt better about the reports and the students. Parents also appreciated the new form of the reports since many other interactions with educational agencies had stressed the negative aspects of their child's scholastic performance. The opportunity to discuss diagnostic results with the students in terms of their skill strengths was perhaps the most important result. Such conferences with students left them feeling worthwhile.

When diagnosing for strengths, teachers must look for student performances that demonstrate comfort, fluency, accuracy, and speed. These can be observed during instruction or testing. Satisfactory test scores evaluated without these characteristics of performance may be misleading in attempts to identify strengths. The following are examples of diagnostic activities for strengths:

- ☐ Instead of listing skill weaknesses on a phonics test, list those skills that were noted as accurate and well developed.
- ☐ Determine comprehension levels at which students can respond with comfort and accuracy. Report those levels as suggested starting levels for instruction.
- ☐ Note skills demonstrated in oral reading and report them as skills that should be practiced and reinforced.
- ☐ Ask the student to indicate his or her perceived reading strengths. Then set up a diagnostic situation in which those strengths can be demonstrated.

Diagnosis for strengths does not preclude noting areas in need of attention; however, it does add a pleasant and positive dimension to diagnosis.

SUMMARY

The three types of diagnosis discussed in this chapter have an important place in reading diagnosis. Each uses data that are available and procedures that are effective in that type of diagnosis. Guidelines for diagnosis are provided to help teachers avoid some of the activities that interfere with effective diagnosis. Diagnosing for strengths is recommended.

SUGGESTED READINGS

Cheek, Earl H., Jr., and Cheek, Martha C., *Diagnostic-Prescriptive Reading Instruction.* Dubuque, Iowa: William C. Brown, 1980. Chapter 2 provides suggestions for the teacher's role in diagnosis and prescription. Chapter 15 contains a discussion of how all the parts of diagnostic-prescriptive teaching fit together.

McGinnis, Dorothy J. and Smith, Dorothy E., *Analyzing and Treating Reading Problems.* New York: MacMillan, 1982. Chapter 4 discusses the classroom teacher's role in analyzing and treating reading problems, while chapter 5 explores the reading specialist's role in diagnosis of reading problems.

Rupley, William H. and Blair, Timothy R., *Reading Diagnosis and Remediation.* Chicago: Rand McNally, 1979. The authors make a strong case in chapter 6 for a study of the educational environment. Included is a teacher effort scale that should be of interest if you plan to assess the environment.

Editorial

Patricia Alexander
is an assistant professor of education at Texas A&M University.

I've learned two important and contrasting bits of knowledge about reading diagnosis. First, diagnosis is essential to good teaching. We must provide students with appropriate and meaningful instruction based on the learner's strengths as well as needs. Diagnosis provides this information.

Secondly, I've found that many teachers feel alienated by and isolated from the diagnostic process. They think of diagnosis as formal tests administered in a formal setting by someone unknown and unaccustomed to classroom realities. These teachers don't realize diagnosis is an inherent part of reading instruction that benefits both the learner and teacher.

We need to destroy these myths. Diagnosis is, indeed, more than formal tests, and, without question, can and should be performed by classroom teachers as well as trained clinicians. It is also important for those engaged in reading instruction to realize that certain learning situations, such as oral reading and questioning, are natural opportunities for effective diagnosis.

Further, teachers need to know that while there are times when informal or classroom diagnosis is appropriate, there are also instances when more formal, clinical diagnosis is warranted. Those involved in teaching reading should learn about the diagnostic options available to them, and the circumstances under which these options should be applied.

One of the threads of similarity that runs through all these diagnostic procedures, whether informal, classroom, or clinic, is the emphasis placed on the learner's strengths. Such a diagnostic focus should be applauded. For too long I have seen diagnosis perceived as a forum from which only the problems of the reader have been reported extensively. The results of this limited view of diagnosis have been very negative feelings and reactions on the part of parents, teachers and learners. It is time we extolled the strengths of learners and used their strengths as our instructional foundation. This does not mean we ignore a learner's needs, only that we approach them by way of that learner's strengths.

Finally, as so aptly stated by the authors, "It should be remembered that the student who is the object of the diagnosis is more important than the accumulation of test scores." All those entrusted with the education of others must comprehend diagnosis as the means by which they can help the learner achieve success within the classroom, a success rightly deserved.

Intellectual, Physical, and Emotional Diagnosis

CHAPTER OUTLINE

CHAPTER EMPHASES

- ☐ An understanding of the role of intelligence and the limitations of intelligence testing is critical in reading diagnosis.
- ☐ Realistic goals can be set when students are measured in terms of their expectancy rather than their grade level placement.
- ☐ Physical factors influence reading growth.
- ☐ Symptoms of emotional disturbances can both cause and be the effect of reading difficulties.
- ☐ Students benefit when teachers make informed referrals.

Reading is not an isolated behavior. It encompasses intellectual, physical, and emotional aspects within the reader. In making an accurate reading diagnosis, student functioning in these areas should be assessed. Diagnosis of intellectual, physical, and emotional problems may require the assistance of professionals with specialized training outside the reading field. However, classroom teachers and reading specialists should be knowledgeable concerning these kinds of diagnoses because teachers are ultimately responsible for their students' daily instruction.

INTELLECTUAL DIAGNOSIS

Estimates of intellectual ability are useful in diagnosing reading difficulties. An estimate of the student's ability can assist the teacher in setting realistic instructional goals. Such goals should be flexible, however, because even the best measures of intelligence are subject to error. Therefore, recognition of the advantages and limitations of measures of intelligence is essential for interpretation of such data in a reading diagnosis.

Low intelligence should not be considered the cause of reading difficulties. In fact, intelligence is related to reading difficulties only in relation to the ability of the school to adjust the educational program to the abilities of various types of students. Intelligence—or lack of it—does not prohibit students from reading up to their potential; rather, school programs, which are often geared to the majority of average students, do not give ample consideration to those at the extremes (intellectually able and less able students), and so difficulty results. The inability of a given situation to provide the necessary adjustments often causes these students to become low achievers. Ross suggests:

> If a child fails to learn, look for a different way of teaching. Don't look for something that is wrong inside the child. Chances are that your teaching method and the child's way of learning are out of phase. Neither the child nor you are to blame for that, but you *can* be blamed if you don't try something else.[1]

Although accurate measures of intellectual performance are essential to the diagnosis of reading difficulties, the intelligence of a given student per se seldom causes the student's failure to learn.

Complications of Intellectual Testing

The educator's tendency to misuse test scores by grasping at high or low scores as the basis for division between low-achieving, average, and above-average readers complicates the use of intelligence tests. How many students have been mislabeled by these tests can only be estimated. A brief review of some of the limitations of intelligence tests will indicate the difficulties encountered when such data are used in diagnosis.

Definitions of Intelligence. Measurement of intellectual ability is complicated by the lack of agreement among authorities as to what constitutes intelligence. To some theorists, intelligence is the ability to think abstractly, while others define it as an individual's learning rate. Still others view intelligence as an individual's ability to adapt to novel situations.[2] With such a lack of agreement about the definition of intelligence, it is not surprising that intelligence tests differ widely in the abilities that they assess. Pragmatically, intelligence can be defined as performance on a given intelligence test.

Reliability. Has the test measured consistently? Has the test measured by chance? If students were to retake the test, would they obtain the same scores? All tests are subject to error; therefore, most test constructors provide information about a test's error factor in the user's guide. Two types of error factors commonly reported are *reliability coefficient* and *standard error of measurement.* Reliability coefficients are usually reported in decimals (such as .93). Reliability coefficients below the .90 level cause concern about test reliability. Test reliability is usually determined by one or more of the following four methods:[3]

1. *Test-retest,* where students take the same test more than once and results are compared.
2. *Parallel forms,* where student performance on alternate test forms is compared (i.e., Form A and Form B).
3. *Split-test,* where total test reliability is estimated from student performance on test halves. (Reliability coefficients obtained by the split-test method are generally higher than those found by the other methods.[4])
4. *Item data,* where the consistency of student responses to single items is compared.

The standard error of measurement is related to test reliability. While the reliability coefficient represents the testing instrument's freedom from error, the standard error of measurement denotes the extent to which error does exist in a test score. It tells the amount a student's obtained score might be expected to vary from that student's hypothetical true score. Suppose Bill obtained a mental age of 9.5 years on a test which had a standard error of measurement of .4 years. If Bill were to take the test repeatedly, he would be expected to score somewhere between 9.1 and 9.9 years about two-thirds of the time. Errors of measurement are greater for students who score very high or very low than for those scoring in the middle or average ranges of the test.

Validity. Does a test measure what it purports to measure? How well does an intelligence test actually measure intelligence? Of the many dimensions that intelligence must surely have, most tests measure only a few; some measure only one. Presumably, the most prominent aspects of intelligence have been included in the best constructed tests. Some tests, however, purport to measure more than can reasonably be expected. Listening comprehension, for example, is sometimes considered a significant aspect of intelligence. If a test of listening comprehension reports a student's score in mental age, however, such a score would be misleading, since mental age constitutes more than the ability to listen and understand. Another complication arises when a given test requires specifically learned skills, such as reading. The test's validity is weakened because the test score also measures the reading achievement of the test taker.

Most test constructors attempt to establish the validity of their measure by comparing the results of their test with another test, usually one of established reputation. This is called *concurrent validity.* A measure may also be valid if the content of the test represents an adequate sampling of the knowledge and skills it is designed to measure. This is called *content validity.* A test is said to have *predictive validity* if that test score can be used to predict some future achievement with accuracy.

Concurrent validity is reported by means of a validity coefficient. These figures usually appear as decimals (such as .70). For purposes of interpretation the decimal must be squared (.49) to find the percent (49 percent) of the variance measured, in common, by each test. Bartz presents a "rule of thumb" for interpretation of validity coefficients when he states: "Validity coefficients may range anywhere from .20 and up, with the .60 to .70 range considered quite high."[5]

If a student takes two different intelligence tests, he or she will probably obtain two different scores. Then the teacher or test administrator must determine which score is more valid, or wonder if the student would have scored differently on yet another measure.

To complicate validity further, many tests contain items that depend on cultural experiences. Students from cultures other than those on which the test was normed may score significantly lower than students from cultures similar to the ones on which the test was normed. In such cases, the test cannot be considered a valid measure of intelligence.

Test Administration and Interpretation. Reliability and validity are crucial factors in accurate test interpretation. When a test has low reliability, interpretation of the test is impossible because the measurement may be error laden. A fairly reliable test which has low validity proves useless because of the uncertainty of what abilities are being measured. A test can be reliable but not valid; however, the reverse is not possible. In order for a test to have high validity, it must measure consistently.

Despite the efforts of the American Psychological Association to prevent it, persons other than qualified psychologists often administer intelligence tests. Many of these people have no training and work without directed supervision. Thus, they often make serious errors in test administration, scoring, and interpretation. Tests administered by untrained personnel should not be considered useful information in a reading diagnosis.

Group Intelligence Tests

Group tests of intelligence are inappropriate for students suspected of having reading difficulties. Many group tests require that students read in order to take the test. Obviously, if they cannot read well, their scores will reflect poor reading as well as low intelligence, and the two will be hopelessly confused. Further, rapport is difficult to establish in group testing. For students who have been subjected to considerable failure, any group test may threaten them further and result in a poor performance. Also, many of the group tests on the market have very poor reliability, making score interpretation nearly impossible. Helms and Turner comment on the disadvantages of group intelligence tests in stating:

> The tests are further limited in that they are highly reliant on verbal abilities, not only for just one dimension of intelligence, but also because the child must *read* all of the directions and questions. Being a poor reader, or simply making an error in reading a statement, may result in a wrong answer. Another, more subtle, disadvantage is the inability of the examiner to know the physical and emotional state of the child.[6]

Awareness of the limitations inherent in measures of intellectual performance will lessen the possibility that intelligence test scores will be used or interpreted improperly. To best assess intellectual performance, at least one of the measures of intelligence must be individual and nonreading in nature. Major discrepancies between test scores constitute justifiable reasons for referral for psychological examination.

Considering the limitations of intelligence testing (particularly group testing) it seems inconceivable that school reading personnel would use such scores to control admission to a program to aid those having reading difficulty. However, many schools limit admission to reading programs to those with group intelligence test scores above a certain score. Such a practice seems indefensible and should be changed, since a student who needs help might well be overlooked. Furthermore, that same student might score much higher on an individual measure. Discrimination of this type is based on a lack of knowledge of the instruments being used. Instead of relying on such scores, other options are available, such as the following tests.

Potential Reading Ability Measures Suitable for Clinical Diagnosis

Revised Stanford-Binet Intelligence Scale. The Stanford-Binet test may only be administered and scored by personnel with formal course work and laboratory experience. The test will yield a mental age and intelligence quotient in a range from preschool to adult. The test measures several aspects of intelligence and is heavily verbal. It takes about one hour to administer, is individual in nature, and requires precise administration and interpretation for reliable results.

Wechsler Intelligence Scale for Children–Revised (WISC–R). Another popular and accurate test of intellectual performance, the WISC–R (see figure 3–1) requires individual administration and should be given by personnel who have had formal course work and laboratory experience. Measuring several aspects of intelligence, the WISC–R yields performance and verbal scores, with the verbal score normally considered the more valid predictor of performance in reading. With poor readers, however, the performance score probably provides the better measure of reading potential. The students' verbal scores may be limited by the same factors that limit their performance in reading. Vance summarized the results of 25 studies which attempted to identify a WISC–R profile that was characteristic of poor readers. Although Vance reported the presence of several general patterns of strengths and weaknesses among poor readers, he cautioned against the application of those patterns to individual students since the findings were based on group results.[7]

WISC-R

RECORD FORM

Wechsler Intelligence Scale for Children—Revised

NAME ______________________ AGE ______ SEX ______

ADDRESS ______________________

PARENT'S NAME ______________________

SCHOOL ______________________ GRADE ______

PLACE OF TESTING ______________________ TESTED BY ______

REFERRED BY ______________________

WISC-R PROFILE

Clinicians who wish to draw a profile should first transfer the child's *scaled scores* to the row of boxes below. Then mark an X on the dot corresponding to the scaled score for each test, and draw a line connecting the X's.*

Scaled Score	VERBAL TESTS: Information	Similarities	Arithmetic	Vocabulary	Comprehension	Digit Span	Scaled Score	PERFORMANCE TESTS: Picture Completion	Picture Arrangement	Block Design	Object Assembly	Coding	Mazes	Scaled Score
	☐	☐	☐	☐	☐	☐		☐	☐	☐	☐	☐	☐	
19	•	•	•	•	•	•	19	•	•	•	•	•	•	19
18	•	•	•	•	•	•	18	•	•	•	•	•	•	18
17	•	•	•	•	•	•	17	•	•	•	•	•	•	17
16	•	•	•	•	•	•	16	•	•	•	•	•	•	16
15	•	•	•	•	•	•	15	•	•	•	•	•	•	15
14	•	•	•	•	•	•	14	•	•	•	•	•	•	14
13	•	•	•	•	•	•	13	•	•	•	•	•	•	13
12	•	•	•	•	•	•	12	•	•	•	•	•	•	12
11	•	•	•	•	•	•	11	•	•	•	•	•	•	11
10	•	•	•	•	•	•	10	•	•	•	•	•	•	10
9	•	•	•	•	•	•	9	•	•	•	•	•	•	9
8	•	•	•	•	•	•	8	•	•	•	•	•	•	8
7	•	•	•	•	•	•	7	•	•	•	•	•	•	7
6	•	•	•	•	•	•	6	•	•	•	•	•	•	6
5	•	•	•	•	•	•	5	•	•	•	•	•	•	5
4	•	•	•	•	•	•	4	•	•	•	•	•	•	4
3	•	•	•	•	•	•	3	•	•	•	•	•	•	3
2	•	•	•	•	•	•	2	•	•	•	•	•	•	2
1	•	•	•	•	•	•	1	•	•	•	•	•	•	1

*See Chapter 4 in the manual for a discussion of the significance of differences between scores on the tests.

	Year	Month	Day
Date Tested			
Date of Birth			
Age			

	Raw Score	Scaled Score
VERBAL TESTS		
Information		
Similarities		
Arithmetic		
Vocabulary		
Comprehension		
(Digit Span)	( )	( )
Verbal Score		
PERFORMANCE TESTS		
Picture Completion		
Picture Arrangement		
Block Design		
Object Assembly		
Coding		
(Mazes)	( )	( )
Performance Score		

	Scaled Score	IQ
Verbal Score	*	
Performance Score	*	
Full Scale Score		

*Prorated from 4 tests, if necessary.

NOTES

Printed in U.S.A.

74-103AS 9-990334

FIGURE 3–1
Record form of the Wechsler Intelligence Scale for Children—Revised. (Copyright © 1974, 1971 by The Psychological Corporation. Reproduced by permission; all rights reserved.)

Moore and Wielan compared the WISC–R performances of students who had been referred for reading diagnosis with those of students from the general population and found that both groups evidenced similar amounts of test-score scatter.[8] While the WISC–R may provide some useful insights into the intellectual abilities of students, teachers should use caution in using WISC–R results to prescribe reading remediation. This test is not intended to be a diagnostic measure of reading ability. The Wechsler Adult Intelligence Scale (WAIS) may be used with older children and adults. Both the WISC–R and the WAIS take approximately one hour to administer.

Kaufman Assessment Battery for Children (K–ABC). Since its publication in 1983, the K–ABC (see figure 3–2) has been generating a great deal of interest. The K–ABC represents an attempt to measure mental processing independently from achievement. An individual intelligence test designed for children of ages 2.5 to 12.5 years, the K–ABC consists of 16 subtests and yields four different scores: Sequential Processing; Simultaneous Processing; Mental Processing Composite, a combination of the sequential and simultaneous measures; and Achievement. Because the intelligence batteries and the achievement battery were standardized on the same populations, a student's problem-solving abilities may be compared to that student's general knowledge and grasp of school-related learning. These comparisons may have a special application in the identification of learning disabled children.

The K–ABC can be administered in 30 to 50 minutes to preschoolers and in 50 to 80 minutes to older children. As with the Stanford-Binet and the WISC–R, the K–ABC requires a specially trained examiner for administration and interpretation of the test. The testing battery includes a Nonverbal Scale for use with hearing-impaired students, language-impaired students, or students for whom English is a second language. The items on the Nonverbal Scale are administered in pantomime and the students are directed to respond through gestures. A Spanish version of the K–ABC is available, as are separate sociocultural percentile rank norms for use with other minority students. One unusual departure from other intelligence tests is the K–ABC authors' decision to describe intelligence without the use of the term *intelligence quotient.*

Quick Assessments of Intelligence. The Slosson Intelligence Test, The Detroit Tests of Learning Aptitude (DTLA), and the Peabody Picture Vocabulary Test–Revised (PPVT–R) are examples of easy-to-administer, quick assessments of some of the

K-ABC Kaufman Assessment Battery for Children
by Alan S. Kaufman and Nadeen L. Kaufman
INDIVIDUAL TEST RECORD

Name Mary B. Sex F
Parents' names Rita and James
Home address 807 S. Lincoln
Home phone 782-4602
Grade 4 School Central Elementary
Examiner Norma Ehrhardt

SOCIOCULTURAL INFORMATION (if pertinent)
Race black
Socioeconomic background mother finished 3rd. grade, housewife, father finished 6th. grade construction worker.

	YEAR	MONTH	DAY
Test date	82	17	15
Birth date	72	8	11
Chronological age	10	9	4

Achievement Subtests $\bar{X} = 100$; $SD = 15$	Standard score ± band of error ___% confidence	Nat'l. %ile rank Table 4	Socio-cultural %ile rank Table 5	S or W Table 11	Other data
11. Expressive Vocabulary	±				
12. Faces & Places	87 ± 8	19	35		8-9
13. Arithmetic	92 ± 8	30	70		9-6
14. Riddles	99 ± 9	47	90	S	10-6
15. Reading/Decoding	73 ± 8	4	10	W	7-6
16. Reading/Understanding	67 ± 8	1	5	W	7-3

Sum of subtest scores: 418 — Transfer sum to Global Scales, *Sum of subtest scores* column.

Mental Processing Subtests $\bar{X} = 10$; $SD = 3$	Scaled Score: Sequential	Scaled Score: Simultaneous	Scaled Score: Nonverbal	Nat'l %ile rank Table 4	S or W Table 11	Other data
1. Magic Window						
2. Face Recognition						
3. Hand Movements	10			50		11-9
4. Gestalt Closure		14		91	S	above 12-6
5. Number Recall	11			63		above 12-6
6. Triangles		8		25		8-0
7. Word Order	6			9	W	6-6
8. Matrix Analogies		9		37		9-9
9. Spatial Memory		7		16		8-3
10. Photo Series		9		37		9-9
Sum of subtest scores	27	47				

Transfer sums to Global Scales, *Sum of subtest scores* column.

Global Scales $\bar{X} = 100$; $SD = 15$	Sum of subtest scores	Standard score ± band of error ___% confidence Table 2	Nat'l. %ile rank Table 4	Socio-cultural %ile rank Table 5	Other data
Sequential Processing	27	93 ± 8	32	50	10-3
Simultaneous Processing	47	95 ± 6	37	80	9-8
Mental Processing Composite	74	93 ± 6	32	70	9-10
Achievement	418	81 ± 4	10	30	8-8
Nonverbal		±			

Global Scale Comparisons

	Indicate >, <, or ≈		Circle the significance level
Sequential	≈	Simultaneous (Table 10)	(NS) .05 .01
Sequential	≈	Achievement (Table 10)	(NS) .05 .01
Simultaneous	>	Achievement (Table 10)	NS .05 (.01)
M P C	>	Achievement (Table 10)	NS .05 (.01)

AGS®

FIGURE 3–2
The Individual Test Record from the Kaufman Assessment Battery for Children. (Copyright © 1983 by American Guidance Service Inc. Reproduced by permission; all rights reserved.)

behavior that indicates intelligence. Although, strictly speaking, the Peabody Picture Vocabulary Test–Revised is a test of receptive vocabulary for Standard American English and not general intelligence, the Peabody is included here as a quick assessment of intelligence because it is used as such by many. Although the PPVT–R does tap hearing vocabulary and experience, two important abilities related to reading potential, it does not accurately assess innate ability.[9]

Each of these quick tests may be given by a teacher who is familiar with the instrument and has had practice in administering it. These abbreviated measures should be treated cautiously, since their brevity can lower their reliability. If scores obtained on these tests are exceedingly high or low, a more careful assessment of intelligence should be conducted. Since the test can be administered quickly, the constructors had to eliminate many of the aspects of intelligence and rely, in some cases, on only one. This raises the question of validity. The predominantly verbal composition of the Slosson, PPVT–R, and several of the subtests of the DTLA may cause many poor readers to score low. For all of these reasons, such tests should be used only as initial indicators of student potential.

Listening Comprehension. Listening comprehension, or *auding,* is another quick and easily assessable indicator of reading potential. It usually requires that the student listen to read aloud passages of increasing difficulty and then answer comprehension questions about their content. Listening comprehension is considered an indicator of reading potential because it reveals, in part, the level at which concepts can be understood and language interpreted independent of word recognition abilities. It is most appropriate for use with younger students since many secondary readers will have silent comprehension levels that exceed their listening comprehension levels. Other difficulties, such as poor attention and general comprehension deficits, may also adversely affect an auding score.

Arithmetic Computation. For students who have attended school for two or more years, a test of arithmetic computation, not involving verbal problems, may be useful in estimating reading potential. Arithmetic computation requires three abilities related to reading achievement: abstract reasoning, manipulation of a symbol system, and visual perception. However, it cannot be used routinely for estimating reading potential. Many students who experience difficulties with reading also have difficulties with arithmetic. Further, when students react with emotional rejection toward the school environment, their achievement is likely to suffer in both reading and arithmetic. Arithmetic computation should be viewed only as a possible indicator of reading potential when students score significantly higher in tests of arithmetic computation than in reading tests. Even then, arithmetic computation should not serve as the only indicator of reading potential because it is essentially an achievement measure.

Other measures of intellectual performance are available for clinical diagnosis; however, most of them require special preparation and laboratory experience, as do the Stanford–Binet, the WISC–R, and the K–ABC.

Potential Reading Ability Measures Suitable for Classroom Diagnosis

The Stanford–Binet, WISC–R, and K–ABC. These tests are not normally administered by the classroom teacher, but their scores are often found in the school records of students experiencing reading difficulties. The other tests mentioned under clinical diagnosis can be administered by a classroom teacher as part of normal school procedure or as a part of classroom diagnosis.

Group Intelligence Tests. Although group intelligence tests are inherently unsatisfactory in reading diagnosis, several of them do separate reading and nonreading factors. The California Test of Mental Maturity, for example, provides a mental age (M.A.) and intelligence quotient (IQ) for both language and nonlanguage performance. The teacher who uses this type of test and finds a major discrepancy between the two scores (such as nonlanguage IQ = 125, language IQ = 100) should be looking for other signs of intellectual performance because the student may be capable but hindered in the language section by lack of reading ability. Other measures of reading potential, such as those mentioned under clinical diagnosis, should then be checked, or the student should be referred for an individual intelligence examination. However, unless group intelligence tests have nonlanguage features, they are not useful in estimating the reading potential of students who read poorly. Even then, their usefulness is highly questionable.

Teacher Observation. The experienced teacher often can estimate reading potential through direct observation of the student's response to various school activities. Students demonstrate their intellectual abilities thousands of times each day in school tasks and problem-solving situations. Specifically, observable examples of intellectual abilities include:

- ☐ Ability to listen and speak effectively in class discussions.
- ☐ Ability to achieve more successfully in arithmetic than in subjects that require reading.
- ☐ Ability to interact effectively in peer group activities.
- ☐ Ability to demonstrate alert attitudes toward the world.
- ☐ Ability to perform satisfactorily on spelling tests.
- ☐ Ability to think in abstract terms and mentally perform complex functions.
- ☐ Ability to understand scientific concepts.

Such observations obviously cannot be considered reliable indicators of reading potential. Teacher observation always includes the possibility of teacher bias; teachers often see just what they are looking for. As an example, a teacher's observation may be influenced by previous test scores and prior impressions of the student. However, lack of ability in these observable areas often provides the first indication of a difficulty. By such observations, students who have been intellectually misjudged may be referred for more accurate evaluations.

Grade Level Expectancy

How often have you read an editorial in the newspaper which decries the fact that many students graduate from high school unable to read at a twelfth grade level? This reflects a common expectation held by most parents and many teachers that all students should be reading at or above grade level. If a pupil is reading below grade level, many individuals would target that student for remedial attention. Grade level expectancy, while well intentioned, is misguided and stems from a lack of knowledge of how standardized, norm-referenced tests are constructed, and lack of awareness of the other alternatives that exist for helping to set reasonable goals for students. The following example may help illustrate some of the problems involved when students' achievement is compared merely to their grade level in school.

Example: Lynne, Claire, and Jane

Lynne, Claire, and Jane are all in the same fourth grade class. Their teacher, Mr. Johnson, gave them a reading test at the beginning of the year and found the following reading grade levels: Lynne, 3.3; Claire, 4.4; and Jane, 4.9. From this evidence

Mr. Johnson concluded that Lynne was reading poorly, Claire was reading well, and Jane was reading very well. He resolved to see that Lynne receive as much extra help as possible.

Suppose, however, that Mr. Johnson also knew the information about the girls provided in table 3–1. Should it change his assessment of their achievement and his expectations for their progress?

TABLE 3–1
A Comparison of Three Fourth Grade Students

Name	Grade Level	Reading Level	Chronological Age	IQ	Grades Repeated
Lynne	4.0	3.3	9.4	82	0
Claire	4.0	4.4	10.2	101	1
Jane	4.0	4.9	9.3	140	0

Comparing Reading Achievement to Reading Expectancy

An alternative to comparing students' reading achievement to their grade level is to compare students' achievement to the best indication of their reading potential or expectancy. Reading potential can be estimated in many different ways, but in each case the underlying idea is similar. Instead of comparing a student's reading achievement to the student's grade level, the student's achievement is compared to facts known about the student's true ability. This can help teachers set realistic goals for the student and identify candidates for remedial attention.

A comparison of the best estimates of reading potential with the best estimates of reading achievement will result in an arithmetical difference. When potential exceeds achievement, the concern is that the student is not working up to capacity. The larger the difference, the more serious the degree of reading difficulty.

Mental Age Formula. Perhaps the most common technique of estimating the seriousness of the reading difficulty is a simple comparison of mental age with reading age. Mental age can be computed as follows:

$$\text{M.A.} = \frac{\text{C.A.} \times \text{IQ}}{100}$$

M.A. = mental age
C.A. = chronological age
IQ = intelligence quotient

Reading achievement scores are most often reported as grade equivalents. In order to convert a grade equivalent to a reading age (R.A.), it is necessary to add 5.2 to the grade equivalent. When a student's reading age is subtracted from the student's mental age, the resulting difference is interpreted as the student's degree of reading difficulty.

Harris Formulas. Harris has proposed two formulas for estimating reading expectancy (R.E.) which give priority to the student's mental age, but which also consider the student's chronological age.[10] The first formula contends:

$$\text{Reading Expectancy Age} = \frac{2(\text{M.A.}) + \text{C.A.}}{3}$$

The resulting reading expectancy age (R Exp A) can be converted to a grade equivalent by subtracting 5.2. This reading expectancy grade equivalent can then be compared to the student's reading achievement scores to give an estimate of the student's degree of reading difficulty.

Another means of comparing the student's reading achievement to the student's reading expectancy or potential is to compute a reading expectancy quotient (R Exp Q). In this formula, reading age is divided by the student's reading expectancy age as found by the previous formula.

$$\text{Reading Expectancy Quotient} = \frac{\text{R.E.} \times 100}{\text{R Exp A}}$$

Harris provides general guidelines for interpreting the reading expectancy quotient. In general, the lower the R Exp Q, the greater the degree of reading difficulty indicated. Quotients below 85 are interpreted as representing a *severe disability,* quotients in the range 85 to 89 represent a *probable disability,* and quotients of 90 to 110 represent *normal limits.*[11]

Bond and Tinker Formula. Bond and Tinker use the number of years that the child has received formal reading instruction as a factor in estimating reading expectancy.[12] Their formula yields a reading expectancy grade equivalent which can be compared to a student's reading achievement scores to give an indication of the student's degree of reading difficulty.

$$\text{R.E.} = (\text{IQ}/100 \times \text{yrs. of reading instruction}) + 1.0$$

The Bond and Tinker formula assumes that most children, regardless of their intellectual ability, will begin first grade with an expectancy of 1.0 and that thereafter their reading expectancy will climb as a function of their general intelligence and the amount of reading instruction that they receive. A student of average intelligence would be expected to achieve one year's growth in reading for each year of reading instruction. A more able student would be expected to make accelerated progress, while a less able student would be expected to achieve at a slower than average rate.[13]

In using the Bond and Tinker formula, teachers should consider three factors. First, they must understand that the term *years in school* does not mean the student's grade placement, but rather, the actual number of school years completed. Therefore, for a student who has a grade placement of 4.8 and who has not accelerated or repeated a grade, the appropriate entry would be 3.8 for years in school. (For this formula, kindergarten does not count as a year in school.) Second, teachers must have accurate data concerning the grades repeated or accelerated. Third, they should be aware that the addition of 1.0 years in the formula is to compensate for the manner in which grade norms are assigned to tests, 1.0 being the zero month of first grade.

Cleland Formula. Cleland prefers to average four factors, giving each equal weight, in arriving at a reading potential score that can be compared to reading achievement.[14] In this formula, he computes the grade equivalents of chronological age, mental age, arithmetic computation, and the Durrell-Sullivan Reading Capacity Test. Note that grade equivalents of M.A. and C.A. are obtained by subtracting five for the five years the child did not attend school.

$$\text{R.E.} = \frac{(\text{C.A.} - 5) + (\text{M.A.} + 5) + (\text{A.C. gr. eq.}) + (\text{D-S gr. eq.})]}{4}$$

This formula has several advantages.

1. Although mental age is used without the compensation that Bond and Tinker give, it is equalized somewhat by the use of chronological age.
2. The use of reading capacity adds auding as a factor (any auding test can be substituted for a capacity score).
3. The use of arithmetic computation provides measures of the student's ability to do nonverbal school work.

Advantages and Limitations of Expectancy Formulas

Each of these expectancy formulas has its own unique advantages and limitations. The mental age formula, while easy to use, relies on mental age as a single factor in estimating reading expectancy. As a result, expectancies tend to be unrealistically high for young students of superior ability. In effect this formula expects that bright students will be reading when they enter school. For example, a student who is 6.0 years old on the first day of first grade and who has an IQ of 140 would have a mental age of 8.4 and a reading expectancy grade equivalent of 3.2.

The Harris formulas seek to mitigate the effect of mental age somewhat by including the student's chronological age in the expectancy computation. Once again, however, schooling or lack of it is not directly considered. In the case of the student described here who is just entering first grade, the Harris formula would yield a reading expectancy grade equivalent of 2.4.

The Bond and Tinker formula includes years of reading instruction as a variable and so gives a more realistic estimate of expectancy for very young students. The beginning first grader in our example would have zero years of reading instruction and so would be assigned a reading expectancy grade equivalent of 1.0 by the Bond and Tinker formula. However, this formula tends to overestimate the reading expectancy of very low-functioning students and underestimate the reading expectancy of older highly able students.

The Cleland formula has the advantage of considering multiple factors in determining reading expectancy. Ebel notes that:

> The broader the basis of observations on which evaluation rests, the better, provided only that each observation carries no more weight in determining the final result than its appropriateness and accuracy warrant.[15]

As we have noted earlier, both auding and arithmetic computation have some limitations in their use as measures of reading potential that raise some question about their appropriateness in computing reading expectancy. The Cleland formula tends to compare more favorably with the Bond and Tinker formula than with other formulas which rely more heavily on mental age.

Degree of Difference between Achievement and Expectancy

When selecting candidates for remedial attention by comparing students' achievement and expectancy, teachers should consider the grade placement of the students. Many students may fall slightly short of their reading expectancy, yet would not be viewed as having serious reading difficulties. Older students can bear a larger variance between potential and achievement without the severe ramifications that occur with younger students.

The scale in table 3–2 may be useful in selecting a cut-off point between a tolerable difference and one that is sufficient to interfere with the child's progress in reading and other subjects. Tolerable differences are presented in this table by individual grade groupings. Although this scale should not be adhered to rigidly, it does provide reasonably useful limits. However, since diagnosis includes considerably more analysis than the estimation of potential and achievement, the educator should not evaluate progress in reading by this technique alone.

TABLE 3–2
Degree of Tolerable Difference Between Potential and Achievement

End of Grade	Tolerable Difference (in Years)
1, 2, and 3	.5
4, 5, and 6	1
7, 8, and 9	1.5
10, 11, and 12	2

When selecting the method for computing the degree of reading difficulty, the following factors should be considered:

- ☐ The number and type of students selected as candidates for remedial attention in reading will vary with the method employed.
- ☐ Each method is only as good as the instruments used to obtain the scores for its computation.
- ☐ A student with a specific skill deficiency may not be discovered by these types of formulas.

In figure 3–3, a student's scores have been plotted. This ten-year-old boy has a 5.5 word recognition level and a 6.0 silent reading comprehension score. His reading expectancy level is

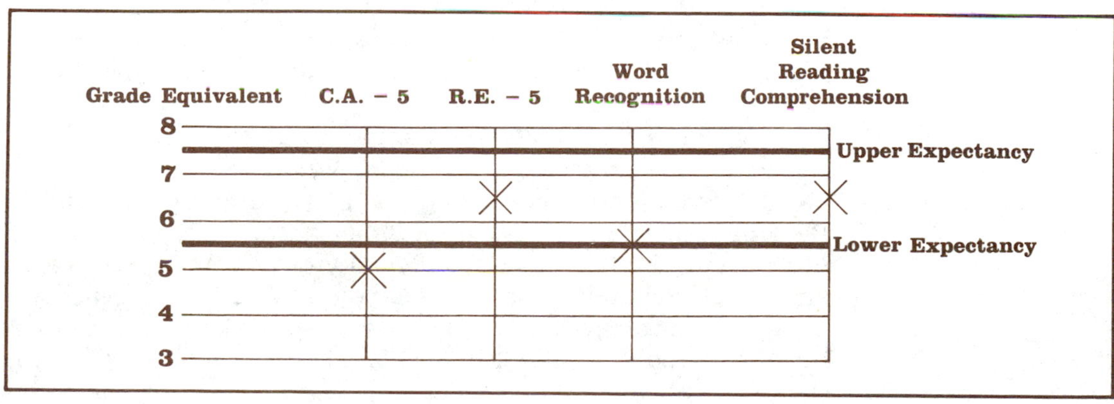

FIGURE 3–3
Comparing Expectancy Range with Other Reading Variables

6.5 and the two heavy lines reflect the standard error plus and minus the actual potential score.

Although neither reading performance score is as high as the reading expectancy, both fall within the standard error of the reading expectancy score. This treatment of expectancy scores expresses to all who receive the report that the score should not be taken as a precise measure.

Example Revisited

Returning to the example of the three fourth grade students (see table 3–1), Mr. Johnson decided to compute reading expectancies to see if his initial impressions about the girls were justified. This is what he found.

Lynne's mental age was computed to be 7.7. When Mr. Johnson placed this mental age in the Harris formula, he found that she had a Reading Expectancy Age of 8.3 and a reading expectancy grade equivalent of 3.1. These expectancies compared favorably with Lynne's reading age of 8.5 and her reading achievement level of 3.3. Mr. Johnson found Lynne's Reading Expectancy Quotient of 102 to be well within normal limits. Using the Bond and Tinker formula, Lynne's Reading Expectancy level was found to be 3.5. Mr. Johnson concluded that, although Lynne was reading below grade level, she was reading pretty well in terms of her potential or expectancy.

Claire's mental age of 10.3 led Mr. Johnson to a Harris Reading Expectancy Age of 10.3 and a reading expectancy grade equivalent of 5.1 (due primarily to the fact that she was older than the average fourth grader). He found, however, that Claire's Reading Expectancy Quotient of 93.2 still fell within normal limits. Mr. Johnson further noted that Claire's Bond and Tinker Reading Expectancy level was 5.0 as a consequence of her repeating a grade. Nevertheless, Claire's reading achievement level of 4.4 was within a tolerable difference of her potential.

In Jane's case Mr. Johnson found mixed results. Her Harris Reading Expectancy Age was 11.8. When Mr. Johnson compared this to Jane's reading age of 10.1, he found that Jane's Reading Expectancy Quotient of 85.6 placed her in the range of probable disability. Surprised, Mr. Johnson computed a Bond and Tinker Reading Expectancy for Lynne and found it was 5.2. This figure compared much more favorably with Lynne's reading achievement level of 4.9. Mr. Johnson resolved to talk with the reading specialist about Jane.

Thus, reading expectancy formulas can provide a better standard for judging reading achievement than grade level expectancy alone. However, expectancy formulas are not without their problems. Although they helped to explain Lynne's below-grade-level achievement, two different formulas painted two different pictures in Jane's case. Once again, the teacher is encouraged to consider reading expectancy as a measure against which to compare reading achievement, but not to put undue emphasis on any single test score or reading expectancy computation.

Some Additional Cautions

Many students could fail to receive the help they need if potential formulas are used as the only indicators of need. Students with specific skill deficiencies or attitudinal problems might well be missed. Students with low potential scores might need a language development program prior to or in conjunction with the start of a reading program.[16] On any one given day, a student might score differently on the reading tests. These and many other problems call for examiners to evaluate the total reader, not just the test scores. Attention to the reader's responses during testing may be more important than the resulting score. How the use of potential fits into classroom and clinical diagnosis is discussed in chapters 4 and 5.

PHYSICAL DIAGNOSIS

When a physical limitation interferes with a student's potential or performance it can be considered a cause of a reading difficulty. Whose job is it to assess the severity of a physical disability? Although physical limitations are recognized first in a classroom or clinical diagnosis, medical personnel or other specialists are responsible for specific identification of the problem, prescription of corrective measures, and making recommendations to teachers for adjusting instruction. Both the reading specialist and the classroom teacher can refer students either on the basis of reliable patterns of symptoms or as a result of certain screening devices available to educators.

Specifically, the areas of physical diagnosis of reading difficulties include general, visual, auditory, and neurological health. Limitations in these areas that are serious enough to interfere with performance in reading will most likely also interfere with general educational performance. However, a general educational deficiency does not necessarily indicate a physical disability, nor does a physical disability always cause a learning deficiency.

General Health

Large numbers of students are not healthy enough to profit efficiently from the instruction provided, even under the best conditions. Educators should know these aspects of general health that should be evaluated in the diagnosis of reading difficulties.

Malnutrition. Malnutrition causes the student to lose weight or lag behind in physical and mental vitality. Malnutrition does not necessarily show itself in loss of weight, however. Many suffering from nutritional imbalance are quite chubby due to an overconsumption of starches. The sluggish behavior that results may interfere with school performance.

Glandular Defects. The endocrine system regulates many important bodily functions. Endocrine disturbances, particularly those involving the thyroid, may adversely affect reading performance. Hypothyroidism, a thyroid deficiency, often causes obesity and a lack of mental alertness. Hyperthyroidism, a thyroid excess, may cause extreme weight loss, irritability, and an inability to concentrate on school tasks.

Mental or Physical Fatigue. Caused by lack of sleep, poor sleeping habits, lack of exercise, or overexertion, mental or physical fatigue can cause students to be inattentive and easily distracted in a learning situation. Unfortunately, in recent years we have seen an upswing in the number of students who come to school both mentally and physically fatigued due to late night television viewing.

Poor General and Physical Condition. Often characterized by frequent illness, poor general physical condition causes a lack of stamina with resulting gaps in the educational program. Factors such as overweight, underweight, dental problems, or hay fever can result in difficulty with school tasks. Alertness to signs of poor health is essential in a reading diagnosis. Many such cases are first identified by individual attention to a student's performance during diagnosis.

The classroom teacher also uses information from school records, reports from the school nurse and the family doctor, information from the parents, and observable symptoms that are characteristic of students with general physical deficiencies to identify physical problems. Sluggishness, inattentiveness, failure to complete assignments, apparent lack of interest, sleeping in school, and general lack of vitality often are symptoms that cause a student to be labeled *lazy* or *indifferent*. Classroom teachers should observe these symptoms, contact the home to report the problem, and make medical referrals when appropriate. At the same time, they should adjust the instruction to make the learning environment as comfortable as possible for the student. This adjustment may take the form of relaxing the tension caused by the student's apparent indifference, allowing the fatigued student a program of varied activities and necessary rest periods, and, when necessary, following the recommendations of medical personnel.

It does not take a medical report to make us aware that all students, not just those with reading difficulties, need good health for optimal school performance. Necessities such as adequate rest, a balanced diet (particularly a good breakfast), annual physical checkups, and large doses of play activity after school are vital requirements for good school performance.

One of the reading specialist's responsibilities in diagnosis is to evaluate reports received from medical personnel in terms of the total case picture of the student involved and to recommend the appropriate classroom adjustment or remedial program.

Visual Diagnosis

Deficiencies in visual ability and ocular comfort may impede a student's reading growth. Recent reports state that from 15 to 40 percent of students need professional visual attention. The relationship of vision to low achievement in reading is complicated, since many students with visual problems are not low achievers. Carefully conducted research shows a relationship between certain types of visual deficiencies and failure in reading, and also that certain visual disabilities and ocular discomfort greatly interfere with students reaching their reading potentials.[17] In general, functional problems such as awkward eye movements and poor fusion cause reading difficulties more often than organic difficulties such as nearsightedness, farsightedness, or astigmatism. A review of some of the aspects of vision and ocular comfort will clarify the relationship.

Acuity. Acuity, the clearness of vision, is normally measured at far-point targets (a Snellen Chart twenty feet away from the student). Such screening tests of acuity provide information concerning the student's acuity at the far point (such as the ability to see the chalkboard). The results of this type of visual screening are expressed in terms of what the average person can see at twenty feet. The term *20/20* means that a person can see at twenty feet the same target that a person with normal vision can see at twenty feet. However, this test, when used alone, cannot detect all visual deficiencies. People do not normally read targets that are twenty feet from the eyes; neither do they read with one eye at a time. The eyes must efficiently move from one target to another, rather than merely fixing on and identifying a target. Kelley claims, "The misconception that the Snellen Chart will do an efficient job of screening out students who need visual care is a major block in the road of those trying to establish good school visual screening programs."[18]

Screening devices to measure near-point acuity should be used in diagnosing a low achiever, although they generally require more time and training to administer properly. One who successfully reads the Snellen Chart may still have a visual deficiency that is causing problems in reading. The farsighted reader, seeing far-point targets better than near-point targets, may pass the Snellen Chart yet not see efficiently enough to read with comfort at the near point. The nearsighted reader, who sees near-point targets better than far-point targets, is likely to fail at reading the Snellen Chart; but, while obviously limited by a visual defect, he or she may still read effectively in most cases. Therefore, effective visual screening must measure both far- and near-point acuity. This need has been partially met by the development of a type of chart for use at a fourteen inch distance. The following additional techniques are generally desirable for accurate near-point screening.

Binocular Fusion. Binocular fusion involves the ability of the brain to blend or fuse the image from each eye into a single adequate image. If the eyes do not work in perfect harmony, a double image or blurring may result. In an effort to ease the discomfort of seeing a double image, the brain will often suppress the vision of one eye. Such a condition is called *amblyopia* or *lazy eye.* Undetected, amblyopia may cause a loss of acuity in the suppressed eye. *Strabismus* involves poor coordination of the eye muscles necessary to focus effectively, and often results in double vision or blurring of the image. Students experiencing binocular fusion difficulties should be referred to a vision specialist. Left untreated, students may confuse letters and words, frequently lose their place when reading, and experience visual discomfort or fatigue.

Ocular Motility. Effective reading requires the efficient operation of the eye in motion. In particular, ocular motility refers to fixations, pursuit, saccadic movement, accommodation, and convergence. Although these important abilities are seldom evaluated in a school screening, classroom teachers and reading specialists should be aware of these and refer students suspected of having difficulties with ocular motility for a thorough vision examination.

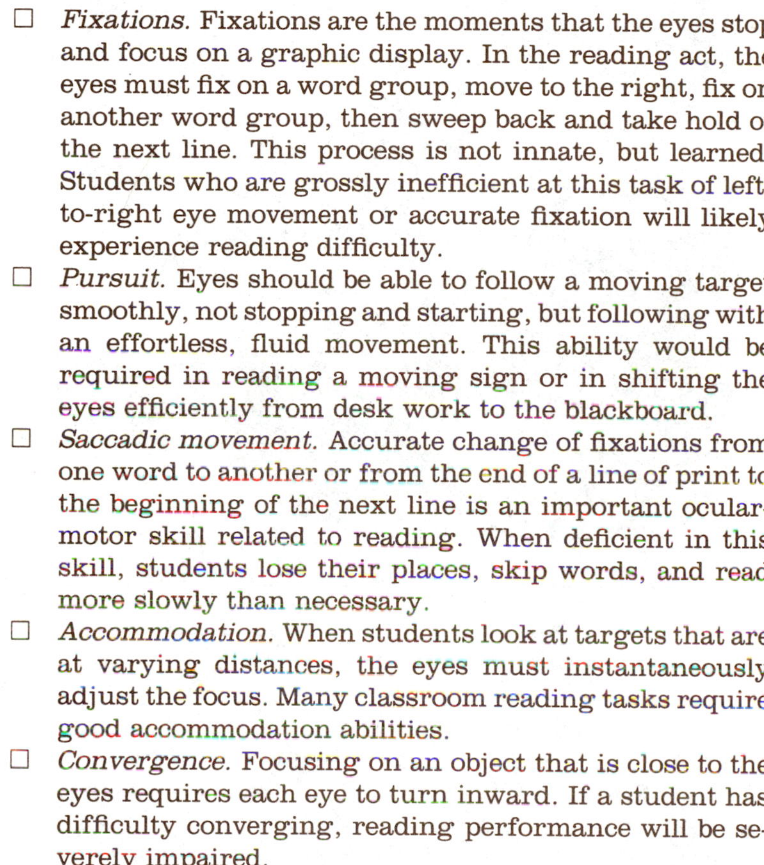

- ☐ *Fixations.* Fixations are the moments that the eyes stop and focus on a graphic display. In the reading act, the eyes must fix on a word group, move to the right, fix on another word group, then sweep back and take hold of the next line. This process is not innate, but learned. Students who are grossly inefficient at this task of left-to-right eye movement or accurate fixation will likely experience reading difficulty.
- ☐ *Pursuit.* Eyes should be able to follow a moving target smoothly, not stopping and starting, but following with an effortless, fluid movement. This ability would be required in reading a moving sign or in shifting the eyes efficiently from desk work to the blackboard.
- ☐ *Saccadic movement.* Accurate change of fixations from one word to another or from the end of a line of print to the beginning of the next line is an important ocular-motor skill related to reading. When deficient in this skill, students lose their places, skip words, and read more slowly than necessary.
- ☐ *Accommodation.* When students look at targets that are at varying distances, the eyes must instantaneously adjust the focus. Many classroom reading tasks require good accommodation abilities.
- ☐ *Convergence.* Focusing on an object that is close to the eyes requires each eye to turn inward. If a student has difficulty converging, reading performance will be severely impaired.

A number of screening devices and procedures are available that a teacher might be trained to use. In screening visual abilities related to most school reading tasks, these procedures represent a marked improvement over the traditionally used Snellen Chart.

A test using a telebinocular provides near- and far-point screening of visual acuity, binocular fusion, color perception, and stereopsis (the ability to judge the relative distance between two objects). The proper administration and analysis of this test requires supervised experience to assure reliable results. The telebinocular screens the visual skills related to the ability of the eyes to fix only on a stationary target (see photo and figure 3–4).

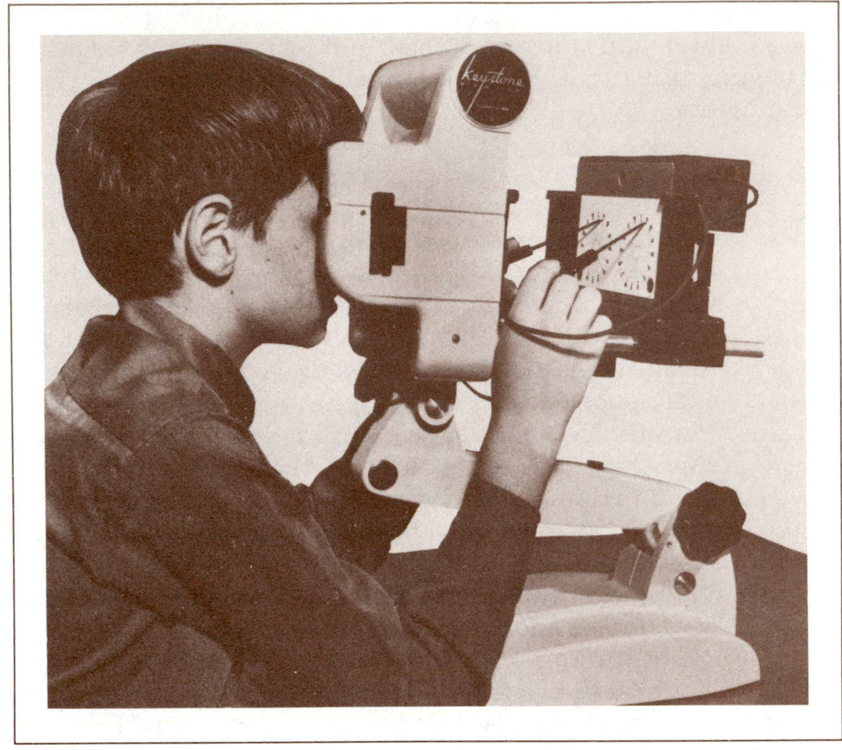

An example of a student using the Keystone Telebinocular.

The reading specialist must also be concerned about the eyes as they operate in reading situations. The Spache-Binocular Reading Tests provide an analysis of binocular vision during the reading act. In these tests, the student looks at a card that has been placed in the telebinocular and reads a story containing some words that only the right eye can see and some that only the left eye can see. By marking the student's responses, the examiner can determine the degree that each eye operates in the reading act. Referral is based on certain characteristics that are identified in the accompanying manual.

A pocket flashlight is used to screen pursuit, saccadic eye movements, accommodation, and convergence. Holding the light upright in front of the eyes, the examiner asks the student to look at the light. The examiner then moves the light in an area eighteen inches from the eye in straight vertical, horizontal, and diagonal lines twelve to eighteen inches in length, and, then in a circle with a radius of about twelve inches clockwise and counterclockwise. Referral should be considered if (1) students cannot follow the light without moving their heads, even after being

KEYSTONE
School Vision Screening

FOR USE WITH THE KEYSTONE TELEBINOCULAR SCHOOL SURVEY CUMULATIVE RECORD FORM NO. 5-B (CATALOG ORDER NO. 5522-B)

RAPID VISION SCREENING TESTS

DISTANT VISION TESTS	Pass	Fail
1A. Dog should be seen jumping over pig	___	___
The 4 blocks should be seen merged into 3	___	___
2A. Balloon No. 2 is farthest away } Balloon No. 5 is closest	___	___
Balloon 2 is red; balloon 5 is green	___	___
Letters in Block A: D C Z P T	(Trainingonly)	
Letters in Block B: Z P D T C *	___	___
Letters in Block C: L D T C Z *	___	___
NEAR VISION TESTS (16 INCHES)		
3A. Yellow line should pass through white square	___	___
The 4 balls should be seen merged into 3	___	___
4A. Letters in Block A: L O Z P C	(Trainingonly)	
Letters in Block B: T Z O D L *	___	___
Letters in Block C: O P T D C *	___	___

* *Passing score: at least 4 letters*

Failure on any test above indicates need for full test at right.

COMPREHENSIVE TEST BATTERY: QUESTIONS

1. What do you see?
2. Does the yellow line go through, above, or below the red ball?
3. To what number, or between what numbers, does the arrow point?
4. How many balls do you see?

4½. In each signboard there are five diamonds (point). In one diamond is a dot. (point to first signboard, show dot in the left diamond.) *Ask:* Where is the dot in Nos. 2, 3, 4, 5, etc.? *Tests 5 and 6 are the same as No. 4½. Ask:* Where is the dot?

7. (Point to the top line of symbols and name each one. Show by pointing that the cross stands out in 3-D.) *Ask:* Which symbol stands out in each of the next lines?
8. What number is in the upper circle? The lower left? The lower right? *(Test 9 is the same as Test 8.)*

10. To what number, or between what numbers, does the arrow point?
11. How many balls do you see?
12. In the three circles in the center (point) you see black crossed lines, black dots, and solid gray. Starting with No. 1 of the outer circles, you see black dots. No. 2 has black lines. What do you see in No. 3? Go as far as you can. *Tests 13 and 14 are the same as 12:* Name what you see in each of the circles.

 73-6386

Name ________ Sex ________ School ________ City ________ Grade ____ Room ____ Teacher ________ Date of birth ________ Date of test ________

Wearing glasses? Yes: For reading only____ for distance only____; both____. No____

Snellen Standard (if desired)

With glasses: RE______ LE______

Without glasses: RE______ LE______

	TEST	LEFT EYE ONLY	RIGHT EYE ONLY	UNSATISFACTORY Underconvergence and/or low usable vision	RE-TEST AREA	EXPECTED RESPONSE	RE-TEST AREA	UNSATISFACTORY Overconvergence
FAR POINT TESTS	1 (DB-10A) Simultaneous Vision							
	2 (DB-8C) Vertical Posture	only	only					
	3 (DB-9) Lateral Posture	Arrow only	Numbers only	15 | 14 | 13 | 12	11	10 | 9 | 8	7	6 | 5 | 4 | 3 | 2 | 1
	4 (DB-4K) Fusion	only	only	Far apart | Close				Close | Far apart
	4½ (DB-1D) Usable Vision Both Eyes			1 L 49% | 2 B 70% | 3 T 84% | 4 L 88% | 5 R 92%	6 T 96%	7 L 98% | 8 B 100% | 9 B 103% | 10 R 105%		
	5 (DB-3D) Usable Vision, Right Eye		No Dots Seen Unless Left Eye Is Occluded	1 T 49% | 2 R 70% | 3 L 84% | 4 T 88% | 5 B 92%	6 B 96%	7 L 98% | 8 R 100% | 9 T 103% | 10 R 105%		
	6 (DB-2D) Usable Vision, Left Eye	No Dots Seen Unless Right Eye Is Occluded		1 B 49% | 2 L 70% | 3 R 84% | 4 R 88% | 5 T 92%	6 L 96%	7 B 98% | 8 L 100% | 9 R 103% | 10 T 105%		
	7 (DB-6D) Stereopsis	+ only	only ●	+ ○ * ○ □ □ ♡ +	*	+ | ♡ | ○		
	8 (DB-13A) Color Perception	Top 32 | Left 79	Right 23	NONE CORRECT | 1 Out of 3	2 Out of 3	ALL CORRECT		
	9 (DB-14A) Color Perception	Top 63 | Left 92	Right 56	NONE CORRECT | 1 Out of 3	2 Out of 3	ALL CORRECT		
NEAR POINT TESTS	10 (DB-9E) Lateral Posture	Arrow only	Numbers only	10 | 9 | 8	7	6 | 5 | 4	3	2
	11 (DB-5K) Fusion	only	only	Far apart | Close				Close | Far apart
	12 (DB-15) Usable Vision, Both Eyes	1 D 10% | 2 L 20%	3 D 30% | 4 D 40%	5 L 50% | 6 D 50% | 7 D 60% | 8 L 60% | 9 D 70% | 10 D 70% | 11 G 80% | 12 L 80%	13 L 90% | 14 D 90%	15 L 100% | 16 D 100% | 17 L 102% | 18 D 102% | 19 G 103% | 20 D 103% | 21 D 105% | 22 L 105%		
	13 (DB-16) Usable Vision, Right Eye	1 D 10% | 2 D 20%	3 L 30% | 4 D 40%	5 L 50% | 6 D 50% | 7 D 60% | 8 L 60% | 9 D 70% | 10 L 70% | 11 D 80% | 12 G 80%	13 L 90% | 14 L 90%	15 D 100% | 16 D 100% | 17 G 102% | 18 D 102% | 19 L 103% | 20 D 103% | 21 D 105% | 22 L 105%		
	14 (DB-17) Usable Vision, Left Eye	1 L 10% | 2 D 20%	3 D 30% | 4 D 40%	5 L 50% | 6 D 50% | 7 L 60% | 8 D 60% | 9 D 70% | 10 D 70% | 11 L 80% | 12 L 80%	13 G 90% | 14 D 90%	15 L 100% | 16 D 100% | 17 L 102% | 18 D 102% | 19 L 103% | 20 G 103% | 21 D 105% | 22 L 105%		

Examined by: ________

FIGURE 3–4
Record form of the Keystone School Vision Screening Test. (Copyright © 1972 by the Keystone View Company. Reproduced by permission; all rights reserved.)

told to hold still; (2) the reflection of the light cannot be seen in both of a student's pupils at all times; or (3) the eye movements are saccadic (that is, they follow the light jerkily instead of smoothly). To test converging power, the light is again held eighteen inches from the eye, moved slowly to a position one inch directly between the eyes and held for one second. Since some students do not understand what they are to do the first time, referral should be recommended only if this fixation cannot be held after three attempts. (Caution should be observed in screening vision through use of a pocket flashlight since some individuals may not be able to tolerate the direct light.)

Not having any of this screening equipment available, classroom teachers must rely on a pattern of symptoms observable in the reading act or other school situations. The checklist in figure 3–5, prepared by the American Optometric Association, includes a list of these symptoms.[19] Note that this checklist recommends that all students who are not performing well in terms of their capacity should be referred for visual examinations.

Students who exhibit the symptoms described in figure 3–5 normally will be referred to the school nurse; however, if screening equipment is limited to the Snellen Chart, the classroom teacher should report the observed behavior to the parents with the recommendation of a complete visual examination by a vision specialist. Until the student receives treatment, the teacher should make every effort to provide a most comfortable and efficient visual environment. This may be accomplished by placing the student in a position of optimal lighting, eliminating glare, adjusting seating to ease board work, or reducing the reading load.

Vision Referral Problems. Because most educators have little or no formal background in vision assessment, referral decisions are fraught with uncertainty. Does this student *really* have a vision problem? Are the student's difficulties severe enough to warrant referral? What if I refer this student and then find that there was no visual difficulty? Abrams places the referral process in perspective:

> The responsibility of the teacher or educator is to *detect* the visual problem, not to *diagnose* visual difficulties. . . . The diagnosis and treatment of a visual problem rightly belongs in the realm of the vision specialist who is trained to handle such problems.[20]

To aid teachers in detecting the children who should be referred for complete visual analysis, the American Optometric Association Committee on Visual Problems in Schools has compiled a list of symptoms—a guide to vision problems. The committee recommends

1. That all children in the lower third of the class, particularly those with ability to achieve above their percentile rating, be referred for complete visual analysis
2. That every child in the class who, even though achieving, is not working within reasonable limits of his own capacity be referred for a complete visual analysis

Following are other symptoms that may indicate a visual problem, regardless of result in any screening test.

Observed in Reading:

Dislike for reading and reading subjects
Skipping or re-reading lines
††Losing place while reading
Slow reading or word calling
Poor perceptual ability, such as confusing *o* and *a*, *n*, and *m*, etc.

Other Manifestations:

Restlessness, nervousness, irritability or other unaccountable behavior
Desire to use finger or marker as pointer while reading
††Avoiding close work
††Poor sitting posture and position while reading
Fatigue or listlessness after close work
Inattentiveness, temper tantrums, or frequent crying
Complaint of blur when looking up from close work
Seeing objects double
Headaches, dizziness, or nausea associated with the use of eyes
††Body rigidity while looking at distant objects
Undue sensitivity to light
Crossed eyes—turning in or out
Red-trimmed, crusted or swollen lids
Vocalizing during silent reading, noticed by watching lips or throat
Reversals persisting in grade 2 or beyond
Inability to remember what has been read
Complaint of letters and lines "running together" or words "jumping"
††Holding reading closer than normal
††Frowning, excessive blinking, scowling, squinting, or other facial distortions while reading
††Excessive head movements while reading
Writing with face too close to work
Frequent sties
Watering or bloodshot eyes
Burning or itching of eyes or eyelids
††Tilting head to one side
††Tending to rub eyes
Closing or covering one eye
Frequent tripping or stumbling
Poor hand and eye coordination as manifested in poor baseball playing, catching and batting, or similar activities
††Thrusting head forward
††Tension during close work

Only a complete case study will determine whether inadequate vision is a significant factor in nonachievement.

††Found to be particularly significant in a recent study

FIGURE 3–5

Teacher's Guide to Vision Problems Checklist. (Copyright © 1953 by the American Optometric Association. Reprinted by permission; all rights reserved.)

Kelley comments on the reluctance of educators to overrefer:

> The cardinal purpose of school visual screening procedures is to refer children who may need visual care. It generally is considered more serious for a screening program to *fail to refer* a child in real need of care than for it to *refer* a child not actually in need of care.[21]

The schools, through their reluctance to refer, have permitted many students to operate daily with eye strain that leads to more complicated, permanent problems. All students should have periodic visual examinations by a specialist. Since most schools do not assume this responsibility, it remains a parental obligation. The teacher, then, should not hesitate to refer any student who demonstrates symptoms of visual difficulties.

Changes in the eyes will occur even following visual adjustment, complicating the referral decision even more. The nature of school, requiring hours of near-point visual activities, may make it necessary for lenses to be changed periodically. Therefore, the teacher should not hesitate to refer students who have symptoms of visual discomfort even if they are wearing glasses.

Another complication of referral occurs when the strongly motivated student, despite experiencing visual strain and discomfort, completes school work and shows no signs of academic deficiency. Again, this student, showing symptoms listed in figure 3–5 should be referred without hesitation before possible damage occurs.

Finally, the choice of to whom the referral should be made is often confusing. The term *vision specialist* has been used to avoid confusion. A *vision specialist* may be an optometrist, an ophthalmologist, or an oculist. A competent specialist in any of these fields should be considered satisfactory for referral. Ophthalmologists and oculists are medical doctors who have specialized in vision problems. The optometrist has a doctor's degree in optometry. Each is qualified to prescribe corrective lenses and visual training. In the case of eye disease, an optometrist will refer the patient to the ophthalmologist or oculist. Regardless of the type of degree held by the vision specialist, educators should make an effort to seek out those who have a special interest in the visual development of students and in the problems of functional vision that relate to reading achievement.

A form such as the one illustrated in figure 3–6 will aid the vision specialist in understanding the reasons for referral and provide him or her with basic educational information which can aid in a complete diagnosis.

Walter was screened visually and did not perform satisfactorily in the following area(s):
near point acuity   near point fusion

His/her present reading level is beginning third grade, but his/her reading potential is about upper 6th grade.

Will you please inform us if, after your examination, a visual deficiency may have been causing this student some difficulties in reading?

Ms. Carlotta Vasquez
(Signed)

FIGURE 3–6
A visual referral form.

The educator's tone when making a referral is especially important. If the educator's tone is dictatorial, conflict with both vision specialists and parents may occur. The referral should be stated in a manner such as "Since Jason appears to be having serious difficulties reading and since he has not had his eyes checked recently, we would like you to take him to a specialist for an examination. As we start to work with Jason, it will be best to correct any visual disorder first. If he has none, then we will not need to be concerned about visual disability."

In summary, both the reading specialist and the classroom teacher should be alert to the possible presence of visual problems in students who are experiencing reading difficulties. Teachers should observe students' classroom behaviors and use screening devices to guide referral of possible problem cases. Under no circumstances should the classroom teacher or the reading specialist consider a battery of screening devices, no matter how highly refined, as a substitution for a thorough eye examination and visual analysis. Screening tests, at best, are limited to their designed function—the identification of those in need of visual attention.

Auditory Diagnosis

Obviously, students who cannot hear adequately face problems in school. Many students with auditory limitations are placed in special schools or special classes for the deaf and hearing impaired so that they can receive specialized education. Many others with hearing losses, however, remain in regular school situations. School nurses have usually been able to identify these students early and to refer them to specialists.

Auditory problems affect reading in several ways. Students with a significant hearing loss are likely to find phonic instruction beyond their grasp because of a distortion of sounds or the inability to hear sounds at all. Most auditory deficiencies concern high frequency sounds; therefore, because of the high frequency of many of the consonant sounds, the most common limitation that a hearing deficiency places upon a reader is in consonant recognition and usage. Hearing losses in lower frequency ranges may result in vowel difficulties. Students with hearing difficulties are also hindered by inability to follow directions since they may not hear them clearly. They are likely to lose their places in oral reading activities when listening to others, fail to complete homework assignments, and appear inattentive and careless.

Teachers should understand the difference between the student who is unable to hear a word and the one who is unable to discriminate between sounds. In the first case, the student has a hearing loss that is a physical problem, and, in the latter, the student has an auditory discrimination problem that has educational implications. (Auditory discrimination will be discussed in chapter 4.)

Ideally, auditory screening should include a test of pitch (frequency) ranging from low to high and one to measure varying loudness (decibels). This screening can be adequately conducted using an audiometer (see photo and figure 3–7), an instrument adaptable for either group or individual auditory testing. Although opinions vary concerning a satisfactory audiometer score, a screening score that reports a loss of twenty-five decibels at 500, 1,000, 2,000, and 6,000 frequencies, and thirty decibels at 4,000, adequately indicates possible interference with reading instruction and that such a student should be referred.[22]

It is unlikely that the classroom teacher has the time, experience, or equipment to conduct the screening mentioned here. Classroom teachers have been advised that a watch-tick test or a whisper test is possible in the classroom. However, classroom teachers are reluctant to use these tests, perhaps because they have not had enough supervised experiences with them and the possibilities of overreferral are too great. Therefore, the classroom teacher should rely on a pattern of the symptoms listed in table 3–3 that, when observed in a student who has failed in reading, is justifiable cause for referral.

Normally, the student is referred to the school nurse for audiometric screening. Then in an effort to encourage as much

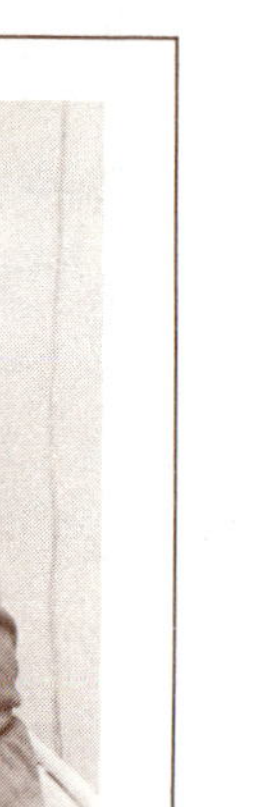

When the audiometer makes a loud sound, the student raises his hand.

success as possible in the classroom, the teacher should move the student's seat so that it is in the center of a discussion area, close to the teacher, and away from outside distractions such as radiators, fans, air conditioners, and traffic noises. A teacher must

TABLE 3–3
Symptoms justifying auditory referral

Physical Symptoms	Behavioral Symptoms
Speech difficulties (particularly with consonant sounds)	Inability to profit from phonic instruction
Tilting the head to listen	Inability to follow directions
Cupping of the ear with the hand in order to follow instructions	General inattentiveness
Strained posture in listening situations	Excessive volume needed for comfortable radio listening
Persistent complaints of earaches	
Inflammation or drainage of the ear	
Reports of persistent buzzing or ringing in the head	

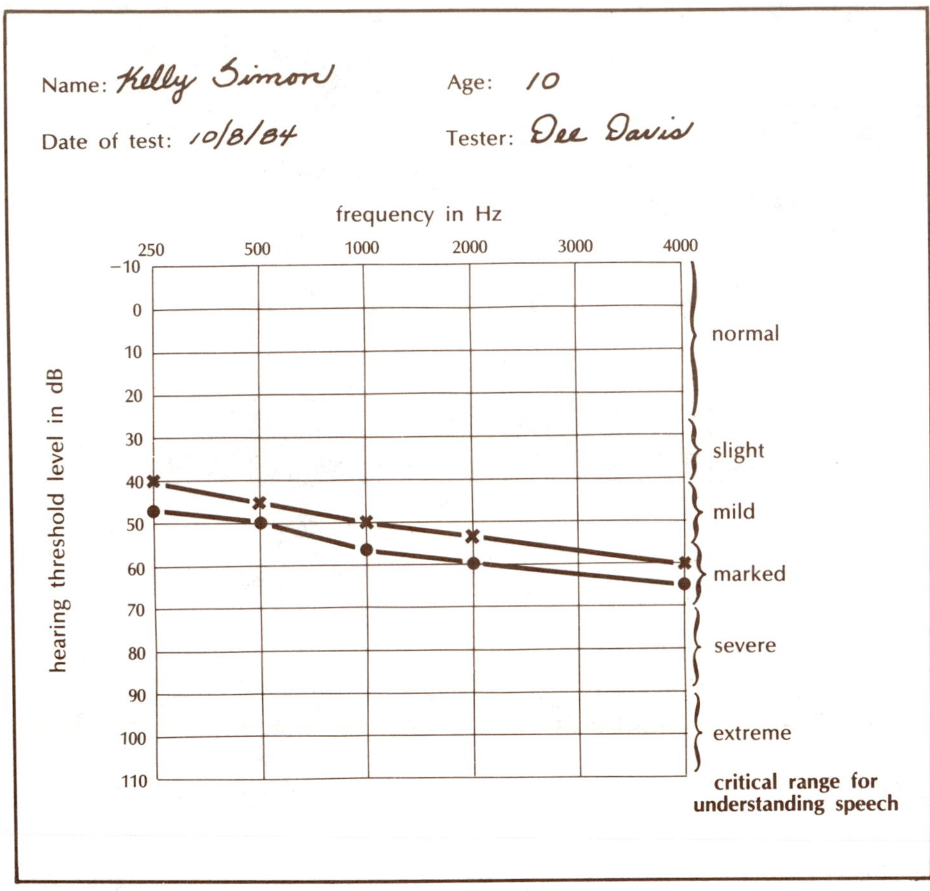

FIGURE 3–7
An audiogram charted for a student with a mild hearing loss (***x*** = *left ear*, ● = *right ear*).

also be willing to repeat assignments for this student to assure that they have been properly understood.

Referral outside the school normally would be made to a general practitioner, an audiologist, or to an otologist. An audiologist is a professional who has particular expertise in hearing assessment and rehabilitation. An otologist is a medical doctor who specializes in physical examinations of the ear. Often an audiologist and an otologist will function as a team. Referrals to one of these specialists should be made in terms of the observed symptoms of auditory difficulty which prompted the referral, with a request for results of the audiometric examination and suggestions concerning appropriate classroom adjustments if an educationally significant hearing loss is found.

Although the reading specialist may not plan to conduct an audiometric examination with every student, such an examination should be made when the student exhibits difficulties in speech or phonics instruction which may be related to a hearing problem. The specialist should take into consideration the observed onset of hearing related difficulties since this will have an important impact on educational planning for the student. For example, if a hearing loss occurs sometime after the primary grades, the student will have had the benefit of receiving basic instruction in sound-symbol correspondences while having unimpaired hearing. The remedial program for such a student would differ from that recommended for a student who began school with an educationally significant hearing loss.

Neurological Disorders

Neurological disorders remain the most confusing of the physical factors which may impede reading growth. Authorities differ markedly regarding the incidence, identification, referral, and treatment of students who are neurologically impaired. Often these differences can be traced to varying perspectives on the problem: medical, educational, or psychiatric. However, even among professionals of similar background, there are often differences due to the imprecise nature of diagnostic knowledge and procedures.

Neurological disorders may be divided into two groups: cases of established, known brain damage; and cases in which brain damage is suspected, but not verified. Little evidence can be found to support the idea that neurological disorders resulting from known brain damage are a major cause of low achievement in reading. Bond, Tinker, Wasson, and Wasson state, "Among children who have not yet acquired the ability to read, there are a very few who have sustained known brain damage before, during, or after birth."[23] In the case of suspected brain damage there is considerably less agreement. Some would attribute virtually all reading disabilities to presumed brain damage. Others would place the incidence of suspected brain damage among poor readers at a much more modest level. Robinson named neurological disorders as one of the causal factors in 18 percent of the cases in her classic study.[24] (In working with poor readers who have been referred to a university reading clinic, it is found that much less than 18 percent show symptoms of abnormal neurological patterns.)

Teachers, faced with the prevailing confusion in the field, may be uncertain about their role in the identification of neurologically impaired students. As with other factors which may contribute to a reading difficulty, the teacher's primary responsibility is to carefully observe and decide which students may warrant referral for a neurological evaluation. Referral of a student should always be based on an observed pattern of symptoms and should only be made when a student fails to respond after the best available diagnosis and remedial instruction or when identification of the student will enable the student to receive needed special services. In the absence of these two cases, a referral may cause the student more harm than good. In recent years, a proliferation of classification labels that have been associated with neurological disorders has emerged. Dunn reports 23 different terms that are used to describe brain damaged children ranging from "clumsy child" to "psychoneurologically disordered child."[25] Unless identification results in either better educational planning or better services for the student, the negative label, an unfortunate by-product of identification, may hinder more than help the student.

Symptoms of neurological problems fall into two categories—physical and educational. Physical symptoms include:

- ☐ *Physical incoordination.* Grossly awkward walking, running, writing, etc., in relation to overall physical development.
- ☐ *Hyperactivity.* Inability to concentrate that causes the child to rarely complete assignments, annoy others, and appear disinterested.
- ☐ *Headaches.* A history of persistent headaches.
- ☐ *Speech impediments.* Persistent blockage of speech, or articulation difficulties that are peculiar for the child's age.
- ☐ *Visual incoordination.* Poor saccadic eye movements, inability of the eyes to focus or to hold to a line of print.

Educational symptoms of neurological problems include:

- ☐ *Average or better than average intelligence.* General educational development deficient in terms of valid measures of intelligence.
- ☐ *Phonic blending deficiency.* Knowledge of sounds but inability to blend them into words.
- ☐ *Poor contextual reader.* Knowledge of a sight vocabulary but difficulties when those words are encountered in sentences.
- ☐ *Slow reading speed.* Poor reading rate, even with easy or familiar material.

- ☐ *Poor auditory discrimination.* Inability to discriminate between sounds of letters, without evidence of an auditory acuity deficiency.
- ☐ *Distractability.* Inattentiveness to designated tasks.
- ☐ *Abnormal behavior.* Overreaction to stimuli (e.g., laughing after others have stopped).
- ☐ *Poor ability to remember sequences.* Although apparently normally intelligent, difficulty in remembering verbal and nonverbal sequences.
- ☐ *Difficulties with visual perception.* Difficulty with spatial orientation often manifested in reversals of letters or words.

Obviously, these symptoms in isolation do not necessarily indicate a neurological disorder. A *pattern* of these symptoms that includes four or more of these indicates that a neurological disorder might exist. Students with this quantity of symptoms, whether identified in classroom or clinical diagnosis, should be considered legitimate referrals for neurological examinations.

Clements summarizes the ten most frequently cited characteristics of minimal brain dysfunction from over 100 publications in the following list:[26]

1. Hyperactivity.
2. Perceptual-motor impairments.
3. Emotional lability.
4. General coordination defects.
5. Disorders of attention.
6. Impulsivity.
7. Disorders of memory and thinking.
8. Specific learning disabilities in reading, arithmetic, writing, or spelling.
9. Disorders of speech and hearing.
10. Equivocal neurological signs and electroencephalographic irregularities.

An initial referral should be made to a pediatrician who has a background in diagnosing neurological disorders and is sympathetic to the educational realities of the classroom. During the first office visit, the pediatrician will conduct a neurological examination and obtain a detailed case history. If he or she detects evidence of a neurological disorder or notes a history of such factors as birth difficulties, head injury, or severe diseases accompanied by prolonged periods of high fever, further specialized testing may be recommended. (Hartlage and Hartlage discuss diagnostic evaluation in more detail.[27])

The reading specialist, upon receipt of the neurological report, relates the findings to other information gathered for the case study. The relationship of neurological problems to the entire case history must be considered in the recommendations for educational adjustment.

The classroom teacher, while waiting for the neurological report, should relieve the student from unnecessary frustration by relaxing tension and providing reading experiences in the area of the student's strengths. If the report indicates that the student does not have a neurological problem, the teacher will continue with the classroom diagnosis in an effort to find the area where correction should start. However, if the report does reveal a neurological problem, the classroom teacher should refer the student to a reading specialist, who will conduct a careful case evaluation, noting all educational aspects and precise recommendations concerning remedial techniques.

In attempting to meet the needs of the neurologically impaired student, cooperation and communication among professionals is essential. Medical personnel need to remember that a label alone does nothing to help a student. Neurologically impaired students represent a heterogeneous group for whom no single treatment routine may be expected to be successful. Medical specialists should attempt to be as descriptive as possible of the student's specific neurological strengths and weaknesses. This will enable the reading teacher to make informed educational decisions concerning remedial approaches to pursue for that particular student.

Likewise, educators can perform an excellent service to medical specialists in providing feedback concerning the observed effect of medical treatment. Classroom teachers can be invaluable in monitoring the effects of drug therapy treatment. Students who evidence attention deficit disorders are most often prescribed one of two central nervous system stimulants, methylphenidate (Ritalin) or dextroamphetamine (Dexedrine).[28] Teachers are in ideal position to notice changes in a student's attention to school-related tasks as well as the student's general ability to function in the classroom. These observations can aid the physician in evaluating the treatment's benefit or detriment to the student, and in adjusting subsequent prescriptions.[29]

Finally, Abrams reminds us that neurologically impaired students may be frustrated by events and conditions beyond their control. These students deserve an extra measure of our compassion and understanding.

> We must recognize that children who have experienced severe reading disabilities have packed a lifetime of pain into a few years. Much of this pain has been associated with the struggle to maintain their dignity in spite of an organism that refuses to

> be efficient. . . . The best thought out strategies and programs established by the most learned people can have little lifelong value or durable impact if the interpersonal relationship patterns are impersonal, insincere, or patronizing. We strongly believe that it is the manner in which contact with the child is maintained that determines the success or failure of anything else.[30]

EMOTIONAL DIAGNOSIS

Emotional difficulties, when considered in terms of reading difficulties, create cause-and-effect confusion. Sometimes emotional disturbances cause reading difficulties; however, many emotional problems are not the cause, but the result, of reading failure. Unfortunately, often no clear line of distinction exists. When emotional disturbances cause reading difficulties, performance in all learning areas suffers. Often, it is in the diagnosis of a reader that this area of difficulty is first uncovered; however, assessing the severity of the difficulty is properly the task of psychological personnel. Conversely, although emotional reactions may complicate a reading diagnosis, they are often not the cause, but rather an effect of the reading failure itself. Most students who encounter difficulty in learning to read exhibit some symptoms of emotional conflict, and these symptoms often diminish or disappear with effective instruction after the diagnosis. In summarizing the research, Bond, Tinker, Wasson, and Wasson conclude, "Examination of all the evidence does make it fairly clear that emotional maladjustment is much more frequently the effect than the cause of reading disability."[31] An effective diagnosis may result in relieving the student of some home and school pressures by exposing the fact that the student's difficulty is not due to a poor attitude or a low level of intellectual potential, but rather to a skill deficiency, which, when corrected, will permit the student to perform as expected.

The classroom teacher and the reading specialist must be aware that most students with reading difficulties react emotionally to their failure through such behavior patterns as refusing to read, not enjoying school, disliking their teachers, or causing problems at home. Assessment of emotional adjustment is complicated for several reasons. First, an individual's behavior is often inconsistent and unpredictable. For example, when frustrated an emotionally disturbed student may lash out in defiance on one occasion, and another time, with similar provocation, may react by being withdrawn and quiet. Secondly, an individual's personality traits change over time. Therefore, an assessment of personality must be considered as an indication of a student's personal adjustment at a given point in time. Thirdly, an individual's personality is complex and is made up of the interactions of many factors. Nunnally states, "One of the impediments to discussing the measurement of personality is that there are so many different kinds of attributes that are included under the name."[32] The more thorough an understanding the teacher has of the intrafamilial, peer, and school relationships, the better the likelihood of an effective diagnosis. The teacher should observe the student in reading situations, note pertinent emotional reactions, include those reactions in the diagnosis, and consider them in the recommendations. However, these reactions should be labeled cautiously as causative of a reading difficulty because their presence does not necessarily make the student a candidate for referral.

Realistically recognizing their limitations as detectors of emotional difficulties and at the same time recognizing the emotional entanglement of these types of students, teachers and reading specialists follow similar diagnostic procedures. Through the cooperation of all the educators in contact with the student, information may be assembled concerning the student, the home, the school situation, and the student's behaviors in peer group encounters.

Information Concerning the Student

Due to their daily contact with the student, classroom teachers are in a unique position to obtain valuable information about the student's reactions to many situations. Often the reading specialist must rely on information supplied by the teacher, the parents, or from a personal interview with the student. Useful information would include the following:

- ☐ The student's attitude toward family, school, teacher, and friends.
- ☐ The student's awareness of behavior and learning problems and the student's suggestions for their improvement.
- ☐ The student's attitude toward reading and the student's self-assessment of his or her own reading skill.
- ☐ The student's development of worthwhile personal goals and the student's level of commitment toward reaching those goals.

Gathered informally by the classroom teacher or formally by the reading teacher, all information in doubtful areas must be checked for reliability. One can do this easily by comparing reliable sources. A student may have claimed to be earning *B*s and

*C*s in school. The educator will rely more readily on the student's other statements about school if, when checking the school records, one finds that the student does indeed make *B*s and *C*s.

Formal personality testing can also prove useful in determining emotional difficulties. The California Test of Personality, one of the more popular instruments for classroom use, provides standardized evaluations of the student's reactions to questions concerning personal and social adjustment. This test may be administered individually or in classroom-sized groups. Since adequate performance requires that the student possess reading skills close to the grade level of the test, the very poor reader will be unable to read the questions. In evaluating The California Test of Personality, one should not place undue emphasis on any low set of scores; however, such scores may be considered indicative of areas of potential personality problems. (Scores indicating the necessity for referral are described in the test manual.) Final verification will not come from this type of testing, but rather from careful teacher observation and referral to psychological personnel.

Personality testing using incomplete sentences provides an informal way of obtaining valuable information. The student is expected to respond to several incomplete sentences, such as "I like books, but . . . ," "My home is . . . ," "I like my brother and . . . ." The most reliable use of this type of information is noting patterns of responses and verifying them by direct observation of the student in situations where these responses may be reflected in behavior. Again, the examiner should be cautioned against excessive analysis of any slightly deviate responses and urged to leave to psychological personnel the final assessment of the emotional stability of the individual being tested.

Paper-and-pencil personality tests are considered inherently weak, since students often anticipate what they consider acceptable responses. Ebel notes:

> Much of personality has to do with typical behavior in actual situations. But the behavior exhibited on a paper-and-pencil test is a limited, artificial kind. Even if a student knows with reasonable accuracy how he would behave in the situation described (and often he does not know) he may find it advantageous to report something else. It is possible for an examinee to "fake good" on most personality tests if he chooses to do so.[33]

Furthermore, these tests tend to record "of-the-moment" responses. Those who have had bad days may score poorly on such tests; however, twenty-four hours later, they may score many points higher. When this occurs, the scores obtained obviously have severely limited use in the diagnosis of emotional problems.

To note personality characteristics in a more natural situation students should be observed at play. An investigation of play behavior may be based on the following types of questions: Do they play with others their own age? Does it appear that they are accepted by their peers? Do they play fairly? Do they play enthusiastically? Answers to such questions provide further analysis of the total behavior pattern without the limitations of paper-and-pencil tests. Caplan and Caplan believe that the analysis of free play has definite advantages in emotional diagnosis:

> Since it is impossible to determine exactly what goes on in a child's mind or to get children to talk like adults, specialists who work with distressed children have found that much can be learned about them from watching them at play during which most children are able to reveal both their imaginary and real life.[34]

Silvern summarizes the current research:

> All of the studies reviewed take the position that the child's social ability/social-interaction is reflected in the child's play. By observing a child's play we can make assumptions about the child's social interactions. Play, then, is the vehicle for *examining* socialization.[35]

Both of these authorities suggest that play analysis has particular value with younger children.

A Study of the Home

Although home visits are uncommon as a result of a reading diagnosis, under certain circumstances such visits are profitable. When it appears that situations at home are impeding the student's language or emotional development, the educator who hopes to improve these conditions must make a home visit. However, teachers should make home visits only when accompanied by another school professional. In cases where a home visit would be of little value, one may gather information concerning home conditions through parental interviews or questionnaires. These are constructed to obtain information on the socioeconomic status of the home, availability of books, intrafamilial relations, parental efforts to assist the child, general family activities, and overall acceptance of the child in the home.

Abnormal home conditions should be brought to the attention of appropriate personnel (school officials, home-school visitors, social workers, and psychologists). Neither the classroom teacher nor the reading specialist can justifiably offer unsolicited advice to parents about home conditions unrelated to the student's educational progress. At times parents will turn to an educator and ask for consultation. Although it depends upon the individual situation, an educator is normally acting outside the proper professional role in offering advice in such cases. Offering advice concerning domestic affairs implies that one has training or information about effective solutions.

Tragically, many students today live under the specter of child abuse and neglect. An estimated 3 percent of school age children are at risk of serious physical injury from their parents each year. Add to that number the many other children who suffer each year from physical neglect and emotional mistreatment, and the number of children affected is staggering. Teachers are in a unique position to help these students by being in daily contact with them. Although other professionals may see children only infrequently, teachers see children every day and should be alert to physical and behavioral signals that may indicate the need for referral. Symptoms of child abuse and neglect include the following:

- ☐ Evidence of repeated injuries that are unexplained and apparently nonaccidental in origin.
- ☐ Frequent complaints of abdominal pain.
- ☐ Recurrent bruises, welts, wounds, fractures, or burns.
- ☐ Consistent hunger, underweight, or failure to thrive.
- ☐ Poor hygiene, inappropriate dress, or unattended physical problems.
- ☐ Evidence or report of sexual abuse.

In addition to the physical signs of abuse, teachers should be alert to behavioral indicators of child abuse. Students who display severe changes in mood, unusual apprehension of adults, or irrational fear of punishment may be victims of abuse.[36]

When child abuse is suspected, the teacher's professional duty is to report those suspicions to the proper authorities. In some areas this will be the building principal or other school administrator; in other areas abuse cases should be reported directly to local child service agencies. Because the physical safety of the child may be at stake, the teacher should not hesitate to refer any suspected case. If abuse is suspected, the teacher should neither interview the parents concerning the matter nor conduct a home visit. The teacher or school need not *prove* abuse—that is up to the appropriate child protective agency. The teacher's sole responsibility is to initiate timely referral.

Social workers may also be helpful in less severe instances if the teacher has reason to attribute a student's poor classroom performance to difficulties at home. These professionals are skilled in working with parents and investigating home situations. Some large school systems have found it worthwhile to have professional social workers on their staffs.

A Study of the School

The classroom teacher gathers relevant data for a classroom diagnosis and submits it to the reading specialist for case analysis. Information relating to attendance, ability to work and play with others, and reactions to various types of frustration should be obtained from the school. Teachers should note the student's behavior patterns in a wide variety of group settings. In this day of increased parental access to student records, subjective comments and anecdotal records are seldom included in a student's school records. When such notations are available, they should be considered in the diagnosis. When behavior patterns are not described in a student's records, they should be sought out through interviews or questionnaire responses from the teacher. Diagnosis that attempts to suggest instructional directions, without considering student behaviors, is incomplete and probably faulty.

If the educator is to be effective in obtaining such information, students and parents must be assured that it will be handled confidentially. A confidential approach on the part of both parents and educators is necessary for reliable data collection.

A number of characteristics exhibited in the school setting may serve to identify a student as a candidate for psychological referral. According to the definition of *seriously emotionally disturbed* included in Public Law 94-142, this student is one who exhibits one or more of the following characteristics over a long period of time and to a marked degree, which adversely affects educational performance:

1. An inability to learn which cannot be explained by intellectual, sensory, or health factors.
2. An inability to build or maintain satisfactory interpersonal relationships with peers and teachers.
3. Inappropriate types of behavior or feelings under normal circumstances.
4. A general pervasive mood of unhappiness or depression.
5. A tendency to develop physical symptoms or fears associated with personal or school problems.[37]

Each of these characteristics obviously can be expected to interfere with a student's ability to benefit from reading instruction. Once again, the proper response of the classroom teacher is to refer the student for examination and to make appropriate classroom adjustments pending the outcome of the evaluation.

Classroom adjustments for the student suspected to be emotionally disturbed or for the student who consistently displays antisocial behavior should be designed around clear limits and planned successes. Students should be clearly told what is expected of them in the classroom and should be aware of the consequences of their actions. Sometimes teachers are reluctant to be firm with the emotionally disturbed student, and yet, the resulting ambiguous standards for classroom behavior may be confusing to the student. At the same time, teachers should be both fair and consistent. Vacc recommends "straight talk" in working with these students.

> Some children, however, will change their behavior for the better almost immediately if it is clearly stated by the teacher how they should behave. The teacher should tell the child that they are going to work together to change the behavior that is causing problems in school and with friends and that the child is going to participate in changing his or her own behavior with the instruction of the teacher.[38]

Another key to working with emotionally disturbed students is to plan for success. Failure situations that produce frustration should be minimized so that students come to expect success. This, in turn, will help to build trust and rapport between the students and the teacher. Students learn that the teacher will not ask them to do something they are incapable of doing. This new-found confidence often will inspire a student to greater achievement. If the frustrating situations are removed that caused either avoidance or hostility in the past, the undesirable behaviors may also diminish. Glass, Christiansen, and Christiansen give some insights into how these suggestions may be translated into classroom practice.

> Since it is understood that many students have a fear of failure in addition to anxiety over learning, traditional testing is minimized and academic lessons are made as informal and relaxing as possible. Emphasis is placed on pointing out correct responses rather than incorrect responses. As the students' academic skills and self-confidence increase, more challenging academic tasks are provided.[39]

The classroom teacher must be willing to give such students special considerations; negative reactions can only drive the student to further reject the learning process and environment. At the same time, the teacher has an obligation to the other students in the classroom to provide an environment conducive to learning. If disruption occurs, alternative strategies for dealing with the emotionally disturbed student must be found.

Classroom teachers should also work to prevent complex emotional disorders. Their reactions, for example, to a student's initial signs of frustration and failure to a situation may cause the student's acceptance or rejection of a temporary solution. Although students must be challenged in school, not all will meet these challenges with the same degree of success. Teachers may relax tensions and feelings of failure by their attitudes toward the efforts of the less successful. All students must succeed in school. Teachers should emphasize the successes of all, but particularly the less successful. However, they should beware of false praise—students resent it. Instead of false praise, they should structure situations in which, with a little effort, a student can legitimately succeed and be praised. More of these types of techniques are discussed in later chapters.

All information and notations concerning the student's emotional behavior should be included and evaluated in the case analysis. The reading teacher should apply the recommendations for the necessary educational adjustment. If the classroom teacher, after instituting these recommendations, finds further complications, the student should be referred to the reading specialist.

Referral decisions are never easily made. The teacher must carefully weigh the potential benefits to the student against the anxiety that referral often creates on the part of students and parents. Teachers are reminded to base referral decisions on a pattern of behaviors and not on test performance alone. Test scores may be a first indicator of student need; however, abnormal scores should always be confirmed by systematic teacher observation of the student's performance. Clearly, in the final analysis, students are better served when a referral is made and no difficulty is found than when no referral is initiated and a problem is allowed to persist.

SUMMARY

Reading is a complex act made up of the interaction of many factors. Intellectual, physical, sensory, emotional, social, and neurological factors all contribute to reading success or failure. The teacher must possess an awareness of the manner in which each of these areas influence the development of reading skill. Knowledge of diagnostic procedures and of referral avenues will enable the teacher to make the most complete assessment of a student's reading difficulties.

Often the types of assessment discussed in this chapter must be undertaken by a specialist from outside the education field. However, teachers should understand the relationship of these areas to reading achievement and be familiar with some of the technical terminology associated with diagnosis in these varied areas. Just as reading itself is a complex act composed of a variety of aspects, a complete reading diagnosis must sometimes encompass the expertise of specialists from many fields.

NOTES

1. Alan O. Ross, *Psychological Aspects of Learning Disabilities and Reading Disorders* (New York: McGraw-Hill Book Company, 1976), 168.
2. Arnold J. Lien, *Measurement and Evaluation of Learning* (Dubuque, Iowa: Wm. C. Brown Company, 1976), 142.
3. David A. Payne, *The Specification and Measurement of Learning Outcomes* (Lexington, Massachusetts: Xerox College Publishing Company, 1968), 129–40.
4. Albert E. Bartz, *Basic Statistical Concepts in Education and the Behavioral Sciences* (Minneapolis: Burgess Publishing, 1976), 343.
5. Bartz, *Basic Statistical Concepts,* 343–44.
6. Donald B. Helms and Jeffrey S. Turner, *Exploring Child Behavior* (Philadelphia: W. B. Saunders Company, 1976), 492.
7. Booney Vance, "Intellectual Characteristics of Reading Disabled Children," *Journal of Research and Development in Education* 14 (Summer 1981): 11–21.
8. David W. Moore and O. Paul Wielan, "WISC–R Scatter Indexes of Children Referred for Reading Diagnosis," *Journal of Learning Disabilities* 14 (November 1981): 511–14.
9. Eugene A. Jongsma, "Test Review: Peabody Picture Vocabulary Test–Revised," *Journal of Reading* 25 (January 1982): 360–64.
10. Albert J. Harris and Edward R. Sipay, *How to Increase Reading Ability,* 7th ed. (New York: Longman, 1980), 154–55.
11. Harris and Sipay, *How to Increase Reading Ability,* 155.
12. Guy L. Bond, Miles A. Tinker, Barbara B. Wasson, and John B. Wasson, *Reading Difficulties: Their Diagnosis and Correction,* 5th ed. (Englewood Cliffs, New Jersey: Prentice-Hall, 1984), 42–45.
13. Bond, Tinker, Wasson, and Wasson, *Reading Difficulties,* 42–43.
14. Donald L. Cleland, "Clinical Materials for Appraising Disabilities in Reading," *The Reading Teacher* 17 (March 1964): 428.

15. Robert L. Ebel, *Essentials of Educational Measurement* (Englewood Cliffs, New Jersey: Prentice-Hall, 1972), 87.
16. John J. Pikulski, "Assessing Information About Intelligence and Reading," *The Reading Teacher* 29 (November 1975): 162.
17. Charles R. Kelley, *Visual Screening and Child Development* (Raleigh, North Carolina: North Carolina State College, 1957), 11.
18. Kelley, *Visual Screening and Child Development,* 11.
19. *Teacher's Guide to Vision Problems* (St. Louis: American Optometric Association, 1953).
20. Jules C. Abrams, "The Psychologist-Educator Views the Relationship of Vision to Reading and Related Learning Disabilities," *Journal of Learning Disabilities* 14 (December 1981): 566, 567.
21. Kelley, *Visual Screening and Child Development,* 11.
22. John Salvia and James E. Ysseldyke, *Assessment in Special and Remedial Education* (Boston: Houghton Mifflin, 1978), 336.
23. Bond, Tinker, Wasson, and Wasson, *Reading Difficulties,* 61.
24. Helen M. Robinson, *Why Pupils Fail in Reading* (Chicago: The University of Chicago Press, 1946), 218.
25. Lloyd M. Dunn, "Minimal Brain Dysfunction: A Dilemma for Educators," in *Brain Damage in School Age Children,* ed. H. Carl Haywood (Washington, D.C.: Council for Exceptional Children, 1968), 163.
26. Sam D. Clements, *Minimal Brain Dysfunction in Children,* (Washington, D.C.: GPO, 1966), 13.
27. Lawrence C. Hartlage and Patricia L. Hartlage, "Application of Neuropsychological Principles in the Diagnosis of Learning Disabilities," in *Brain Function and Reading Disabilities.* ed. Lester Tarnopol and Muriel Tarnopol (Baltimore: University Park Press, 1977), 111–46.
28. Laurie L. Humphries, "Medication and Reading Disability," *Journal of Research and Development in Education* 14 (Summer 1981): 54–57.
29. Barbara Bateman, "Educational Implications of Minimal Brain Dysfunction," *The Reading Teacher* 27 (April 1974): 662–68.
30. Jules C. Abrams, "Minimal Brain Dysfunction and Dyslexia," *Reading World* 14 (March 1975): 227.
31. Bond, Tinker, Wasson, and Wasson, *Reading Difficulties,* 83.
32. Jum C. Nunnally, *Educational Measurement and Evaluation,* 2d ed. (New York: McGraw-Hill, 1972), 469.
33. Ebel, *Essentials of Educational Measurement,* 520.
34. Frank Caplan and Theresa Caplan, *The Power of Play* (Garden City, New York: Anchor Press/Doubleday, 1973), p. 54.
35. Steven B. Silvern, "Play as an Avenue for Social Growth," *Journal of Research and Development in Education* 14 (Spring 1981): 110.
36. Donald F. Kline, *Child Abuse and Neglect: A Primer for School Personnel* (Reston, Virginia: Council for Exceptional Children, 1977), 17–25.

37. Department of Health, Education, and Welfare, "Education of Handicapped Children," *Federal Register* 42 (August 23, 1977): 42478.
38. Nicholas A. Vacc, "Coping with the Behaviorally Disturbed Child in the Classroom," *Viewpoints in Teaching and Learning* 55 (Summer 1979): 32.
39. Raymond M. Glass, Jeanne Christiansen, and James L. Christiansen, *Teaching Exceptional Students in the Regular Classroom* (Boston: Little, Brown and Company, 1982), 88.

SUGGESTED READINGS

Cleland, Donald L. "Clinical Materials for Appraising Disabilities in Reading." *The Reading Teacher* 17 (March 1964): 428. This interesting, easy-to-read article presents summaries of the various appraisal materials available for clinical diagnosis. The discussion of reading capacity and appropriate techniques for determining it is particularly interesting.

Geoffrion, Leo D. and Schuster, Karen E. *Auditory Handicaps and Reading*. Newark, Delaware: International Reading Association, 1980. This annotated bibliography provides an excellent starting point for anyone researching information on this important subject.

Harris, Albert J. and Sipay, Edward R. *How to Increase Reading Ability*, Seventh Edition, New York: Longman, 1980. Harris and Sipay discuss several techniques for the use of mental age in determining reading expectancy scores.

Hartlage, Lawrence C. and Hartlage, Patricia L. "Application of Neuropsychological Principles in the Diagnosis of Learning Disabilities," in *Brain Function and Reading Disabilities*, ed. by Lester Tarnopol and Muriel Tarnopol. Baltimore, Maryland: University Park Press, 1977, pp. 111–46. The authors discuss neuropsychological assessment instruments, their interpretation, and subsequent prescription. A comprehensive neurological assessment battery is listed and several illustrative cases are presented.

Salvia, John and Ysseldyke, James E. *Assessment in Special and Remedial Education*, Boston, Massachusetts: Houghton Mifflin Company, 1978. Although a number of the topics contained in this chapter receive excellent treatment in this text, the reader is particularly urged to review chapter 16 which discusses visual and auditory assessment.

U.S. Department of Health, Education, and Welfare. *Child Abuse and Neglect*, Washington, D.C.: HEW, 1977. This self-instructional text developed for Head Start personnel presents useful information regarding the characteristics, reporting, treatment, and prevention of abuse and neglect.

Editorial

Gerald L. Fowler
is a reading supervisor for the Carlisle Public Schools, Carlisle, Pennsylvania.

Anthony did not like school. More specifically, he did not like being in my reading class. I took some solace in the fact that records indicated that he had not liked being in previous classes either. But now Anthony was a sixth grader with developing emotional problems. Also, he could not read very well. Standardized tests placed him about four years behind his peers, with a general weakness in most skill areas. Still, Anthony seemed bright. He could argue his case logically in class discussions and he was a leader among his classmates. He took charge of most playground activities, and other children would collect at his desk during any free moments of the day. When it came time for reading, Anthony would often become sullen and look for other things to do. Frequently, he would begin an emotional outburst with a statement intended to hurt or anger a designated target. It was obvious to me that he was embarrassed by his reading problem. Unfortunately, there seemed to be no way to relieve this apparent embarrassment.

One day, however, an interesting thing happened. Anthony came to me and said that his mother's birthday was coming soon and he had saved about three dollars to buy her a present. He asked my opinion as to a gift and I could tell by his expression that he had far more expensive hopes. I suggested an alternative plan. He would surrender his money to me and I would get the ingredients for a cake, a cake he would bake and decorate in school. Anthony liked the idea. The cake was magnificent and it was made with the help of the school secretary and cafeteria staff. No less amazing than the cake was the change in Anthony's attitude over the ensuing weeks. He attempted most of the reading assignments without quarrel and even filled his free time with independent reading. I suspect that Anthony realized that his reading problem did not diminish his value to his teacher and his friends. We liked him just as much anyway! Buy the end of the year, Anthony was reading in sixth-grade materials and as cocky as ever. I remember a final challenge to me to "pick any book in our room, pick any page" and he would read it. I did and he did.

Organize Materials
Choose a Quiet Spot
Highlight the Main Ideas

4

Classroom Diagnosis

CHAPTER OUTLINE

CHAPTER EMPHASES

- ☐ The first task in classroom diagnosis should be assessing the learning climate.
- ☐ Classroom diagnosis involves the observation of student behavior, limited testing, and assessment of interests and attitudes.
- ☐ Student strengths and needs should receive equal attention.
- ☐ Records of classroom assessment are essential.

Note: All tests mentioned in this chapter are included in appendix A, which provides a detailed checklist indicating each test's characteristics.

The classroom teacher, who has a relatively long acquaintance with a student, relies heavily on informal observation, systematic observation, informal testing, and student self-assessment for educational diagnosis of difficulties in reading. The classroom teacher considers the learning climate, the various causes of reading difficulties, the possible instructional adjustments that can be made, and the continuous assessment of student progress.

THE LEARNING CLIMATE

When teachers notice that certain students are experiencing difficulties in reading, their first step should logically be to conduct a quick assessment of the learning climate. While it would be impossible to note all aspects of the learning climate in each teacher's classroom, a brief look at some important factors may prove helpful.

1. Is the climate one in which students are comfortable? Are such aspects as ventilation, lighting, and room cleanliness appropriate for learning? Since reading requires vigorous attention to the tasks at hand, physical discomfort can easily cause difficulties. Most of the physical aspects of discomfort can be adjusted easily once noticed.
2. Is the climate one that fosters communication? Are there any signs that students are experiencing difficulty communicating with the teacher or with other students? The threat of ridicule or failure can discourage some students from even attempting to communicate. Students are well aware of the risks involved in attempting to communicate. When risk taking is not worthwhile, communication becomes difficult and it may appear as though the students are not able to respond. Risk taking and communication can be improved by:
   - ☐ Starting comprehension discussions with personal questions that all students can answer without the fear of being wrong. For example, if the starter question is, "What did you like most about this story?" all students can respond without the fear of being wrong.
   - ☐ Focusing on a discussion about what has been read, as opposed to a teacher-questioning session. For example, after using a personal starter question, the teacher and students can discuss agreements and disagreements about the responses of others.

By staying away from a questioning session in which the students are penalized for being wrong, the spirit of communication can be developed.

- ☐ Staying at the eye level of the students instead of standing in front of them.
- ☐ Encouraging student-to-student communication and teaching students to regard the thoughts of others as important even when they disagree.

These and other aspects of facilitating risk taking and communication will be discussed in detail in chapter 9.

3. Are the materials for instruction appropriate? Are the materials suited to the reading levels of the students who are experiencing difficulty in reading? If not, then there may be no need for further assessment. The materials should be adjusted and the students observed to see if the difficulties disappear.
4. Are there opportunities for individualizing portions of instruction? Do all students have to complete the same assignments in the same amount of time or are there alternatives? If alternatives do not exist, can they be developed? Many readers appear to be having difficulty when they are attempting activities that are not appropriate for them, either because the activities are not geared to the students' strengths, or the time allotted for completion is not sufficient.

Numerous aspects of the learning climate may be assessed to determine if reading difficulties can be attributed to the climate instead of to the student. The four mentioned here are common causes of difficulties that incorrectly appear to be within the student. Other common aspects that may be examined include inappropriate class size, inappropriate instructional strategies, discriminatory treatment of students, and the effect of labels that are attached to certain students.

Observing Student Behavior

If the learning climate seems appropriate and if a student is not able to respond when the climate is adjusted, then the classroom teacher needs to observe and assess that student's behavior to determine where the difficulties might lie. Some examples of the types of behaviors to look for follow.

1. Do the students have difficulty with reading comprehension activities? If students are not effectively gaining meaning from their reading, then they are reading

nonsense. When reading without gaining meaning, the student makes many errors that may appear to be vocabulary problems or problems with word attack skills. In this chapter several approaches to assessing comprehension skills will be presented.

2. Are the difficulties most apparent when the students are reading in the content areas? Many students do satisfactory work in teacher-directed reading lessons but seem to have considerable difficulty with independent reading in content-area books. The particular books, the assigned activities, and the nature of the difficulty need to be assessed. For example, the answers to the following questions would be helpful:
   - ☐ Are students having difficulty with all content books or just certain ones? If certain ones, why?
   - ☐ What features of the books creating the difficulty can be identified? Are readability levels too high?
   - ☐ Can the assigned activities be changed to make the reading of content books an easier task? Are new concepts introduced prior to independent reading? Are new vocabulary words discussed?
   - ☐ Are study guides available for student use? If not, are the students certain of the specific tasks in the assignment?
3. Do oral reading activities seem to be difficult for these students? Many students can read silently and answer questions but cannot read that same material orally with fluency. Assessment of the nature of the difficulty should be made before further oral reading activities are planned.
4. Do these students read accurately and with good comprehension, but so slowly that they never finish their reading when others do? A slow reader causes real problems for the teacher. These readers hold up the entire group while others wait until they finish their reading.

IMPLEMENTING CLASSROOM DIAGNOSIS

Classroom diagnosis can take place before, during, or after instruction. Each technique has distinct advantages and limitations and most teachers use each of them at times.

Diagnosis before Instruction

Prior to planning instruction, the level of skill development of students should be known. This information can be collected

Appropriate classroom climate is important for effective independent reading.

from sources such as past school records, student self-assessments, and tests.

School records contain a variety of information ranging from very useful to completely useless in nature. When using this information, teachers should first try to assess the reliability of the data found on school records. Teacher comments, test scores, health information, and past scholastic performance are usually found in school records. Unfortunately, much of this information is in the form of global information and is of little use. For example, test scores usually indicate total test scores and give little indication of how those scores were obtained. A low score on an IQ test may appear in the records as an intelligence quotient; however, if the test itself were available it might show that the student did satisfactorily on all but one section, and that that section lowered the total score. In many instances, however, useful data are found in school records, so they should be examined prior to initiating testing. If, for example, a teacher is curious about a student's intellectual ability, the school records may contain several indicators of that ability, making additional testing unnecessary. When those indicators provide consistent data and have been collected at different times in the student's schooling, they can be used with some degree of confidence. If, however, these indicators are not consistent or have been collected over a short period of time, one should use them cautiously.

Student self-assessment provides surprisingly useful information. Numerous professionals use self-report as one of the first steps in diagnosis: the doctor wants to know how you are feeling, the dentist wants to know which tooth hurts, and the lawyer wants to know a client's opinion of the problem. Many students have very accurate perceptions of their difficulty and are willing to discuss those perceptions. The following questions are useful in getting the students thinking about how reading is working for them:

1. Do you think you read better, worse, or about the same as other students in your class?
2. What do you do best when reading?
3. What causes you the most difficulty when reading?
4. Are you reading a book for fun? (If the answer is *yes*, ask for the name of the book.)
5. If you were to describe reading to a kindergarten child, what would you say?
6. Why do you read books? For fun, information, because you have to, or for another reason?
7. What could your teacher do to make reading easier for you?

After assessing the reading skills of the students who have already provided teachers with a self-report, teachers can better help them understand themselves as readers. Students make accurate self-reports more than 50 percent of the time. Accuracy is determined by comparing student self-reports with data collected during diagnosis. Many teachers attempt to determine the strengths and weaknesses of their students by testing them before instruction. They use these test results as they plan future instruction and as they plan for grouping students. Six basic types of testing instruments are available for classroom diagnosis: standardized tests, prepared informal inventories, teacher-made informal inventories, cloze tests, maze tests, and criterion-referenced tests.

The type of information needed for diagnosis should determine which testing instrument is selected. Some instruments are designed to measure the progress of groups of students, while others are designed to provide information on individual students. Some help teachers obtain information concerning the reading levels of students, while others provide information on skill development. By first determining what type of information they need, teachers can make intelligent choices. The following descriptions provide an overview of the various types of instruments available for classroom diagnosis.

Standardized Tests. Most schools test regularly with one of the major standardized tests (Iowa Test of Basic Skills, California Reading Test, Comprehensive Test of Basic Skills, Stanford Reading Test, Metropolitan Reading Test, or the Gates MacGinitie Reading Test). These tests are commonly used and many teachers already have student scores available to them. The tests usually yield total reading, vocabulary, and comprehension scores. Students usually take these tests in class-size groups, and their performance is to be completed within specified time limits; the reading section of most of these tests can be administered within an hour. Some of the tests have subscores relating to various types of reading vocabulary and comprehension skills. Standardized test scores are norm based (the scores obtained are compared to the score distribution obtained from the population upon which the test was normed). This procedure assumes approximately equal numbers of students scoring above and below the test's normed mean for a given grade level.

Standardized test scores are nearly useless for classroom diagnosis.[1] The tests' limitations have been discussed by many authorities in reading. First, since they are administered to groups, multiple-choice answers are required, which encourages guessing. Second, the standardizing procedures are subject to error, which causes considerable concern about their reliability. Third, their ability to match the student with a given reading level is constantly under question. Finally, the use of subtests has been discouraged because of the extreme lack of reliability of these measures.

However, since schools administer tests to determine generally how well students are doing, two diagnostic uses of standardized test scores are recommended.

1. While the earned scores do not reflect accurate reading grade levels, extremely low scores usually indicate reading difficulty. Therefore, prior to instruction, teachers can gain an idea of which students may experience difficulties; they may be able to identify those students most in need of informal diagnosis. If the scores in table 4–1 were obtained at the beginning of fourth grade, Jack and Portia logically would be selected as those most in need of further diagnosis due to their extremely low performance.
2. While subtest scores do not meet reliability standards, extreme differences in subtest scores can serve as indicators of possible skill difficulties. For example, in table 4–1, Jack and Marcia exhibit extreme differences between word meaning and paragraph meaning scores.

TABLE 4–1
Standardized test grade equivalents

Student	Word Meaning	Paragraph Meaning
Jack	1.3	2.3
Portia	1.9	2.0
Larry	3.4	3.5
Marcia	2.7	3.7
Cheryl	3.5	3.8
Judy	3.6	3.7
Pat	3.7	3.9
Juan	4.1	4.0
Robin	4.2	3.9
Dolores	4.1	4.1

The teacher should not accept these scores at face value. Instead, the scores should suggest that something may be wrong. The teacher should continue the diagnosis, usually through the use of informal techniques.

Teachers will find standardized test scores recorded in either grade equivalents, percentiles, or stanines. Since grade equivalents are often incorrectly confused with grade levels and since they do not reflect a student's relative position with other students, the use of stanines or percentiles is preferred. Stanine scores range from a low of 1 to a high of 9. Percentiles range from 1 to 99, 1 again being low.

The two uses of standardized test scores are suggested only if scores are available. Tests should not be administered solely for the purpose of obtaining such scores, however, since they are more reliably obtained from other sources.

Prepared Informal Inventories. Several publishing companies and many school districts have prepared informal testing instruments that are useful for classroom diagnosis. Informal inventories are usually developed by teachers from the actual materials the students will be expected to use during instruction. Inventories already prepared for teachers generally use a sampling technique, where words are selected from a sampling of commonly used reading materials. Other inventories include paragraphs for oral and silent reading. Teachers using these instruments can obtain measures of the student's oral reading accuracy and silent reading comprehension as well as skill development. The paragraphs are usually evaluated through the use of readability formulas or taken from materials that have been graded previously.

One commercially prepared informal instrument is the Botel Reading Inventory (Revised). This inventory contains four major sections. The Word Recognition Test requires students to read graded lists of words orally. The Word Opposites Test requires the student to identify antonyms in graded word lists. It can also be used for reading expectancy when the teacher reads the words to the student (see figure 4–1). The Decoding Test contains four sections: letter naming, beginning consonant sound/letter awareness, rhyme sound/letter pattern awareness, and decoding syllable/spelling patterns. The Spelling Placement Test consists of frequently used spelling words. Parts of this inventory are group tests, while other parts must be administered individually. Testing can be conducted quickly and provide teachers with a survey of their students' strengths.

Results, such as those in table 4–2, can be useful in placing students in suitable books and in making initial decisions about areas of needed instruction.

A third grade teacher with this type of diagnostic data early in the school year can make grouping decisions and book placements with considerable confidence. Betty and Simone's scores look very much alike on the first two subtests, but not so much alike in spelling. The same can be said for Linda and Maria.

The data in table 4–2 from the Botel Reading Inventory is obviously more useful than the data in table 4–1, because it

BOTEL READING INVENTORY **B**

Word Opposites Test (Reading)

Directions: Pick a word in each line which means the opposite or nearly the opposite of the numbered word. Draw a line under it.
Example:
1. work find play stop

Name ____________

Date ____________

Teacher ____________

	A		a	b	c
(First)	1.	father	birthday	mother	children
	2.	boy	shoe	train	girl
	3.	in	eat	one	out
	4.	big	away	little	around
	5.	here	live	find	there
	6.	morning	please	night	horse
	7.	up	there	from	down
	8.	him	bag	ask	her
	9.	go	stop	boat	kitten
	10.	yes	saw	no	fish

Score ______%

FIGURE 4–1
The Word Opposites Test from the Botel Reading Inventory by Morton Botel. (Copyright © 1978 by Follett Publishing Company. Used by permission.)

TABLE 4–2
Botel Reading Inventory sample results

Student	Word Recognition*	Word Opposites*	Spelling % correct** Grade 1	Grade 2	Grade 3	Grade 4
Betty	2–1	2–2	100	85	70	—
Simone	2–1	2–2	85	70	—	—
Janet	2–1	2–2	100	90	70	—
Les	2–2	2–2	100	80	60	—
Mae	3–1	3–2	90	90	80	60
Linda	3–1	3–1	100	100	90	60
Maria	3–1	3–1	100	80	60	—
Jane	3–2	4	100	100	90	70
Joan	3–2	5	100	100	100	90
Jose	4	5	100	100	90	70

*Grade level equivalents.
**Testing stops when a student scores below 80 percent.

relates more closely to instruction. When teachers add data concerning oral reading and comprehension, it can be even more useful.

Another prepared informal inventory, the Individual Evaluation Procedures in Reading,[2] features passages taken from the content areas of literature, science, and history. It measures ability levels from primer level to tenth grade and has two forms. The examiner starts by administering a word recognition test to determine probable starting levels for the graded passages. Since some readers do well when reading basal-type stories, but have difficulty in content materials, this inventory proves particularly useful.

Teacher-made Informal Reading Inventories (IRIs). Teachers can develop informal tests having the same features as those prepared commercially. Using the material from which they intended to teach the students, teachers can assess a reader's abilities to recognize words, read orally, and read silently for comprehension. Many school systems develop IRIs for use by their teachers. Constructing such instruments can be time consuming and requires considerable knowledge of both the reading process and test construction. Interpretation can be even more difficult. Powell raises serious questions concerning traditional norms used on informal inventories.[3] Others also have found the subject of norms for informal inventories rather perplexing.[4] Betts is acknowledged as creator of the IRI as a functional measurement instrument.[5] Since then, Powell has conducted numerous studies attempting to establish criteria that teachers can use when interpreting informal inventories.[6]

Powell's latest study of criteria for interpretation of informal reading inventory results can be applied by a study of comprehension, word recognition, and other systematic behavior. Powell states, however, "The comprehension dimension is the most important of the three in determining final placement. When comprehension drops below the criterion for a given level, then it matters not what happens on the other two dimensions."[7]

Powell contends that the comprehension and word recognition criteria will vary with the difficulty of the material. His criteria can be seen in table 4–3.[8]

These criteria are based on oral reading at first sight. The criteria were determined by comparing IRI scores with scores on cloze tests. Word recognition errors in oral reading include insertions, omissions, mispronunciations, substitutions, unknown words, and transpositions. Other errors such as repetitions, disregarding punctuation, nonfluent reading, etc., should be noted and evaluated diagnostically, but should not be used for determining word recognition scores for IRIs.[9]

A student reading a second-grade book would be considered to be reading independently when making only one word recognition error per seventeen running words. A student reading from a fourth-grade book would be considered to be reading at

TABLE 4–3
Informal reading inventory scoring criteria by performance grade level

Performance Level	Word Recognition	Comprehension
Independent		
1–2	1/17	80+
3–5	1/27+	85+
6+	1/35+	90+
Instructional		
1–2	1/8–1/16	55–80
3–5	1/13–1/26	60–85
6+	1/18–1/35	65–90
Frustration		
1–2	1/7–	55–
3–5	1/12–	60–
6+	1/17–	65–

the frustration level when making one or more word recognition errors for every twelve running words. Powell checked this criterion against a dependent criterion, on a test of comprehension at each level cited. Test results can be used in much the same manner as that suggested for commercially prepared informal inventories. A major advantage of teacher-made inventories centers around the ability to make the test cover a wider range of reading materials than do many commercially prepared tests. The larger sampling tends to produce more reliable results. However, two serious problems occur with their construction. The teacher may have difficulty selecting materials and asking questions that are accurate measures of the student's development, and grading the materials accurately.

However, with some training, teachers can select materials and ask questions that are accurate measures of the student's development. Also, they are more capable of interpreting the results when they have developed the instrument themselves. However, without training and without a thorough knowledge of the skills of reading, many sloppy, inaccurate, relatively useless instruments have been developed. Also, publishers tend to pay little attention to the readability level of materials even if they place grade-level numbers on the books.[10] Even then the readability level is generally an average of the readability levels of the individual pages. Through readability checks on several basals, teachers become aware that a "fifth-grade" basal can range in readability level from second- to eighth-grade.[11] If the teacher uses these materials for an informal inventory and happens to select pages that are at the extremes of the ranges (second- and eighth-grade levels in the examples), the assessment of a student's reading ability will be inaccurate. For example, the *Autobiography of Malcolm X* was rated at readability levels of fifth, eighth, and tenth grade when the examiner used three different readability formulas.[12]

A problem exists with matching performance prior to instruction with any given material. In fact, mismatching probably occurs all too frequently. A student tendency to change reading ability with the material's content contributes to the mismatching. Books tend to be inaccurately matched with their grade level, particularly in the content areas. Informal inventories provide more useful information than standardized tests, even considering their limitations. With teacher made inventories, mismatching is reduced since the student is tested from samples of the same material in which instruction will take place.

Cloze Tests. Closure testing may help circumvent the problem of mismatching and labeling. Cloze tests constructed from the types of materials students are expected to use can provide useful information concerning the students' abilities to work with various types of printed materials. The procedure for closure testing is to select several passages of at least 150 words from the various books to be used and retype the selection, deleting every fifth word. All proper nouns as well as the entire first sentence should be left intact, as in the following example.

> Mary had a little lamb. Its fleece was white _______ snow. Everywhere that Mary _______ the lamb was sure _______ go.

Then the student reads the selection, supplying the omitted word. Older students can write the words in; younger students can read the passage to you orally. A score is determined by counting the number of words actually used by the author as *correct* responses.

A score of 40 percent or higher indicates that the book should not be above the reader's level.[13] A score below 40 percent indicates that the book is probably too difficult. The student will need more help reading it or should be permitted to use easier material. The use of closure eliminates the necessity of matching a grade-level score with a book because the test derives from the various types of material that the student will be expected to read. Closure tests are easily constructed, scored, and interpreted. While they are not flawless, they may be the most useful type of testing instrument available to the classroom teacher for use prior to instruction.

A word of caution is necessary. Considerable research is being conducted with closure testing materials. Adjusted norms have been reported indicating possible differences from the 40-percent criterion mentioned. As one works with students of different ages and with materials from different content areas, adjusted norms can be expected. The teacher should watch for reports of such changes for the most useful application of closure in reading diagnosis.

Two problems arise when using cloze tests for reading diagnosis. First, the tests are usually very frustrating to students who are operating in reading material above their instructional level. If, after five or six deletions, the student has made serious mistakes concerning the meaning of the passage, then the reader is working with nonsense. Many give up—refusing to try any more items because they know that what they are doing does not make sense.

The second problem concerns grading a cloze test. The exact word of the author must be presented in order to be considered correct. Synonyms do not count, nor do creative entries. This scoring procedure is annoying to many teachers who must mark an entry as an error when they know that the student has obtained the meaning of the author. The following example illustrates this.

> Test item: The owner of the ______ dog was Mike.
> Correct response: The owner of the *huge* dog was Mike.
> Incorrect student response: The owner of the *big* dog was Mike.

The student is not helped at all if, in the next sentence, the clue is "Mike's big dog likes ______." Now the response "big" looks accurate. Nevertheless, the teacher must mark *big* if the 40-percent criteria is to be used.

Maze Tests. An adjustment to cloze tests called *maze tests*[14] has been made to overcome some of the objections raised to cloze testing. As in cloze tests, every fifth word is deleted. However, three alternatives are given. So, given the sentence, "The men were working at the oil well," a maze test would look like

at
"The men were working in the oil well."
big

Two of the alternatives are the same part of speech so that they would both be syntactically correct. The other is not acceptable syntactically and makes nonsense out of the sentence.

Maze tests require the students to obtain scores of 70 percent or better for the material to be appropriate for their instruction. Scores from 65 to 75 are an indication that teacher direction is necessary for successful comprehension of the material.

Some school faculties develop maze tests for all of their basic texts. Assembled by a faculty, these tests can be constructed easily and placed in the school office for future use. New students can be given a few of these and placed with a high degree of accuracy. When other students are experiencing difficulty with working in a given book, a quick use of a maze test can provide data concerning the difficulty of that material for those students.

When a maze test seems to indicate that the material is above a student's instructional level, a new sample of material can be selected for the maze test.

Criterion-Referenced Tests (CRTs). Unlike standardized norm-referenced tests that compare students with one another, CRTs are designed to reveal any one student's ability to demonstrate a specific skill. However, the CRT's effectiveness in reading diagnosis is limited to whether the objective of the test is important and whether the test can measure the objective.

For each objective judged important, several test items are developed. The student's ability to respond to the test items in relation to that specific objective will become one indicator of the degree to which the student has learned the objective. It is easier to develop items for some objectives than others. For example, one can easily construct a test item to determine if a student can substitute the initial consonant *t* to make new words from *mop, sip,* and *sin,* but it is much more difficult to construct a test item to determine if a student can obtain the main idea from a complicated paragraph.

Numerous CRTs are finding their ways into classrooms. Table 4–4 shows Stallard's[15] report on some of the variables that need to be considered when choosing a CRT for classroom use. The wide range of objectives and items for sampling each objective, and the variance in what is considered mastery make test selection and interpretation difficult. The tests are often justified as a management system for teachers; however, unless interpreted cautiously, they can lead to mismanagement, calling for the teaching of unimportant subskills and locking all students into the identical path to reading. The teacher should use only those parts of such tests that relate to what they think is important. This applies particularly to phonics subskills.

Teacher-constructed CRTs give the teacher the opportunity to develop large numbers of items to sample the students' behavior. Large sampling tends to increase the reliability of tests. When few items are included to measure a given type of behavior, CRTs have the same reliability problems as standardized tests.

Diagnosis during and after Instruction

In classroom diagnosis, observation of the student's ability to respond to instruction is of prime importance. Through the direct observation of the student's responses, the teacher can avoid some of the time-consuming, costly, and sometimes questionable testing commonly linked to diagnosis. Also of prime importance is the continued assessment of the learning climate. That climate can change rapidly and without notice unless continuous assessment is made. Student self-assessment should also occur continuously. As students' attitudes and self-concepts as readers change, teachers should note the changes and adjust instruction according to those changes. Instead of the formal questionnaire, as was suggested in diagnosis before instruction, self-assessment can be informal and occur during and after instruction. A simple, "How well do you think you did on this

TABLE 4–4
Characteristics of fifteen objective-based reading programs. (From Cathy Stallard, "Comparing Objective-Based Reading Programs." *Journal of Reading,* October 1977. Reprinted by permission of the International Reading Association.)

[a]	1	2 A/B	3	4
Rationale presented in book or booklet form			X	X
Grade levels included in program	K–Adult	K–6 K–6	1–6	1–6
Categories of skills included in program				
Bilingual reading skills				
Comprehension skills	X	–/X	X	X
Creative reading skills		–/X		
Interpretive or critical reading skills		–/X		X
Oral reading skills				
Readiness skills	X	X/–	X	X
Secondary or content area skills	X	–/X	X	
Self-directed or independent reading skills				
Study skills		–/X	X	X
Vocabulary skills	X		X	X
Word attack skills	X	X/–	X	X
Total number of objectives in program	450	32/31	428	343
Percent of test items correct to demonstrate skill mastery	95%	100/ 84%	75–100%[c]	50–80%
Average number of test items per skill	2–3	17/12	3	5
Average number of specific activities for teaching each skill		10+/ 20+		
Consultant services available		X/X	X	X
In-service training of teachers available	X	X[f]/X[f]	X	X[e]
Procedures for including teacher-made objectives in tests	X	[e]		
Purchaser selects desired objectives from catalog				

1. Criterion Reading
2A. Croft Word Attack
2B. Croft Comprehension
3. Fountain Valley
4. IPMS
5. Performance Objectives
6. PRI
7. Read-On
8. SCORE
9. SOBAR
10. ICRT
11. Wisconsin Design
12. ORBIT
13. PLAN
14. High Intensity
15. SARI

5	6	7	8	9	10	11	12	13	14	15
X	X		X			X	X	X	X	
K–6	K–6.5	1–4	1–8	1–6	1–8	K–6	K–12	K–12	1–Adult	K–8
				X						
X	X	X	X	X	X	X	X	X	X	X
						X				
	X		X	X	X	X	X	X	X	
								X	X	X
	X	X	X					X		
X			X		X	(X)[b]	X	X	X	
						X		X	X	
			X	X	X	X	X	X	X	
X		X	X	X	X	X		X		X
X	X	X	X	X	X	X	X	X	X	X
312	172	60	800+	463	329	309	335	1100	475	95
	80%	90%	66.7 75,100%[d]	[d]	[d]	80%	75%	66–80%[d]	80%	90–100%
	3–4	15–20	3+	3	4	12–25	4	3–4	10	20
	8					14+		5+		2+
X	X[e]		X			X	X		X[e]	X
X	X		X		X	X[f]	(X)[b]	X	X	X
			X						X	
X			X	X			X		X	

[a]Each number designates a particular program. [b]Being developed. [c]75% is "proficiency" level, 100% is "mastery" level; individual user chooses criterion level desired for the class. [d]Mastery level is established by individual user of program. [e]Available on request. [f]In-service programs are also designed to be training sessions for district personnel who intend to conduct in-service training for others in their district.

activity?" can provide important information for the teacher. If the students think they did very well and the teacher assesses their performances poorly, then conferences should be held. During conferences it can be determined whether the students understood the assignment, the expectations, and the form of the final product.

Skills assessment during and after instruction depends heavily on the teacher's ability to observe various types of student behavior. Equal weight should be given to the student's performance on individual seat work and on teacher-made tests. Attention to task, enthusiasm, cooperative spirit, and efficient study habits can also be observed during instruction. At times teachers are too busy to make accurate observations during instruction and must rely on the cooperation of others. Other teachers, the principal, the reading specialist, an aide, or a parent volunteer can be asked to help. If three or four students are experiencing difficulty, these students can be observed using a checklist for several minutes apiece. If an observation is made every fifteen seconds for five minutes, the teacher will have twenty pieces of data. Information from observations can be noted on a form such as in figure 4–2.

Using this form, an entry for each activity is used to indicate whether the student is working with the teacher in a group, with the teacher individually, or independent from the teacher. Only two checkmarks are needed for each observation: (1) was the student on-task, off-task, or was it not possible to determine and (2) with what type of materials was the student supposed to be working? If the pattern in figure 4–2 were to continue, it

FIGURE 4–2
Example of systematic observation record keeping

Student's Name Rebecca **Date** 5/14/84
Activity a independent **b** ________ **c** ________

	On task?			Working with		
Observation	**Yes**	**No**	**?**	**Letters**	**Words**	**Sentences**
1	✓					✓
2	✓					✓
3		✓		✓		
4		✓		✓		
5	✓				✓	
6	✓				✓	

would tell the teacher that Rebecca goes off task when working independently with letter-type activities, but is on task when working with sentences.

The teacher can now examine those letter exercises and see if they can be made more appealing; talk with Rebecca about her on-task and off-task behavior to see if she has any ideas about how to improve her concentration; or change to more sentence exercises so that Rebecca can benefit as much as possible from her school activities. Obviously, any behavior could be substituted for those shown; however, it is important to observe as few as possible at one time. Trying to observe too many types of behavior at one time can be confusing, and produces unreliable results.

To assess reading behavior during and after instruction, the teacher will want to identify the context in which that behavior occurs. Is behavior during teacher-directed instruction the same as behavior while working independently or with an aide? Does a given student work better alone or with another student? When working alone, does the type of activity seem to generate different kinds of behavior? For example, some students may work quite well with the teacher, be completely inadequate when working at assigned work independently, and then work quite well again when working with a classmate. If the only sample of behavior were taken when working at assigned seat work, a distorted perception of the student's reading behavior would be obtained.

For the purpose of diagnosis, student behavior should be assessed in four reading situations.

1. Behavior while working with word recognition and word meaning activities.
2. Behavior while reading orally.
3. Behavior while reading silently.
4. Behavior while responding to silent reading to demonstrate understanding of what has been read.

The order of these activities does not indicate their importance. Usually the last one will be the most important source of data. Given a specific objective, however, any one of the four may be the most important in a given situation. For each activity, the teacher will try to obtain answers to the following questions:

- ☐ *What is the instructional level?* Teachers must determine at which level each student can respond most effectively to instruction; normally, it is a point at which the student makes errors but does not fail completely. Teachers have numerous opportunities to observe students reading different types of materials. They realize that students do not have one instructional level, but several. In social studies materials, a given student may read at levels considerably above materials read in other areas. As a student encounters materials that are obviously too hard, teachers must adjust instruction by either increasing assistance through word introduction and concept development prior to reading or reducing the difficulty of the material by selecting different books.

- ☐ *Specifically, what types of skills do the readers possess? What are their reading strengths?* Diagnostically, the teacher looks for those skills that the students have apparently mastered. For example, if a student always attacks the initial portion of the word accurately, initial consonants may be listed as mastered. The teacher also notes observed patterns of errors. Thus, both strengths and needs are noted.
- ☐ *What classroom adjustment can be used to teach to the students' strengths? What adjustments can be made to assist students in areas of needs?* By starting with adjustments that permit students to demonstrate strengths, success experiences can be developed. Awareness of adjustments that will help students in the areas of need will help teachers plan for continued student development.
- ☐ *Which activities seem to generate the most enthusiasm on the part of the student?* Teachers should note the expression of interest or enthusiasm for learning since all teachers need to know which types of activities motivate their students and which types seem to bore or frustrate them.

To answer each of these questions, teachers directly observe students in three reading situations: word recognition and word meaning exercises, oral reading, and silent reading. Reading situations differ from skill areas in that each situation requires the use of one or more of the skills for acceptable performance. Improvement in the skill areas usually results in improvement in reading situations when the diagnosis has been effective in establishing the instructional strengths and needs of students. Word recognition exercises provide teachers with information concerning the ability of a student to handle words in isolation. Since almost all reading activities require dealing with words in context, word recognition diagnosis is of little value. However, it does give the teacher some insight to the student's word knowledge. Word meaning exercises focus on the various meanings of words. Again, in isolation most word meanings are vague. What does *bank, ball, run, happy,* or *awkward* mean without a sentence of support? And service words such as *if, and, on,* and *when* carry meaning only as they relate to other words. Observation of students in oral reading provides teachers with the best insight into their overt reading behavior. It provides teachers with their only observation of the overt reading behavior of students when reading in context. Obviously, oral and silent reading require somewhat different behavior. Oral and silent reading probably are more similar for beginning readers and become less similar as readers gain maturity. Silent reading provides teachers with the best situation to determine the comprehension performance of students. Observations in each situation provide important information for teachers to complete the picture of a student's reading performance. Teachers add these observations to any testing information that they may have and formulate diagnostic hypotheses that they will attempt to interpret into instructional adjustments.

Word Recognition and Word Meaning. Scores from word recognition and word meaning assessment activities can be used as a basis for selecting passages for initial oral and silent reading diagnosis. Some analysis of performance with words in isolation can be conducted. Teachers need to observe patterns of performance in the various reading situations in order to develop sound diagnostic hypotheses. Each observed behavior pattern should be followed by a statement of diagnosis that considers both strengths and weaknesses. Strengths generally indicate areas in which a student is making a positive effort; therefore, attitudes as well as skills are reflected. The following are examples of observed student behavior and possible assessment implications.

1. The student refuses to pronounce words even after a delay of up to five seconds.
   - *strengths:* none known
   - *weaknesses:* may not know the word; may lack word attack skills
2. The student hesitates, but finally pronounces a word after a delay of two to five seconds.
   - *strength:* may be using word attack skills or delayed recall of word form at sight
   - *weakness:* may not be in sight vocabulary

3. The student partially pronounces the word but fails to pronounce entire word accurately (e.g., *ta* for *table*).
    strength: uses graphic cues for the portion of word pronounced (in this case, initial consonant and vowel sound)
    weaknesses: may not be in sight vocabulary; may have difficulty in word attack with unpronounced portion of word (in this case, word ending)
4. The student substitutes one word for another while maintaining the basic word meaning (e.g., *kitten* for *cat*).
    strength: may have clue to word meaning through association
    weakness: may be disregarding graphic cues
5. The student can pronounce a word accurately but does not know its meaning.
    strength: uses graphic cues
    weaknesses: may need concept development; may have worked so hard to pronounce the word that attention to meaning was not possible
6. The student reverses letter order (e.g., *was* for *saw*, *expect* for *except*).
    strength: may be observing graphic cues
    weaknesses: may have directional confusion (orientation); may not be in sight vocabulary

Observations noted during word recognition activities should be verified in oral and silent reading activities.

Oral Reading. Teachers should observe oral reading to determine how students use graphic and semantic contextual cues in reading. Some signs of thoughtful oral reading are:

1. The student repeats words or phrases. Four type of repetitions should be considered.
    - ☐ Student successfully changes first response to match text.
        strengths: may be using context (semantic) clues; may be using graphic cues
        weaknesses: none known
    - ☐ Student attempts to correct but is unsuccessful.
        strength: may be aware of semantic cues

weakness: may be unable to utilize graphic cues in semantic setting

- ☐ Student simply repeats portion that was initially correct.
  - *strength:* may be attempting to improve intonation
  - *weakness:* may be biding for time to attack forthcoming segment of the passage
- ☐ Student changes an initially correct response.
  - *strength:* may be changing passage into a more familiar speech pattern
  - *weakness:* may be biding for time to attack forthcoming segment of the passage or searching for meaning.

2. The student omits words. Two types of omissions should be considered.
   - ☐ The omission distorts meaning.
     - *strengths:* none known
     - *weaknesses:* may not be reading for meaning; may not be in sight vocabulary
   - ☐ Omission does not distort meaning.
     - *strength:* may be reading for meaning
     - *weaknesses:* may have too large an eye–voice span; may not be in sight vocabulary

   Omissions occur infrequently and account for less than 7 percent of oral reading errors; 93 percent of the time they do not distort the meaning of the sentence.[16]
3. The student inserts words. Two types of insertions should be considered.
   - ☐ The insertion distorts meaning.
     - *strengths:* none known
     - *weakness:* may not be using semantic cues
   - ☐ The insertion does not distort meaning.
     - *strength:* may be embellishing the author's meaning
     - *weakness:* may have too large an eye–voice span

   Insertions also occur infrequently and account for less than 6 percent of oral reading errors; 94 percent of the time they do not distort the meaning of the sentence.[17]
4. The student substitutes a word or nonword for the word in the passage. Substitutions account for more than 87

percent of oral reading errors.[18] When such a substitution occurs, it can be analyzed according to graphic, syntactic, and semantic information.[19] Such an analysis considers qualitative as well as quantitative considerations. The qualitative aspects rest heavily with the student's reaction to the passage in a meaningful context.

Example: Student reads: "the big title was"
Text was: "the big table was"
Graphic: initial—accurate
medial—error
final—accurate
Syntactic: accurate, a noun for a noun
Semantic: error, major change in meaning

Example: Student reads: "boy hurried down"
Text was: "boy hustled down"
Graphic: initial—accurate
medial—variance
final—accurate
Syntactic: accurate, a verb for a verb
Semantic: not accurate, but acceptable

These three types of oral reading behavior need to be considered in terms of how they relate to one another. Individually the strengths and weaknesses include the following:

☐ Student fails to use graphic cues.
strengths: uses graphic cues for portions of words accurately pronounced; may be using syntactic and semantic cues
weaknesses: may fail to use all graphic cues available; may not be in sight vocabulary

☐ Student fails to use syntactic cues.
strength: may be using graphic cues
weaknesses: may fail to use syntactic cues in the language; may not be in sight vocabulary

☐ Student fails to use semantic cues.
strength: may be using graphic and syntactic cues
weaknesses: may not be in sight vocabulary; may be concentrating on pronunciation instead of meaning; may not be familiar with concepts

5. The student fails to observe punctuation.
strengths: none known

weaknesses: decoding may be so difficult that punctuation is ignored; may be unaware of the function of punctuation

6. The student observes all punctuation via pauses and inflection.
   strengths: using semantic cues; knows cues implied by punctuation
   weaknesses: none known
7. The student loses place during oral reading.
   strengths: none known
   weaknesses: may have directional confusion; may be reading meaninglessly; may have visual problem; may be overconcentrating on decoding
8. The student reads word-by-word (all words pronounced accurately, but slowly, with pauses between them and without much expression).
   strength: may be using graphic cues
   weaknesses: may not be using semantic cues; may have insufficient sight vocabulary.
9. The student exhibits difficulty when asked questions, although he accurately pronounces all words.
   strength: may be using graphic cues
   weaknesses: decoding may be so consuming that comprehension does not occur; may have inadequate conceptual development; may have poor verbal memory

Reading assessment does not normally include oral reading comprehension as an important skill, especially when the reader is reading orally without reading silently first. Teachers should ask questions after oral reading to help the readers know that all reading should be purposeful. Comprehension errors of passages read orally should always be confirmed in silent-reading situations.

Symptoms observed during oral reading should be based on materials that the student can read at 90 to 95 percent accuracy. All symptoms observed during attempts to read frustrating material are invalid because the difficulty of the material creates unnatural error patterns.

Silent Reading. Assessment of silent-reading tasks can be made during the silent reading itself and in comprehension activities that follow silent reading. Comprehension assessment is difficult, but very important. If all other reading skills are functioning well but the readers are not obtaining meaning, then they are not reading. On the other hand, if other reading skills are incomplete but the readers are obtaining meaning, then they are functioning as readers. During silent reading, teachers can observe several instances of overt behavior that may aid in the total diagnosis:

1. The student moves lips and makes subvocalized sound during silent reading.
   strength: appears to be working on graphic cues
   weaknesses: may be overworking decoding; may be trying to remember what is read; may be a habit carried over from excessive oral reading
2. The student points to words with fingers.
   strength: may be using touch to keep place or to emphasize words
   weaknesses: orientation skills may need touch support; may be having decoding difficulties
3. The student shows physical signs of reading discomfort (e.g., rubbing of eyes, extreme restlessness, constant adjustment of book).
   strength: may be persevering with task
   weaknesses: possible difficulty of material; possible physical deficiencies (vision, nutrition, etc.); possible emotional reaction to frustration

The important diagnostic aspect of silent reading is, of course, the ability of the student to demonstrate an understanding of the author's message. Five important considerations must be noted.

1. What types of questions are to be asked: literal questions that call for facts and details; interpretive questions that call for paraphrasing and drawing inferences; or problem-solving questions that call for critical and creative response and evaluative thinking?
2. What situation is the student facing when answering questions? A recall situation calls for the reading material to be unavailable during questioning. A locate situation encourages the student to find the answer in the reading material. Locating opportunities appear to have a great effect on a student's ability to respond to questions at all levels.
3. Was the student aware of the purposes for silent reading?

The student's ability to demonstrate an understanding of the author's message is important in diagnosis of silent reading problems.

4. How much exposure has the student had to the reading material? Are the responses expected after a single reading or after study and reexamination of the material? Different performances may obviously be expected depending on the amount of exposure to the material.
5. How much time has elapsed between the reading of the material and the student's response to it?

The following procedure is suggested for silent reading comprehension diagnosis.

1. Have the student read the story for a set purpose. At times the purpose is set by the teacher and at other times it is set by the students.
2. After the students have finished reading, give them a few minutes to think about what they have read and then ask them to retell as much of the story as they can. From this the teacher can assess the personal meaning that various students were able to derive from the story.
3. Start questioning in a recall situation and with interpretive questions. Davey found that students answer literal questions more accurately when questioning starts with interpretive questions than they do when questions start with literal questions.[20] Then ask literal and problem-solving questions.

4. Permit students to return to the passage and locate the answers to questions missed in a recall situation.

Steps 3 and 4 give teachers six comprehension scores from questioning. Using the number or percent of accurate responses, these scores can be charted, as in figure 4–3.

The following behaviors may be observed during the question-reaction period of a silent reading lesson.

1. The student can decode the material but cannot respond to literal questions in a recall situation.
   strength: may be using graphic, semantic, and syntactic cues
   weaknesses: may have poor (visual) memory; may need concept development related to material read; may be overconcentrating on graphic cues
2. The student can decode the material and can respond to literal questions in a locate situation.
   strengths: may be using graphic, semantic, and syntactic cues; may be able to locate literally stated ideas
   weaknesses: none known
3. The student can respond to literal understanding questions but cannot interpret those ideas into own words.
   strengths: may be using graphic, semantic, and syntactic cues; uses literal understanding
   weaknesses: possible overconcentration of graphic cues; possible load difficulty; possible failure to reflect on the author's ideas

Student: Sarah	**Grade:** 7	
	Reading situation	
Type of response	**Recall**	**Locate**
Interpretive	60%	80%
Literal	50%	100%
Problem solving	70%	80%

FIGURE 4–3
Example of comprehension record keeping form for diagnostic use

4. The student can respond literally and can interpret the author's ideas but cannot apply ideas to problem-solving situations.
   strengths: may be using graphic, syntactic, and semantic cues; uses literal understanding; uses interpretation
   weaknesses: may lack problem-solving skills; possible misunderstanding of the problem
5. The student can retell the story accurately but cannot answer teacher-made questions related to it.
   strengths: shows literal understanding; uses sequence skills
   weakness: may have inability to anticipate teacher questions
6. The student can answer teacher-made questions when alllowed to study and reexamine passage, but not after a single reading.
   strength: gains meaning when allotted sufficient time
   weakness: may need repeated exposure for comprehension
7. The student can answer teacher-made questions immediately after reading but is unable to do so a day or so later.
   strength: may have short-term memory
   weakness: may not have adequate long-term memory
8. The student can answer questions covering short passages but is unable to do so on longer passages.
   strength: may have short-term memory
   weaknesses: may have inadequate long-term memory; may lack organizational skills

Teachers should collect observational data relating to comprehension over a period of time. A given comprehension failure might be as attributable to story content, reader interest, or reader motivation on a given day as it is to reading ability. Once a consistent pattern is observed, teachers can make diagnostic hypotheses and start to make needed instructional adjustments in the reading program.

Three Cautions

Teachers must be cautioned of three aspects in observing reading behavior. First, observation of reading behavior is a learned skill. Teachers must consistently practice, habitually keep careful records, and double- and triple-check findings. Obviously one repetition in an oral reading situation cannot determine a diagnostic hypothesis. Also, classroom observations may lead to a dangerously fractionalized view of the reader. Every reader is more than the sum of skills listed on the preceding pages. The classroom teacher needs to pull back periodically during diagnosis and observe the whole reader. Such observations may reveal that the reader is always on-task, enjoying the reading activities, helping others, and happy. Perhaps such observations are more important than a listing of skill strengths and weaknesses. At least they should be recorded as equally important information.

Second, many readers do very poorly during the initial efforts to respond in a diagnostic setting. They are attempting to determine what is expected of them and may be quite nervous since they do not know what is going to happen next. For this reason, students should be allowed to respond to a practice passage of relatively easy material. In this case, student performance on the first passage read orally would not be counted in the assessment. Likewise, the student response to the first silent reading passage would not be counted. Our interest is in determining how well these students can read, so we want to provide the best assessment situation as possible.

Third, in comprehension assessment the reader's prior knowledge of the content of the passages being read is going to have an effect on how well that story is comprehended. It is possible to be fooled completely about a reader's comprehension skills or lack of them. For example, most adults have considerable knowledge about the events surrounding the assassination of President John F. Kennedy and would feel very comfortable reading a passage or two about the day of his assassination in Dallas. If, however, the passages to be read were about the Battle of Hastings, most of these adults would be a bit uncomfortable because they cannot bring much prior knowledge to that event in history. If comprehension were to be assessed using one of these two events in history, undoubtedly, most would choose the passages about President Kennedy's assassination. Therefore, in classroom assessment of reading comprehension it will prove helpful to assess comprehension over a period of time using a variety of passages.

QUESTIONS TO PINPOINT DIAGNOSTIC FINDINGS

From word recognition, oral reading, and silent reading data, teachers should seek answers to questions in the following skill areas.

Prereading-Readiness Skills. If answers to questions in this area are *yes,* remedial suggestions can be found in chapter 7.

1. Do language skills appear to be underdeveloped?
2. Do speech skills appear to be underdeveloped?
3. Does dialect usage appear to cause difficulty?
4. Do visual or auditory problems appear to be causing discomfort?
5. Do visual discrimination skills appear to be underdeveloped?
6. Do auditory discrimination skills appear to be underdeveloped?
7. Do reversals occur frequently enough to cause confusion?
8. Does student frequently lose place during reading?

Sight Vocabulary. If answers to questions in this area are *yes*, remedial suggestions can be found in chapter 8.

1. Does student misread small, similar words?
2. Do words missed represent abstract concepts?
3. Do word meanings appear to be confused?
4. Does student know words in context but not in isolation?
5. Does student appear to know words at end of a lesson, but not the next day?

Word Attack. If answers to questions in this area are *yes*, remedial suggestions can be found in chapter 8.

Phonics

1. Does student use graphic cues? Which graphic cues are used?
2. Does student attack small words accurately, but not larger ones?
3. Does student seem to know sound-symbol relationships, but seem unable to use them during reading?

Structural

1. Do words missed contain prefixes or suffixes?
2. Are words missed compound words?

Contextual

1. Does student appear to ignore syntactic cues?
2. Does student appear to ignore semantic cues?
3. Does student appear to ignore punctuation cues?

Comprehension. If answers to questions in this areas are *yes*, remedial suggestions can be found in chapter 9.

1. Do large units of material seem to interfere with comprehension?

2. Do comprehension difficulties occur with some types of comprehension and not others? (Literal comprehension is weak but interpretive is strong.)
3. Does student respond when given opportunities to retell stories from a personal point of view?
4. Does student have difficulty using locating skills?
5. Does student have difficulty understanding material read in content areas?
6. Does student reorganize what has been read so that it makes sense from a personal point of view?
7. Does student fail to comprehend most of what has been read?

INTERESTS, HABITS, AND ATTITUDES

An evaluation of student interests, habits, and attitudes is an important part of classroom diagnosis. Teachers, through regular observation of student performances, are in the ideal setting to note changes in interests, habits and attitudes. Effort should be made to note effective and ineffective habits that seem to vary considerably from those of the average student. The reading specialist will likely ask the classroom teacher for information concerning interest, habits and attitudes; therefore, observations should be noted carefully. Specifically, classroom teachers should obtain answers to the following questions:

1. What uses do students make of free reading opportunities? Do they appear eager to use free time for reading, or is reading only the result of constant prodding?
2. Do students appear anxious or reluctant to read orally? Silently? Does there appear to be a difference in attitude between oral and silent reading situations?
3. Are signs of reluctance noticeable in reading situations only or in all learning situations? If difficulty occurs only in reading then it may be the act of reading that is causing the reluctance. If reluctance is observed in all learning situations, then an analysis of the learning environment is needed.
4. In what reading situations are students most or least effective? Do students tend to enjoy providing answers orally as opposed to writing them? Do questions that call for summaries get better results than specific questions? Students often develop habits as a result of what has been expected by other teachers.
5. Do students have to be prodded to finish reading assignments? If they cannot work without supervision even when specific assignments have been made, unsu-

pervised reading situations should be avoided in initial remedial instruction.

6. What types of book selections do the students make in the library? Considerable information can be obtained about interests by noticing the types of books chosen from the library. Remedial efforts should start with the type of material in which students have indicated an interest.

Answers to these questions will become important guides to the initial remedial sessions. Teachers will find it useful to record these findings so that they will have a record of accurate data. Although these questions will be answered mostly by informal observation, teachers should give them special attention and become active agents in collecting information.

At times, it is not possible to obtain precise *yes* or *no* answers to such questions. In these cases, teachers should continue to observe the readers until they can substantiate accurate error patterns. Specifically, teachers may provide students with individualized exercises to do independently, go over their responses, and have a short conference about their responses. As a part of informal, on-the-spot diagnosis, this technique can be useful in verifying classroom diagnosis. Suppose, for example, that one has diagnosed irregular patterns of difficulty with final consonant sounds. Several carefully prepared exercises with final consonant sounds can be developed, administered, and analyzed for the purpose of verification. Further verification can come from information available in school records, parental interviews, past observations, classroom diagnostic tests, and subsequent instruction.

Pencil-and-paper interest surveys can be used to obtain information about areas that motivate students. However, interests change rapidly, making the results of a survey inappropriate several weeks from the time it was administered. Sample questions for an interest survey might include:

1. What things do you like to do when you get home from school?
2. If you could wish for three things for your future, what would they be?
3. Name three of your favorite television shows.
4. Do you enjoy participating in sports? If so, which sports?
5. Do you have any hobbies? If so, what are they?

Such questions tend to provide the teacher with natural areas of interests. Books and articles about these areas can now be read in the classroom by these students. Lessons can be planned to feature activities related to the interests of the students.

RECORD KEEPING

Classroom diagnosis effectiveness will rest to a large extent upon the records teachers keep. The type of records will vary with the purpose of the diagnostic activities. Figure 4–4 shows an example of group record keeping. An entire class can be monitored by this type of record using no more than two sheets of 8″ × 11½″ paper. Another type of group record can be used to monitor student progress over time. The teacher can determine what data are available and periodically assess student behavior in those areas.

Name	Botel WO	Oral Reading Accuracy	Comprehension	Placement Reader Level
Pat	3^2	97%	Good	3^2
JoEllen	4	99%	Fair	3^1
Otto	3^1	95%	Poor	3^1
Maria	3^1	90%	Good	4

FIGURE 4–4
Example of group record keeping

Students in this record were placed according to the Botel Word Opposites (Reading) Test. The teacher periodically asks individual students to read orally a 100-word passage. Their oral reading accuracy is sampled in this manner. Note that in figure 4–4 Ron appears to be having considerable difficulty with his accuracy in the 3^1 reader. Then, over time, the teacher jots down impressions received about each student's responses during comprehension lessons. Ron again seems to be doing poorly. Having obtained this type of information, the teacher may consider placing Ron in material that he can handle with better comprehension and better oral reading accuracy. Using this type of record and updating the data several times during the year will assist in keeping students in appropriate materials for instruction.

Another type of record keeping involves a detailed account of the reading skill development of individual students. Such records are time consuming to develop and probably would be maintained only on the students about whom a teacher is most concerned. These records would include test scores and data from teacher observations and would be collected periodically. Figure 4–5 can be adapted for individual record keeping.

Name *Klyde Martin* **Age** *12* **Teacher** *D. Keller*
Grade *6* **Date record initiated** *October 1983*

	Date Scored *Oct. 83*	Date Scored *May 84*
Scores:		
Word Recognition	*3.5*	*4.5*
Oral Reading Accuracy	*4.0*	*5.5*
Silent Reading		
Recall Comp.	*4.5*	*6.0*
Locate Comp.	*6.0*	*7.0*
Strengths:		
Word Recognition		
Oral Reading Behavior		*greatly improved*
Silent Reading Comprehension	*comprehension using locating skills*	
Weaknesses:		
Word Recognition	*pronounced words in isolation*	*improved*
Oral Reading Behavior		
Silent Reading Comprehension		*improved*

Interests and Attitudes *He is interested in music art, and the outdoors. He plays center for the school basketball team.*

Comments: *He is sensitive about his inability to read well and is embarrassed when talking about it. Interest in art could be spring-board to reading activity.*

FIGURE 4–5
Example of individual record keeping form

Records can also be kept on an informal basis. Using a 5″ × 8″ index card for each student, the teacher can jot down important behavior noted during any lesson. Dates and behavior observed serve as a suitable record of student progress. Figure 4–6 shows the types of entries that may be recorded:

9/12	Administered Botel Word Opposites Test—Jim scored at 3^2 level.
9/15	Jim comprehended well in the 3^2 material.
10/3	Jim appears to have trouble completing assignments in his social studies book. I'll try to introduce new concepts.
10/7	After introduction of new concepts, Jim comprehended material in his social studies book well.

FIGURE 4–6
Example of informal record keeping

As the teacher makes decisions about record keeping formats, care should be taken to assure that the records do not create unreasonable time demands. Careful records should be maintained on a few important types of behavior instead of inaccurate records on many types.

FOUR FINAL QUESTIONS

Teachers should reflect on the answers to the following four questions to complete an effective classroom diagnosis and to assist them in establishing more clearly the validity of their findings.

1. Did the students make the same error in both easy and difficult material, or did the observed errors indicate frustration with the material? Teachers are most interested in the errors made at the instructional level, the level at which they hope to make improvement. All readers make errors when reading at their frustration level; these errors, however, normally do not lead to diagnostic conclusions, for these are not the errors upon which remediation is based.
2. Were the errors first interpreted as slowness actually an effort on the part of the reader to be especially careful and precise and to be reflective? Beware of diagnostic conclusions drawn from the students' responses to questions, especially when timed standardized tests are used or when testing situations make the reader aware of being evaluated. Many students have been taught to

be impulsive with their responses when, in fact, reflective behavior may be considerably more desirable.

3. Can students be helped as a result of classroom diagnosis, or is further diagnosis necessary? Further testing with any of the instruments mentioned under clinical diagnosis is appropriate when the teacher has the knowledge of their proper use and interpretation, and has the time to use them. At this point, however, the services of a reading specialist may be required.
4. Did the students appear to concentrate while being directly observed, or did they seem easily distracted? Children who appear to be distracted during observation may have produced unreliable symptoms.

The diagnostic task consists of observing individuals through analysis of symptoms and associating the symptoms to appropriate skill areas. Then, the significance of the errors must be determined and that information organized in terms of practical classroom adjustments. Under only a few circumstances will diagnosis be concluded at this point. An ongoing process, diagnosis will normally continue during the remedial sessions, always attempting to obtain more precise information concerning the readers. Morris believes that this is the important advantage for the classroom teacher. He states, "To the teacher . . . the challenge is to get to grips more directly with the problem and by working with the individual pupil try to understand what is leading him astray."[21] We would add that an additional challenge would be to determine more precisely the skill, strengths, and deficiencies of the student.

EARLY IDENTIFICATION

Teachers are capable of making early identifications of children who are likely to experience difficulty in school. In Maryland, a multidisciplinary task force worked two years to develop assessment instruments to identify children with potential learning handicaps."[22] They found the best device for such identification to be systematic teacher observations. At the University of Maryland reading clinic, we found a similar result when asking teachers to identify potential reading problems. They identified them more accurately than did the tests that we administered. In some schools, early identification occurs in kindergarten. When accompanied by specific symptoms, such identification assists teachers in modifying educational programs to increase the possibilities of success. Some children might best start with a phonics-based program; others might profit from one that stresses sight learning. Some succeed best when the initial program uses the language-experience approach, and others need multisensory techniques. Such programs have the potential to assist students' successful start in school and avoid several years of failure.

Several problems are related to early identification programs. First, if they stop with identification, thus only labeling a student they may do more harm than good. Second, when tests are relied upon heavily, many students become erroneously identified and others are not identified when they should be. Thirdly, providing teachers with checklists of behavior that may cause learning problems may result in self-fulfilling prophecies. For example, if a teacher is told that children in first grade who make reversals may have serious reading problems, teachers might react to children so identified in such ways that create nonlearning. Finally, parents can be aroused to such a state of anxiety as to alarm the child.

If early identification programs are implemented, several safeguards should be applied to avoid these problems. Early identification should never be made using a single testing instrument. Children who have been initially identified should be reevaluated periodically. Early identification programs should be accompanied by instructional adjustments. Parents should be informed of the program and the advantages it offers their children. All early identification programs should be carefully monitored and periodically evaluated to be certain they are effective.

SUMMARY

Classroom diagnostic assessment involves the observation and testing of student behavior. It also involves the assessment of the learning climate. Classroom diagnostic assessment can take place before, during, or after instruction. Teachers are encouraged to diagnose for strengths as well as for needs. Evaluation of student self-appraisal is a recommended tactic for classroom diagnosis.

Teachers should develop some type of record keeping to reflect classroom diagnosis. These records are used to assess skill development, to aid in communication with other teachers and parents, and to evaluate the success of instructional adjustments.

NOTES

1. Roger Farr, *Reading: What Can Be Measured?* (Newark, Del.: IRA, 1969), 97, 212–18.

2. Thomas A. Rakes, Joyce S. Choate, and Gayle Lane Waller, *Individual Evaluation Procedures in Reading*, Englewood Cliffs, N.J.: Prentice-Hall, Inc., 1983.
3. William R. Powell, "The Validity of the Instructional Reading Level," *Diagnostic Viewpoints in Reading* (1971): 121–33.
4. William K. Durr, ed., *Reading Difficulties* (Newark, Del.: IRA, 1970), 67–132.
5. Emmett A. Betts, *Foundations of Reading Instruction* (New York: American Book Co., 1946).
6. William R. Powell, "Revised Criteria for the Informal Reading Inventory" (Speech presented at International Reading Association, New Orleans, La., May 3, 1974).
7. Ibid., 11.
8. William R. Powell, "Measuring Reading Informally," (Paper presented at International Reading Association, Houston, Texas, 1978): 9.
9. Ibid., 8.
10. Robert E. Mills and Jean R. Richardson, "What Do Publishers Mean by Grade Level?" *The Reading Teacher* 16, no. 5 (March 1963): 359–62.
11. Mae C. Johnson, "Comparison of Readability Formulas" (Ph.D. dissertation, University of Maryland Reading Center, 1971).
12. Lowell D. Eberwein, "The Variability of Basal Reader Textbooks and How Much Teachers Know About It," *Reading World* 18, no. 3 (1979): 259–72.
13. Earl F. Rankin and Joseph W. Culhane, "Comparable Cloze and Multiple Choice Comprehension Test Scores," *Journal of Reading* (December 1969), 194.
14. John T. Guthrie et al., "The Maze Techniques to Assess, Monitor Reading Comprehension," *The Reading Teacher* 28, no. 2, (November 1974): 161–68.
15. Cathy Stallard, "Comparing Objective Based Reading Programs," *Journal of Reading* 21, no. 5 (Oct. 1977), 36–44.
16. Karen D'Angelo and Robert M. Wilson, "How Helpful is Insertion and Omission Analysis?" *The Reading Teacher* 32, no. 5 (February 1979): 519–20.
17. Ibid.
18. Ibid.
19. Kenneth S. Goodman, "Analysis of Oral Reading Miscues: Applied Psycholinguistics," *Reading Research Quarterly* 5 (Fall 1969): 9–30.
20. H. Beth Davey, "The Effect of Question Order on Comprehension Test Performance at the Literal and Interpretive Levels," (Faculty research paper, University of Maryland, Reading Center, 1975).
21. Ronald Morris, *Success and Failure in Learning to Read* (London: Oldbourne, 1963), 159.
22. *Reading in Maryland* (Baltimore, Md.: Division of Instruction, Maryland State Department of Education, 1974–75).

SUGGESTED READINGS

Cunningham, Patricia Marr, Arthur, Sharon V., and Cunningham, James W. *Classroom Reading Instruction,* Lexington, Mass., D. C. Heath, 1977. This text provides numerous examples of classroom diagnosis through the use of teacher observation of student behavior during instruction.

Deboer, Dorothy L., ed. *Reading Diagnosis and Evaluation.* Newark, Del.: International Reading Association, 1970. This IRA collection features early identification, use of testing, and formal approaches, emphasizing the diagnostic aspects of reading.

Durr, William K., ed. *Reading Difficulties.* Newark, Del.: International Reading Association, 1970. The second section, "The Informal Inventories," includes six articles by different authors on the various aspects of informal inventories. Readers who are unfamiliar with informal techniques will want to study this section.

Farr, Roger. *Reading: What Can Be Measured?* Newark, Del.: International Reading Association, 1969. An excellent paperback that looks at the value and limitations of the various measuring instruments used in reading. A valuable resource for teachers.

Geyer, James R., and Matanzo, Jane. *Programmed Reading Diagnosis for Teachers: with Prescriptive References.* Columbus, OH: Charles E. Merrill, 1977. For those who want practice coding and analyzing reading behavior, this book may be interesting. Aside from specific practice exercises, case studies are included for prescription writing. Suggested answers are provided throughout.

Goodman, Kenneth S. "Analysis of Oral Reading Miscues: Applied Psycholinguistics." *Reading Research Quarterly* 5 (Fall 1969): 9–30. Goodman states his case for oral reading analysis in this article. This view of the reader as a processor of language cues is important for those who wish to become skilled diagnostic teachers.

Johns, Jerry L. et. al., *Assessing Reading Behavior.* Newark, Del.: International Reading Association, 1977. This monograph is an annotated bibliography on the topic of informal reading inventories and will provide the reader with useful reference to many of the issues involved in the use and interpretation of them.

Stallard, Cathy. "Comparing Objective Based Reading Programs." *Journal of Reading* 21, no. 1 (Oct. 1977), 36–44. Stallard discusses criterion-referenced testing programs and instructional programs. The coverage is useful for those considering a commercial program for their students.

Editorial

Rachel Kaufmann
is a reading specialist for the Baltimore County Public Schools in Maryland.

Mrs. Jones and her son Davey arrived at school one October morning. They had just moved into the area from another state and she wanted to register Davey in our fifth grade. After the appropriate papers were filled out, Davey was screened by the transient resource teacher. While talking with Davey, she discovered that he had been in five other elementary schools and had repeated first grade. Also, his dad didn't live with them, and his mom was looking for a job.

The transient resource teacher found that Davey was functioning considerably below grade level in reading, math, spelling, and language, and placed him in the lowest fifth grade class. He was very quiet and withdrawn in the classroom. After a week it became obvious to the classroom teacher that Davey was having difficulty in all academic areas. She felt that perhaps he just needed some time to adjust to his new environment—both at school and at home.

Meanwhile, a concerted effort was being made to obtain Davey's previous school records, but to no avail. They appeared to be lost. It was up to the school to collect data and determine an appropriate program for Davey. He was beginning to adjust well socially, but his academic progress was extremely limited. By working with Davey and observing him in a variety of situations, the classroom teacher began to compile information about his strengths and needs. She listened to him read orally and administered an informal reading test and a maze test. Using her data and that of the transient resource teacher, she and the reading specialist worked together to plan the most appropriate program for Davey. He also was referred to the Pupil Services Team.

During one of the teacher's conversations with Davey, he mentioned that his present class was much larger than the one in his previous school. Further questioning revealed that there had been two teachers in the room, and only three people in his reading group. A conference with Davey's mom confirmed the teacher's suspicions—Davey had been in a special education class and his mom had neglected to inform the school.

The Pupil Services Team recommended a medical, psychological, language, and educational battery for Davey. The results indicated that he indeed did belong in a special education program, and he was placed in the school's intermediate learning disabilities class. Davey made steady progress throughout the year and is presently well on his way to completing the goals of his Individualized Education Program. Davey will spend one more year in elementary school before he goes on to middle school. With careful program planning, based on continuous classroom diagnosis, and the individualized attention he is receiving, he should continue to make steady gains.

In a school with a highly mobile population teachers must be aware of the many problems a transient student may have. Davey is just one of many children who are meeting success due to an alert and knowledgeable classroom teacher who saw the need for diagnostic testing.

House

5

Clinical Diagnosis

CHAPTER OUTLINE

REFERRAL
INITIAL SCREENING
THE INTERVIEW
EXTENDED DIAGNOSIS
CASE REPORTING

CHAPTER EMPHASES

- ☐ Clinical diagnosis is individual.
- ☐ Clinical diagnosis is systematic.
- ☐ Clinical diagnosis is not problem free.
- ☐ Clinical diagnosis involves varying levels of assessment.
- ☐ Clinical diagnosis relies on behavior patterns.
- ☐ Clinical diagnosis relies on diagnostic lessons.
- ☐ Clinical diagnosis relies on data interpretation.
- ☐ Clinical diagnosis relies on record keeping.

Note: All tests mentioned in this chapter are included in appendix A, which provides a detailed check list indicating each test's characteristics.

Clinical diagnosis is conducted by a reading specialist using a variety of assessment techniques to collect the data needed to plan instruction or make recommendations for instruction. In clinical diagnosis, the student is usually evaluated outside the classroom. This involves taking the student to a testing area in the building or to a testing facility out of the building.

Clinical diagnosis features an individual evaluation of the reader and the reading situation, and is required when the best efforts at the classroom level have not resulted in helping the student become a successful reader. Its purposes are the same as those of classroom diagnosis, as are the questions that are asked. When all or portions of the classroom diagnosis are not effective, the classroom teacher makes a referral request. However, sometimes parents, resource people, or teachers may make the referral. Occasionally a student will make a self-referral, asking for specific help in some aspect of reading.

The major advantages of clinical diagnosis are:

1. It is individual in nature.
2. It is conducted by specially trained professionals.
3. It uses the best assessment instruments available.
4. It releases the classroom teacher to perform other responsibilities.
5. It uses a variety of professional resources.
6. It uses data from a variety of sources.

These advantages may make clinical diagnosis sound superior to and more desirable than classroom diagnosis, and sometimes it is. But clinical diagnosis is complicated with severe limitations, such as:

1. Evaluating a reader in an individual setting does not necessarily provide information about that reader's behavior in a group setting.
2. Matching clinical data with instructional procedures and materials is an error-ridden procedure.
3. Conflicting clinical data can lead to confusion instead of enlightenment.
4. Clinical diagnosis tends to focus on the deficiencies of the reader while overlooking deficiencies in the learning climate.

This chapter will offer suggestions of ways to overcome, or at least minimize, these limitations. Clinical cases lead to the belief that clinical diagnosis should be continuous. That is, once the initial assessment recommendations are made, the reader's progress should be continuously monitored to assure a successful outcome. Most readers who receive adjusted instruction recommended by a clinical assessment make spectacular progress; however some do not. And some of these do not respond even after continued instruction adjustments and continued assessment. In other words, all of the questions as to why students fail in learning to read have not yet been answered. Some of the difficulties seem to be caused by subtle, untestable problems in the learning climate or within the reader.

Development of an "I-can't" attitude is one of the most severe problems within the reader experiencing difficulties. The likelihood that remediation will prove ineffective due to a reader's low self-esteem increases when he or she has a severe failure syndrome; has seldom or never experienced success in reading; and has been in this situation for three or more years. The reading specialist should approach clinical assessment with these thoughts in mind. The following suggestions for clinical diagnosis can be adapted to each unique situation.

REFERRAL

Various systems are used to refer students to reading specialists. These systems not only refer the readers, but also serve as starting points for collecting data to be used in clinical diagnosis.

In the school setting, a screening committee might be the referral agency. That committee gathers all available information concerning the referred readers and forwards that data with the referral. When referrals are made outside the school (to a college reading clinic, for example) the receiving agency usually asks for data from the referring agency. The referral form shown in figure 5–1 is used when parents refer their children to the University of Maryland Reading Clinic. It provides important preassessment data and often prevents serious mistakes in assessment activities. For example, by using the information on the form in figure 5–1, the specialist knew in advance that this child was deaf so could be sure that an interpreter was present at the initial evaluation session.

Besides obtaining information from referring parents, outside agencies should examine existing school records. They contain information regarding test scores, classroom diagnosis, health, and school progress that can help in a clinical diagnosis.

University of Maryland **College of Education** **Reading Center**

Date *September 9, 1981*

Child's Name *Daniel C. Wagner* Birthdate *02-08-72* Grade *6*

Mother's Name *Frances C. Wagner* Occupation *store manager*

Business Phone *1-203-445-8394*

Father's Name *James E. Wagner* Occupation *Cabinet Maker*

Business Phone *1-203-445-8394*

Home Address *222 Poquonnock Rd.* Child's School ______

College Park, Ct. 06340 Address ______

Zip Code

Home Phone *445-4216* Principal *Mrs. Mildred Brown*

Reason for referral to University of Maryland Reading Clinic *Classroom teacher suggested it. They have met with no success at his school.*

Please be sure to fill out the attached questionnaire, and return all of this to the University of Maryland, College of Education, Reading Center, College Park, Maryland 20742.

Place an X on the line following each question and add comments when appropriate.

	Not at all 1	Perhaps 2	Certainly 3
1. Do you believe health problems have affected your child's reading?	X		

If 2 or 3, please comment ______

	Not at all 1	Perhaps 2	Certainly 3
2. Do you believe attitude problems have affected your child's reading?	X		

If 2 or 3, please comment ______

FIGURE 5–1
A referral form for clinical diagnosis.

	Not at all	Perhaps	Certainly
	1	2	3
3. Do you believe teaching procedures have affected your child's reading?		X	

If 2 or 3, please comment *They use the same set of readers for all children even when a given set does not work well.*

	Not at all	Perhaps	Certainly
4. Do you believe teacher attitude has affected your child's reading?	1	2	3
	X		

If 2 or 3, please comment ______

	Not at all	Perhaps	Certainly
5. Do you believe problems at home have affected your child's reading?	1	2	3
		X	

If 2 or 3, please comment *I never learned to read well. Maybe it is my fault.*

	No	They tried, but	Very well
6. Do you believe the school authorities have responded to your child's problem?	1	2	3
	X		

Please comment *The teachers seem to care but the school does not even provide special help for those having trouble with their reading.*

	No	Yes
7. Is this your first referral of your child for help with reading problems?		X

If no, please explain ______

8. How many schools has your child attended? (1) 2 3 4 5
9. If your child was retained a grade, what grade? *2nd*

FIGURE 5–1
Continued

10. Do you believe your child believes that reading is valued in the home?

Not at all	Some	A lot
	X	

11. How frequently did you read to your child when he/she was:

	Not at all	Occasion-ally	Almost daily
2–4 years old?		X	
5–6 years old?		X	
7–8 years old?	X		
9+ years old?	X		

12. Is your child now reading a book that is not a school requirement?

No	Yes
X	

If yes, what book ________

a. Is the mother?

No	Yes
X	

If yes, what book ________

b. Is the father?

No	Yes
	X

If yes, what book *Beautiful Swimmers.*

13. Have there been other reading problems in the family?

No	Yes
	X

If yes, please comment *As I mentioned, I never learned to read well.*

14. Do you help your child with his/her reading at home?

Not at all	Some	A lot
X		

If "some" or "a lot," what do you do? ________

Use back side to tell us anything not included on this side.

FIGURE 5–1
Continued

INITIAL SCREENING

Since most reading specialists lack the time to adequately service all of the students referred to them, they should establish a screening procedure. The purpose of screening is to obtain a rough estimate of the students' reading skills. The screening results can then be evaluated by the referring committee who will decide what sort of help the student needs. Screenings in out-of-school clinical agencies save hours of diagnostic time. It is estimated that about one-third of the students referred for clinical diagnosis have no reading difficulties. These referrals are usually based on a decline in school grades, concern raised by an article in the press, or interest in the reader's development without concern that difficulties exist. Obviously, a full-blown clinical diagnosis in such cases is unnecessary.

Screenings should include some indication of mental ability, oral reading behavior, comprehension after silent reading, word-attack or study skills, and a diagnostic lesson. Screenings can usually be conducted within two hours.

The following sections explain the steps involved in clinical diagnosis. To make the process more understandable, a fictional student named Walt will be used to illustrate each step and how it helps in accumulating information for a successful diagnosis.

Establishing Rapport

Purposes

a. Relax the reader and develop a communicative atmosphere.
b. Obtain information from the reader.

Procedures

a. Using the referral form, discuss areas that appear to be strengths.
b. Use a student self-assessment procedure.
c. Use an interview guide form to gain interest information.

Time needed

Generally about five minutes. At times a very shy student may need more time to relax and feel comfortable.

Walt example

Age 12 Grade 7

Likes school, football, mathematics, cooking, and skateboards.

Does not care for water sports or history.

Says he has few friends.

Establishing rapport helps relax the reader and develops a communicative atmosphere.

Indication of Mental Ability

In a screening situation a reading specialist seeks to obtain only an *indication* of mental ability. The careful testing of mental ability would take more time than the entire screening. Therefore, the indication must be evaluated liberally. Using the standard error for a range score is advisable.

Purposes

a. Determine a reading expectancy level or range.
b. Determine the need for further testing of intellectual ability, i.e., excessively high or low scores or scores that do not fit other available data (teacher observation, listening comprehension, other scores on tests of mental ability). In these cases, further testing is recommended.

Procedures

In a screening conduct a quick test of mental ability, which will be supplemented with the reading specialist's observation during the screening. For example, if a reader scores poorly on a test of mental ability, but has a good speaking vocabulary and scores well in reading comprehension, then the ability score's accuracy may be doubted.

Examples of tests

Listening section of the Diagnostic Reading Scales (Test 4)
Peabody Picture Vocabulary Test
Slosson Intelligence Test

Verbal Opposites of the Detroit Tests of Learning Aptitudes
Time needed
Five to fifteen minutes

> **Walt example**
> Age 12   Grade 7
> Likes school, football, mathematics, cooking, and skateboards.
> Does not care for water sports or history.
> Says he has few friends.
> Ability range: Age 10–12

Oral Reading Testing

This testing can be divided into two subsections, oral reading of isolated words and oral reading in context.

Oral Reading of Isolated Words (Word recognition).
Purpose
To obtain a quick estimate of reading level to determine the starting point for further testing.
Procedures
Many word recognition tests are available. A few examples are:

Botel Word Recognition
Diagnostic Reading Scales
(see figure 5–2)
Woodcock Reading Mastery
Slosson Oral Reading Test
Informal reading inventory

Time needed
Five to ten minutes

> **Walt example**
> Age 12   Grade 7
> Likes school, football, mathematics, cooking, and skateboards
> Does not care for water sports or history.
> Says he has few friends.
> Ability range: Age 10–12
> Word recognition: Grade 4

Some authorities suggest using rather sophisticated procedures for testing word recognition which employ both timed and untimed responses. Others suggest an analysis of word recognition errors. In a screening situation such procedures are too time-consuming and are not warranted. These two procedures will be discussed later in this chapter during discussion of extended diagnosis. Note that the only purpose for word recognition testing in a screening is to place students in other tests.

Oral Reading in Context.

Purposes

a. Determine oral reading level.
b. Determine oral reading comprehension.
c. Evaluate oral reading behavior to gain insight into the reader's oral reading strategies.

The procedures for purpose c are different from those for purposes a and b. Since a given screening may involve all three purposes, the procedures for each are presented.

Procedures for purposes a and b

Many test instruments are available for these two purposes. Examples are:

Diagnostic Reading Scales
Gilmore Oral Reading Tests
Gray Oral Reading Test
Informal reading inventory

Although the directions for administering these tests vary, they all have the following basic ingredients:

- ☐ The student reads aloud from graded selections, ranging from simple to difficult.
- ☐ The examiner records the reader's responses as outlined by the manual.
- ☐ Scores are based on a frequency count rather than a qualitative analysis.
- ☐ Several comprehension questions are asked that normally provide a measure of the reader's ability to recall specifically stated facts from the story.

The value of oral reading comprehension scores is questionable. During oral reading, most readers are concentrating on pronunciation and fluency. The valuable insights gained from an analysis of oral reading relate to those processes that the reader demonstrates. Comprehension skills are best measured after silent reading. Questions asked after oral reading can be used to show students that reading is a purposeful activity if the teacher begins a lesson with purpose-setting questions and follows oral reading with those same questions.

As with word recognition, many reading specialists prefer to construct informal oral reading tests. Passages are selected from graded materials that the student may be expected to read.

______	1. look	______	26. good		
______	2. come	______	27. girl		
______	3. in	______	28. name		
______	4. the	______	29. away		
______	5. you	______	30. this		
______	6. one	______	31. bed		
______	7. she	______	32. call		
______	8. mother	______	33. time		
______	9. me	______	34. sleep		
______	10. yellow	______	35. fish		
______	11. pig	______	36. morning		
______	12. it	______	37. seen		
______	13. big	______	38. children		
______	14. milk	______	39. live		
______	15. dog	______	40. around		
______	16. tree	______	41. barn		
______	17. are	______	42. other		
______	18. day	______	43. under		
______	19. run	______	44. cry		
______	20. all	______	45. chicken		
______	21. father	______	46. breakfast		
______	22. door	______	47. chair		
______	23. like	______	48. rain		
______	24. ball	______	49. asleep		
______	25. eat	______	50. peep		

WORD RECOGNITION

list 1

total score ______

placement ______

Number Correct	Grade Placement
11-13	1.3
14-20	1.6
21-32	1.8
33-44	2.3
*45-50	2.8

*If student achieves this level, administer List 2.

FIGURE 5–2
A word recognition test from the Diagnostic Reading Scales. (Copyright © 1963 by CBT/McGraw-Hill, Inc. Reproduced by permission; all rights reserved.)

Accuracy is recorded as it is on standardized tests of oral reading. Using informal oral reading tests during diagnosis offers the advantage of evaluating students from longer selections and a variety of content. An inherent disadvantage of informal oral reading tests lies in the possibly false assumption that the graded materials used for the tests are, in fact, accurately graded. For example, if a given selection taken from a fifth-grade book is actually at the sixth-grade level, diagnostic conclusions that come from it are faulty. Another limitation relates to how such tests are interpreted. Pikulski states that an informal inventory's usefulness in diagnosis is related to how well the testing material matches the material to be used for instruction.[1] Obviously, if they are mismatched, interpreting results is difficult.

Using oral reading tests as diagnostic tools has several limitations. Disagreement abounds about what constitutes an oral reading error. Certainly, one would recognize such errors as mispronounced words, hesitancy on unknown words, or disregard of punctuation marks as obvious limitations to effective oral reading. But is it an error when a reader repeats words to correct oral reading mistakes? Is it an error when a student stops to use word-attack skills on words not known at sight? Or are these examples of the type of behavior teachers want readers to display? Are all errors of equal importance, or do some interfere with reading efficiency more seriously than others? If weights could be developed for various types of errors, would the same weight hold at various grade levels? (For example, would a vowel error made by a first grader be as serious an error as a vowel error made by a fifth grader?)

Test constructors, in an effort to standardize oral reading tests, have had to establish some easily recognizable arbitrary standards for accurate oral reading. Although these arbitrary systems vary, most of them include markings similar to those listed in the Gilmore Oral Reading Test.[2] Substitutions and mispronunciations are written above the word on which the error was made; omissions are circled; repetitions are underlined; words inserted are put in the appropriate place; punctuation that is disregarded is marked by an *X*; hesitations of two seconds or more are marked by a checkmark above the word, and at five seconds these words are pronounced for the reader and two checkmarks are made. The following paragraph has been marked according to this system.

A spaceman has stepped onto the surface of Mars. He is very careful as he steps from his capsule. Live television brings the moment to the entire population of the planet earth. It is a an exciting moment.

This system gives an exact representation of the student's reading. This student made the following errors: hesitated on the word *has* and failed to pronounce the word *stepped* in five seconds; mispronounced *surface* and disregarded the period after *Mars*; repeated *He is very*; substituted *telephone* for *television* and *a* for *an*; omitted *entire*, and added *planet*.

This paragraph illustrates not only the marking system but also the fact that all errors are not equally important. (For example, hesitation on the word *has* is a less serious error than the failure to pronounce *stepped*.[3]

One can also observe reader strengths from this test. For example, although the first sentence is somewhat distorted, this student seemed to get the passage's basic meaning. The second sentence was read perfectly. The omission of the word *entire* and the addition of the word *planet* did not distort meaning.

Beside the disagreement about what really constitutes an oral reading error, another limitation of oral reading tests concerns their dependence on the ability of the examiner to hear and record accurately the errors that the reader makes. Clinicians need supervised practice to gain proficiency in oral reading test administration. If the examiner is not able to hear or record the responses accurately, the results of testing will be invalid. Through practice, competency can be developed to assure satisfactory administration and interpretation of oral reading tests. However, unsupervised testing without adequate practice can lead to extremely unreliable results.

Time needed for testing oral reading level and determining oral reading comprehension depends, of course, on how many passages need to be read to get to the instructional level. Oral reading diagnosis can usually be conducted in five to fifteen minutes.

Walt example

Age 12 Grade 7
Likes school, football, mathematics, cooking, and skateboards.
Does not care for water sports or history.
Says he has few friends.
Ability range: Age 10–12
Word recognition: Grade 4
Oral accuracy: Grade 5
Oral comprehension: Grade 5

Procedures for purpose c

Testing for evaluation of the student's oral reading behavior should be conducted on longer passages than those used for purposes a and b. Goodman and Burke[4] have developed passages for this purpose. Teachers can select passages from materials that students would normally be expected to read in school.

As discussed in chapter 4, the work of Kenneth Goodman has influenced the way many are using oral reading in clinical diagnosis.[5] He discourages using oral reading to obtain reading level information and emphasizes using it for linguistic processing information (miscues). Student responses during oral reading are classified qualitatively in terms of the appropriate use of cues. The Gilmore coding system mentioned earlier is also changed to reflect the qualitative classifications.

Many reading specialists have made adaptations of Goodman's ideas for clinical use.[6] Staff members at the University of Maryland reading clinic, for example, have adapted his ideas as a way of looking at oral reading behavior (ORB). Those ideas that most directly affect the ability to make useful recommendations to teachers were modified and used. Basically, with this approach, every response that is in variance to the text is recorded, leaving one word of text on each side of the variant word, for example:

Text: in *the* street
Student response: in *a* street

Then a judgment is made to classify the student variance as a regression, insertion, omission, or substitution. Regressions are further analyzed using the following questions:

1. Did the student change the first response to make a correction?
2. Did the student appear to attempt a correction but fail?
3. Did the student simply repeat a portion that was initially correct?
4. Did the student change a response that was initially correct?

In each of these cases the student might be self-monitoring his or her own comprehension; the reader might have thought that the oral reading did not sound correct or make sense. With such an analysis, one can see that a regression may be classified as good oral reading behavior as well as poor.

Omissions and insertions are judged in terms of whether they changed the meaning of the context. If they do not change the meaning, we can assume that the reader is using semantic cues.

Substitutions, the most important student response in studying oral reading behavior, are evaluated as follows:

1. When making the substitution, did the reader use graphic cues? In what way did the reader display knowledge of phonics or structural analysis?
2. Did the reader use semantic cues? In what ways did the reader demonstrate use of the context?
3. Did the reader use syntactic cues? In what ways did the reader show knowledge of grammar? If the reader uses semantic cues, one assumes the use of syntactic cues. However, if the reader does not use semantic cues but does use syntactic cues, valuable information is obtained about the student's awareness of language.

Obviously, each of these analyses involves some subjective judgment. But with them the reader can be given credit for oral reading strengths even when responses are different from the text. Each of these responses is recorded and all responses in a category are totaled. Then the specialist can say how much of the time a student demonstrates a specific type of oral reading behavior; for example, when the reader makes substitutions, semantic cues are used effectively 75 percent of the time.

The use of this type of oral reading behavior analysis calls for considerable practice. Examiners are urged to use tape recorders, at least during initial efforts, to record variances for this type of analysis.

Goodman and Burke's work may be referred to for a detailed explanation of oral reading miscue analysis.[7] Oral reading diagnosis is of most value for students reading between second- and seventh-grade reading levels. Beginning readers' responses may be related to the method used for instruction. If language experience has been used, the reader may rely heavily on semantic cues; if a phonics method has been used, the reader may indicate heavy reliance on graphic cues. Once the reader is beyond the initial stages of learning to read, one can better determine which cues the reader relies on. Older readers probably use very different behavior in oral reading than in silent reading. Perhaps oral reading analysis becomes less useful as an insight into silent reading behavior as the reader matures. Diagnostic information from oral reading should be interpreted with this caution in mind.

Time needed for purpose c

Usually oral reading behavior analysis is conducted on one passage and takes little testing time (5 to 10 minutes); however, if the passage is one on which the reader either makes no errors or makes so many that he or she is reading nonsense, another passage should be selected and more time allotted.

Obviously, a screening can be conducted using all three purposes. If so, time will be added to the screening. Most reading specialists will want to decide which oral reading purpose best suits their needs and evaluate oral reading accordingly.

Walt example

Age 12 Grade 7

Likes school, football, mathematics, cooking, and skateboards.

Does not care for water sports or history.

Says he has few friends.

Ability range: Age 10–12

Word recognition: Grade 4

Oral accuracy: Grade 5

Oral comprehension: Grade 5

Oral reading behavior: High use of semantic cues at fifth-grade level.

Low use of graphic cues at fifth-grade level.

Comprehension after Silent Reading

Comprehension diagnosis is difficult because so much depends on the diagnostic procedures used. Comprehension levels can vary several grade levels when different procedures are used. The content of the passages being used, the setting for silent reading, and the assessment procedures can all influence any reader's comprehension performance.

Purposes

a. Determine the reader's skills in responding to three different methods of obtaining comprehension.
b. Determine the reader's skills in understanding passages at various degrees of difficulty.
c. Determine the reader's skills in responding to various types of questions.

As in oral reading, the procedures needed to achieve these purposes are different; however, the procedures can be combined so that each purpose is attained in a screening situation. By using an informal reading inventory, the reading specialist has the flexibility to manipulate the reading setting so that important diagnostic information can be obtained.

Procedures for purpose a

Since the procedure used for assessing comprehension affects reader response, teachers and reading specialists should administer informal reading inventories using three different methods:

1. Have the reader read for the purpose of retelling the story in the passage, which gives a personal response that indicates what the reader saw as most meaningful.
2. Have the reader respond to questions about the story from recall, without the printed material available for referral.
3. Have the reader respond to questions that could not be answered in recall by locating the answers in the material.

Procedures for purposes b and c

The reading specialist will need to decide what type of instrument will be used to assess comprehension. These instruments include prepared tests, informal inventories, cloze or maze tests, and criterion-referenced tests. These same tests are used in classroom diagnosis; however, when used for clinical assessment, they are used on an individual basis, allowing time for different tests and more careful evaluation of reader behavior.

Prepared Tests. Several examples of prepared tests that are available for clinical diagnosis are the Diagnostic Reading Scales, Gates-McKillop-Horowitz Reading Diagnostic Tests, Durrell Analysis of Reading Difficulties, and Woodcock Reading Mastery Tests.

Tests such as these provide information about the reader's ability to understand material at different levels. They can also provide information about the reader's ability to respond to various types of questions. The reading specialist will want to be certain that different types of questions are provided, since some tests provide questions that ask for literal responses only.

When selecting a test, the reading specialist should make certain that it is reliable and valid. Information concerning validity and reliability can be found in the technical manual that accompanies each test. Tests that lack validity do not reflect the variables that the test was constructed to measure. Tests with low reliability are measuring too much chance score and are not dependable.

Informal Inventories. Informal inventories, whether prepared commercially or by teachers, provide clinical diagnosis with flexible instruments to assess reading comprehension. The flexibility is feasible because the tests are not standardized, allowing for the three types of assessment suggested under purpose a. The manipulation of standardized tests interferes with their norms so that the results are meaningless. Some prepared informal inventories are The Classroom Reading Inventory, The Standard Reading Inventory, Pupil Placement Test, and Analytical Reading Inventory. The reading specialist will want to examine each of these and make selections most suited to their school situation. (Each of these is presented in detail in appendix A.) Considerations should include:

1. Are alternate forms available? Alternate forms provide flexibility needed for pre- and posttesting, use of alternate passages for starter examples, and use when assessment about the performance on a given passage can be doubted.
2. Do the questions reflect varying types of comprehension? As discussed previously, various types of questions are needed to assess purpose c.
3. Do the passages reflect the type of reading material being used in the reader's school? If the reader is placed in content materials and the passages are narrative, then a mismatch has occurred.
4. Have the readability levels of the passages been checked? If so, how? Passages with unchecked readability levels should be held suspect. It is not enough that the passages have been taken from graded books.
5. Are the cutoff scores realistic? Since the work of William Powell was made available in 1978,[8] some inventories may be using outdated cutoff scores.

Teacher-developed informal inventories have long been used to assess reading comprehension. Generally these inventories are developed using the materials that the students will be reading in school, eliminating the problem of matching test materials with instructional materials. For best results a group of reading specialists should work together to develop the informal inventory. By checking and double checking the passages and the questions, easily made errors can be avoided. Passages should be field tested and replaced when they do not yield accurate results. Inventory developers should apply the same questions to their tests that apply to commercially-developed informal inventories.

The following steps are suggested for developing an informal inventory for clinical diagnosis:

1. Select passages from instructional material. Passages should be varied in topic, complete in thought, and of interest to the grade level of the students. Passages should be between 125 and 175 words in order for error patterns to stabilize.
2. Develop questions on each passage. About ten questions should be developed to assess comprehension. Questions should elicit literal, interpretive, and problem-solving responses. The number of each type of question will vary with the passage content.
3. Field test each passage on students known to be reading satisfactorily at the passage's grade level. When reading silently most students should be able to answer 70 percent of the questions. If they fall below that, the questions should be reworked. If the students are tested after oral reading the acceptable correct response level is lowered to 55 to 65 percent. How one field tests the inventory will depend on the purposes one has for developing it in the first place. Preferably, the inventory should be used as a measure of silent, not oral, reading comprehension. If students answer all of the questions, then the questions may be too easy. If adjusting the questions does not change student performance, the readability level of the passage may be inappropriate. Even though a passage was selected from instructional material, it may have a higher or lower readability level than that listed on the instructional material. In such cases, a different passage should be selected.
4. After making necessary adjustments use the inventory keeping notes on its effectiveness.
5. If difficulties occur, continue to adjust questions or search for more appropriate passages.

Cloze and Maze Tests. Cloze tests are constructed directly from the material used in instruction. Every fifth word is deleted, and the student is to supply the missing word. Accuracy scores of 40 percent reflect the 70-percent mark (or instructional level) on the tests previously mentioned. Using a passage with fifty deletions is suggested.

Cloze tests can be used informally to determine how well students use syntactic and semantic cues when reading. In these cases, certain words are deleted (for example, all verbs) to see if the students can supply appropriate words.

Maze testing is a modification of cloze procedures. In maze tests, instead of deleting every fifth word, a three-word choice is provided. For example:

street
The boys walked down the house.
run

The student is to select the most appropriate word. In this type of testing, students are expected to score 70-percent accuracy to determine instructional levels.

Cloze and maze tests can be used to supplement information obtained from informal inventories.

Criterion-Referenced Tests. Criterion Referenced Tests (CRTs) can be used in clinical diagnosis, although they are usually more useful for classroom diagnosis since they are group instruments. Reading specialists often develop short CRTs for use in screenings to measure one or more specific objectives. For example, if a screening indicates that the student is having difficulty grasping the author's major ideas, the reading specialist may select several paragraphs and have the student read the paragraphs to obtain the author's main idea. By adding these data to that which was already available, the reading specialist would be adding reliability to the findings of the screening. (See discussion on CRTs in chapter 4.)

From these possibilities for comprehension diagnosis, the reading specialist will need to make a decision concerning what would be most useful. No one decision is appropriate for every case; however, the following suggestions have proven useful in most.

1. Select a good informal reading inventory.
2. Administer it for the retelling purpose.
3. Ask specific questions in a recall situation for important items missed in retelling.
4. Ask specific questions in a locating situation for important items missed in recall questioning.

Time needed
About twenty minutes. The time needed depends on the number of passages that need to be read to obtain an instructional level.

Walt example

Age 12 Grade 7
Likes school, football, mathematics, cooking, and skateboards.
Does not care for water sports or history.
Says he has few friends.
Ability range: Age 10–12
Word recognition: Grade 4
Oral accuracy: Grade 5
Oral comprehension: Grade 5
Oral reading behavior: High use of semantic cues at fifth-grade level.
Low use of graphic cues at fifth-grade level.
Comprehension using Informal Reading Inventory:
4th-grade passage retelling good, recall 90% + locate 10% = 100%
5th-grade passage retelling fair, recall 70% + locate 30% = 100%
6th-grade passage retelling poor, recall 50% + locate 20% = 70%
7th-grade passage retelling poor, recall 20% + locate 30% = 50%

By adding the recall and the locate percentages, the percent of questions answered accurately can be obtained. These data show that Walt's retelling dropped off immediately after the fourth-grade passage and recall dropped off after the fifth-grade passage. Therefore, his retelling comprehension level is fourth grade, his recall level is fifth grade, and his locate level is sixth grade.

At this time in the screening a decision must be made. Is further testing desirable? If so, in what direction should it go? Since Walt scored into the fourth-, fifth-, and sixth-grade levels on all tests, a decision was made to extend the screening to include an assessment of Walt's study skills. If he had scored at the first-, second-, or third-grade level, continued assessment of his word attack skills would have been the next step.

Study Skill Assessment

Purposes

a. Determine if the reader can use reading skills in content materials.

b. Determine if the reader uses effective study techniques.

Obtaining an accurate assessment of a student's use of reading skills in content materials can be difficult. This assessment generally would be obtained in an extended diagnosis or during instruction.

Procedures

a. Collect interview data from content teachers. Types of questions for content-teacher interviews include:

1. Is the student able to complete independent assignments for class?
2. In what areas does the student show strengths?
3. What is your assessment of the student's weaknesses?
4. What adjustments have you been able to make for the student's lack of reading skills?
5. How does the student handle maps, charts, and graphs?
6. How does the student use dictionary skills?

b. Collect interview data from student. Types of questions for student interview include:

1. How much homework do you get each evening?
2. How long do you work on your homework?
3. Where do you do your homework?
4. What do you find easiest to do?
5. What is most difficult for you?

c. Sample the student's reading in content material at his or her instructional level. By taking a content book at the student's instructional level, the reading specialist can teach a directed lesson and note the student's ability to respond.

Time needed

Five to ten minutes

Walt example

Study skill assessment:

Good in completing mathematics assignments.
Weak in completing social studies and science assignments.
Weak in spelling.

Word Attack Assessment

Purposes

a. Determine if important word attack subskills may be causing reading comprehension difficulties.
b. Identify those important word attack subskills that are the reader's strengths.

Procedures

The usual procedure is to administer a test of identified important word attack skills. (The word *important* is used here because many word attack tests include the assessment of skills that are not useful to the reader.) The reading specialist will need to determine which word attack skills need assessment and then select an instrument or a portion of an instrument that assesses those skills. Some instruments that can be considered are:

Botel Reading Inventory (revised): Decoding Test
Diagnostic Reading Scales
Roswell-Chall Diagnostic Reading Test of Word Analysis Skills
Sipay Word Analysis Tests
Woodcock Reading Mastery Tests

The amount of time needed to administer the tests varies greatly. At this point in a screening, time becomes crucial since the reader is likely to be weary of testing. Perhaps the selection of a short survey-type test would be most appropriate, saving the more time-consuming tests for extended diagnosis. (Each of these tests is described in appendix A.)

Time needed

Ten to thirty minutes, depending on the test selected.

Walt example

We had already decided that Walt did not need a word attack assessment. But, if he had, perhaps the results would show:
Knowledge of initial consonants: Excellent
Rhyming word skills: Excellent
Syllabication skills: Weak

Diagnostic Lesson

The final step in the screening is to test out the hypotheses developed from the available data through an instructional lesson. In Walt's case, the data available look like this:

Walt example

Age 12 Grade 7

Likes school, football, mathematics, cooking, and skateboards.

Does not care for water sports or history.

Says he has few friends.

Ability range: Age 10–12

Word recognition: Grade 4

Oral accuracy: Grade 5

Oral comprehension: Grade 5

Oral reading behavior: High use of semantic cues at fifth-grade level.

Low use of graphic cues at fifth-grade level.

Comprehension using Informal Reading Inventory:

- 4th-grade passage retelling good, recall 90% + locate 10% = 100%
- 5th-grade passage retelling fair, recall 70% + locate 30% = 100%
- 6th-grade passage retelling poor, recall 50% + locate 20% = 70%
- 7th-grade passage retelling poor, recall 20% + locate 30% = 50%

Study skill assessment:

Good in completing mathematics assignments.

Weak in completing social studies and science assignments.

Weak in spelling.

From these data several hypotheses may be developed:

- ☐ Although Walt is having some difficulty with reading, he has a good attitude toward school and likes mathematics, so opportunities should be developed for him to demonstrate his math skills.
- ☐ Walt comprehends best when using both recall and locate situations. He should be encouraged the use of both recall and locate situations for comprehension in all school subjects.
- ☐ Walt's use of semantic cues in oral reading indicates little need for concern. However, it is useful to determine which graphic cues are used and which are ignored. This analysis may help explain some of his difficulty with spelling.

What diagnostic lesson could be useful to deal with these hypotheses? Two possibilities are:

1. A directed lesson with content material, using locating skills at sixth-grade level.
2. A lesson directed toward Walt's locating comprehension skills, using different passages at fifth- and sixth-grade levels.

Of these two, the first is clearly preferable since Walt is in seventh grade and independent work in content areas is needed. In other cases, the diagnostic lesson could be used to:

1. Determine if the student can respond to the language experience approach.
2. Determine if the student can respond to the VAKT technique.
3. Determine if the student can respond to different types of questioning procedures.
4. Determine if the student can read material in a teacher-directed lesson that the student was unable to read independently.

The goal is obvious. The diagnostic lesson is used to verify the working hypotheses generated from the data of the screening. If it does verify the screening data, then recommendations can be made with assurance. If it does not verify the data, then extended diagnosis is recommended, or, if the diagnostic lesson justifies it, the hypotheses can be adjusted to reflect it.

Caution on Initial Screenings

The data collected in this brief manner lead to the formation of working hypotheses that must be tested through extended diagnosis and instruction. The results are *not* conclusive. Although every effort is made to be thorough, there is simply too much involved in the reading process for it to be thoroughly evaluated through a screening. The interview session with the parents and possibly with the student should be approached with caution. No pronouncements of cause and effect and no absolute conclusions are yielded in initial screening; rather, it is the first careful look into the situation.

THE INTERVIEW

The interview allows the reading specialist and the parents to obtain more information about the student's reading difficulties. Parents come to the interview with a lot of information about their perceptions of their child's reading difficulties, and may have difficulty listening until they have the opportunity to share

The interview between the parent and the specialist should start with information from the parent.

these perceptions. Therefore, the interview should start with a solicitation of information from the parents. Some starter questions might be:

1. Why do you think your child is having difficulty with reading?
2. What has the school personnel told you about your child's difficulty?
3. Why did you refer your child for this screening?

Most parents will respond to these types of questions willingly and unload their concerns. The person conducting the interview should listen carefully, showing interest, but not showing approval or disapproval. When the parents pick up signals that they are on unacceptable ground, they tend to become guarded and less communicative.

Most parents are very perceptive about the difficulties their children are experiencing. Often their comments reinforce or clarify the findings of the screening. In these cases, the interview is a confirming activity. In some cases, the parents tend to concentrate on one aspect of reading, one teacher, or one instructional activity (usually phonics). This type of concentration keeps them from gaining a broad perspective about their children's reading. In these cases, the interview becomes an enlightening activity.

After the parents have expressed their concerns the reading specialist can then discuss the results of the screening. The following procedures can be followed:

1. Explain each test, give an example of an item from it, and discuss the student's performance on that test. The test score and its interpretation should be given.
2. Summarize all observed behavior.
3. Present implications in the form of working hypotheses. Suggesting conclusions as a result of a screening should be avoided. Rather, state that adjustments will be the first things to try and then reevaluation will be conducted.
4. Ask for questions from the parents.

Some guidelines to follow for conducting interviews that follow initial screenings include:

1. Do not take notes during the interview. Wait until the parents have gone and then write down a record of what transpired. Notetaking during an interview tends to make parents uneasy.
2. Do not tape record an interview. Tapes make parents uncomfortable. If you must tape the interview, be certain that all involved know that it is being taped.
3. Do not take sides with the parents against a teacher or a school program. Taking sides in these matters is unethical because both sides of the story are not known.
4. If the screening is to be shared with other school personnel, be certain that the parents know this and approve. An out-of-school agency should have written permission from the parents to share any testing report.
5. Attempt to offer plausible recommendations. When possible, make the recommendations so that the parents have some decisions to make. For example, it may be that the school could offer some additional services or that a private tutor could be found.

A written report of the screening data with implications and suggestions for instruction or extended diagnosis is usually prepared. Such reports, when developed by school personnel, are useful for reference during school staffing meetings. When prepared by out-of-school agencies, they are usually mailed to the school principal.

This text has presented clinical screening procedures in detail. Reading specialists in the schools report that this screening procedure is their most common request for diagnosis; seldom is more detailed diagnosis requested. In a recent survey of a Maryland school district, reading specialists averaged 85 individual assessments each year. If this figure is typical for other reading specialists, then time-efficient diagnostic procedures such as those suggested here must be used for thorough assessment.

EXTENDED DIAGNOSIS

After measuring the reader's strengths and weaknesses in sight vocabulary, oral reading, and silent reading, tentative hypotheses are made. From these hypotheses, the reading specialist obtains clues to the reader's strengths and weaknesses in the skill areas and plans further diagnosis. The procedures here are identical to those used by the teacher in classroom diagnosis. Although the questions asked in relation to each skill area are those asked in classroom diagnosis, the resulting conclusions may culminate in further diagnosis, since the reading specialist has more diagnostic tools available and is more qualified to interpret the results. Using these tentative hypotheses, the reading specialist may need to extend the diagnosis to those skill areas that have been identified as needing further analysis.

One basic consideration in clinical diagnosis concerns the possibility that a student may have strength in a certain mode of learning. For example, a reader who may learn effectively when tactile experiences are combined with visual stimuli may not learn through visual stimuli alone. These strengths and weaknesses should serve as guides for instruction.

Learning Modalities

To assess learning modalities, the reading specialist has such tests as the Mills Learning Methods Tests, the Monroe-Sherman Group Diagnostic Reading Aptitude and Achievement Tests, the Detroit Tests of Learning Aptitude, the Gates Associative Learning Test, and the Illinois Test of Psycholinguistic Abilities. These tests attempt to identify strengths in visual or auditory sensory systems; the Mills test adds tactile and combination techniques. For severely handicapped readers, identification of strong learning modalities seems especially helpful. Modality identification is illusive, however. The examiner must realize that students may have many strengths not noted when using a specific instrument, making scores only partially helpful.

Intellectual Abilities

Diagnosis may also be extended into intellectual abilities. As discussed in chapter 3, the WISC–R and the Stanford-Binet are most commonly used for these purposes. The Illinois Test of Psycholinguistic Abilities (ITPA) claims to provide a different look at the student's linguistic functioning. Newcomer and Hammill caution, however, that ITPA's value is limited to gathering broad, descriptive information and is seriously limited for specific educational diagnosis.[9] Furthermore, correlations between ITPA subtest scores and reading achievement are very low.

Visual Discrimination

If visual discrimination skills appear to be deficient, the Monroe-Sherman Group Diagnostic Reading Aptitude and Achievement Tests, standardized readiness tests, or informal measures can be used for further diagnosis. The clinician should be certain that diagnostic data will aid in the development of an educational prescription. Generally informal measures are of most value. Informal testing, using a simple passage or experience story, can be conducted by asking the reader to circle all words that begin with a specific letter after identifying the letter; by asking the reader to underline all words that have a certain ending; or by finding specific letters in a paragraph. The advantage of such informal testing is that the testing medium consists of the actual reading passage.

Auditory Discrimination

If auditory discrimination appears to be causing a problem, further testing through measures such as the Wepman Auditory Discrimination Test can provide valuable input into diagnosis. Then further identify auditory discrimination abilities in terms of initial sounds, medial sounds, or final sounds. Informal measures are equally useful and easily constructed. The clinician can read lists of words in pairs ("cat"/"fat") and ask the student to indicate whether they are the same or different. Perhaps a better way to determine auditory discrimination skills is to ask the student to repeat the two words. This eliminates his or her confusion about what *same* and *different* mean.

Orientation

If the tentative hypothesis identifies orientation as a reading problem, diagnosis often is extended to include an evaluation of eye motion during both oral and silent reading. The student's eyes are monitored closely to determine if they move with an acceptable number of fixations across a printed line, and if they move backwards excessively in regressions. Since everyone makes a certain number of regressions while reading, diagnosis in this area can prove difficult.

Reading specialists should observe groups of good, fair, and poor readers so that they can learn what is expected in the observation of eye movements. Other observations that can lead to suspicions about lack of orientation are behaviors such as peculiar reading posture, placing the book at unusual angles, and losing one's place.

Dominance Preference

Another extension of diagnosis of orientation often focuses on the area of dominance preference. After screening thousands of cases, the staff of the University of Maryland reading clinic found no relationship of dominance to orientation problems, nor did they find any remedial solutions based on such diagnosis. While many students have symptoms of confused dominance, such cases are not restricted to reading problems. Thus, continued efforts to link reading difficulties to dominance problems cannot be justified. Such diagnosis often even leads educators away from the symptoms that will best offer solutions to the student's educational difficulties.

Sight Vocabulary

If the tentative hypothesis identifies sight vocabulary as the problem, a more careful analysis of tests previously administered may determine patterns of sight vocabulary errors (see chapter 4). Durrell suggests that when time is not a factor the word not known at sight should be used to determine if the reader can analyze the word using word attack skills.[10] In such cases, the word recognition answer sheet will have two columns, one for instant pronunciation and one for delayed pronunciation. If the reader does not know the word at sight but does know it when permitted to examine it, that reader obviously has skills to attack the word properly but has not mastered the word for his or her sight vocabulary.

Word Attack

If the tentative hypothesis finds a student's word attack skills in need of further diagnosis, the specialist should analyze the errors made in word recognition and oral reading, as was done in the classroom diagnosis (see chapter 4). Tests are also available for clinical diagnosis that measure specific word attack skill performance. The Botel Reading Inventory; the Diagnostic Reading Test by Bond, Balow, and Hoyt; the Roswell-Chall Diagnostic Reading Test of Word Analysis Skills; the Doren Diagnostic Reading Test; and the Sipay Word Analysis Tests are six well-known, quite different evaluations of word attack skills. Each of these tests may be administered to groups of students who respond to oral presentations by the teacher. The Botel test is quite short; the Bond, Balow, and Hoyt test takes about forty-five minutes; and the Doren test takes three hours. The Sipay test can be given in sections taking ten to twenty minutes per section. The various diagnostic test batteries also contain an analysis of word attack skills; however, they heavily emphasize phonics. Teacher-made, criterion-referenced tests of the various word attack skills often provide the best insight into skill strengths and needs in this area. For example, if analysis of word recognition and oral reading responses indicates that the student has difficulty with word endings, then a test can be constructed that measures only skills dealing with word endings. A standardized word attack test would waste valuable time in such a case.

Reading specialists generally want to see how well a student with specific word attack problems performs on a spelling test. This test should be given at the student's instructional level. Through an analysis of spelling errors, the reading specialist can extend the diagnosis and verify previous findings. The Spelling Placement Test of the Botel Reading Inventory can provide the data needed for such an analysis.

The reading specialist should be aware that many readers have learned to attack words adequately in isolated drill-type exercises but are not capable of performing the same task when they see these words in context. It would be erroneous, therefore, to conclude that students do not have word attack deficiencies simply because they perform successfully on diagnostic tests of word attack skills. Evaluation must be made in an oral reading situation where the student is faced, not with the single unknown word, but with the unknown word in a group of familiar words.

Comprehension

If the tentative hypothesis identifies the need for further diagnosis in comprehension, attention must again be directed to those questions asked in classroom diagnosis (see chapter 4). Clinical diagnosis will be extended to review the history of approaches used in the student's reading instruction. From this type of analysis, the reading specialist can often understand gaps in instruction areas and suggest remedial programs to fill these gaps. In the area of comprehension, the specialist should establish the answers to four questions before proceeding to remediation:

- ☐ *Is the reader's poor performance on a comprehension test due basically to weak comprehension skills, or is it more closely related to inadequate vocabulary?* One technique for determining the answer to this question is to make a careful comparison between word-meaning and paragraph-meaning scores. Poorer performance in word meaning usually indicates that a student's vocabulary skills are prohibiting maximum performance in comprehension.
- ☐ *Is there a need for further comprehension testing to verify conflicting test scores?* It may be necessary to administer a test that has more items, one that has a better variety of items, or one that measures a certain type of comprehension skill not measured in the previously administered silent reading test. When students have serious comprehension difficulties, the reading specialist seldom finds one silent reading test satisfactory. If another test is administered, the results of that test should undergo the same diagnostic scrutiny as the previous test. Scores of such tests should not be averaged, however. When more than one test of silent reading is used to diagnose skill strengths and weaknesses, analysis of the responses to types of questions rather than a composite score is critical to clinical diagnosis.
- ☐ *Is the reader's poor performance on a comprehension test due basically to slow reading?* In classroom diagnosis, the ability to complete the reading assignments in a specific time period is considered; in clinical diagnosis, equal consideration must be given to the reader who fails to complete reading tests in the allotted time or is very slow on untimed tests. There is no possibility of obtaining this information from the grade scores on silent reading tests; rather, a careful inner test analysis will reveal the amount of material covered. The Reading Versatility Test is designed to determine the flexibility with which a student attacks print designed for different purposes.
- ☐ *Is the reader's poor comprehension on specific text exercises caused by the lack of experiences in the content area of the material being read?* A city student unfamiliar with farm life may score poorly on a test story about

farming, yet be quite capable of comprehending a similar story about city life. Diagnosis, however, is not so easy. While broad areas of experience may be identified, a reader's background of experiences is quite personal and involved, and can be difficult to ascertain.

Reading Habits and Attitudes

If the tentative hypothesis identifies reading habits and attitudes as a problem, the reading specialist has found that the student has the basic skills to read adequately, but does not care to read. This diagnosis involves a careful consideration of the information from the areas of emotional and physical diagnosis. The student may indicate a poor attitude toward school-type tasks and books or physical discomfort. Two study habit questionnaires are available to assist in extended diagnosis in this area: California Study Method Survey and Survey of Study Habits and Attitudes (SSHA) (see Form H for grades 7–12 of SSHA in figure 5–3). Further evaluation is needed of past efforts made by the school to encourage the student to read, the availability of books in the school and at home, and the general atmosphere that may encourage or discourage reading in these situations. A student who can read but normally doesn't is not considered in need of a specialist's attention. The reading specialist is obligated only to make specific recommendations to the classroom teacher. However, fully aware that interests are always changing, the reading specialist will attempt to assess the student's interests either formally through an established interest inventory or informally through interest inventories or a personal interview with the student, his parents, and his teacher. Many students, although they are reading as well as possible, are placed in frustrating reading situations daily in school. It does not take a specialist to realize that reading is painful for these students and that they may easily develop a negative attitude toward reading. Information gleaned in such a manner should be included in the diagnostic report.

Diagnostic Batteries

Diagnostic batteries used in clinical diagnosis consist of a group of tests used in a single unit. These tests are designed for use as a complete reading analysis. The more prominent of these batteries are the Durrell Analysis of Reading Difficulties, Gates-McKillop-Horowitz Reading Diagnostic Test, Diagnostic Reading Scales, and Monroe-Sherman Group Diagnostic Reading Aptitude and Achievement Tests.[11] The first three are individual in nature, while the last is a group test. A careful examination of these diagnostic batteries is essential for an appropriate selection for clinical diagnosis. The only items that all these tests have in common are measures of silent or oral reading and work attack skills. Some tests also include word recognition, oral reading, arithmetic, spelling, auditory and visual discrimination, and auding. The main advantage of using a diagnostic battery is that the scores of the subtests are comparable since they are standardized on the same population. Another advantage is that there is only one manual and one test to learn to administer and interpret; one does not have the overwhelming job that occurs with some other types of testing combinations. The resulting information will provide an individual analysis of how a student is reading and how the student's skill development is related to total reading scores.

These diagnostic batteries are not without limitations, however. Some are too brief and some are standardized on very small populations, thereby causing reliability problems. Most importantly, reading specialists will find that the tests do not measure the types of quantities of skill that they wish to measure, thus causing validity problems. Therefore, in clinical diagnosis, it is unlikely that any one of these diagnostic batteries will be adequate for a complete diagnosis. Note that subtests of diagnostic batteries are recommended for use in diagnosing areas of strengths and weaknesses that can be studied in more depth.

In a recent survey of 100 college and university reading clinics by Rogers, et al.,[12] the data in table 5–1 were reported concerning the frequency of use of various diagnostic instruments.

Diagnostic Teaching

Formulating diagnostic hypotheses from data based on testing situations can lead to a distorted view of the reader. The reader's behavior during instruction must also be considered. An instructional session provides additional data for extended clinical diagnosis.

Specifically, reading specialists should provide lessons that check their findings concerning reading level, major skill strengths, and major skill needs. For example, if the diagnosis supported an instructional level at 3^1, skill strengths in beginning consonants and directly stated recall, and skill weaknesses in vowels and problem solving, a lesson should be designed to see how the reader operates in each of these areas. Several books—one at the 2^2 level, one at the 3^1 level, and perhaps one at the 3^2 level—can be selected with silent reading followed by questioning in the area of strengths and needs. A short phonics lesson

TABLE 5–1
Test instruments and techniques used in diagnosis

Instrument/Technique	Rank	Incidence
Informal Reading Inventory	1	57
Visual Screening	2	53
Background Information Form	3	29
Audiometric Hearing Tests	4	26
Phonic Inventories	5	22
Spache Diagnostic Reading Scales	5	22
Informal Interest Inventory	7	21
Slosson Intelligence Tests	8	20
Test of Auditory Discrimination	9	18
Durrell Analysis of Reading Difficulty	10	16
Full Scale IQ (i.e., Wechsler, Stanford Binet)	10	16
Peabody Picture Vocabulary Test	12	15
Gates-MacGinitie Reading Tests	13	14
School Achievement Records/Grades	13	14
Woodcock Reading Mastery Test	15	12
Reading Miscue Analysis Inventory	15	12
Basic Sight Word Lists (i.e., Dolch)	16	11
Stanford Diagnostic Reading Test	17	10
Gates-McKillop Reading Test	17	10
Wide Range Achievement Test	19	10
Slosson Oral Reading Test	19	8
Gray Oral Reading Test	21	7
Detroit Test of Language Aptitude	21	7
Gilmore Oral Reading Test	22	6
California Reading Test	23	5
Ekwall Reading Inventory	24	4
Botel Reading Inventory	24	4

can be developed to see how well the reader handles consonants and vowels.

If the hypotheses are confirmed, the diagnosis becomes more reliable. However, if the student can perform during instruction, new hypotheses should be formulated and tested. Rarely are all hypotheses confirmed. Clinicians who skip the step of diagnostic teaching place themselves in the position of drawing faulty conclusions. Preparing a report on a student that contains faulty conclusions has serious consequences. If specialists expect teachers to use their reports to adjust instruction, they should test their findings in instructional situations. In the reading center at the University of Maryland, diagnostic lessons that follow testing have been found to be of the utmost value. Occasionally a full case study seems necessary to complete a diagnostic evaluation. To develop a full case study, in-depth test-

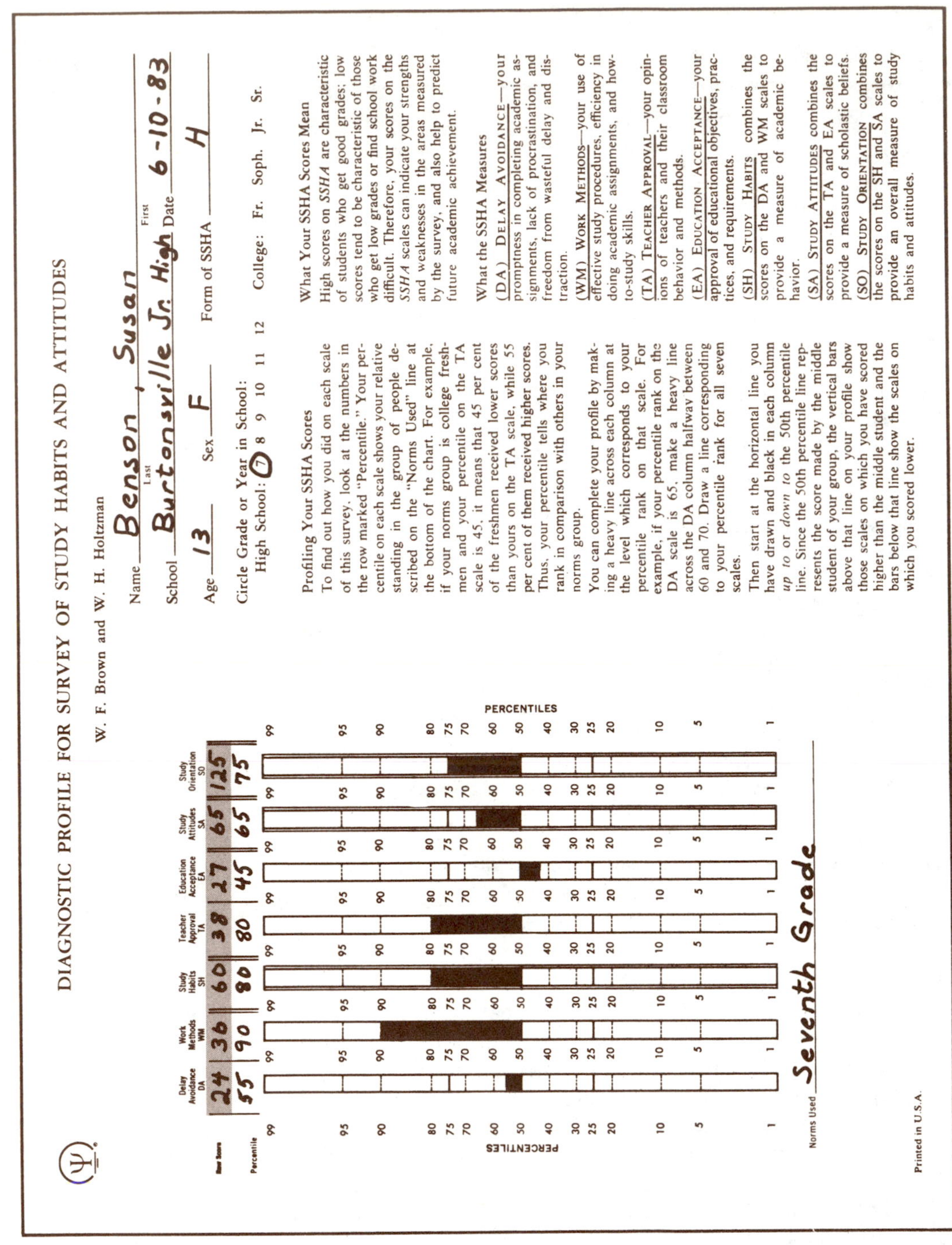

DIAGNOSTIC PROFILE FOR SURVEY OF STUDY HABITS AND ATTITUDES

W. F. Brown and W. H. Holtzman

Name Benson, Susan (Last / First)
School Burtonsville Jr. High Date 6-10-83
Age 13 Sex F Form of SSHA H

Circle Grade or Year in School:
High School: (7) 8 9 10 11 12 College: Fr. Soph. Jr. Sr.

	Delay Avoidance DA	Work Methods WM	Study Habits SH	Teacher Approval TA	Education Acceptance EA	Study Attitudes SA	Study Orientation SO
Raw Score	24	36	60	38	27	65	125
Percentile	55	90	80	80	45	65	75

Norms Used Seventh Grade

Printed in U.S.A.

Profiling Your SSHA Scores

To find out how you did on each scale of this survey, look at the numbers in the row marked "Percentile." Your percentile on each scale shows your relative standing in the group of people described on the "Norms Used" line at the bottom of the chart. For example, if your norms group is college freshmen and your percentile on the TA scale is 45, it means that 45 per cent of the freshmen received lower scores than yours on the TA scale, while 55 per cent of them received higher scores. Thus, your percentile tells where you rank in comparison with others in your norms group.

You can complete your profile by making a heavy line across each column at the level which corresponds to your percentile rank on that scale. For example, if your percentile rank on the DA scale is 65, make a heavy line across the DA column halfway between 60 and 70. Draw a line corresponding to your percentile rank for all seven scales.

Then start at the horizontal line you have drawn and black in each column *up to* or *down to* the 50th percentile line. Since the 50th percentile line represents the score made by the middle student of your group, the vertical bars above that line on your profile show those scales on which you have scored higher than the middle student and the bars below that line show the scales on which you scored lower.

What Your SSHA Scores Mean

High scores on *SSHA* are characteristic of students who get good grades; low scores tend to be characteristic of those who get low grades or find school work difficult. Therefore, your scores on the *SSHA* scales can indicate your strengths and weaknesses in the areas measured by the survey, and also help to predict future academic achievement.

What the SSHA Measures

(DA) DELAY AVOIDANCE—your promptness in completing academic assignments, lack of procrastination, and freedom from wasteful delay and distraction.

(WM) WORK METHODS—your use of effective study procedures, efficiency in doing academic assignments, and how-to-study skills.

(TA) TEACHER APPROVAL—your opinions of teachers and their classroom behavior and methods.

(EA) EDUCATION ACCEPTANCE—your approval of educational objectives, practices, and requirements.

(SH) STUDY HABITS combines the scores on the DA and WM scales to provide a measure of academic behavior.

(SA) STUDY ATTITUDES combines the scores on the TA and EA scales to provide a measure of scholastic beliefs.

(SO) STUDY ORIENTATION combines the scores on the SH and SA scales to provide an overall measure of study habits and attitudes.

FIGURE 5–3
A page from the Survey of Study Habits and Attitudes. (Copyright © 1967, 1964, 1953 by the Psychological Corporation. Reprinted by permission; all rights reserved.)

ing is required in the areas of intelligence, verbal performance, auditory skills, visual skills, word recognition, oral reading behavior, silent reading comprehension, and word attack skills. To these are added medical reports and a developmental history, as well as detailed information from the school and home.

The decision to proceed with a full case study will stem from lack of information on the student and failure of the initial screening to satisfactorily identify the student's strengths and weaknesses. An evaluation of every aspect of the student's educational development, as well as his or her intellectual, emotional, and physical development, is needed. Because of the time, money, and coordination of efforts required, case studies are reserved for those students with the greatest apparent difficulties.

CASE REPORTING

As in classroom diagnosis, the information accumulated in a clinical diagnosis is useless unless it can be organized for easy understanding. A case report is the typical approach to preparing diagnostic information for clinical use. Although the precise form may vary, the following format should be used so that persons unfamiliar with the student can make optimum use of case information:

1. The first page should contain a concise summary of the essential data included in the report: name; age; address; school; degree of reading retardation; and a summary statement of diagnostic findings including intellectual, physical, emotional, and educational diagnosis.
2. The first page should be followed by as many pages of explanation as necessary. The explanation should include all test scores, the dates the tests were administered, and the name of the test administrator, as well as diagnostic interpretations of the test performance and evaluations of the student's responses. It also should include data from screening tests and referral reports. It is here that the relative importance of each piece of data is evaluated and interrelated and that causative factors may be identified.
3. The third section should consist of a page or two of complete description of the successes of the diagnostic lesson.
4. The last pages of the case report should include specific recommendations and referrals. Recommendations are

made to the clinic, classroom teacher, and parents, specifying preventive as well as remedial procedures.

The report can best be explained to the teacher in a face-to-face interview. Teachers nearly always have questions about the report that can be answered during the interview. The report will be better understood by the teacher if it has been discussed.

Not long ago, parents were denied specific information concerning test results. Today that has changed; parents have become aware of the need for such information, and often demand it. Indeed, they have the right to know this information. It is essential to give parents copies of anything sent to teachers. If reports are misfiled or lost, parents must have copies to replace those lost. Furthermore, parents can often implement adjustments at home to assist with the correction of difficulties.

Since reports often contain technical language, parents will find it helpful to receive the report during a conference. Technical language can then be explained and questions answered.

Pitfalls of Diagnosis

Both clinical and classroom diagnosis may be plagued by certain pitfalls. They include the following.

Overgeneralization. The tendency to use total test scores without examination of the pattern of test scores; the tendency to draw conclusions before all facts are in; the tendency to rely on the first significant symptom; and the tendency to hazard guesses outside the professional field are all examples of overgeneralizing in diagnosis. Overgeneralizing can be controlled, in part, by making couched statements when all data are not available. For example, instead of saying that a student has a poor home life, one can say that from the data available the home conditions bear watching as a possible cause of the student's lack of educational development. More than merely playing with words, couched statements protect the educational diagnostician and lead to more accurate reporting of diagnostic results.

Overextension of Diagnosis. Extending diagnosis beyond areas which will help arrive at an accurate picture of the student may cause the student to become overconcerned about a reading problem and is therefore a waste of time. In commenting on the disadvantages of extended diagnostic periods, Strang concludes, "He may feel more strongly than ever that something may be wrong with him.[13] Overextension of diagnosis occurs more commonly in the clinic than in the classroom because the clinic provides the most careful study of the reader and a variety of tests. Some clinics suggest that each student receive a complete diagnostic analysis regardless of need. This can only be justified in the interest of gathering research data; however, the expense to the student must always be considered, for not all students can accept large quantities of diagnosis. Nevertheless, every effort must be made to arrive at a true picture of the difficulty. Through the use of initial screenings, selective studies, and in-depth case studies, diagnosticians have choices available and can avoid overextension of diagnosis.

Abbreviated Diagnosis. A hurried diagnosis often does not investigate a given reading difficulty properly. Insufficient diagnosis is most common in the classroom, where lack of time and materials exert constant pressure on the teacher's efforts. Regardless of the limitations of the classroom situation, the teacher must use all available data to insure that the information obtained is reliable and valid. Abbreviated diagnosis commonly leads to wrong conclusions and, in effect, to waste of time that would have been saved through a more thorough diagnosis. If diagnosticians include the diagnostic teaching lesson as part of their diagnosis, the chance of an abbreviated diagnosis is lessened because unknown factors usually come to light in a diagnostic lesson.

Overstepping Professional Boundaries. Educators sometimes make statements that are beyond their professional boundaries. The diagnostician must refrain from playing psychiatrist or medical doctor and, instead, refer willingly when necessary. As with overgeneralizing, couching terms in a diagnostic report that goes beyond the field of education will help avoid overstepping professional boundaries. For example, if a telebinocular examination indicates the need for referral, the clinician may write that "poor performance on test four of the telebinocular indicates the need for a professional visual examination." That type of statement is more appropriate than one stating that the poor score on the telebinocular indicates visual problems that need professional attention.

Unfounded Statements of Fact. Positive, factual statements made by educators based on evidence that does not justify so strong a statement should be avoided. Couching terms to indicate suspicious areas where more testing may be needed or areas where referral is necessary will be beneficial to all those who are attempting to arrive at a student's difficulty area. An examiner must be certain that positive statements concerning a student's observed difficulties are backed by highly reliable data.

Isolation of Factors. Isolated pieces of diagnostic data, test scores, and the like must not be examined without consideration for their relationship to the entire diagnosis. The significance of particular data are often lessened when they are placed in the total picture of a student's reading difficulty. A single group of data or a single test score used in isolation is likely to lead to a distorted picture of the difficulty. Even in the classroom, where time and materials are at a premium, this pitfall should be avoided.

Previous Bias. The examiner must be alert to the possible interference of data that are tainted by bias. Bias is often found in the remarks of parents or teachers and can have a definite effect on the direction the diagnosis may take. To circumvent this effect, the examiner may intentionally avoid evaluating data from the parents and teachers until tentative hypotheses are reached.

Difficult Diagnostic Problems

The So-Called Nonreader. Unfortunately, not all diagnosis falls into neat packages of specific skill deficiencies. Some students appear unable to profit from even the best instruction in any of the skill areas. They cannot learn to read by conventional methods. Abrams estimates this population to be less than 1 percent of the total population of disabled readers.[14] While diagnosis of these students may be the basic responsibility of the reading specialist, the entire resources of the school should be consulted.

Commonly referred to as *dyslexic, neurologically deficient, minimally brain damaged, learning disabled,* or as having a *specific reading disability,* nonreaders have disabilities complicated by multiple factors. They are almost always emotionally involved in their gross failure. They are likely to be physically deficient and may appear slow. Trying to please the teacher often no longer interests them. Diagnosis has failed to identify a consistent behavior pattern. Educators have attempted to teach them by all known methods; each of these methods has failed.

Effective diagnosis calls for an interdisciplinary approach to these students. Every effort should be made to seek out the sources of difficulties. It is often necessary for these students to be diagnosed in clinics that have been established to work efficiently with them. Diagnosis and initial remediation will be accomplished most effectively in these clinic-type situations. Some school districts are establishing special schools for such students. Carefully trained teachers work in coordination with personnel from other disciplines to establish meaningful educational programs for these very troubled learners.

In some cases, despite all efforts, these students continue to fail. Multidisciplinary efforts are continuously explored in hopes of establishing new areas of diagnosis and remediation for them. Screening committees assure that the most appropriate resource personnel work to diagnose and remediate these students. Early identification programs followed by early intervention hold some promise. Multisensory techniques are often employed effectively. However, the search continues for diagnostic and instructional techniques that will make school life more pleasant and successful for these students.

While educators working in these areas may be well qualified and well intentioned, some caution is advised. First, labeling students as dyslexic is little help and can cause serious damage to a learner's self-concept. Rather, clinicians should present information about the students' strengths and needs as specifically as possible and avoid the use of general terms which have no diagnostic use. Second, the formation of special schools and special classes is a procedure that might cause more harm than good to the student. Chapter 10 presents some of these difficulties. Finally, the attempt of some educational groups to specialize in one or more of these labeled groups of students can run the risk of creating a feeling among other educators that these students are not their concern. The notion that someone else should deal with difficult students is faulty and should be challenged.

The Culturally Different. Another group that appears to be experiencing severe difficulty in traditional programs consists of students with cultural backgrounds that differ from the general population. Their language and their experiences are not likely to correspond to the instructional materials that they are expected to use. Mismatching students from low-income homes with books designed for middle- and upper-class children has been common.

Diagnostic instruments that use stories based on middle-class concepts (Dick and Jane going on a vacation in the suburbs) put poor students at a disadvantage in the testing situation. Interpretation of low reading and intelligence scores must be in terms of the students' different cultural backgrounds.

Aside from considerations such as these, culturally different students should be diagnosed using the questions suggested in this chapter. Strengths should be noted and used. Deficiencies should be worked with through the students' demonstrated strengths. Focusing on strengths is extremely important for establishing good diagnostic and remedial relationships with these students.

In all likelihood these students will be urged to try harder and make more effort while being compared with successful students from the cultural majority. McDermott, discussing the high rate of failure among some groups, states, "Almost invariably, such problems arise when a group in power educates the children of a minority group."[15] He attributes the problem to lack of communication and failure to understand what motivates those who are different from ourselves.

McDermott's position is confirmed by Williams and Associates who developed the BITCH test (Black Intelligence Test of Cultural Homogeneity).[16] They found that inter-city black students could perform well on this test but suburban whites found passing it impossible. The test is used to help develop an awareness of the cultural bias that exists in many of the commonly-used tests.

If some students come to school and hear a strange language and experience strange customs, it is likely that they will not enter into a situation conducive to communication. The error clinicians and teachers can make is to assume that their silence indicates lack of ability. Once that error is made, the entire diagnostic effort becomes invalid.

Due to the immigration of large numbers of Asians, Hispanics, and Africans into American society, many students attending school do not use English as their first language; indeed, many do not use English at all. These students and their teachers are usually assisted by English-as-a-Second-Language (ESL) trained educators. However, the day-to-day education of these students is the responsibility of the entire school staff. Efforts must be made to help them learn English while at the same time respecting their first languages and the cultural customs that go with them. The work of Hancock, DeLorenzo and Ben-Barka should be helpful for educators working with these children.[17]

SUMMARY

Clinical diagnosis is normally conducted on individual students. It relies heavily on observations of student behavior and the results of testing. Clinical diagnosis has obvious advantages and several severe limitations.

Understanding the purposes and procedures involved in an initial screening is crucial to clinical diagnosis. Initial screenings involve interviews, questionnaires, testing, and diagnostic lessons. Initial screenings are followed by instruction with continuous evaluation or extended diagnosis. Extended diagnosis relies heavily on testing.

The reading specialist must avoid the seven pitfalls that can lead to erroneous diagnostic conclusions and invalid diagnosis. The reading specialist must also be aware of the difficulties in diagnosing nonreaders and readers from different cultural backgrounds.

If clinical diagnosis is seen as a part of an ongoing diagnostic and instructional program and not as an end in itself, then successful learning can be provided for many readers who do not now experience it.

NOTES

1. John Pikulski, "A Critical Review: Informal Reading Inventories," *The Reading Teacher* 28 (November 1974): 143.
2. "Gilmore Oral Reading Test," *Manual of Directions* (New York: Harcourt Brace Jovanovich, 1952), 8–9.
3. For opportunities to practice oral reading coding, see James Geyer and Jane Matanzo, *Programmed Reading Diagnosis for Teachers: with Prescriptive References* (Columbus, OH: Charles E. Merrill Publishing Co., 1977).
4. Yetta M. Goodman and Carolyn L. Burke, *Reading Miscue Inventory—Manual* (New York: Macmillan Publishing Co., 1971).
5. Kenneth S. Goodman, "Analysis of Oral Reading Miscues: Applied Psycholinguistics," *Reading Research Quarterly* 5 (Fall 1969): 9–30.
6. Ibid.
7. Yetta M. Goodman and Carolyn L. Burke, *Reading Miscue Inventory—Manual* (New York: Macmillan Publishing Co., 1971).
8. William R. Powell, "Measuring Reading Performance Informally," (Paper presented at International Reading Association, Houston, Texas, 1978), 2.
9. Phyllis L. Newcomer and Donald D. Hammill, "ITPA and Academic Achievement: A Survey," *The Reading Teacher* 28, no. 8 (May 1975): 731–41.
10. Donald D. Durrell, *Manual of Directions: Durrell Analysis of Reading Difficulty* (New York: The Psychological Corporation, 1980).
11. The Woodcock Johnson Psycho-Educational Battery is another useful instrument.
12. Sue F. Rogers, Shirley B. Merlin, Mary M. Brittain, Robert A. Palmatier, and Patricia Terrell, "A Research View of Clinic Practicums in Reading Education," *Reading World* (December 1983): 134–46.

13. Ruth Strang, *Diagnostic Teaching of Reading* (New York: McGraw-Hill Book Co., 1969), 8.
14. Jules Abrams, "Minimal Brain Dysfunction and Dyslexia," *Reading World* 14, no. 3 (March 1975): 219.
15. Ray P. McDermott, "The Ethnography of Speaking and Reading" in *Linguistic Theory,* ed. Roger Shuy (Newark, Del.: IRA, 1977), 176.
16. Robert L. Williams, "Misuse of Tests: Self Concept," in *Report of the Tenth National Conference on Civil and Human Rights in Education* (Washington D.C.: NEA, 1972), 17–19.
17. Charles R. Hancock, William E. DeLorenzo, and Alba Ben-Barka, *Teaching Pre- and Semi-Literate Loation and Cambodian Adolescents to Read* (Baltimore: Maryland Dept. of Education, 1983).

SUGGESTED READINGS

Abrams, Jules. "Minimal Brain Dysfunction and Dyslexia." *Reading World* 14, no. 3 (1975): 219–27. A useful discussion, this article places these problems in perspective for teachers.

Buros, Oscar K. *Reading Tests and 1983 Reviews, 1 & 2.* Highland Park, N.J.: Gryphon, 1975, 1968. This publication is a listing of all available reading tests available as of 1983. Most tests receive critical reviews. An essential book for those selecting testing instruments in reading.

Dechant, Emerald. *Diagnosis and Remediation of Reading Disabilities,* Englewood Cliffs, N.J.: Prentice-Hall, Inc, 1981. Chapter 4 discusses types and severity of reading problems and deals with the characteristics of students with specific types of reading difficulties.

Farr, Roger. *Reading: What Can Be Measured?* Newark, Del.: International Reading Association, 1967. Chapters 2 and 3 discuss the use and misuse of available testing instruments in reading. Readers are encouraged to study Farr's discussion.

Geyer, James R., and Matanzo, Jane. *Programmed Reading Diagnosis for Teachers: with Prescriptive References.* Columbus, OH: Charles E. Merrill Publishing Co., 1977. The opportunity for specific practice in various parts of diagnosis and prescription is provided in this book. Reading specialists would do well to work through all aspects presented by Geyer and Matanzo.

Goodman, Kenneth S. "Analysis of Oral Reading Miscues: Applied Psycholinguistics." *Reading Research Quarterly* 5 (Fall 1969): 9–30.

Harris, Albert J. *How To Increase Reading Ability,* 4th ed. New York: David McKay Co., 1970. Chapters 7 and 8 present rather interesting discussions of the topics discussed under educational diagnosis. Harris's book is considered required reading by all those seriously interested in the diagnosis of reading problems.

McDermott, Ray P. "The Ethnography of Speaking and Reading" in *Linguistic Theory,* ed. by Roger Shuy. Newark, Del.: IRA, 1977, 144–52. Presents an interesting case for the ways in which readers are treated differently. Instances are cited when both communication and motivation are missed, causing certain groups of readers to fail.

Editorial

Darryl Quinn Henry
is a senior engineering writer and monitor for the Bendix Field Engineering Corporation

Summer clinic was only a week away, and we were still screening the few stragglers whose applications were the last to arrive. I had done several before and felt downright cocky about my ability to correctly diagnose reading problems.

My last screening of the day was Gary, a thirteen-year-old boy who was to be retained in the sixth grade for the second time. I carefully studied all of the notes written by his teachers and the parent referral form. They made Gary sound like Attila the Hun with a week-old sinus headache and aspirin yet to be invented. I suspected by reading between the lines that if his teachers had been asked to list his strengths, about the only thing they could have offered would have been that Gary didn't show up very often. His mother wrote that he was unpopular with other kids and rude to adults. Although she tried to be positive in her description of his behavior at home, I suspect he wouldn't have been her first choice for a Dale Carnegie award. According to everything I read, not only did Gary have the personality of a pit viper, but the poor kid couldn't read either.

You can imagine how overjoyed I was at the thought of spending the next hour or so in his company. Just like the referrals said, Gary really turned on the "charm" as soon as he came in. He didn't respond to my half-hearted attempts to establish rapport before beginning the testing. I, not being a masochist, decided that a longer interview was a waste of time, so we plunged directly into the testing. Now I had the situation under control; Gary wasn't recalcitrant, and the testing was quickly finished. According to the preliminary findings, Gary definitely had a reading problem. His silent comprehension was 3^1 in a recall situation and 3^2 in locate. I completed all of the paperwork and thought to myself, "God help the poor sucker who has to work with him for the next six weeks."

Being a terrible conniver, I explained to my partner that Gary and I had a personality conflict at the screening and talked her into spending more time working with him. I certainly didn't bother to recite chapter and verse of his past history to her.

Gary made some progress socially and academically almost daily after an initial week of negative behavior. It was soon obvious that he could read with comprehension far above what the initial screening indicated. Thanks to my partner acting as a buffer, Gary and I worked out a tentative truce by the end of the third week. He turned out to be likeable and enjoyed clinic. By the fifth week my conscience and curiosity got the best of me. I retested Gary with amazing results. He could now recall on a fifth-grade level and locate on sixth.

After the initial unjustified feeling of euphoria that we had accomplished so much in five weeks, we had to look at the results realistically. Try though we might, it just wasn't possible for us to take credit for the jump in his scores. I finally asked Gary why he had performed so poorly at the initial screening. Three years later, I'm still ashamed to tell you his answer. Gary said, "I could tell right away that you didn't like me, so I tried to finish the testing as fast as I could."

6

Insights Into Remediation

CHAPTER OUTLINE

GUIDELINES FOR REMEDIATION
PITFALLS OF REMEDIATION

CHAPTER EMPHASES

- ☐ Effective remediation is based on careful diagnosis.
- ☐ Remedial programs should seek to guarantee and illustrate success to the student.
- ☐ The same techniques are used in classroom and clinical remediation.
- ☐ Several recent research studies have yielded important insights into remediation.
- ☐ Successful remedial programs require careful planning and skilled implementation.
- ☐ Microcomputers can have an effective role in remediation.

Remediation of reading difficulties is not based on mysterious techniques that are impossible for the classroom teacher to understand. Rather, remediation is based on sound instructional principles focused on the strengths and needs of the students that have been determined by careful diagnosis. Since remediation calls for skillful teaching, anyone who works in a remedial program should be a skilled teacher who keeps up-to-date by reading and studying.

As previously discussed, there is seldom one cause of reading difficulties; therefore, there is seldom one approach to their solution. The public has often been led to believe the opposite, thereby causing pressure on educators to teach by certain methods which incorporate a little of all known teaching techniques. Instead, remediation should be in direct response to diagnostic findings, necessitating the use of the most suitable educational techniques as solutions to the diagnostic findings. These findings contain information concerning skill strengths as well as needs.

GUIDELINES FOR REMEDIATION

Teachers will find remediation most effective if they adhere to the three following guidelines.

- ☐ *Remediation must guarantee immediate success.* In the remedial program, initial instruction should culminate in a successful, satisfying experience. In this way, students who have experienced frequent failure in reading begin the remedial program with the attitude that *this* educational experience will be both different and rewarding. Without this attitude, the best remedial efforts are often wasted. Successful learning situations also are assured by directing learning toward those activities that the diagnosis has indicated are the students' strengths and interests. All initial lessons should be directed toward student strengths. As remediation progresses, the time devoted to strengths is likely to decrease. When the students start to ask for instruction in the areas of their weaknesses, changes in instructional strategy can take place. However, throughout the entire program, a large portion of every lesson should be directed to strengths.
- ☐ *Remedial successes must be illustrated to the student.* Successes must be presented so that the readers' awareness of them is assured. As students progress, charts, graphs, word files, and specific teacher comments can be used to illustrate successes.

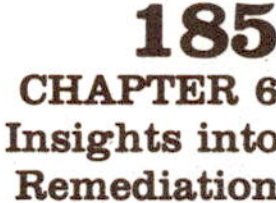

Students need individualized instruction.

- ☐ *Remediation must provide for transfer to actual reading situations.* On some occasions in a remedial program isolated drill in various areas will be required; however, drill activities should always come from contextual reading material and should always conclude in contextual reading situations. The mastery of all skills takes place best in actual reading situations.

Types of Remediation

Unlike diagnosis, classroom and clinical remediation involves the same teaching strategies. The students need individualized instruction. Instruction is based on sound learning theory, and is constantly adjusted to students' responses. While remediation in a clinical setting may be easier because of small group size, the strategies used do not differ. No materials, techniques, or learning theories are reserved for the clinical setting. In fact, the opposite may be true. Many teachers are able and willing to apply skills learned in a clinical setting to their classrooms. Many reading specialists find it useful to conduct remedial efforts without taking the readers from their classrooms. Thus, teachers can easily pick up teaching strategies used by the reading specialist, and reading specialists can often learn from the classroom teacher's teaching strategies.

Implications from Research

The findings of the following six research reports are cause for alarm in considering the plight of students with reading difficulties. Teachers should channel that alarm into constructive use by considering the implications of these studies as they plan remedial lessons.

1. Allington found that poor readers read very little during remedial reading classes.[1] The mean number of words read during a given session was forty three. He recommends less skill instruction and much more reading time.
2. Clay observed first graders and found that good readers read 20,000 words during the year and poor readers read 5,000 words.[2] These findings support Allington's, in that poor readers do not get much reading practice. Clay also noted that good readers would correct one error in three, whereas poor readers would correct only one error in twenty. If poor readers made nine errors in a twenty-seven word passage without correction, it would appear that they were not reading for meaning and practicing poor reading habits.
3. Allington also found that good readers and poor readers are treated differently during instruction.[3] When good readers made oral reading errors, they were interrupted by the teacher 24 percent of the time. Poor readers were interrupted 68 percent of the time. With good readers the interruptions were made at the end of a meaningful unit; poor readers were interrupted at the point of the error. Two implications can be gleaned from these data: good readers get to read more because they are interrupted less; and poor readers, interrupted at the point of the error, have difficulty understanding what they read and are not given the opportunity to self-correct.
4. Durkin conducted observational research and found almost no comprehension instruction in grades 3 and 6.[4] Comprehension was assessed, but not taught. She also found almost no instruction in the area of study skills. Content knowledge was assessed, but the skills to acquire that knowledge were not being taught. If readers can comprehend what they read, they do well in assessment; and if they cannot comprehend they will do poorly in the assessment sessions.
5. Gambrell, Wilson, and Gantt found that good and poor readers were treated differently in an observational

study of fourth graders.[5] Good readers were all reading in material that was very easy (their error rate was one in 100 running words). Poor readers were placed in material that was very difficult (one error in nine running words). Good readers were observed reading 57 percent of the time; poor readers were reading only 33 percent of the time. Poor readers spent twice as much time in phonics skill activities as good readers. Finally, good readers were observed to be on task 92 percent of the time but poor readers only 81 percent of the time. These findings may be explained as follows: poor readers are placed in difficult material and sound inaccurate. The teacher therefore increases the skill work, thereby decreasing reading time. Skill work tends to be meaningless, so the poor readers go off task.

6. An NIE study involving both reading and mathematics found that time spent on successful learning activities resulted in increased achievement.[6] Time spent on difficult activities that resulted in failure decreased achievement.

As these six studies illustrate, readers with difficulties are experiencing different treatment during instruction which probably contributes to their reading problems. A series of instructional adjustments should be implemented to change the frustrating learning environment to one of success.

Assure Positive Attitude. Remedial activities, while based on diagnosis, should concentrate on the interests of students. The sense of self-worth must be developed early. Helping readers realize success with materials that are of interest has tremendous impact. The "I-can't-do-it" attitude quickly turns around to "I can do it." Handicapped readers should not be *talked into* feeling good about themselves; their success experiences should be *realized.* Students should also feel that those success experiences are important. Further, teachers should use materials that highly interest students, such as newspapers, auto magazines, model construction, and cookbooks. One student, reportedly not able to read above the third-grade level, could read football articles in the *Washington Post* with a high comprehension level. The following suggestions can be used as starter ideas.

1. When a student performs successfully, let him or her teach the activity to another student.
2. Provide rewards for successful performance.

Remedial activities should concentrate on the students' interests.

3. Build small group rapport: "We can read—we are worthwhile."
4. Provide teaming situations for successful learning. Let pairs of readers work toward an objective.
5. Make certain the students understand the objectives and know when they have reached them.
6. Keep parents and other teachers informed about successes so that they may reinforce them.

Plan for a Balanced Program. Two types of balance make remedial programs effective. First, a balance must be struck between reading narrative material and reading content material. As students see reading skills transferred to content material, they realize that they can be successful in science and social studies activities and that they can achieve overall success in school.

Second, an even balance should be kept between skills and reading. Each skill lesson must result in a successful reading activity. Three steps are appropriate in maintaining this balance.

1. Teachers give the skills lesson.
2. Students practice the skills on an individual lesson.
3. Students do free reading applying the skills.

The research previously cited would seem to indicate that reading time to apply skills should be a major portion of each remedial lesson.

Without these types of balance, remedial instruction can become segmented and distort the purposes for learning to read well. Success in phonics lessons is useless unless those learned skills can be applied in free reading. Teachers need to plan for balance in order to assure a complete remedial program.

Encourage Risk Taking. Years of unsuccessful attempts in reading activities tend to discourage students from trying. They risk being corrected, ridiculed, embarrassed, and defeated. If they decide not to try, there is no risk of failure. Remedial lessons must encourage risk taking by:

- ☐ Assuring that students are not penalized for inaccurate responses.
- ☐ Placing students in material that they can handle with ease.
- ☐ Encouraging students to work together toward an answer to a problem.
- ☐ Creating a discussion atmosphere during comprehension lessons rather than a teacher-questioning session where only the teacher holds the correct answer (see chapter 11).
- ☐ Setting attainable goals for each student; when the goals are reached, the student should be recognized for those successes.

Plan for Student Decision Making. Teachers can encourage students to be enthusiastic toward a lesson by involving them in setting objectives, selecting activities, and participating in evaluation. Many handicapped readers sit through activities designed to improve their reading skills but have no idea what the lesson is designed to teach them.

During orientation activities to a lesson, students should be free to add objectives and question others. Of course, students cannot make all decisions, but they can have input. Generally students are inclined to put forth more effort once they understand why they are doing an activity.

Allowing students to contract to complete a certain number of activities in a certain amount of time has great impact. The teacher provides a list of possible activities that will satisfy skill drill, skill practice, and free reading requirements. From this list, the students and teacher pick those that are of most interest and appear to be most possible for them. Negotiation is important in contracting. Both the students and the teacher should have input. At times certain activities are required; at other times, two activities are selected from a list of five. At other times, students may have completely free choice. A form such as figure 6–1 is useful in deciding which activities are chosen.

The student is instructed to self-evaluate by placing a smile or frown in the box beside the activity completed. When all activities are completed, no further work is assigned. The payoff for completing assignments must not be more assignments.

The teacher and students then discuss the quality of the completed activities and plan for the next day's lessons. Activities evaluated positively should be discussed in terms of what made the students feel good about them. Those evaluated negatively should also be discussed. Students should not be made to feel badly about an honest evaluation. Their reactions can be used as clues in future planning. Experience with such contracts shows that many students become increasingly positive about

Name________________ Date________________
Pick one activity from box 1, 2, 3.
Pick one activity from box 4, 5, 6.
Pick one activity from box 7, 8, 9.
Activity 10 is required.

1. Play initial consonant game. ☐	2. Teach consonants to your partner. ☐
3. Complete skills sheet on consonants. ☐	4. Find words beginning with *s*, *t*, *c*, *b* on page 34. ☐
5. Read story about Pat the Rat. ☐	6. Read aloud with teacher. ☐
7. Read story from book on library shelf. ☐	8. Make display advertising book you are reading. ☐
9. Read aloud with your partner from book of your choice. ☐	10. Participate in ten-minute sustained silent reading. ☐

FIGURE 6–1
A sample contract.

reading; they often ask for more activities, a good sign that reading is becoming interesting and worthwhile to them.

The students then feel very involved with their lessons. They become trusting and enthusiastic. The teacher, always in control, then knows what does and does not interest the students; therefore, better planning results.

Conduct Task Analysis. When students have difficulty with an activity, task analysis can be used as a diagnostic teaching tool. Task analysis allows the teacher to uncover which subskills may be missing in order for the student to complete the given task. Since all students master skills in very personal ways, pat formulas for why a given student cannot respond are of little use. The University of Maryland's reading clinic identifies the following five steps in task analysis[7] by applying the ideas of Ladd.[8]

Step 1 A problem is identified.
Example: A student cannot respond satisfactorily to questioning about the material read, even when reading silently.

Step 2 The teacher determines the strengths and weaknesses the student has in this skill area.
Example: Can read orally with satisfactory accuracy at the fourth-grade level.
Cannot answer literal questions asked from this material.
Can answer literal questions when working at the third-grade level.

Step 3 The teacher forms hypotheses concerning the possible reasons for this difficulty.
Example: The student is not interested in the material.
The passage is too long.
The questions are threatening.
The student does not have purpose for reading.

Step 4 Through diagnostic teaching, the teacher tests each hypothesis.
Example: For the first hypothesis, the teacher may attempt to determine the student's interest areas and find material at the fourth-grade level in these areas. For the second hypothesis, the teacher may break the passage into smaller parts, asking the questions following each part.

Step 5 The teacher keeps a record of each diagnostic lesson and forms a tentative conclusion to be tested in further instruction.

Example: This student responded well when material was in the area of sports and motorcycles. He also responded better when he jotted down his purposes for reading before he started. Passage-length adjustment did not change his ability to comprehend, and the questions did not seem threatening in this new situation.

Of course task analysis is a strategy that has been used by good teachers for a long time. However, it can be helpful to formalize the process in this manner so that all can profit from its power as a diagnostic tool.

Task analysis for reading diagnosis proves especially valuable because people do not all learn through the same set of subskills. What stops one person from comprehending a given passage differs from what stops another. And what one person needs as a subskill to read better may well be a subskill that another person does not need. Task analysis provides a highly suitable, flexible strategy for getting at the unique learning styles of each reader.

Computer-Assisted Learning. With the increasing use of microcomputers as instructional aids, publishing companies are producing software for all instructional areas, including reading. The educational objectives and the quality of that software vary greatly. Since obtaining software for review purposes can be difficult, other techniques for its selection are necessary, including the following.

1. Obtain reviews from a local resource network (clearinghouse). These networks are usually established by colleges, universities, and state education departments. Users of software are encouraged to evaluate it and report that evaluation for distribution to network users. Any educators who plan to use microcomputers for reading instruction should be encouraged to contact their local resource network.
2. Obtain reviews from a national resource network. Software evaluations are available from the Northwest Regional Educational Laboratories.[9]
3. Take courses that provide hands-on review of available software. Most colleges and many school districts offer such courses.
4. Attend conferences where publishing companies display their latest software. While evaluating software thoroughly at a conference may be difficult, one can quickly spot those that are developed with the most care.

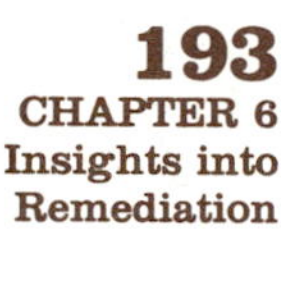

Microcomputers can be helpful tools in comprehension development.

5. Subscribe to computer journals. These journals usually contain reviews of recently developed software and include addresses, costs, and the level for which it is intended.

Some teachers take course work to learn computer language so that they can develop their own software. This can be a long and difficult process. Most educators will rely on published software until computer languages are made easier to use.

Students usually find learning on a microcomputer highly appealing. Sometimes it is difficult to get readers to share the use of the microcomputer with others. They want to spend a great deal of time using it and are almost always on task while using it. Using a word processor for student writing proves very successful. Since writing is revised easily, the students are willing to proofread and revise—an activity they usually resist in pencil-and-paper writing.

However, microprocessor programs should do more than provide an enjoyable time for the students. These programs should meet important educational objectives. Some programs consist of nothing more than workbook pages adapted for the computer. Bradley reviewed others that contained long passages to be read on the screen.[10] Others contained loops, were personalized, and reinforced important reading skills.

All teachers should have some degree of computer literacy to keep up with current educational trends. Some colleges and universities already require graduating education majors to complete at least one computer course. In the future, teachers without computer skills will certainly be at a disadvantage, and indeed, may even be unemployable.

Involve Others. Teachers must use all possible resources when their students are having difficulty learning to read. The student's problem may best be solved by involving a physical education teacher, speech therapist, parent, psychologist, or family doctor. Even if others do not have suggestions for helping such students, communication channels should be open so that all involved stay informed. Many good instructional programs have become ineffective when members unintentionally work against one another.

Peers can team together with a reader on activities that the reader cannot do alone. They can also help conduct some time-consuming, drill-type activities, so teachers are freed to perform more productive tasks; in this way the peers can also profit from the student's strengths. For example, a certain boy was always the poorest in every activity. He always saw himself as a follower, never as a leader. As a field trip approached, he was taken on a "dry run" to familiarize him with the features of the field trip. He became excited and served as a group leader on the actual field trip. The other children appreciated his leadership and assistance. By getting everyone involved, the teacher can change a student's life from one of failure and frustration to one of success and excitement.

By considering these ideas before starting a remedial program, teachers can make adjustments that provide for a greater chance of success.

The Older Handicapped Reader. Secondary school students who encounter serious problems while learning to read require special consideration in planning a remedial program. Materials for instruction and instructional techniques should be selected in terms of appeal to the secondary student. Driver's manuals, job information, consumer education materials, and newspaper articles are examples of appealing materials.

Secondary students who have many unsuccessful experiences tend to be very poor risk takers. They believe that if they do not try, they cannot fail again; of course they fail to realize that they won't learn either. Teachers must plan lessons so that risk taking is encouraged, not punished.

Contracting with these students can also prove effective. The contracts differ from those used with younger students, in that the secondary students are more involved with the decisions made in each part of the contract (i.e., planning, selecting activities, and evaluating). Secondary students with severe reading difficulties can also be excellent tutors for younger students. They take great pride in such roles and obtain excellent results; they probably learn more than the student being tutored. Teachers should also organize instructional activities around problems that the students have identified as important to them. Secondary students can "get turned on to" reading when the learning activities have immediate application in their lives.

Teachers should avoid teaching with the same instructional techniques that have in the past resulted in failure for the student. Specifically they should:

- ☐ Avoid teaching isolated phonics, but instead teach students to read for meaning.
- ☐ Encourage students to read for retention of ideas, not isolated details.
- ☐ Relate reading skills to those academic areas holding the most interest for students.
- ☐ Help students recognize that reading is the key to success in school.

While all of these suggestions have application to students of all ages, they have particular application to secondary students with severe reading problems because almost all of these students have been "turned off" to reading somewhere in their school experience. The teacher must therefore work on improving the students' attitude and self-concept by providing successful reading experiences.

PITFALLS OF REMEDIATION

The classroom teacher and the reading specialist should consider the following pitfalls that, when not avoided, disrupt the efficiency of many remedial programs.

Fragmented Programs

Remedial programs that focus on the development of skills without providing opportunities for practice and use of the skills generally fail. Students in such programs often develop faulty concepts about the purposes for reading. Similarly, programs that do not provide balance between materials at the independent and instructional levels of the students are limited in their effectiveness. Many packaged remedial programs are seriously fragmented and should only be used if supplements for balance can be provided.

Compulsion to Teach

Many well-designed programs are ineffective due to the teacher's compulsion to teach. Involving students in planning, materials selection, purpose setting, and follow-up activities really works. By using contracting, the D-R-T-A, survival reading, and other strategies that involve students, remedial programs stand excellent chance for success.

Teaching to Needs

Constant attention to needs or weaknesses tends to overwhelm students. Every remedial program should be designed to focus on student strengths a large portion of the time.

Oral Reading

Many programs stress oral reading (and often oral reading at sight). Although students should develop fluency in oral reading, and oral reading gives teachers useful diagnostic information, no justification can be found for using it as the major emphasis of the program. Oral reading stresses word pronunciation, an important part of the reading process, but not the ultimate objective. In this chapter, silent reading comprehension has been stressed. Teachers should be certain that silent reading is a part of every lesson.

Oral reading at sight has no place in a remedial program. Students should always be permitted to prepare for oral reading by practicing silently or practicing orally by themselves. With such preparation, students will be able to produce their best, most fluent oral reading. (Of course, oral reading at sight should be used for on-the-spot diagnosis during remedial programs.)

Illustrating Progress

While often delighted with the progress of their students, many teachers fail to relate this to them. Through contracting, students can understand their progress when each contract is evaluated. Personal progress charts in sight vocabulary development, books read, and skills mastered are effective. Without recognition of success, the students often become discouraged and quit trying.

Sharing Information

When more than one educator is working with a student, a communication system should be developed. Each person should know what the other is doing. Without communication, the student is likely to be exposed to conflicting strategies that serve to confuse rather than help. This becomes very complicated when the student is being tutored outside of the school. In such cases, regular communication from one educator to another is necessary.

SUMMARY

Effective remedial programs focus on the student's self-concept. Strengths must be practiced, recognized, and approved. Students must be decision makers in their instructional activities along with the teacher. All school resources must be used to assist readers in realizing that they can and do read.

NOTES

1. Richard Allington, "If They Don't Read Much, How They Ever Gonna Get Good?" *Journal of Reading* 21, no. 1 (October 1977): 57–61.
2. Marie Clay, *Reading: The Patterning of Complex Behavior* (London: Heinemann Educational Books, 1972), 102.
3. Richard Allington, "Are Good Readers and Poor Readers Taught Differently?" American Research Association, Toronto, March 1978.
4. Dolores Durkin, "What Classroom Observations Reveal About Reading Comprehension Instruction," *Reading Research Quarterly* 14, no. 4 (1978–79): 481–533.
5. Linda B. Gambrell, Robert M. Wilson, and Walter N. Gantt, "Classroom Observations of Task-Attending Behaviors of Good and Poor Readers," *Journal of Educational Research,* vol. 74, no. 6 (August 1981): 400–405.
6. Carolyn Denham and Ann Lieberman, eds. *Time to Learn,* (Washington D.C. National Institute of Education, 1980).
7. Robert M. Wilson, "Comprehension Diagnosis Via Task Analysis," *Reading World* 14, no. 3 (March 1975): 178–79.
8. Eleanor Ladd, "Task Analysis," *Reading: What Is It All About?* (Clemson, S.C.: Clemson University, 1975), 68–77.
9. Northwest Regional Educational Laboratories, 300 South West 6 Ave., Portland, Oregon 97204.
10. Virginia N. Bradley, "Reading Comprehension Instruction in Microcomputer Reading Programs," unpublished dissertation, Univ. of Maryland, 1983.

SUGGESTED READINGS

Carbo, Marie. "Research in Reading and Learning Styles," *Exceptional Children,* vol. 49, no. 6 (1983): 486–94. Presents a review of the literature on the need for designing instruction to the learner's style strengths.

Durkin, Dolores. "What Classroom Observations Reveal About Reading Comprehension." *Reading Research Quarterly* Vol. 14, No. 4, 1978–1979; 481–533. A detailed description is presented of the observed behavior of teachers during reading and social studies lessons. This article should be studied by all who are planning remedial lessons.

Gambrell, Linda B., and Wilson, Robert M. *Focusing on the Strengths of Children.* Belmont, Calif.: Fearon Publishers, 1973. Detailed accounts of techniques for focusing on strengths of all students are provided. Ideas for making school enjoyable are included throughout.

Heller, Rachelle S. and Martin, C. Dianne. *Bits 'N Bytes About Computing: A Computer Literacy Primer.* Rockville, Md.: Computer Science Press, 1982. This is a beginning book about computers, what they can do for us, and how they can affect our lives. These authors also produce the "Bits 'n Bytes Gazette," a periodical newsletter for children.

Prentice, Lloyd R.; Beckelman, Laurie; and Caputo, Phyllis. *Computer Confidence,* Instructo/McGraw-Hill, 1983. A resource book for teachers. Includes ideas about the use of computers for instruction, references to clearinghouses, and reference lists of books and periodicals about computers and software.

Smith, Frank. *Understanding Reading,* 2d ed. New York: Holt, Rinehart, and Winston, 1978, chapter 2. The problems of risk taking are discussed in this and other chapters. This book is important reading for those who are going to work with students who have experienced large amounts of failure.

Wilson, Robert M., and Gambrell, Linda B. *Contract Teaching.* Paoli, Pa.: Instructo/McGraw-Hill, 1980. Numerous examples of contract teaching with detailed explanations are included. Record-keeping strategies and reinforcement techniques make this a useful source.

Editorial

Marcia M. Wilson
is the principal at Broad Acres Elementary School in Montgomery County, Maryland.

As a classroom teacher, realizing the need to provide for alternatives and student involvement was easy; but identifying an organizational plan that could account for the varying strengths and needs of thirty heterogeneously grouped third graders seemed overwhelming. However, as the time progressed, I was continually unable to deny the frustration I witnessed as many handicapped readers tried and failed with reading, writing, and spelling activities that were too difficult for them. The need for individual students to become aware of and involved in the setting of attainable goals convinced me to try contract teaching.

There are many observations I can reflect upon that have convinced me that contract teaching is a viable and desirable way for teachers to provide for decision making, student involvement, and individually paced instruction, but there is one instance that was so delightful that I'm sure I'll remember it vividly for a long time to come.

I had a class of thirty third graders who were mastering the concept of contract spelling. My class included students from below pre-primer level to sixth-grade level. The spelling book issued to me contained twelve words—a number that had proved very easy for some children and totally unreachable to others.

We had passed the stage where children had learned to select, with teacher involvement, those words that they felt they could successfully learn by Friday. We had also talked about various study methods that could help us learn to spell new words, and we were currently experimenting with a limited variety in order to identify those specific techniques that were most beneficial to each individual student.

On Friday, the class was taking the posttest, with each student writing only those words that he or she had contracted to learn. While I was reading the list, I realized that some students, while waiting for me to read a word they had contracted for, had free moments when they could sit back and wait, or look around.

Being familiar with the efforts to copy that can occur if students are frustrated, I immediately asked the students to cover their papers and remember to keep their eyes on their own work area. No sooner had the thoughtless remark left my mouth when one student looked up at me and said, "*Why* would anyone cheat in this room?"

That question caused me to think about and isolate the following changes that were occurring in my room: (1) Being involved in the attainment of a task that was attainable was removing the syndrome of failure and reducing the negative effects of unrealistic competition. (2) The development of an atmosphere where success was possible for all had created an atmosphere where students were encouraging and supportive of one another. (3) Continued experience with success was encouraging students to become risk takers. (4) Involvement of students had developed an awareness of the need for learning as well as a commitment toward learning.

Not only did contracting offer me, as the teacher, a manageable system for offering differentiated learning opportunities, but it proved to be a technique that resulted in a learning climate that was positive and assured success. Had I taken the time to put words to the changes I was witnessing, I might have had a better answer for the boy who asked me, "Why would anyone cheat in this room?"

Cloudy
4
5
6
7
8
9

Readiness Activities

CHAPTER OUTLINE

LANGUAGE INTERFERENCE
AUDITORY DIFFICULTIES
VISUAL DIFFICULTIES
ORIENTATION

CHAPTER EMPHASES

☐ Language differences reduce the chances that students will take risks.
☐ Instructional programs should start where the developing student can respond with success.
☐ Auditory and visual discrimination skills are best taught with written passages.
☐ When students seem to be disoriented, teachers should be certain that the difficulty is not in the learning climate.

Note: All instructional materials cited in this chapter are listed in appendix B, giving details.

Some readers need help in the basic readiness areas of reading—language, auditory, visual, and orientation. These readers often appear to be slow, immature, and limited intellectually. With effective instruction, however, these characteristics tend to disappear. In some cases it will be determined that the reader needs time to develop. Most of the time, however, waiting will not help the student develop readiness skills and instruction will be necessary.

Readiness activities for readers experiencing serious difficulties with reading are similar to readiness activities for beginning readers, except that the instructional materials are adjusted to assure student interest.

LANGUAGE INTERFERENCE

When students develop an awareness that their language is different from their peers', they tend to withdraw from oral communication. It's too risky. Everyone has searched for a synonym rather than attempt to use words he or she is unsure how to pronounce. Thus, criticism that usually follows is avoided. Imagine, then, the students who have developed that feeling about every utterance they make. If one doesn't attempt oral communication, one won't be criticized. Risk taking is essential, however, for language development. Teachers must develop a climate in which oral communication is enjoyable and rewarding. By reducing the threat of criticism the teacher increases risk taking and facilitates the use of oral communication. Language difficulties can arise when the student's language does not match the language used in school, is underdeveloped through limited experiential language background, or reflects limited conceptual development.

Dialect Language Mismatching

Students whose dialect differs from that used in school and in the instructional materials are often found in remedial reading classes. Their difficulty lies in attempting to learn to read a language that differs to some degree from the one they speak. How seriously the problem of dialect mismatching affects reading ability is uncertain; however, one may safely assume that it causes a degree of discomfort that, when coupled with other learning difficulties, can interfere with learning to read. Of course, many students with mismatched language do learn to read effectively.

Instruction must start with the teacher's acceptance of their language. Teachers must have a genuine respect for the language that students bring to school. Criticisms of language differences attack not only the students but their families and friends. Specifically, the teacher should demonstrate acceptance by doing the following:

1. Respond to language differences without initial correction.
2. Respond to the students' thoughts with enthusiasm regardless of their language.
3. Don't repeat the students' responses in a correcting effort.

Anyone can work better and faster with a student who feels comfortable and accepted. However, teachers demonstrate considerable concern about dialect usage because they feel that they are responsible for improving language. But the concept of "improving" in itself implies nonacceptance. The teacher must recognize the students' language as being good for them and acceptable for their purposes.[1] The teacher also can help students become aware of language forms other than those more commonly used in school. Most importantly, students must feel accepted so that they can receive further instruction. Specifically, the following instruction techniques are useful.

When Using Prepared Materials, Accept Students' Use of Dialect. If the sentence is "I see two dogs," and a student says, "I see two dog," accept it without correction. By so doing, meaning is stressed and language accepted.

Use Language-Experience Stories that Students Can Dictate to You. (See chapter 8 for specifics on the use of language experience.) In writing student contributions, be certain to spell words accurately (e.g., if a student says, "da dog," write "the dog"). When the student reads the story aloud and says "da dog," it should be accepted. Teachers should not change the syntax. For example, if a student says, "I ain't got none," it should be written as spoken. To change the syntax to "I don't have any" is a correction, denying the principle of acceptance and reducing risk taking.

Allow Numerous Opportunities for Students to Hear and to Respond to Language Commonly Found in Books and Used in Other Segments of our Society. Read to them. Read every day. Read good literature. Talk with them about what you have read. Let them discuss it with you. Always serve as a model. Enunciate precisely and use standard English forms. Teach students to respond to your language. Use tape recorders to provide stories and directions for activities to provide even more modeling opportunities.

Provide Structured Lessons to Develop Students' Abilities to Use the Language They Will Find Elsewhere in Society and Particularly in School. Feigenbaum suggests the following three steps:[2]

1. *Auditory discrimination.* Help the student to hear differences in language form. Take one type of difference (negation, for example) and say, "Tell me whether these two sentences sound exactly alike or different: 1. I ain't got none. 2. I don't have any." As the students develop auditory discrimination skills between their language and school language, move to step two.
2. *Identification of school language.* From the two sentences, help the students pick the one they are more likely to hear the teacher use or to read in books. Auditory awareness of school language is not difficult to develop, but is not to be assumed merely from the ability to discriminate auditorily.
3. *Dialect transfer.* Say one sentence and have the students respond in the other language. Such transfer should be practiced both ways (i.e., from home language to school language and the reverse). For example, the teacher says, "I ain't got none," and the students attempt to put the expression into school language ("I don't have any"). Then the teacher uses school language, and the students respond in their language. When conducting structured lessons, the teacher should start with a structure common to the students' language and stay with that structure until dialect transfer is mastered. All lessons must be conducted without reference to *right* and *wrong* or *good* and *bad.*

   Once dialect transfer is mastered, the teacher should encourage the students to use school language in school but should not encourage them to use it in their informal conversations at play or at home. De Stefano refers to the use of different dialects in different social situations as using registers.[3] Everyone uses different registers at times to adjust to the social situation. The register one picks to use at a football game is quite different from the one selected to use when teaching a class. The use of registers should be discussed with students, using examples. As students with language mismatch problems gain skill in dialect transfer, instruction with materials using school language can be used effectively.

Foreign Language Mismatching

Many students come to school with a native language other than English. Their mismatch with school language is nearly total. Even if they become skilled at getting the printed code into a spoken code, nothing makes sense. Ten percent of school-age children were classified as having non-English language backgrounds in 1978; the most common were Spanish speakers. Four million persons reported Spanish as their first language; of that number over fifty percent reported having trouble speaking or understanding English.[4]

The type of difficulty students have depends on whether they use English as a second language or whether the students are fluent in English but are just more comfortable using their native language. If they use English fluently, they can be taught with regular school materials. However, if they know little English and are nonfluent, a major block is in the way of successful reading. For example, the Puerto Ricans who are recent immigrants and live in Puerto Rican communities in New York may well go to school with little knowledge of English. In such cases, beginning reading instruction should be in Spanish, not English. As these students become fluent in Spanish, transfer can be made from Spanish to English. In this way these students can become successful readers in two languages.

Instructional assistance should be obtained through programs offered by the schools. If no program is offered in a given language, attempts should be made to enlist community volunteers who are fluent in the students' native language.

If teachers try to teach these children in English and fail, the students will not be able to read in either English or their native languages. If they return to their native country after three years of failure in learning to read English, they will have difficulty in reading their native language because that language was not used to teach reading.

If native language materials are not available, these students should be taught in their native language by the language-experience approach.[5] However, this may prove difficult with the wide range of languages spoken by recent immigrants.

Underdeveloped Language

Students who come to school seriously deficient in experiences simply do not have the conceptual framework to read effectively.

Sticht stresses the importance of language development in reading by stating, "Reading ability is built upon a foundation of language abilities both developed and expressed largely by means of oracy skills of auding and speaking."[6] Those students from isolated rural poverty areas and those from severe large city poverty areas may be considered to represent these types of students. In the following discussion, it is assumed that they lack experiences but not mental ability. They may appear to lack mental ability because they fail to understand situations that are comprehended easily by others. They may lack primary experiences with mountains, lakes, automobiles, and airplanes. The teacher may make the following specific educational adjustments.

Emphasize Language Experiences. Everything that happens during the school day can be discussed. Linking language directly to the students' experiences helps them develop concepts for the things they encounter. Trips, pictures, films, and audiotapes can be used to develop language experiences. Activities within the classroom, special programs in the school, and visitors in the classroom also stimulate language. Every experience must be discussed to make language a constant part of the experience. For example, if a class makes a trip to the zoo, the students should talk about what they are experiencing, and the teacher should both encourage the students to talk, and provide explanations of what they are experiencing.

Start with the Language-Experience Approach. Just as it does for students with different dialects, the language-experience approach assures a successful start in reading, since the concepts students encounter are their own.

Use Available Commercial Programs. Several companies have commercial programs designed to aid language development. Most of these programs involve stimulation with pictures, video- or audiotapes, or films. Teachers are directed to help students explain what they are seeing or hearing. Vocabulary and English usage and syntax are developed as they listen to each other and to the teacher. Synonym and antonym activities also stretch students' conceptual framework. (See appendix B for a listing of such programs.)

Facilitate Continuous Language Exposure. Activities that permit students to talk with one another and to listen to the teacher make language improvement possible. Activities may include the following.

1. Role playing in which students are encouraged to act out roles of story characters or persons whom they admire stimulate students to talk with each other.
2. A telephone corner with toy phones can be used to stimulate talking.
3. An older person can come to the room to talk about an exciting experience.
4. Activities that stimulate one-to-one conversations are needed in abundance for those with underdeveloped language backgrounds. Activities which encourage students to talk on a one-to-one basis include a question chair placed close to the teacher's work area (a student with a question comes to the chair, and the teacher discusses the concerns with the student); simple repetition games that call for students to repeat what the teacher has said; and eating lunch and chatting with several students every day.

Activities such as these place value on language as communication and expose students to modeled language. However, since reading is not withheld until large vocabularies are developed, the language enrichment technique must continue for several years.

Conceptual Development

Some language problems arise from slow conceptual development. Students may be six years old but react to language like four year olds. Many of these children have compounding problems, such as poor motor coordination or physical defects. Although many find their way into programs for the mentally retarded, many others are mainstreamed into regular classrooms so teachers must learn how to work with them.

As a first suggestion, every teacher should be urged to view each student as a developing human being. As such, they should accept all students as being as developed as they can be. Instructional programs are planned in accordance with where students are, not where teachers would like them to be. Categorizing them under labels or locking them into slow-moving groups indicates a lack of acceptance and is of little educational value. At the same time, expectations of learning rate, learning quantity, and retention ability should be realistic. Programs must be adjusted for these students in order to make use of their strengths. Teachers should use patience and supply many rewards for successful performances. Successes must be highlighted, and failures must be minimized or ignored.

Having an older student visit the classroom to relate experiences can be highly motivating

Contracting should be considered as a strategy in working with these students. Contracting permits the teacher to adjust the amount and type of learning for each student. Completing the contract is regarded as educational achievement and recognized as a success. For example, students may be contracted to learn *x* number of words each week (*x* is used to indicate that it could be any number and would vary from student to student). Words could come from any context (i.e., teacher talk, books, other students, posters, food labels, etc.). The objectives are to develop vocabulary and success experiences. The teacher considers the rate and type of learning that will allow each student to succeed. Contracts can be renegotiated when students or the teacher believes that the rate or type of learning is no longer appropriate. For best results, a contract should not be longer than a week for these students.

Regardless of the type of language deficiency, the students' education must continue. Starting points must be identified, and progress should be documented. The teacher should keep in mind that all students can learn and that all can profit from reading programs if the programs are adjusted to their strengths.

The classifications for language deficiencies suggested in this chapter are not as clear-cut as they may seem. Many students may be handicapped by two or all three types of language limitations. But these students *can* learn. Educators cannot use the lack of language development as an excuse for not teaching; students cannot use it as an excuse for not learning.

AUDITORY DIFFICULTIES

Some students enter school without the necessary auditory skills to profit from normal instruction. When ignored by the teacher, these auditory skills can remain undeveloped, thus causing considerable discomfort to the struggling reader. For this discussion on remediation, auditory skills will be classified into hearing problems and auditory discrimination problems.

Hearing Problems

While teachers can do nothing to correct hearing problems aside from referring the student to a hearing specialist, they can make temporary classroom adjustments to facilitate a comfortable learning situation by:

1. Arranging the seating so that the students with hearing problems are close to the teacher during group instruction.
2. Standing close to those students' desks during group instruction and increasing their voice volume so that students with hearing problems can hear the instruction. They can also face the students, thereby providing opportunity for lip reading.
3. Creating a "buddy" system. When a student does not hear the teacher or the other students, another student can repeat the information and help that student understand it.
4. When possible, stressing visual learning activities (i.e., reading instead of listening). Instruction for independent work should be written, as should rules, regulations, and announcements. The writing can be on the chalkboard, on chart paper, or in personal notes to students with hearing problems.

Auditory Discrimination

Many students have normal hearing skills but underdeveloped auditory discrimination skills. They experience difficulty distinguishing one sound from another. Their difficulty is likely to be incorrectly identified as speech impairment or trouble with phonics. Because students come to school with most speech skills developed one would believe that their auditory discrimination skills are also developed. However, for teachers with students who have underdeveloped articulation skills or who are not in the habit of listening carefully, the following suggestions can prove valuable:

1. Request the assistance of a speech and hearing therapist who can work with the students, help diagnose their difficulties or offer suggestions for classroom adjustments.
2. Serve as a speech model. Enunciate distinctly and read with articulate speech patterns.
3. Provide exercises that stress gross auditory differences. For example:

   Tell me whether the words that I repeat are the same or different:

   catch—catch
   big—dog
   many—some

   Tell me whether the first sounds you hear in the words that I repeat are the same or different:

   big—belt
   butter—lettuce
   boy—sail

4. Gradually provide exercises involving finer auditory discriminations. For example:

   Tell me whether the words that I repeat are the same or different:

   catch—catch
   corn—scorn
   can—tan

   Tell me whether the first sound you hear in the following words is the same or different:

   big—pig
   bite—tight
   best—best

5. Provide exercises that demand longer auditory memory. For example:

   Listen to the first word that I give you. Then tell me whether the following words are the same or different:

   pig: pig—small—big—pig—dig

   Listen to the first sound in the word I give you. Then tell me which of the following words have the same beginning sound:

   pig: bite—pick—pencil—dig—picnic

6. Provide exercises that call for listening for sound in different parts of the word. For example:

   Listen for words that end in the same sound as the word *pig:*

   dig—ditch—park—twig—dog

7. Provide exercises that indicate the ability to hear rhyming words. For example:

   Listen to the first word I give you and tell me whether the following words rhyme with that word:

   cat: rat—sat—pot—pat

8. Provide a stimulus word and ask the student to say some words that rhyme. For example:

   Listen to the first word I give you and tell me some words that rhyme with it:

   cat:

Techniques for conducting drill lessons such as these can include placing items on tape and having students do the exercises independently; having an aide or a skilled student read what you have prepared; and calling the students who need such work to you while the others are working independently. These students need daily practice to assist them in developing auditory-discrimination skills. As the skills are mastered, a periodic review should be made. It is also necessary to review the skills prior to developing phonics lessons. Auditory-discrimination skills are also easily developed and reinforced through game activities.[7]

Some students will not respond to these activities due to serious problems in auditory orientation. These students need in-depth training through the cooperative efforts of the reading specialist, classroom teacher, and speech teacher. Phonics instruction should be withheld until a thorough program in auditory sequencing has been completed. These students have difficulty distinguishing initial, medial, and final sounds as they hear them. They also have difficulty associating auditory with visual sequences. Understandably these are different skills; auditory sequences occur in time and visual sequences occur in space. Because most students come to school with these skills in hand, some teachers assume that all students have them. Programs such as *Auditory Discrimination in Depth* provide instruction in sound formation, sound sequences, and sound placement.[8] These programs require one-to-one instruction and complete cooperation of all who work with the student.

VISUAL DIFFICULTIES

As with auditory problems, visual problems also can be grouped into two categories: those dealing with the skills and functions of vision and those dealing with visual discrimination. Numerous students find giving visual attention difficult, either as the result of a physical disability or a developmental lag.

Vision Problems

Visual problems can be adjusted and corrected by vision specialists. The teacher, in the meantime, must work with those students daily. Several suggestions for helping students with vision problems include:

1. Arrange seating so that the reader has the best light, the least glare, and the optimum distance for easy viewing. Those who are farsighted can sit in the back of the instructional area and those who are nearsighted can sit in the front.
2. When writing on the board, use larger letter size than usual.
3. Supplement writing on the board or on chart paper by providing auditory reinforcement.
4. Use the "buddy" system. By working with a student who has normal sight, a student with visual difficulties can seek help when visual difficulties interfere with getting needed information.
5. Stress auditory learning. A student with visual problems may respond better to a phonics approach or to sound reinforcement. Tracing also helps, for it develops opportunities for reinforcing weak visual skills.
6. Make visual activity periods short. When students show signs of discomfort (e.g., rubbing of eyes and inattentiveness), they should be released from the visual tasks involved in reading.

Adjustments such as these are not the answer to the basic problem but can make learning comfortable for a student.

Visual Discrimination

Difficulties with visual discrimination skills are usually the result of inexperience or inability to attend to the task. In either case, successful experience can usually develop comfort in visual-discrimination skills. The following suggestions can be valuable in developing them.

Start with the Students' Language. As students talk, write down what they say. For example, if a student wants to talk about what was seen on the way to school, the following story may develop:

> I saw a big dog. His name was Rex. The dog frightened many of us. But I picked up a stick and scared the dog. Everyone thinks I am very brave. Do you?

Once the story is written, two copies are prepared for each student, one to use for visual-discrimination activities and one to save for reading. On the copy that the students can mark, the following activities can be tried:

1. Ask the students to pick words that they know. Write the words on cards and then have them find the words in the story. They do not need to say them, but they do have to match them.
2. Write the letter *s* on a card and ask the students to underline that letter every time they see it in the story.
3. Ask the students to circle all the words that begin with the letter *a* (give them *a* cards).
4. Write a phrase on cards. Have the students find it in the story and draw two lines under it.
5. Ask the students to draw a box around every word that ends with the letter *e*. (Give the students *e* cards.)

From duplicated story copy have the students cut out words and phrases and match them with the story on chart paper. This activity enhances transfer from activities at the seat to activities at the board. Depending on the story, visual-discrimination activities can be formulated to help students develop the required skills. Matching, seeing letters in words, finding letters in specific parts of words, and finding groups of words in a certain order are only a few examples. By asking the students to do something different in each activity (underlining, circling, drawing a box), the teacher can easily see how well each activity has been completed. As with auditory discrimination, the teacher should start with gross discriminations and move to fine discriminations. For example, beginning with the letter *s* is easier than starting with *d*. Finding a word is easier than finding a letter; finding a letter or a group of letters in a certain position in a word is even more difficult. Discover where the students are in the development of visual discrimination abilities and work from there. Teachers should also provide a stimulus with which the students are to work visually. Auditory reinforcements are fine, but the activities must be visual to visual (i.e., the students see a word on a card and match it with a word on the board).

Use Word Cards. Cards on which the students have written words they mastered can be used to develop visual discrimination skills. For example, teachers can ask the students to complete these tasks:

1. Find all the words in their files that end in *e*, like *ate*.

2. Find all the words that end in *ing*, like walk*ing*.
3. Find all the words that have double consonants, like te*ll*.

The suggestions for such activities could be endless, but two points about them are important: (1) teachers are working with visual clues and from words that the students know; and (2) through teaching from strengths, students can develop strong visual-discrimination skills.

Provide a Magazine Area in the Room. Teachers should instruct the readers to look through magazines for ads with certain kinds of words (e.g., words about people, words that describe things, etc.). Provide a pair of scissors or some paste, and a place to post these words when found.

Use Game-Type Activities. Game-type activities hold considerable merit in developing visual discrimination, just as they do in developing auditory discrimination. (Suggestions can be found in Sullivan.[9]) For example, teachers can give students a set of cards with letters on them. Then starting with a small group of letters, such as *s, t,* and *w,* they hold up a letter and have students hold up the same letter. Then they hold up two letters and have students hold up the same two letters in the same sequence. Such an activity can gradually increase in difficulty, thus developing the attention to detail and visual-discrimination skills needed for reading. Once the game idea is developed, students can play without direct teacher supervision.

Use Newspapers to Develop Visual Skills. The newspaper is useful because of its availability, its expendability, and its motivational appeal. Students can work at the following activities.

1. Make a collage of all the various forms of a given letter that they can find in advertisements and headlines.
2. Circle all the occurrences of a given letter in the comic strips after a lesson on that letter.
3. Conduct word hunts for words that are in their word banks. Cut them out and paste them on their word bank cards.
4. Find words in advertisements that have unique features and make a collage out of them—for example, all words with ascending letters or that end in *s*.

These and numerous other ideas can be developed from available newspaper supplies and provide motivation in themselves. The students notice that they are working with the same type of material that they see adults use in their homes.

Use Commercially-Prepared Materials. Workbook-type activities, spirit duplication master sheets, and pencil-paper activities are commonly used commercially-prepared materials. Many such activities start with form identification. For example, five balls are placed on a sheet; four of them are green and one is red. Students are to mark the one that is different. However, such activities should be reserved for only the most severely handicapped and even then seem to be of questionable value in the reading process. (Several of the more popular commercial materials are listed in appendix B.) However, teachers themselves can make materials that are more relevant to the reading process with relatively small commitments of time and energy. Students respond very well to such homemade materials.

When making materials for students to use in visual discrimination activities, several precautions are necessary:

1. Printing should be done very carefully; however, typing is preferred.
2. Printing only should be used on working copies. These copies should contain no art work, photographs, or other distractions.
3. At first, only small amounts of print should be used on a page. Do not smother the reader with too many words and sentences.
4. Make activities short and (if possible) self-correcting. Provide answer keys or models of marked copies.
5. Make the print of beginning activities look like that which the children are accustomed to seeing. For very young children, each new sentence should start a new line. With older students, material can appear in paragraph form. To make the material too much like a preprimer is insulting to older students.
6. Always end the activity by reading the story. If the students cannot read it, read it to them. Always apply the activity to reading for thought by discussing the story and its meanings with the students.
7. When students do well, tell them so. Praise for legitimate successes is important in all drill work, but students should not be praised for incomplete or inaccu-

rate work. Instead, the activity should be restructured so that students can complete it. Then they can be praised.

Visual-discrimination activities should be continued as the students begin to read. Review as well as more advanced activities should be part of the visual-discrimination program until students are operating comfortably.

ORIENTATION

Orientation difficulties are reflected by the inability to visually follow the print in words or sentences. Orientation skills are commonly listed under visual discrimination; however, difficulties in this area seem to be peculiar enough to justify separate classification. Visual-discrimination skills are related to seeing likenesses and differences; orientation skills are concerned with the left-to-right controlled visual movements necessary for effective reading.

Readers' orientation errors cannot be corrected by simply calling the errors to their attention. Remedial procedures for correcting orientation skills are most effective when they help students feel the comfort and success that accompanies correct orientation and when they provide practice to extend the skill into a habit. Three specific questions should be addressed in considering orientation problems:

1. Does the student exhibit visual difficulty in following the print from left to right?
2. Does the student habitually reverse words or letters?
3. Does the student habitually lose his or her place?

The symptoms suggested by these questions are closely related at times because thay all pertain to directional attack on the printed page. As a result, remedial techniques are often quite similar. However, these areas are differentiated here in an effort to make remediation as understandable as possible.

Failure to Move Left-to-Right

Difficulty in moving from left to right on a printed page can normally be traced to a faulty habit and, therefore, is usually alleviated by concentrated practice. Many suggestions for improved left-to-right movement across the page are available in the basal readers' manuals. The following specific suggestions have worked with those who need more practice than is suggested in these manuals.

Provide Opportunities for Writing Experience. Through writing students can clearly see the necessity of the left-to-right word formation across a line. Students should observe the teacher writing on the board, and those who are able to write should be given every opportunity to do so.

Illustrate that Sentences Involve a Left-to-Right Word Progression. An initial approach would be to have the students write sentences containing their sight words, thereby actively involving them in developing effective left-to-right sequence. Students demonstrate understanding of this concept when they are able to create their own sentences from their resource of sight words.

Have Students Point to Words While Reading. The finger can be used as a crutch until the habit of left-to-right eye movements can be developed more fully. Clay discusses the issue of pointing to words under the topic "Is Pointing Good or Bad?"[10] While most teachers have heard about the ill effects of pointing to words while reading, Clay points out that most students have adequate left-to-right behavior. Some, however, reveal gross difficulties when asked to point to the words they are reading. When this type of difficulty is noted, some time can be spent instructing students to point to the words they are reading to fix the concept of left-to-right eye movements.

Use Choral Reading Activities. Reading orally in unison with the teacher or with others allows students to experience left-to-right word movement within a group. There should be one good oral reading model in the group.

Use the Michigan Tracking Program. The *Michigan Tracking Program* (figure 7–1) has been useful in working with students with severe orientation problems. These materials are constructed to teach readers to move from left to right on a printed line, and from the top to the bottom of a page. Students must complete the entire activity in the order it is presented. The materials are constructed so that if they miss one item they cannot finish the activity.

The tracking concept can be adapted to any material. For example, teachers can take any printed unit and provide a sentence with words from the unit that students are to find in order, such as the following:

Look for: *See the dog run.*
Unit of print: I have a dog. You can *see* him on Saturday. He can run into *the* house. My *dog* can *run* very fast.

Mechanical Aids. Mechanical aids are available to help students with orientation skills. Tracking, for example, can be reinforced by the use of the *Controlled Reader.* Students watch a

1. The man walked.
She This The Them
me may mad man
talked waked walked walled

2. Joe ran here.
Jim Joe John Jack
run ray ran ram
there then head here

3. Dad is big.
Day Dad Dab Dog
it at as is
bag buy big bog

4. Boys play ball.
Bugs Bays Buys Boys
plan play park page
bill pull ball balk

5. I saw birds.
A I It As
was say way saw
bids birds burst birch

Fill in:

Boys	ball.		saw birds.
Joe	here.	Dad is	
The man		Min	Sec

6. Girls, go home.
Grills Girls Guys Goods
go got get golf
house horse home come

7. Look at him.
Cook Lake Took Look
it as at is
his her him hem

8. Are you there?
Car Are Far Tar
one your you once
here then were there

9. Who was that?
Why How Who What
saw was way wash
this then that they

10. Call her up.
Came Tell Tall Call
him her has his
up on down in

Fill in:

Who was	?		at him.
Call her	?	Are	there?
Girls,	home.	Min	Sec

FIGURE 7–1
A sample of word tracking from the Michigan Tracking Program by Donald E. P. Smith. (Copyright © 1967 by Donald E. P. Smith. Published by Ann Arbor Publishers. Reprinted by permission.)

story from a film that is paced either a line at a time or by a left-to-right exposure control, and that can be regulated for speed. Mechanical aids can help motivate the students to attempt activities that are otherwise rather dull. However, when one considers the costs of such devices and the excitement that can be created with teacher-made materials, it would appear that the use of controlled reading machines in remedial reading is of a seriously limited value. First, they place readers in reading situations that are unnatural. Reading is not a mechanically-paced activity; rather, it is a stop-and-go activity. Readers stop to use word-attack skills and to reread certain passages; they then go quickly to other sections. The notion all words and phrases deserve the same amount of reading time must be seriously questioned. When mechanical aids are used, they should be followed by practice with normal reading materials without the use of the aid. In such a way, students are assisted in transferring from practice situations to real reading situations.

Tendency to Reverse Letters, Words, and Phrases

The tendency to reverse letters, words, and phrases is one of the common orientation difficulties, particularly with young readers. Different from failure to move left-to-right across a line, reversals involve inappropriate left-to-right progression in words and phrases within a line. The reader not only must consciously attack words from left to right but must develop this into a habit. After awareness is developed, the problem can be solved by specific practice.

Kindergarten and First-Grade Teachers Should Emphasize Directional Progression Both Directly and Subtly. Through writing on the board in front of students and calling their attention to the direction that the letters flow to form a word, the teacher can give the children opportunities to grasp this concept. The students may also write on the chalkboard since they are less inclined to make directional errors when doing board work. Directional progression is a more difficult concept for some students to grasp than the left-to-right movement across a line of print, especially when whole-word techniques have been stressed in initial instruction. The sense of touch involved in writing reinforces the left-to-right progression within words. When individual language-experience stories are being written, the teacher should sit beside each child so that the child can watch the words being formed. If the teacher sits across the table, the child watches the words being formed right-to-left instead of left-to-right. If the teacher types the story, the child should sit at the typewriter to watch the words form.

Phonics Lessons Provide Opportunity for the Reinforcement of Proper Progression through Words. This is particularly true in initial- and final-consonant substitution activities where the position of the letters in words is emphasized. In phonics lessons where stress is placed on the initial sounds in words, teachers can often place words on the board to illustrate the similarities or differences in the initial sounds. This practice, of course, emphasizes the left-to-right concept as it applies to word attack.

Spelling Activities Help Reinforce the Proper Image of the Word. The concept of the position of the letters in each word is of primary importance. Through the spelling of commonly confused words, the teacher is able to reinforce the proper sequence of letters.

Students Can Trace Words that Are Missed so that They Sense Left-to-Right Progression. As the students trace words, they are expected to pronounce them correctly. If they cannot do this, the problem is more likely one of inadequate sight vocabulary. Special instructions for the kinesthetic technique follow.[11]

1. The reader is exposed to the word symbol and its pronunciation. (Since these words are usually taken from the reader's experience stories, teachers can assume that he or she knows their meanings.)
2. The reader is directed to trace the word while saying it. (This tracing procedure is to be repeated until it appears that the reader has mastered the word. The teacher demonstrates as often as necessary when beginning this approach.) Fernald notes that finger contact with the letters is essential, especially in these early stages.[12]
3. The reader then is directed to reproduce the word without the copy, again pronouncing it. This technique is not one in which the reader spells the word or sounds the letters; rather, it is a whole-word technique. The benefits of tracing are not limited to orientation skills; other uses will be noted under sight vocabulary and word attack where a more detailed explanation is presented (see chapter 8).

Teachers will find several variations of the kinesthetic technique in the literature. Some prefer that all tracing be done in sand; some prefer to use a chalkboard; others feel that tracing the word in large copy is entirely adequate. Some suggest that the word be printed, providing the best transfer to actual reading. Others prefer that the word be written in script to reinforce the flow and connection between the letters. Regardless of the system, the left-to-right progression of words is reinforced, and the readers, sensing the total results of their efforts, often learn to pronounce words properly. Teachers will find many opportunities in other reading activities to reinforce left-to-right progressions. Teachers need to help students with meaning cues when reversals are made by asking questions such as, "Did that make sense to you?" or "Did that mean anything to you?" Since the ultimate check of reading accuracy is always making sense from the passage, meaning cues are always appropriate.

Tendency to Omit Words without Distorting Context

Omissions seldom distort the meaning of a passage. Apparently readers keep their minds on the context and make sense out of it while not necessarily reading every word. While such an omission is not in itself worthy of concern, the *habit* of omitting words *is* of concern, for the word omitted may be an important one. For example, on a medicine label, the message "Do not swallow" may be read "Do swallow." Teachers are interested, therefore, in developing awareness in students that all the words on the page should receive attention. The following suggestions should aid in this process.

A Tape Recorder Can be Effectively Used with Students Who Have this Type of Difficulty. Teachers tape an oral-reading selection and then the students listen carefully to the tape while following the story with their eyes. They then mark each word that was omitted. (Students are generally surprised that they make omissions.) Then the students attempt to reread the story without omitting any words. They listen to the new tape while following the story; again they mark omissions. Teachers often find that students are able to make conscious corrections, although this technique may need to be repeated several times to develop satisfactory performance.[13] Self-diagnosis by students helps to emphasize to them their reading strengths and needs. Followed by practice and reevaluation, it tends to correct most omission errors.

The Reading-Impress Technique for Oral Reading is Valuable for Students Who Make Many Omissions.[14] The teacher and the students read in unison. The teacher is the leader and sets the model of fluency and accuracy. The students follow, reading with the teacher and obtaining the feeling for fluent, accurate oral reading. The teacher may want a student to read the passage alone once it has been read with the teacher. If accuracy is not obtained, then the process should be repeated.

Habitual Loss of One's Place

Habitually losing one's place may be related to a visual problem; therefore, students should first be checked for signs of ocular difficulty manifested by other symptoms (see chapter 3). If there is no indication that the difficulty is visual, the student should be given instruction.

When readers lose their places during reading, they may be having difficulty following the line of print or with their return sweep. As readers move from line to line, their eyes sweep back across the page. Many readers find that movement difficult.

To correct either of these difficulties, students can use a line holder of some type. An index card will serve the purpose. Some teachers instruct students to point to the first word in the line. It is more desirable to use line holders than to encourage the student to point to individual words; however at times pointing is necessary. Pointing to words can lead to word-by-word reading and can slow the pace of reading greatly. The use of all line holders should be eliminated as soon as the student is able to read without losing his or her place.

Students who lose their places during reading may also be indicating a lack of interest and may not be paying attention. They need to be involved in setting the objectives for their lessons and in selecting materials for instruction. These are attention-getting strategies and tend to increase reader awareness of the need to stay tuned to the lesson. At other times, the lesson's tempo encourages the students' minds to wander. As the teacher stops to assist a reader having difficulty, other students may mentally slip away. Teacher attention to the lesson tempo should help to alleviate such problems.

The Seriously Disoriented Reader

Some students display serious difficulties in all of the readiness areas. Their orientation to the printed page is so distorted that there is little chance that they will learn to read. Their difficulties are usually complicated by inability to remember sight words, understand the relationship between letters and sounds, and make any sense out of the passage. Several suggestions are offered for working with students who have these types of difficulties:

1. First the learning climate should be reexamined. Are there any distractors that may be keeping the student from giving full attention to the reading activity? If so, adjustments to those distractors should precede any of the following suggestions.

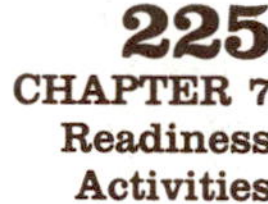

Skill instruction should always end with silent reading time.

2. Physical and psychological assessments should be conducted so that problems in these areas can be understood and adjustments made. If no problems are identified as a result of these assessments, the problem lies somewhere in the school program.
3. A school screening committee should gather as much data as possible, including observation of the student during instructional periods. Considering all of the resources within the school, the screening committee makes decisions concerning which resources can best assist the student. A plan is implemented, and periodic evaluation of progress keeps the screening committee informed and able to make future decisions.
4. Some schools have special programs for those experiencing serious difficulties. Instructors with special training direct the learning of such students. These special programs can involve visual discrimination training, carefully structured phonics activities, visual training, and auditory training. Experienced nursery-school and kindergarten teachers may have highly useful instructional suggestions. Local college personnel who operate clinics and who work with seriously handicapped readers may offer program suggestions and work with specially identified children.
5. Means for providing large amounts of individual attention often need to be developed. Teacher aides, parents,

volunteers, and peer tutors can assist the teacher. They can help students as they work independently from the teacher. They can help these students avoid practicing faulty learning habits, and help them build a sense of self-worth and success that they need so badly.

6. Teachers will need to provide communications with parents. Naturally parents become anxious about their children's difficulties. They also become easy targets for people who think they have all the answers to the student's difficulty. Expensive tutorial programs, often operated to earn profit instead of to help the reader, are easy to find. By helping the parents understand the difficulty and the efforts school personnel make, much of their anxiety can be reduced.

SUMMARY

The activities involved in readiness instruction are not limited to primary-grade teachers. Teachers at all levels must be skilled in identification and treatment of the types of problems discussed in this chapter. Reading specialists must know how to obtain maximum help for teachers who cannot reach students because of readiness limitations. In most cases, no reason exists why reading instruction, directed to the strengths of students, cannot proceed while readiness programs are being conducted. Of course, the effort must be to assist the student in becoming the most successful learner possible.

While some students need direct and intensive instruction in the areas mentioned in this chapter, most student difficulties in these areas can be remediated easily. These students either missed instruction when it was offered or they were not yet ready to profit from it. Short reviews in the areas of difficulty often result in immediate understanding and improvement.

NOTES

1. Kenneth S. Goodman, "Dialect Rejection and Reading," *Reading Research Quarterly* 15 (Summer 1970): 603.
2. Irwin Feigenbaum, "The Use of Nonstandard English in Teaching Standard: Contrast and Comparison," in *Teaching Standard English in the Inner City* (Washington, D.C.: Center for Applied Linguistics, 1970), 87–104.
3. Johanna S. De Stefano, *Some Parameters of Register in Adult and Child Speech* (Washington, D.C.: Institute of Applied Linguistics, 1972).

4. *The Prospects for Bilingual Education in the Nation,* (Washington, D.C.: Fifth Annual Report of the National Advisory Council for Bilingual Education, 1980–81), 20–24.
5. Charles R. Hancock, William E. DeLorenzo, and Alba Ben-Barka, *Teaching Pre- and Semi-Literate Loation and Cambodian Adolescents to Read* (Baltimore, Maryland: State Dept. of Education, 1983), 10.
6. Thomas Sticht, et al., *Auding and Reading* (Alexandria, Va.: Human Resources Research Association, 1974), vi.
7. David Russell and Etta E. Karp, *Reading Aids through the Grades* and *Listening Aids through the Grades* (New York: Teachers College, Columbia University, 1951).
8. Charles and Patricia Lindamood, *Auditory Discrimination in Depth,* (Hingham, Michigan: Teaching Resource Corp.).
9. Dorothy Sullivan, Beth Davey, and Dolores Dickerson, *Games as Learning Tools* (Paoli, Pa.: Instructo/McGraw-Hill Book Co., 1978).
10. Marie Clay, *Reading: The Patterning of Complex Behaviour,* (London: Heinemann Educational Books, 1973), 56–57.
11. Grace Fernald, *Remedial Techniques in Basic School Subjects* (New York: McGraw-Hill Book Co., 1943), 35–39.
12. Ibid.
13. Robert M. Wilson, "Oral Reading Is Fun," *The Reading Teacher* 18 (October 1965): 41–43.
14. Paul M. Hollingsworth, "An Experiment With the Impress Methods of Teaching Reading," *The Reading Teacher* 24 (November 1970): 112–14.

SUGGESTED READINGS

Clay, Marie. *Reading: The Patterning of Complex Behaviour.* London: Heinemann Educational Books, 1972. Part II of this book discusses early reading skills in detail. Chapter 6 provides interesting reading regarding directional learning.

Fernald, Grace. *Remedial Techniques in Basic School Subjects.* New York: McGraw-Hill Book Co., 1943. The advantages and specific techniques of the tracing technique are presented in chapter 5. The reader will find this presentation interesting and complete.

Hall, MaryAnne. *Teaching Reading as a Language Experience,* 3d ed. Columbus, OH: Charles E. Merrill Publishing Co., 1981. This book provides a basic background for those unfamiliar with the possibilities for using the language-experience approach in remediation. Chapter 7 deals specifically with teaching prereading skills through the language-experience approach.

Hymes, James L., Jr. *Before the Child Reads.* New York: Row, Peterson & Co., 1958. Hymes presents the viewpoint of an experienced educator of young children. His chapter "You Do Not

Have to 'Build' Readiness," while concerned with preschool children, should be considered required reading.

Kephart, Newell C. *The Slow Learner in the Classroom.* Columbus, OH: Charles E. Merrill Publishing Co., 1971. The reader will find interesting reading covering the motor readiness needs of youngsters. Particular attention is given to motor skills, which the author relates to success in learning.

Monroe, Marion, and Rogers, Bernice. *Foundations for Reading.* Chicago: Scott Foresman and Co., 1964. The authors have presented a series of chapters (chapters 1–5) relating to the beginning reading processes. The educator who is attempting remediation without a thorough understanding of this initial process will find this reading very profitable.

Sticht, Thomas G., et al. *Auding and Reading.* Alexandria, Va.: Human Resources Research Association, 1974. A thorough discussion of the place of language in the reading process is provided in this book.

Editorial

Gerald L. Fowler
is a reading supervisor for the Carlisle, Pennsylvania Public Schools.

Randy was a very shy first grader. He rarely talked to the other children and often responded to me with gestures rather than words. When he did speak, the sounds were often garbled and the messages limited to one or two phrases. By the end of the first month of school, Randy still seemed bewildered and approached every experience as though it were his first. A referral to our speech therapist came back with the response that Randy had the language capacity of a "two or three year old." My own experiences had shown me that he had no knowledge of letters (names or sounds), few labels for common objects, and limited visual discrimination ability for graphic constructions. Also, Randy was not doing well in the readiness program designed to lead into the basal readers used in our school.

Further background information revealed that he lived with his father and a sister who was a few years older than he. His family was very poor, having few modern conveniences. There were no phones, radios, televisions, or books in his apartment. His father had to leave Randy and his sister alone while he worked. They were given strict instructions to keep the door locked and talk with no one during his absence.

I decided that Randy needed a rich language-oriented program to become a successful reader. I began using the language-experience approach with him. In this way we would begin with the few words he already knew and use them as building blocks in many skill areas. Randy enjoyed this approach. He spent another year in first grade, and four years later I happened to be visiting the school (I had since left) and discovered he was doing quite well in grade five. Not the top of the class but well enough to read comfortably in groups and do many of the content-area assignments that required reading.

bed
lion
banana
banana
drum
postman
pitcher
pitcher

8 Word Identification

CHAPTER OUTLINE

CHAPTER EMPHASES

- ☐ The language-experience approach can aid in developing personal sight vocabularies.
- ☐ Sight vocabulary and word-attack activities can be developed from word-bank words.
- ☐ Sight vocabulary and word-attack lessons should be short and end with reading in context.
- ☐ Phonics instruction can be abstract and, therefore, very difficult.
- ☐ Learning centers can reinforce sight vocabulary and word-attack activities.
- ☐ Some students need a system for attacking unknown words.

Note: All instructional materials cited in this chapter are listed in appendix B.

Successful reading requires use of sight vocabulary and word-attack skills. Remedial work in these areas should not focus on teaching a large set of isolated words or skills, but rather should concentrate on total comprehension of a reading passage. This chapter will explore remediation in these areas stressing the relationship between the activities and comprehension.

THE LANGUAGE-EXPERIENCE APPROACH

The teacher and reading specialist who are planning remedial activities in the area of sight vocabulary and word attack must understand the language-experience approach. This approach stresses reading as a meaningful, communicative activity. For students who have experienced difficulty reading, an approach that stresses personal meaning has the following advantages:

1. The language-experience approach focuses first and mainly on understanding meaning and then on isolated skill development so that it has more motivational appeal to students.
2. The words used in developing language-experience stories have personal meaning for the students who developed the stories. The teacher can assume that the students have at least one meaning for the words used.
3. The syntax of the stories is familiar to the students who developed them. No strange grammatical structures interfere with understanding.
4. The content of the stories has personal meaning to the students. This assures comprehension and facilitates motivation.

When language-experience stories are used as a basis for remedial activities in sight vocabulary and word-attack skills, the lessons should start and end with the words in context so that the students are continuously reminded that all of their effort is toward reading for meaning. The following suggestions can serve as possible techniques for using language-experience stories in developing sight vocabulary and word-attack skills.

1. Generate a discussion concerning the experience of a student or group of students. Encourage the students to talk about what they saw or did, how it made them feel, and the meaning the experience had for them.

2. Following free discussion, direct the students to tell a story about the experience. Ask for contributions and write exactly what they say. Always spell words correctly, but do not change the contributor's sentence structure. Some guidelines for writing stories follow.
   - ☐ Encourage all students to contribute.
   - ☐ In the beginning, use some type of identification for each individual's contribution (e.g., "Donald said, 'I see a big dog' " or "I see a big dog" [Donald]).
   - ☐ Read what has been written immediately following writing each sentence. Next have the student who gave the sentence read it; then, the entire group.
   - ☐ For very young readers, start every new sentence on a new line. For older readers, write in paragraphs.
   - ☐ Begin with fairly short stories. If the students have more to say, write the story on two pages with only a few lines on each page. Students with serious reading problems can become discouraged with too much print on a single page.
   - ☐ Have students watch as the story is written. Call attention to the formation of words as they are written.
   - ☐ As students develop skill with beginning consonants, invite them to help spell words (e.g., "How would I begin the word *boy*?").
3. After the story is written, have the students read it in unison several times.
4. Duplicate the story as soon as possible, making at least two copies for each student. One copy can be placed in a folder to become reading material. The second copy can be used for skill development.
5. Skills can be developed from language-experience stories in a variety of ways. In chapter 7, using language-experience stories to develop visual discrimination, auditory discrimination, and orientation skills was discussed. Skills in vocabulary can be developed using the following methods:
   - ☐ Have the students mark all the words that they know. Then have them put several of these words in a private word box or word bank. The students' word banks provide a natural opportunity for meaningful word drills. On the front of the word bank card print the word. On the back write a sentence given by the student using the word.

tiger	The tiger is strong.
(front)	(back)

- ☐ Students can practice their known words in pairs or in small groups. They can match words in their word banks with words in their stories. They can classify words as action words, naming words, people words, words beginning with specific letters, and so on.
- ☐ Once a group of words is developed, students can use their word banks to help them with spelling activities. They can use them to build sentences, make crossword puzzles, and in many other activities.
- ☐ Add words to the students' banks occasionally. When the word *and* or *the* occurs repeatedly in a story, but has not been chosen for placement in the word banks, call it to the students' attention. Such service words will be needed in future reading and in vocabulary activities.

6. Word-attack skills can be developed using the following methods:

- ☐ Using word bank words, have students make a collection of rhyming words, e.g., "Collect all words in your word bank that rhyme with *cat.*" Then have students share their rhyming words. Write them on the chalkboard and discuss how the words found are the same and how they are different. See if the students can brainstorm to build more *-at* rhyming words.
- ☐ Have students search their word banks for all words that begin with a given consonant and share what they have found. See if they can brainstorm to add words that fit.
- ☐ Have students search their word banks for words with common prefixes and suffixes and again share and brainstorm.
- ☐ After studying syllabication generalizations, use word bank words to serve as examples and exceptions to the generalization. For example, if the generalization being taught is *vc/cv,* then the students would find words such as *window, picnic, pencil,* and *problem* as examples that match the generalization, and a word such as *father* as an exception.

7. Comprehension activities can also be developed from language-experience stories (see chapter 9).

PIZZA

1. Preheat oven to 425° F.
2. Put pizza flour mix in a small bowl.
3. Add ½ cup very warm water to mix. Stir with spoon until all flour particles are moistened. Then stir vigorously for 25 strokes.
4. Cover bowl. Let stand in warm place for 5 minutes.
5. Using shortening, grease well a 14" pizza pan or a 14"x11" rectangle on a cookie sheet.
6. Grease fingers then lightly spread pizza edges of pan up edges ¼" to rim.
7. Pour canned sauce over t

Following direction activities can come naturally from the language-experience approach.

These suggestions in no way cover all the possibilities of the language-experience approach for remediation. Additional specific suggestions are provided under various remedial areas in this and other chapters. Those unfamiliar with the language-experience approach will want to study the books of Stauffer and Hall listed at the end of this chapter.

REMEDIATION IN SIGHT VOCABULARY

Sight vocabulary involves instant word pronunciation and word meaning identification. Sight vocabulary study aims at comprehension through decoding and associating a word in context rather than in isolation since word meaning depends on the relationship between the words in a sentence or paragraph.

Remedial procedures will be developed in direct response to the questions asked under the diagnosis of sight vocabulary difficulties. Specifically, those questions are:

1. Does the student miss small, graphically similar words?
2. Do words missed represent abstract concepts?
3. Do word meanings appear to be confused?
4. Does the student know words in context but not in isolation?
5. Does the student appear to know words at the end of a lesson but not the next day?

These difficulties seldom appear alone; rather, they are interrelated. Establishing the answers to these questions helps determine in which areas the interrelationship has taken place so that these areas can be emphasized in remediation. For example, through examination it can clearly be seen that small, graphically similar words are often words with abstract meanings, so dual remedial considerations are required.

Small, Graphically Similar Words

Do the students miss small, graphically similar words or do they falter on words that are obviously different? Quite often, readers will miss small words that have minimal configurational differences (e.g., *when* and *where*), while effectively attacking larger and more obviously different words (e.g., *elephant* and *Christmas*). The latter is considered a skill in sight vocabulary, while the former normally shows difficulty in word attack, especially if the words missed are at or below the instructional level. Whichever, the teacher should work from the readers' strengths. If the students can work with words of maximal differences, the teacher should provide more exercises with those types of words, moving gradually to words that are more similar until skill with those words has developed. Then the students should move to words even more alike until skill with words that have minimal graphic differences has been developed.

Ultimately, the student must receive instruction in the discrimination of words that are minimally different. These exercises should be conducted in phrase and sentence form so that the reader realizes that the minimal difference distorts not only the pronunciation but the meaning of the words: "We took the *dig* (instead of *dog*) for a walk." To clarify the similarities and differences in minimally different words, teachers should pull these words from context for study (*dig-dog*). Any exercise, however, should be followed by returning to context.

In the early grades, the teacher may use experience charts to illustrate the need for careful visual discrimination of minimally different words. In these situations, the teacher should take every opportunity to emphasize how words of similar configuration actually differ in both form and meaning, using the reader's own language contributions as examples. For instance, when writing a student's story, the teacher should look for opportunities to demonstrate how certain words look alike or different.

Using words from the students' word banks (i.e., words that are already known) illustrates teaching to strengths. Locating words in the banks that look very much alike, pronouncing them, noting meanings, using them in sentences, and noting how they look alike and different is extremely useful. Attention should be given to differences in all parts of the words—initial, medial, and final.

Programmed materials are available that are particularly adaptable for classroom use in remediation of this skill difficulty. These materials can help the student see differences in words that have minimal graphic differences (e.g., *hat* and *bat*). As an example of these materials, *Programmed Reading* contains a series of exercises through which the reader can develop skill with a minimum amount of teacher supervision (see figure 8–1). The student must look at the pictures, read the sentence or partial sentence, and use closure to obtain the correct code and message. These exercises progress from the elementary type to complete stories. The forced-choice closure concept, where the reader selects from a limited number of appropriate responses, is maintained at all levels.

The student is reinforced by the appearance of the correct answer after each frame or page, depending on how much material the teacher feels the reader can handle before reinforcement. The skills developed in the workbooks are transferred to reading in prepared storybooks, containing stories with minimally different words. It is unlikely that these materials will satisfy the reader's total reading needs. Programmed materials such as these can be supplemented with the language-experience approach, allowing students to develop their personal word bank of meaningful words.

The linguistic approach can be adapted to almost any type of material, for example, the word banks and programmed materials mentioned previously. The *Let's Read* books and *The Merrill Linguistic Readers* (see figure 9–2) are prepared linguistic materials for beginning readers and are appropriate for individualized instruction of students with serious reading problems. Both of these approaches have a controlled vocabulary of minimally different words, a controlled initial presentation of words with consistent vowel and consonant sounds, and an absence of pictures so that correct visual perception is necessary for accurate decoding. A similar approach, *The Linguistic Readers,* varies somewhat from these, but does maintain the necessity for visual perception of minimal differences. An example of adaptations of *The Linguistic Readers* for instruction is thoroughly described by Botel.[1]

Abstract Concepts

Students often find it particularly difficult to remember words that represent abstract concepts (e.g., *when, these, if, those*). Emphasis in remediation for this type of difficulty should focus

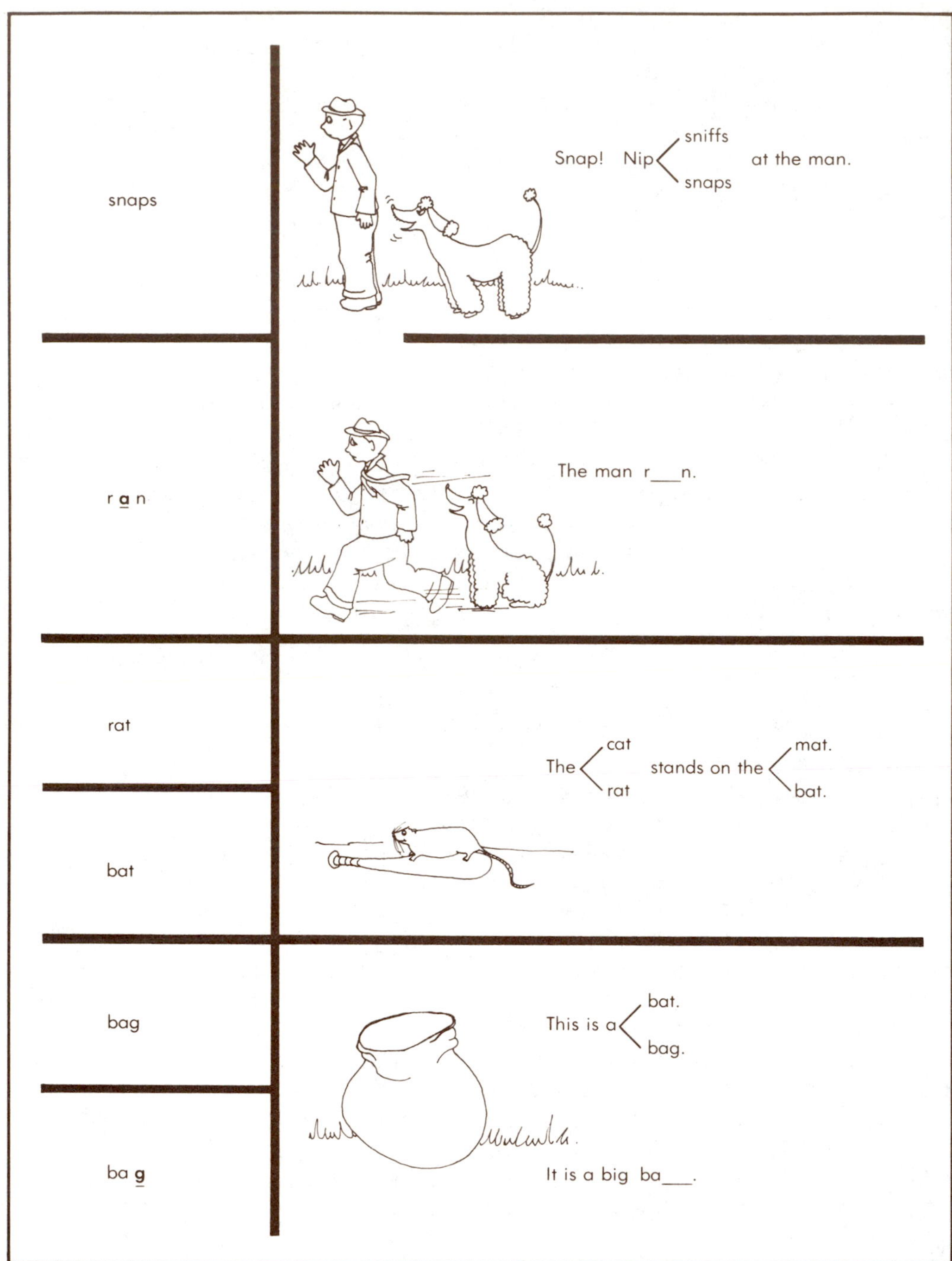

FIGURE 8–1
A sample page of a programmed reader. (Reproduced by permission from *PROGRAMMED READING BOOK 2, Series One.* Copyright © 1963 by Sullivan Associates. Published by McGraw-Hill, Inc.)

A Little Red Hen

A little red hen is in Ben's pen.
Pam looked at the hen and said,
"Can I have the red hen
for a pet?"

Ben said, "If you can get a box
for it, you can have the red hen."

Pam ran and got a red box
with a lid.
She fed the hen and led it
to the box.
The little red hen got into its
little red box.

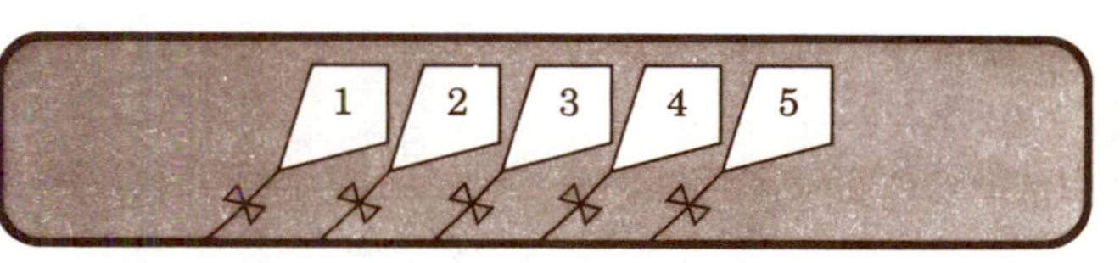

5 The little red hen got into its box.

2 Pam said, "Can I have the hen for a pet?"

4 Pam ran and got a box with a lid.

1 A little red hen is in Ben's pen.

3 "If you get a box for the hen, you can," said Ben.

Use after page 24 of Unit 5. **Arranging Events in Sequence:** Pupils should carefully read the story on page 22 before doing this exercise. Then have pupils read all of the sentences on this page. Have them find the number **1** and read the sentence that tells what happened first. Then have them decide which event happened next and write the number **2** in the correct box. Repeat for the remaining sentences having pupils work independently. Notice that the last one is done for the pupil. Pupils may copy the sentences in correct sequence on a separate sheet of paper.

21

FIGURE 8–2
A sample page from a linguistic reader. (Copyright © 1980 by Charles E. Merrill Publishing Company. *The Merrill Linguistic Reader Catch On, Level C.* Reproduced by permission; all rights reserved.)

on the word as it appears in context since it is from context that these words can be understood. Furthermore, since these words are seldom used in isolation in reading, they should not be taught in isolation.

Once again, experience-story approaches are particularly valuable in developing this type of reading sight vocabulary. Students use these words to formulate their experience stories, allowing a natural opportunity for instruction in the service and function of these words. Although the experience-story approach will probably be used more frequently with younger readers, considerable success with this type of approach has also been found with older students. Experience-story reading allows teachers to determine if words used have meaning for the readers, since they make the contributions. Through these materials, the use and nature of abstract words can be effectively illustrated.

Again, word bank words that carry little meaning of their own (*and, the, of,* and so on) are known to students and can be developed into meaningful activities. For example, using *and, the,* and *of* from a word bank, teachers can ask which word would fit in the blank: bread ____ butter, I see ____ man, and on top ____ the table. The use of such modified closure activities develops skills in the use of abstract words.

Sight vocabulary drills with abstract concepts are most effective when the words are used in phrases (e.g., *in a good spirit*). Prepared phrase cards with the more commonly used word combinations are available in the Dolch game series (e.g., *Match, Basic Sight Cards*).

After a certain amount of sight vocabulary has been developed, students may build sentences from word cards. Here emphasis should be placed on the function of the abstract word as created by the student. With this activity, the unknown word is not placed in a definition situation; rather, it appears in a functional situation—the sentence. Intentional distortions of these types of words in context may be used to illustrate their importance. For example, the text reads, "*In* the table is a lot of money." It is changed to read, "*On* the table is a lot of money." The students either describe or illustrate how the slight change has affected the meaning of the sentence.

Word games, such as *Word Lotto* (see appendix B), that use abstract words reinforce words that have been previously learned (i.e., words from students' word banks). Word games are highly motivating and take the drill atmosphere from reinforcement activities. Games such as checkers can be used with words taped on each square. As players move or jump opponents, they are expected to pronounce the words on the spaces involved. Students become so enthusiastic about such activities that they forget they are being drilled.

Confused Word Meanings

Remedial instruction for confusion of word meanings must be based on the following two considerations.

1. Sometimes students, for one reason or another, fail to develop a background of experience that permits them to associate meaning with the word they have pronounced. If this deficiency is chronic, remediation will necessarily consist of experiential language development as well as instruction in sight vocabulary.
2. Although many students know the meaning of a word and can use it in a sentence, they fail to associate the word with the correct meaning, apparently because of preoccupation with word pronunciation. Remedial activities with these students, then, should be in the area of sight vocabulary, where they must be taught to be conscious of what the word says as well as how it sounds.

As previously stated, every word drill should end with the word in context. In this way the precise meaning and function of the word are best understood; readers with these characteristics must have context emphasized even more precisely. The students begin by reading easy material and demonstrating their knowledge of the words in question by paraphrasing the author's words.

Teachers will often find it useful to establish whether the students know the meaning of a word through definition. If students can give the definition of a word, the meaning of the word as such is not causing the problem; the use of the word in a particular contextual situation, is causing difficulty, however. The presentation of the word in various settings is then the appropriate approach to take.

Since students already understand the meaning of the pronounced words, experience stories using the students' own wording again play an important role in remedial efforts. Teachers of elementary school children are urged to provide numerous opportunities for group-experience stories in which an association between the experiences of the group and the words that represent those experiences exists. This presents a golden opportunity to create situations in which students learn from one another. Frequently students react better to the responses of their peers than to teacher efforts. Two sources of activities to help students develop word meaning skills are Heilman[2] for the younger student and Dale and O'Rourke[3] for the more mature student.

Although frequently not included as a remedial technique, the dictionary can be used to assist older students. Because they know the correct pronunciation of a word in print, they can use the dictionary to find meanings efficiently; consequently, they may develop a habit of consulting the dictionary for unknown words. Techniques for use with the dictionary are discussed in the section "Remediation in Word Attack" later in this chapter.

The *Peabody Language Development Kits* contain programs for numerous language development lessons. Teachers may find this type of program a guide for the entire school year. Among the experiences included with these kits are following directions, brainstorming, critical thinking, memorizing, rhyming, and listening. Pictures, objects, and tapes are used to enrich the child's experiential background.

The *Building Pre-Reading Skills Kit-A-Language* provides the teacher with another program for language development. It consists of pictures through which vocabulary can be stimulated, synonyms developed, and language-experience stories drawn.

For the reader seriously handicapped by the inability to associate the printed word with meaning, the Non-Oral Reading Series may contain the requisites for initial instruction. This approach bypasses completely the vocalization of the printed word and emphasizes instead the word's association with a pictured concept. The task is to match the printed symbol with a picture representing the concept for that symbol. This direct association from print to concept minimizes the importance of pronunciation for those who have been overdrilled in it.

Teachers will also find it useful to have the student respond directly through physical activity to such printed word commands as "jump up," and "shake hands." This approach also minimizes vocalization of the printed word, emphasizing again the meaning of the word through student response. The *Nichols Tachistoscope Slides,* developed for this purpose, appear to be effective in establishing the importance of the concepts covered by words.

Collecting words in categories from the word bank can also help stress word meanings. For example, to collect action words, the student must think of word meaning, not just pronunciation. Words that are names of things can be matched with the action words to make short sentences (e.g., *dogs run, ducks dive, horses jump*). Students can look at the sentences they have built to determine which ones make sense, an extremely mean-

Placing word bank words on a checker board is an enjoyable drill exercise for students.

ingful activity. In addition, stimulating students with incomplete sentences, such as "I like to ____", makes the learning more personal and interesting.

Teachers also may use initial sight-vocabulary exercises consisting of nouns, adjectives, and verbs that can be pictured. The *Dolch Picture Word Cards,* containing ninety six of these types of words, may be used. Several matching games require a student to match a picture with a printed word, thereby reinforcing understanding of word meaning in a gamelike activity. Such activities are self-motivating. *Picture Word Puzzles* provide similar reinforcement with children having association deficiencies.

Active participation can be achieved by having students build sentences from the words that they know. After known words are placed on cards, the cards are scrambled and the students are asked to build either specific sentences or sentences of their choosing. The *Linguistic Block Series* can be used in the same manner by allowing students to fill the blank block with words in their personal vocabularies.

Meaning in Context

Students who know words in context but not in isolation are indicating that context aids their reading. By being aware of the function of words in their language and sentence meaning, these students are demonstrating desirable word-attack processes. Since most words are encountered in context, this difficulty should not be considered critical.

Occasionally, however, a word must be read in isolation and recognition is crucial (e.g., signs which indicate words such as *Stop, Danger, Women*). Such words should be taught in context, then pulled from context and attention placed on meaning. Since meaning clues seem to aid this type of reader, the stress on meaning should also help. These words should also be pointed out in real life whenever possible. For example, teachers can locate a *Stop* sign and see if students know the word when they see it at a street corner.

Sometimes the student recognizes the word in isolation but not in context. While such cases are rare, some consideration should be given to the problem. Usually this happens when the word has been changed from what students had known. If students learn the word *bank* as a basketball term and then encounter it in the sentence, "I can *bank* on you," they may not understand it. In such a case it would be correct to say that the students did not have the word *bank* as a sight word, so they did not know the word in isolation. Some readers have difficulty with certain types of print. Small print on a crowded page can cause them some confusion. The teacher can encourage these students to frame the word by blocking out all of the other words. If the other words were distractors, the student should then be able to read the word and proceed with reading the passage. However, by starting vocabulary instruction with words in context this problem should not occur.

Learning Not Retained

Students often appear to have mastered words for their sight vocabularies, then the next day cannot recall their meanings. This presents a real problem for teachers, who, thinking that the students have learned the words, plan the next lesson using those words as a base. The students also become confused because they cannot remember those words. The solution for such problems is elusive because several causes may be operating alone or in combination.

Teachers may be asking the students to learn too many sight words in a given lesson. If so, pacing must be adjusted. In remedial situations, the teacher and the student should negotiate the pace of sight words to be learned. If the teacher feels that a student can learn four words a day and the student says, "I think I can learn three a day," three words should be the accepted goal with an added, "And be certain to learn them well." If this

Pupils can build sentences from scrambled word cards.

adjustment helps the students remember their sight words, a suitable pace for successful learning has been found. Pace may need to be adjusted daily depending on the difficulty of the words to be remembered, (the meanings of *elephant* and *Halloween* are easier to remember than the meanings of *their* and *there*). Teachers should make certain that the students learn what they study.

Another reason for lack of retention may be that the students have not had enough opportunities to encounter the new words. Everyone has thought he or she has mastered something only to find out that it has slipped from memory. Repeated exposure to such information enables clear recall of it. For students who forget easily, teachers should structure extra practice. Games, learning centers, and working with peers can be ways of helping students retain what they respond to initially. Since some students need more exposure to sight words than others, such practice should be individually prescribed.

Still another possible explanation for students forgetting is that the teacher has assumed too much when planning to use the previous day's words as a base for the next day's lesson. A quick review of the materials assumed to have been learned will quickly let the teacher know if the base is solid. If not, a brief review lesson should strengthen the ability of students to recall the sight words so that the base for the next lesson is established.

Some students need more sensory reinforcement for learning sight words than others. The Visual, Auditory, Kinesthetic,

Tactile (VAKT) technique, for example, can be used to help some students remember sight words. Recently, hand signs developed for communication among the deaf have been explored as possible means to reinforce sight vocabulary.[4] Many signs carry meaning by the way the sign is made (for example, the word *children* is signed by miming patting several children's heads). Students often find learning signs fun and interesting so they have little trouble remembering words associated with the signs from day to day.

Teachers will find that adding signs to sight vocabulary lessons is easy and takes little time. First, the teacher must obtain a book of signs, such as *The Comprehensive Signed English Dictionary.*[5] When students select words to place on their word cards the teacher looks up the signs for the words in the dictionary, and goes through the following steps:

1. Show the word on the word card.
2. Sign the word.
3. Say the word.
4. Have the students perform steps 1, 2, and 3 with the teacher several times.

Students are anxious to learn new words to sign and teach them to others. Often, when students master words with signing, they eliminate the signing without being asked to do so. Two students at the University of Maryland used signing to reinforce sight vocabulary with twenty children who could not retain their sight words. The signing intervention was conducted daily for four weeks. In all twenty cases the children were able to retain their sight words more accurately when signing was used than when more traditional methods of instruction were used. When tested over time, the children retained their signed sight words. Signing may therefore be a strategy for teachers to use for children who cannot remember sight words.

Finally, teachers should make certain that the students have learned words in a contextual situation. If the students' word cards have only the word on the front of a card, then sentences using the word created by the students should be placed on the back. If students do not seem to be able to respond to a word, they can turn the card over and see it in a familiar context. In this manner, they can work with word cards without teacher help even when they run into difficulty.

Additional Considerations in Sight Vocabulary

The following aspects of remediation of sight vocabulary problems should be carefully understood by any person conducting remediation in this area.

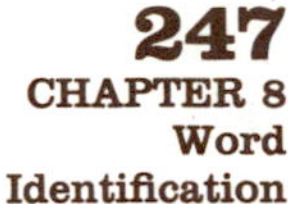

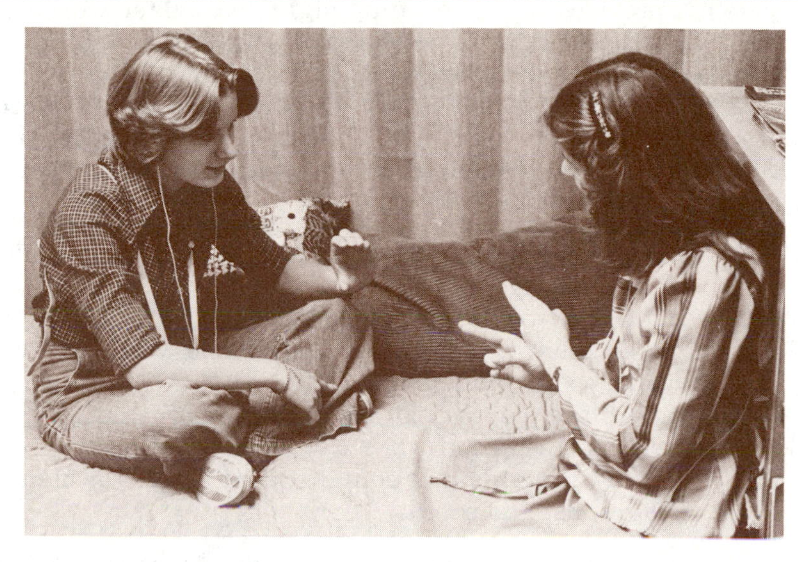

Signing can be used as a language-development activity that is fun and highly motivating.

Skill Segmentation. Students often see no connection between learning sight vocabulary and reading. Efforts to link sight vocabulary training to actual reading situations are essential. Students should be asked why they think they are studying these words. Their verbalization of how sight vocabulary fits into reading helps teachers know how well their students understand the purposes for a given activity.

Tell Students the Word. The teacher will find many situations in which it is advisable to tell students unknown words. Although normally teachers should not provide unknown words, they will often find that students are in situations where they simply do not have the skills needed to attack unknown words. In these cases, telling them the word will permit them to move along with the context of the story, focusing attention on those words they have the skills to attack effectively. In such cases, the teachers should not feel guilty about telling students words, nor should they make the students feel this way.

Overlearning. The very nature of sight vocabulary (instant recognition and meaning) implies that it must be overlearned. Overlearning, not to be conducted in isolated drill activities, is most effective when the reader has opportunities to use the word again and again in context. Many remedial efforts fail because they do not provide for overlearning sight vocabulary words in context. Experience stories, trade books, and similar materials are available to facilitate overlearning.

Reinforcing sight vocabulary through the use of word banks exemplifies the concept of focusing on strengths and meets the need for overlearning. Several suggestions for the use of word banks as reinforcers follow.

1. Find all the words that begin like ________ or end like ________.
2. Find all the words that rhyme with ________.
3. Find all the words that are one-syllable words or two-syllable words (and so on).
4. Find all the words that are examples of ________ (a given generalization).
5. Find all the words that contain silent letters (or blends or digraphs, and so on.)

Likewise games, either commercially developed or teacher made, make overlearning exciting and fun. Games that follow the pattern of a race track and involve spinning a wheel or rolling dice to move around it can be used. Each block on the race track can require the student to demonstrate a skill: initial consonant substitution, syllabication, or vowel knowledge. Remember that the element of chance enters into game activities; a loss is not a matter of intellectual inability, but luck. Teachers should be certain that this chance factor is obvious to students in all games used for these purposes.

Every remedial session should provide opportunities for the students to read materials of their own choosing. Perhaps as much as 25 to 50 percent of the remedial time can be wisely spent on such activities. Readers become comfortable with words that they will meet over and over again. Overlearning is often interpreted as a drill-and-grill type of activity. Obviously, the more motivating the activity, the less it will be viewed as a chore.

Word Length and Sound Length. Some seriously handicapped readers may look at a word such as *mow* and call it *motorcycle.* These readers have not made an association between sound length and word length. Consequently, they have a slim possibility of making progress in sight-vocabulary development without an intervention program in awareness of sound and graphic relationships. (These lessons should not focus on phonics, but rather an awareness that long-sounding words will appear to be longer in print than short-sounding words.) Instruction is directed to the problem by discussing the problem with the stu-

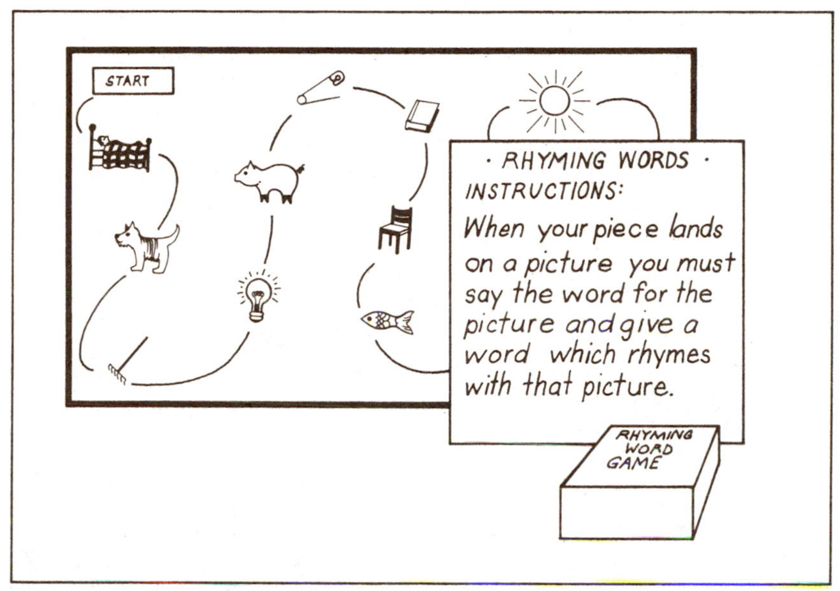

Competitive games enrich otherwise boring phonics activities.

dents and then providing exercises with extreme examples (*mow—motorcycle*) and moving toward instruction with minor changes (*mow—mower*).

Word Boundaries. Some immature readers have difficulty identifying word boundaries even though they sound as though they are reading accurately. Clay reports this type of phenomenon and attributes it to memorization of the passage.[6] The students listen to others and repeat what they have heard. They sound as if they are reading, but they are not. If teachers are concerned that some of the readers are doing just that, they should ask the readers to frame several of the words. If they frame the word *house* as follows, then they show that they do not recognize the boundaries of the word:

I went into (the house to) see Jim.

The students should be shown the word *house* on a card and asked to read a sentence. They should be able to find it in the sentence and frame it. In this way, they can learn the boundaries of the words.

Motivation Techniques

The often subtle developments in sight vocabulary should be illustrated to readers so that they may be encouraged by their progress. The following techniques have been found to be particularly helpful.

1. Transferring every lesson to contextual situations illustrates to students that the effort they are making in sight vocabulary is, in effect, making them better readers. Particularly with older students, this in itself is often ample motivation for further improvement.
2. Recording experience stories in booklet form is interesting to younger students because they can see their progress merely by the quantity of the material they have been able to learn to read. The sight vocabulary implications of that quantity can be pointed out if the student doesn't see it.
3. Charts illustrating the goals toward which the student will work in sight vocabulary seem to trigger some students' efforts to perform better. Ultimately, intrinsic motivation should fulfill the function of such charts. Further, these charts should never place one reader in competition with another. Illustrating success through charts must be carefully planned. Objectives must be short-term and within the realistic grasp of the student. Charts that emphasize long-range goals can discourage as well as encourage students. During a moon shot, University of Maryland clinicians led their students in a vocabulary development race against the astronauts. The students won the race, and the short-term nature (eight days) of the chart made it worthwhile.
4. Sight vocabulary cards maintained in a file or on a ring illustrate visually to students that they have accumulated a number of useful words through which they can become better readers. These words should not be listed in isolation; rather, they should appear in a sentence with the word highlighted with colored ink.

Games have been suggested for teaching several of these techniques. These appear to hold a student's interest and to establish a degree of motivation, while assisting the student in developing sight vocabulary.

As has been mentioned, the use of contracts through which students regulate their learning to some degree are of particular value. The completion of a contract is motivation in itself. Of course, specially constructed rewards and motivational devices can be built in. For example, contract completion can result in an immediate reward through free-reading time, praise, and other encouragement.

REMEDIATION IN WORD ATTACK

Word-attack skills enable students to pronounce words not in their sight vocabularies and to understand them without teacher assistance as they are used in contextual situations.

Many readers have serious difficulties with word-attack skills, so many remedial programs concentrate on them heavily. Consequently, teachers have an abundant amount of material to choose from to teach word-attack skills. Also, many approaches to the problem have been recommended in the professional literature. With this wealth of information, teachers can easily overemphasize instruction in word-attack skills. Heilman proposes, "The optimum amount of phonics instruction that a child should receive is the minimum amount he needs to become an independent reader."[7] Following such advice should lessen the possibilities of overemphasis. Another danger related to word-attack instruction is that it often occurs in isolation away from context. Students often fail to see the purposes for such lessons and interest lags. Teachers should end all word-attack lessons in context so students can see how what they have learned has helped them to read better.

In light of the research on good and poor readers, reading specialists and classroom teachers should assure all readers ample time to practice reading. They should especially remember this as they develop lesson plans in word-attack skills.

In the discussion on the use of criterion-referenced tests in chapter 4, teachers were warned against testing too many objectives. Some programs that accompany CRTs lock students into learning a specific set of subskills prior to moving to the next level. Since these subskill lessons seem to concentrate on word-attack skills, this area presents the greatest problem. Different students need different amounts and types of phonics instruction. Teachers should take care to avoid use of programs that lock students into specific learning sequences. Remedial programs in word attack should be designed to foster independence in reading, not mere proficiency in word-attack drills.

Because various methods exist for attacking words not known at sight, educational focus should be on word-attack skills that assist the reader in attacking words most efficiently in terms of time and most consistently in terms of application. Once overlearned, efficiency in word attack should have the same aims as efficiency in sight vocabulary (i.e., to decode the word and associate its meaning instantly to the context in which it occurs).

As indicated in the diagnosis chapters, word attack falls into three major categories: phonics clues, structural clues, and contextual clues. Dictionary skills, a fourth category of word attack that normally is not considered a remedial necessity, need development in remedial programs at times.

Discovery Technique

Teachers must assume that most students referred for remedial help have had instruction in word-attack skills. Since those skills have not been mastered the teachers can conclude that previous instructional efforts have failed. Therefore, part of the reason for failure in learning word-attack skills must be attributed to the instructional technique. Throughout this section, the discovery technique will be mentioned as a solution to specific problems.[8] A brief review of the discovery technique and some of its possibilities are included as a preface to the discussion of remediation in word attack.

1. Present words that contain the visual clues desired for instruction. For example (using known words):

   index *picnic* *pencil* *chapter*

2. Direct the students to observe visually the patterns in the words. For example:

☐ Place a *v* above each vowel.	v v index
☐ Place a *c* above each consonant between the vowels.	vccv index
☐ Divide the word into syllables.	vc cv in/dex

3. Have the students form generalizations in their own words. For example, one student may say, "*vc/cv*"; another might say, "When you have *vc/cv* divide between the *c*'s" concerning these patterns and this syllabication. Any appropriate response is acceptable. Teachers should avoid forcing their own wording on the students.
4. Have the students turn to material that they are reading to collect words that fit the pattern. For example, refer to a specific page in a book on which there are five words that fit the pattern. The students may also find words in their word banks that fit the pattern.

The major advantages of the discovery technique include the active response of the students, acceptance of their generalizations, and the impact that results from forming a generalization through the use of visual clues. Teachers may choose to vary the approach at times; in fact, Botel suggests that steps 3 and 4 be reversed. Other variations may include a discussion of exceptions to the generalization; help in beginning the wording (e.g., "When a word contains the pattern . . ."); and activities directed from word lists to determine the ability of the students to discriminate the visual pattern. Although the discovery technique takes more time than simply telling the students, the lasting effects are extremely valuable.

Phonics

Remedial efforts in the area of phonics will deal with the questions asked after diagnosis.

1. Does the student appear to not use graphic cues?
2. Does the student attack small words accurately but not large ones?
3. Does the student seem to know sound-symbol relationships but seem unable to use them during reading?

Although in diagnosis the skills of phonics have been delegated to one of three precise areas (letter sounds, syllabication, and blending), the remedial program should combine these areas for instructional purposes. The functional use of phonics skills involves the reader's ability to divide the word into syllables, sound the letters, blend the sounds into a recognizable word, and check the derived pronunciation in the context from which the word was taken.

Auditory discrimination skills are essential to successful phonics instruction (see chapter 7). However, with seriously handicapped readers any phonics instruction should start with auditory discrimination activities. Teachers should make it a policy not to assume prior learning in this area.

Phonics instruction is the most abstract, and therefore most difficult, element of language students must learn. Lessons, therefore, should be short, detailed, and related to some contextual situation.

Graphic Cues. Does the student appear not to use graphic cues? Which graphic cues are used accurately? For each student, the teacher should have a list of all known strengths in phonics. This information has been accumulated during oral reading testing and specific phonics testing. All phonics lessons should start with these strengths. As new skills are mastered, teachers should adjust the list of strengths for each student. In this way, the teacher always has an accounting of each student's phonics knowledge.

Teachers should also make a plan for instruction. Plans should include the approach to be used to teach the skills, methods for practicing the skills, and procedures for using them.

Plans for Teaching the Skill. Teachers must decide whether to teach phonics from whole words or in isolation. In either case, the major decision concerns which approach best suits the student's strengths. Both will call for providing ample opportunity for all students to demonstrate their skills rather than their weaknesses, and the suitability of either approach will depend on the following:

1. The teacher's familiarity with a given technique combined with the availability of materials and results obtained through their use. Although teachers generally work best with familiar techniques and materials, new methods and ideas should not be overlooked. Inflexible and inappropriate teaching can result from the failure to adapt. Teachers should be as objective as possible in assessing the materials and techniques that can be used most effectively.
2. The student's previous experience and reaction to that technique. If, after good instruction, a student fails with a given technique and develops a negative attitude toward it, another approach may be more desirable.

By using these two factors to help make decisions about what approach to use, no doors are closed. It must be remembered, however, that working from known words has a distinct advantage since instruction is related to something already meaningful to the students.

Students should be alert to the idea that each time they decode a word, the sounds that are uttered should be associated with a meaningful concept. Techniques must be used to facilitate this alertness in each phonics lesson. The students may be required to put the pronounced word in a sentence, or the teacher may present words in which classification is possible (e.g., things done at school or names of animals). In either case, attention is called to the fact that the pronounced word has meaning as well as sound.

Several approaches for instruction are outlined here.

1. *Discovery technique.* In phonics instruction the discovery technique is used to help students develop an awareness of the consistent sound-symbol relationship. The teacher starts with visual and auditory stimulation:

   Let's read these words:
   see *sit* *sox* *sun*
   Listen carefully to the first sound in each word.
   They all start with the same sound. Let's hear it.
   With what letter does each of these words start?

Once the students have an awareness of the relationship between the letter *s* and the sound it represents, the teacher has several choices:

> Look in your word banks and see how many words you can find that start with the letter *s.* Pronounce these words and see if they all have the sound that *see, sit, sox,* and *sun* start with.
>
> Look in your book on page ___. There are three words that start with *s.* Find them and let's see if they start with the sound we hear at the beginning of *see, sit, sox,* and *sun.*
>
> Or, I'll give you some word endings. You place the *s* sound in front and let's see which ones make real words:
>
> *s-and* *s-at* *s-im* *s-oz*

Tempo is important. These steps can be dragged out to a point that makes instruction boring. Teachers should make this instruction snappy and move to the generalization step:

> Let's all try to say in our own words what we have learned today.

Teachers should check each effort and help students clarify the generalization. A student may write, "When a word starts with the letter *s,* it will start like the word *sat.*" At this point, instruction is over and students go into a practice activity.

2. *Word families.* Many students develop excellent word-attack skills quickly through the use of word families and initial-consonant substitution. After some instruction on the initial sounds, words can be built quickly.

> You know the initial sounds that the letters *t, s, f,* and *p* represent. This word ending is *-at.* Put your consonant in front and see how many make real words:
>
> *t-at* *s-at* *f-at* *p-at*

Attention is placed on two aspects of reading in these activities: initial-consonant substitution is easy and quick; and when students pronounce words they should always make a check to be sure the word has meaning for them. Other word families such as *-in, -and, -et* can also be used. Teachers should control the pace so that students are not overwhelmed, but keep it moving in a snappy, interesting way.

3. *Speech-to-Print Phonics.* A commercially prepared program that uses parts of all of these techniques, *Speech to Print Phonics,* has been used with success. The program features learning several sounds, applying them through substitution, checking for meaning, and us-

ing repetition. These materials can be used with groups or individual students.

4. *Cloze.* Cloze techniques, which were discussed in the diagnosis chapters, can also be used for phonics instruction. Students can be given sentences with parts of words left out and attempt to insert the correct part so that the sentence will make sense.

   The __oy hit the __all.
   The dog __it the man.
   We had __ean soup for dinner.

   In a teacher-directed activity, the teacher can ask the group for the letter that should go in the blank in order for the sentence to make sense. The teacher then inserts the correct letter. For individual practice, a similar set of sentences can be developed so the students insert the correct letters themselves. This adds the element of writing the letters, which is reinforcing.

   As skill with one sound is developed, other sounds are added, making the activity one that requires more discrimination.

   The __oy baked a __ake.
   Mary __aught the ball.

   These activities can be started as teacher-directed and lead to individual performance.

5. *Word-bank words.* Teachers should use the student's reading sight vocabulary to develop phonics lessons. Use word bank words to:

   - ☐ Collect all words that begin or end with the same sound
   - ☐ Collect rhyming words
   - ☐ Collect words with the same vowel sound and place them in long sound and short sound groups

   Once these collections are made, teachers should help the students draw generalizations about the sounds represented by the letter under investigation. Students will find words with letters that do not fit the generalizations; use these to discuss the exceptions to generalizations.

   City, cell, and *cycle* are exceptions to the *K* (hard) sound of *c* because they are followed by *i, e,* and *y.* Teachers can have the students find other words using the letter *c* followed by either *i, e,* or *y.* Do they fit this exception to the K (hard sound) generalization?

Practice sessions allow students to work with what they have learned.

If none of the instructional techniques prove effective, the teacher is encouraged to employ task analysis techniques. Since all learners respond in terms of their uniqueness, it may be that some logical explanation exists for a reading difficulty. Teachers should examine students for what they are able to do; specifically they should see if students can:

1. Respond to initial, final, medial letters.
2. Recognize familiar parts in unknown words.
3. Know the meaning of the words read to them.
4. Find the word in a dictionary.
5. Distinguish sounds when words are read to them.
6. Respond to a word when it is placed in context.

From such a list of observations, strengths and instructional needs can be recorded.

Practicing Learned Skills. Practice sessions allow students to work with what they have learned so that they can gain a degree of comfort with the skill. The following are suggestions for practicing learned skills.

1. *Games.* Teacher-made or commercially developed games can be used to let students practice what they have learned. *SRA Word Games, Phonics We Use Learn-*

ing Games, Vowel and Consonant Lotto are examples of packaged kits that are available. After instruction, students play those games that contain the skills they have learned. Teacher-made games, although time-consuming to construct, can be made to relate directly to the skills of a given lesson.

2. *Learning centers.* Self-directed activities that relate to skills learned can be made available. Small groups or individual students can work through centers, practicing their new skills. Centers can be either self-correcting or activities can be checked by the teacher. They generally deal with topics that interest students to add an attention-getting dimension. An example of a learning center activity is given in figure 8–3.
3. *Tutoring.* As soon as a teacher determines a skill to be mastered, the students should be allowed to teach the skill to someone else. It does not matter if the other person knows the skill or not. By practicing teaching a skill that has been recently learned, the student plays the teacher's role. Students will love and learn from it.

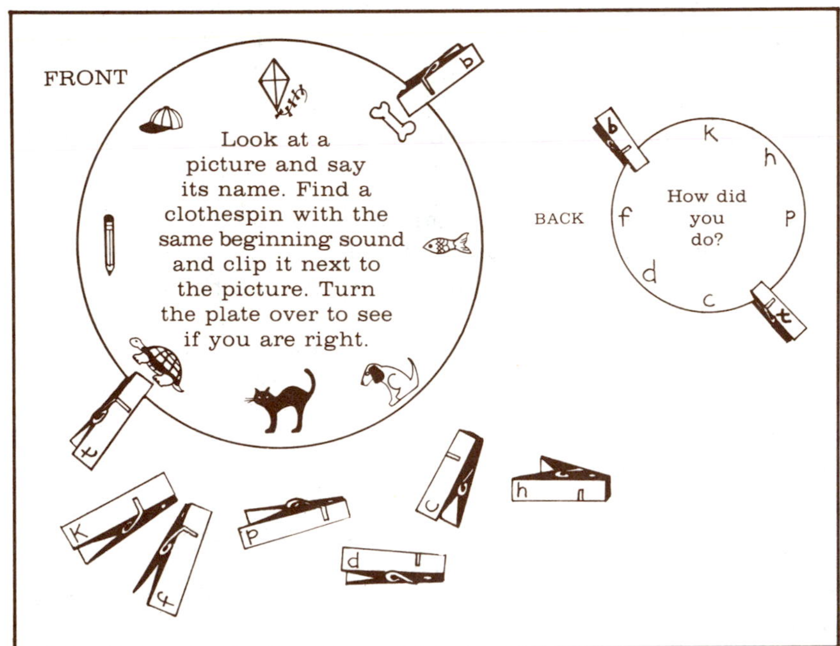

FIGURE 8–3
A learning center using clothespins and a cardboard plate provides manipulative activities. Note that the center becomes self-correcting when students turn the plate over.

4. *Worksheets.* Some workbooks contain highly useful activities for follow-up practice. *Phonics Skilltests, Phonics We Use,* and *Working with Sounds* are a few of the many commercial materials available for practice sessions. Teachers should pull out the pages as they are needed rather than overwhelm the students with the entire workbook at once.

Teachers should try to make practice sessions short and interesting. By paying attention to the students as they practice, teachers can prevent frustration. If the practice activity is too difficult, it should be adjusted so that the students experience success and are not practicing mistakes.

Using Learned Skills. After instruction and practice, students should have opportunities to use their new skills in reading. Each remedial session generally should end with a period of silent reading to show the students that the reason for their effort is to make it possible for them to read on their own. Once they get this idea, these reading periods are valued by the students.

Attacking Small and Large Words. Many students use phonics to attack short words that they do not know at sight, but cannot effectively transfer this use to longer words of more than one or two syllables. This results from a lack of effective means to break these longer words into shorter, more easily decoded parts. Thus, teachers should teach students general rules of syllabication. The instructional level of the students will help the teacher determine the specific generalizations to be taught. However, the following three generalizations are essential for all students in learning the syllabication of words.

1. *The vowel-consonant-vowel generalization.* When a word is structured v-c-v, syllables are usually divided between the first vowel and the consonant.

   v cv
   over = o/ver

   However, vowels that are followed by the consonants *r, x,* or *v* are an exception to the v-c-v generalization: the *r, x,* or *v* is grouped with the preceding vowel.

   vc v
   carol = car/ol
   vc v
   taxi = tax/i

vc v
river = *riv/er*

2. *The vowel-consonant-consonant-vowel generalization.* When a word has the structure v-c-c-v, syllables are usually divided between the consonants.

vc cv
picnic = *pic/nic*

However, blends and digraphs are treated as one consonant.

v c v
achieve = *a/chieve*

3. *The consonant-*le *generalization.* When a word ends in the structure consonant plus *-le,* those three letters form the last syllable.

c-le
ankle = *an/kle*

For students who fail to understand syllabication after learning these generalizations, teachers should use the Fernald technique,[9] modifying it to require students to pronounce syllables where they would be pronouncing words.

Once the word has been dissected, either through syllabication or through actual sounding of each letter of the syllable, the students must be able to blend these sounds to obtain a pronunciation with a meaning. When difficulty with blending arises, the student must be given ample opportunity to obtain a feeling for blending by dividing known words into syllables and blending their sounds to come up with a meaningful utterance. Blending sounds and syllables is an inherent part of each lesson in which the student learns the sound or divides the word into syllables.

Several phonics approaches simplify the problem of blending and pronunciation by teaching the sounds as units rather than isolated pronunciation. In the following case, for example, the sound *b* will be taught in the initial position as it relates to the various vowels: *ba, be, bi, bo, bu.* This then is immediately substituted in word-building exercises.:

bad   *beg*   *bit*   *boss*   *but*

Inability to Use Sound-Symbol Relationships during Reading. Sometimes a student knows sound-symbol relationships but seems unable to use this knowledge during reading. This common difficulty often leads to isolated skill practice; however, the emphasis should be on application of learned skills in contextual reading.

One cause of this difficulty may be that students have learned many phonics subskills and are confused about which ones to use. Of course, different skills should be used in different situations. For example, rhyming elements are useful when they are recognized. When they are not, attention to the initial sound may be most helpful. If phonics instruction is taught with techniques for use, then application may occur. For example, the *Speech-to-Print* program does this. Once the sound-symbol relationship is learned the students are asked to use their new skill in a substitution activity that focuses on the use of context as well as the new phonics skill.

Another cause of this difficulty is that many students learn far too many phonics subskills. Lesson after lesson on the many variations of the vowel sound-symbol relationships can lead to confusion. Smith states that there are far too many rules for the vowel sound-symbol relationships for most young students to master.[10] In one count he came up with 106 vowel rules. Excessive instruction in subskills can lead to a distorted view of reading and a confused reader.

Still another cause may be that initial failure with phonics instruction has created a lack of risk taking while reading. Botel suggests that sound-symbol relationships be taught through the syllable approach.[11] It is easier to learn and blend and it is closer to meaning. This approach involves teaching high-frequency syllables (*-at/-ate, -an/-ane, -ad/ade,* etc.). He lists all possible combinations.[12] Then the reader substitutes initial consonants and consonant blends to develop a word-attack system.

Structural Clues

Deficiencies in the ability to attack compound words are generally not too serious because students can easily be taught to pronounce words if they know the parts. If they do not know the parts, they probably have an inadequate sight vocabulary. Although prefixes cause more difficulty than compounds words, the fact that they are at the beginning of the word, usually a separate, easily pronounceable syllable, and concerned with a meaning that directly alters the base word makes them easier to learn and causes less difficulty in remedial reading. However, in the case of suffixes, where these three factors are often missing, many students experience difficulty. It is with suffixes that the service of the base word is most likely to change, even though a precise difference in meaning is not evident. Note in the following words that when the suffix is removed the base word's spelling and configuration is distorted, causing an additional complication in the study of suffixes:

run	*running*	*runn-ing*
hope	*hoping*	*hop-ing*

The discovery technique is again suggested for its advantage is making students generalize structural patterns from known words.[13] This technique is equally applicable to difficulties with prefixes, suffixes, or compound words. In teaching decoding and interpretations of the prefix *un,* for example, it may be best to follow a procedure similar to this:

1. Present the word *happy* in a sentence such as *John is happy.*
2. Change the word to *unhappy: John is unhappy.*
3. Have the students discuss the difference in meaning.
4. Present several other words in similar manner.
5. Have the students generalize by answering the question, "What does *un* generally do to the meaning of a word to which it is prefixed?"
6. Collect word patterns of this type and see if they apply to the generalization.
7. Note that *un* has a sound that is consistent and that it changes the meaning of the words to which it is attached.
8. As the students read, their attention should be directed to words prefixed with *un.* They should determine if these words fit the generalization.

Word wheels that contain the base word can be made easily: as students move the wheel, they add either a prefix or a suffix to the base word. Suggestions for these can be found in Russell and Karp's *Reading Aids through the Grades.*[14] The teacher is cautioned in the construction of such reinforcement devices to be certain that the students know the base word and to be alert to the spelling changes that occur when the suffix is added. Prepared exercises of this type are found in materials such as the *Classroom Reading Clinic.* In this kit, word wheels on which base words are altered by prefixes and suffixes provide ready-made reinforcement exercises.

Practice. Practice activities for structural skills do not differ from those that follow phonics instruction. Games, learning centers, tutoring, and practice sheets are appropriate here also. For older students *Tactics in Reading* and *Basic Reading Skills* provide mature activities for practice.

Using Learned Skills. The reading time provided at the end of practice sessions is important for the students to develop the understanding that all of these activities have one purpose—to make reading a more enjoyable and successful experience.

Context Clues

Authors provide context clues by redundancy in their writing and through deliberate attempts to help the reader. Readers pick up on those clues through the use of their knowledge of syntax, semantics, and pronunciation. Just how does a reader gain these skills for use in reading? Probably the best way is to read a great deal and read all types of material (fiction, content, newspapers, poetry, and magazines). Obviously seriously handicapped readers find this difficult because very little material is suitable for them to read for practice. Teachers should examine students' reading to determine if they ignore syntactic, semantic, and punctuation cues to uncover whether they have problems with context clues.

Ignoring Syntactic Cues. Students who make substitutions but use the correct part of speech in the substitution are telling their teachers that they understand the language but cannot read the exact word. Those who substitute the incorrect part of speech are telling their teachers the material is so strange to them that they cannot make use of their language knowledge. The teachers' very first task is to make adjustments in material to determine if the students continue to misuse syntactic cues on easier material or material that is of higher interest to them. If adjustment of materials eliminates the problem, practice in reading should be provided in that type of material.

If students continue to substitute incorrect parts of speech, direct instruction in simple closure activities is appropriate. Students may be asked to discuss which word may fit in this blank:

Mary has a ______ baseball bat.

Answers such as *new, big, large, small, green, yellow,* and *nice* can be accepted. Teachers and students should discuss why they fit; then other parts of speech can be eliminated, and the practice can continue. Students enjoy this open-ended type of response and can quickly become aware of the syntactic cues that our language offers.

Ignoring Semantic Cues. If students substitute words in reading that do not distort meaning, they are on their way to being successful readers. However, if they distort meaning with their substitutions, they are missing the ideas of the author. Teachers must first adjust the materials to see if easier materials and materials of more interest can correct the errors. Such adjustments almost always work. If the concepts or technical vocabulary are too complex for students, they stand little chance of using context effectively. Smith talks of readers using prediction as a technique to develop awareness of meaning.[15] For example, teachers read these sentences to the students:

> The team had their high scorer under the basket. The score was 96–94 with three seconds left. Jim thought, "Wow, what a *(blank)* game!"

Then ask, "What words would fit in the blank and what words would be wrong? Why?"

The same types of activities can be used in silent reading. Let groups of students work together to determine which word can be used and why. Authors provide semantic cues in all types of reading.

Some commercial materials may assist the teacher in providing many experiences of this type. *Using the Context* provides numerous activities at various grade levels.

For mature readers teachers can use newspaper articles and words that can be supplied. Students are excited about such adultlike reading and quickly understand how the use of context clues is more than a guessing game.

Ignoring Punctuation Cues. Punctuation errors are often due to the frustration level of the material rather than failure to observe punctuation. Therefore, specific attention to punctuation marks in reading will be useless. Time will be spent more wisely on other skill areas with materials of the proper level. However, if the error is due to lack of knowledge about the use of punctuation marks, instruction in needed.

Choral reading is an effective, subtle way for students to obtain a feeling for the function of punctuation marks. Following group oral reading, the students' attention should be called to the fact that punctuation marks have different functions and call for different inflections. Listening to good oral reading on a tape recorder will make readers aware of the need to observe punctuation marks in their reading materials.

Opportunities for students to follow the teacher's reading to observe effects of punctuation also may prove helpful. Intentionally distorting the punctuation, the teacher can ask students to explain what happens to the author's ideas. When used sparingly, this technique works well with those having trouble hearing their own punctuation errors.

When readers have difficulty using punctuation it is almost always because the materials are too strange or too difficult. Teachers should make certain that practice activities always involve appropriate materials that reduce frustration.

Use of Dictionaries

Dictionary skills are indispensable for word attack. Students with reading problems may benefit from dictionary instruction. Work in programming has produced two publications that may be of use in remediation, *Lessons for Self-Instruction in Basic Skills* and *David Discovers the Dictionary*. These programs have an individualized approach requiring minimum teacher supervision for the student to acquire the skills necessary to use the dictionary.

Teachers should provide a dictionary for every reader. When word-attack problems occur, students should use the dictionaries. The skills needed are quickly formed and lead the readers to independent dictionary use. Of course dictionaries require the use of alphabetizing skills and locating skills, but these can easily be taught and readers can gain self-esteem from the independence that results.

PUTTING IT ALL TOGETHER

As discussed in the phonics section of this chapter, some students seem to know their subskills but have difficulty using them. More instruction with subskills is obviously not the answer; other explanations must be found.

One possible explanation is that instruction was not followed by opportunities for the use of the newly learned skill. Through disuse, the skill gradually becomes weakened and eventually lost. Each lesson must be followed by reading practice, and in some cases it may be well for that practice to be monitored by the teacher so that the transfer of the skill to reading can be verified.

Another explanation may be that the students have received conflicting advice about how to use their new skills. One teacher may suggest starting with the initial consonant, another may suggest using a dictionary, and parents may tell them to spell the unknown word. While many readers withstand such conflicting advice, the handicapped reader can become thoroughly confused.

Teachers should help students establish a minimal strategy for attacking unknown words. All teachers working with the students agree to the strategy and use it consistently with them. Parents and librarians are also informed of it and use it. In this way, the student is seeing that what is learned in reading classes is carried over in other areas of school and even at home. The strategy that any group of teachers would develop should relate to what they stress during instruction. The following is an example of such a strategy:

> When you come to a word you do not know, use this technique.
>
> 1. Read on and look for clues.
> 2. Frame the word.
> 3. Try the first sound.
> 4. Divide the word into smaller parts.
> 5. Consult the dictionary or resource person.

Here the students are asked to use context clues first, configuration clues second, phonics third, syllabication fourth, and then either use a dictionary or ask someone for help. Teachers should then teach each of these strategies. Students have cards they can refer to with the strategies written on them. They can use these for bookmarks. Teachers post the strategies in each room and the media center, send a copy home, and emphasize the strategy in every lesson. In this way, the students get the idea that what they have worked so hard to learn has application for reading.

Using a minimal strategy does not limit those students who have more skills that they can use. It simply gets the readers started on the road to independent reading using word-attack skills.

Motivation

By far the strongest motivation to students for studying word-attack skills is being able to see how this knowledge enables them to become more independent readers. It is essential, therefore, for students to be put in the situation of transferring learned skills to context in every lesson if possible. Game-type activities, as suggested, make reinforcement of these skills more informal and pleasurable.

The discovery technique has motivational appeal, especially to some of the older students who need work in word attack.

Generalizing the concepts of word attack with a minimum of teacher supervision usually becomes a highly motivating situation.

Graphic illustrations of progress usually help motivate students. Teacher-made materials designed to illustrate established goals and the students' achievement within their scope and capabilities are effective motivating devices too.

Programmed materials with immediate feedback contain inherent motivational appeal. These materials, designed to reinforce, correct, and alter incorrect responses, establish situations in which the reader eventually will be successsful—a desirable outcome in all types of remedial programs (see figures 8–4 and 8–5).

SUMMARY

The remedial techniques used in the area of vocabulary deficiencies, whether sight vocabulary or word attack, are based on diagnostic findings. Once these deficiencies are determined, educators have a variety of remediation approaches from which to choose. Starting with those that they believe will serve most adequately, educators remain alert during instruction to the possibility that the original approach may need to be modified as instruction continues.

Constant awareness of the value of incorporating skill activities into contextual situations is the responsibility of both the teacher and the reading specialist. Continued drill, without well-developed transfer opportunities, is of little value.

NOTES

1. Morton Botel, *Forming and Re-Forming the Reading/Language Arts Curriculum* (Washington, D.C.: Curriculum Development Associates, 1975).
2. Arthur W. Heilman, *Smuggling Language into the Teaching of Reading*, 2d. ed. (Columbus, OH: Charles E. Merrill, 1978).
3. Edgar Dale and Joseph O'Rourke, *Techniques of Teaching Vocabularies* (Palo Alto, Calif: Field Educational Publications, 1971).
4. Joanne Greenberg, McCay, Vernon, Jan Hafer DuBois, and Jan C. Knight, *The Language Arts Handbook* (Baltimore: University Park Press, 1982).
5. Harry Bornstein, Karen L. Saulnier, and Lillian B. Hamilton, *The Comprehensive Signed English Dictionary* (Washington D.C.: Gallaudet College Press, 1983).
6. Marie Clay, *Reading: The Patterning of Complex Behaviour.* (London: Heinemann Educational Books, 1972), chapter 6.

Student Record Sheet

THE NFL READING KIT from BOWMAR

D = Details M = Main idea G = Generalization F/O = Fact/Opinion
C = Context clues S = Sequence I = Inference

CARD No.	QUESTION NUMBER 1	2	3	4	5	6	7	8	9	10
1. The Man Who Surprised the Cardinals	D	D	D	C	M					
2. The Great O. J. Simpson	D	D	D	C	M					
3. The Quiet Winner	D	D	D	C	M					
4. George Who?	D	D	D	C	M					
5. Superstar Who Never Played Pro Football	D	D	D	C	M					
6. The Man Who Painted the Helmet	D	D	D	C	M					
7. The Man Called Bronko	D	D	D	C	M					
8. The Greatest Pass Catcher	D	D	D	C	M					
9. The Growth of Pro Football	D	D	D	C	M					
10. The Men in the Striped Shirts	D	D	D	C	M					
11. The Player Who Followed His Father	D	D	D	C	M	S				
12. The Player Who Went for the Top	D	D	D	C	M	S				
13. The Runner Who Became a Receiver	D	D	D	C	M	S				
14. Frank Gifford: Announcer and Player	D	D	D	C	M	S				
15. Roger Staubach: Still a Winner	D	D	D	C	M	S				
16. Joe Namath in Super Bowl III	D	D	D	C	M	S				
17. The President Who Helped Save Football	D	D	D	C	M	S				
18. The Great Passer	D	D	D	C	M	S				
19. The Grand Old Man of Football	D	D	D	C	M	S				
20. The Quarterback Who Was Not Too Old	D	D	D	C	M	S				
21. The Player Who Showed He Belonged	D	D	D	C	M	S	G			
22. The Scrambling Quarterback	D	D	D	C	M	S	G			
23. The Player No One Wanted	D	D	D	C	M	S	G			
24. Coach Who Built Something Out of Nothing	D	D	D	C	M	S	G			
25. The Last-Minute Victory	D	D	D	C	M	S	G			

Teacher Record Sheet

Teacher's name ______________________

School ______________________

STUDENT/STARTING LEVEL	SKILL/DATE MASTERED	Details	Context Clues	Main Idea	Sequence	Generalization	Inference	Fact/Opinion

FIGURE 8–4
Student and teacher record sheets from the *NFL Reading Kit* teacher's guide. (Copyright © 1977 by Bowmar/Noble Publishers, Inc. Reproduced by permission; all rights reserved.)

Comprehension Check

The Man Who Surprised the Cardinals

REMEMBERING DETAILS

1. Terry Metcalf was ___C___ tall.
   a. 6 feet 2 inches
   b. 5 feet 6 inches
   c. 5 feet 10 inches
   d. 7 feet

2. In Terry's first year he went over ___b___ yards on offense.
   a. 2,000
   b. 1,000
   c. 2,058
   d. 500

3. The man from the Cardinals had seen Terry play ___d___.
   a. in high school
   b. for the Chicago Bears
   c. in a baseball game
   d. in college

USING CONTEXT CLUES TO GET WORD MEANINGS

4. "He even got 23 yards when he picked up a loose ball." In this sentence, *loose ball* means ___b___.
   a. ball that fell apart
   b. ball that had been dropped
   c. ball that he found at home
   d. ball with the players' names on it

FINDING THE MAIN IDEA

5. The main idea of this story is that ___C___.
   a. the Cardinals made their players work hard
   b. Terry Metcalf was a poor runner
   c. Terry Metcalf turned out to be a fine player
   d. Terry Metcalf was not strong

SPECIAL WORD MEANINGS

college: a school that people can go to after high school, usually for four years

defense: the players on a football team who are on the field when the other team has the ball

pro: a person who gets paid for doing something (in this case, for playing football); pro is short for professional

offense: the players on a football team who are on the field when their own team has the ball

NFL: the National Football League, a group of teams that play each other in pro football

Comprehension Check

The Great O. J. Simpson

REMEMBERING DETAILS

1. O.J. Simpson talked to Jim Brown at ___b___.
   a. a football game
   b. an ice cream store
   c. a park
   d. a baseball game

2. O.J. broke Jim Brown's record in ___d___.
   a. 1961
   b. 1963
   c. 1971
   d. 1973

3. When O. J. broke the record, the officials stopped the game ___a___.
   a. for a moment
   b. for 30 minutes
   c. for 45 minutes
   d. for an hour

USING CONTEXT CLUES TO GET WORD MEANINGS

4. "In 10 years no one had come close to that mark." In this sentence, *mark* means ___b___.
   a. write
   b. record
   c. time
   d. football

FINDING THE MAIN IDEA

5. Another good title for this story would be ___d___.
   a. Jim Brown Loves Ice Cream
   b. The Long Season
   c. O.J. and the Frozen Field
   d. The 2,003-Yard Season of O.J. Simpson

SPECIAL WORD MEANINGS

rush: to run with the football and try to gain yards

officials: the people on the field who make sure that players follow the rules and play fairly

quarterback: the player who stands behind the offensive line and starts each play by taking the ball from the center

snap: the pass from the center to the quarterback

index finger: the finger next to the thumb

FIGURE 8–5
Sample cards from the *NFL Reading Kit* teacher's guide. (Copyright © 1977 by Bowmar/Noble Publisher's, Inc. Reproduced by permission; all rights reserved.)

7. Arthur W. Heilman, *Phonics in Proper Perspective,* 4th ed. (Columbus, OH: Charles E. Merrill, 1981), 22.
8. Morton Botel, *How to Teach Reading* (Chicago: Follett Publishing Co., 1968), 64.
9. Grace Fernald, *Remedial Techniques in Basic School Subjects* (New York: McGraw-Hill Book Co., 1943), Part II.
10. Frank Smith, *Understanding Reading* (New York: Holt, Rinehart & Winston, 1978), 140.
11. Morton Botel, *Forming and Re-forming the Reading/Language Arts Curriculum* (Washington, D.C.: Curriculum Development Associates, 1975).
12. Ibid., 36–42.
13. Botel, *How to Teach Reading,* 40.
14. David H. Russell and Etta E. Karp, *Reading Aids through the Grades* (New York: Columbia University Press, 1951).
15. Frank Smith, "The Role of Prediction in Reading," *Elementary English* 52, no. 3 (March 1975): 305–11.

SUGGESTED READINGS

Botel, Morton, *How to Teach Reading.* Chicago: Follett Publishing Co., 1968. In chapters 3 and 5 of this well-written book, Botel presents the "discovery" and "spelling" mastery techniques for use in sight vocabulary and word-attack lessons. The teacher will find this a practical guide to developmental and remedial activities.

Burmeister, Lou E. "Usefulness of Phonic Generalizations," *The Reading Teacher* 21 (1968): 349–59. This article reviews the research on phonics generalizations. Reading this review is essential prior to work with children in a program that concentrates on the use of phonics.

Clymer, Theodore. "The Utility of Phonics Generalizations in the Primary Grades," *The Reading Teacher* 17 (1963): 252–58. This article discusses how functional the generalizations commonly taught to children are in terms of the number of times the generalizations hold true and the number of words to which they apply.

Coley, Joan, and Gambrell, Linda. *Programmed Reading Vocabulary for Teachers.* Columbus, OH: Charles E. Merrill Publishing Co., 1977. This book presents the basic knowledge a teacher must have to work with students in the area of sight vocabulary. The material is presented in programmed format.

Forte, Imogene; Pangle, Mary Ann; and Tupa, Robbie. *Center Stuff.* Nashville, Tenn: Incentive Publication, 1973. A useful collection of ideas for developing learning centers on many topics.

Fries, Charles C. *Linguistics and Reading.* New York: Holt, Rinehart and Winston, 1963. One explanation for the linguistic involvement in teaching reading can be found in this book. For those who have difficulty understanding the linguist, this book is a good introduction. Teachers of handicapped readers must acquaint themselves with the works of the linguists.

Greenberg, Joanne; Vernon, McCay; Dubois, Jan Hafer; and Knight, Jan C. *The Language Arts Handbook.* Baltimore: University Park Press, 1982. Presents a case for the use of finger spelling and signing as reinforcers in language arts instruction. Includes many specific lesson suggestions.

Hall, Mary Anne. *Teaching Reading as a Language Experience.* 3d ed. Columbus, OH: Charles E. Merrill Publishing Co., 1981. This book presents basic information for teachers concerning the nature and uses of language experience as an approach to reading instruction.

Heilman, Arthur W. *Phonics in Proper Perspective.* 4th ed. Columbus, OH: Charles E. Merrill Publishing Co., 1981. Heilman has combined an assessment of the place of phonics with a survey of the skills to be taught; he has also included examples and appropriate words lists. The educator who works with handicapped readers will find this book indispensable in working with phonics.

Lee, Dorris M., and Allen, R. V. *Learning to Read through Experience.* New York: Appleton-Century-Crofts, 1963. A combination of philosophy and techniques, this book is a must for those who plan to work with seriously handicapped children. As indicated, this approach will be of particular value with many children, and the book will provide the educator with a thorough background from which to work.

Stauffer, Russell. *The Language-Experience Approach to the Teaching of Reading.* New York: Harper & Row, 1970. Chapters 1, 2 and 3 discuss the theory and uses of language-experience approaches. Chapter 10 discusses special uses of language experience, including clinical cases.

Waynant, Louise R., and Wilson, Robert M. *Learning Centers . . . A Guide to Effective Use.* Paoli, Pa.: Instructo, 1974. Provides numerous ideas about the construction and use of learning centers. Those who want to use learning centers in remedial programs will find this book useful.

Wilson, Robert M., and Hall, MaryAnne. *Programmed Word Attack for Teachers.* 4th ed. Columbus, OH: Charles E. Merrill Publishing Co., 1984. This book presents basic knowledge about word attack needed by teachers for instruction. The material is presented in a programmed format followed by tests that enable teachers to demonstrate their knowledge of word-attack skills.

Editorial

Mary Jo Comer
is a vice-principal for the St. Mary's County Schools in Maryland.

Most handicapped readers avoid reading and have developed skills of avoidance much as other students have developed skills in reading. These avoidance skills have become strengths for these students and must be approached and used as such.

In an Improve Your Reading Club in high school, I found that these very handicapped readers could consistently beat top students (and their teachers!) at a nonreading game, checkers. Many of these same students also had a great need—to be able to read the Driver's Education manual and apply its contents.

My concern was not just that they be able to pass the driver's test, but that they become good, safe, knowledgeable drivers.

Analyzing the task, I recognized that there were three areas where reading skills were involved: vocabulary, symbol recognition, and theory application. Once these areas were identified it became a simple matter to put on index cards words, symbols, or situations in the form of questions. Over seventy-five cards were compiled, each asking for a specific bit of information. These cards contained questions such as these:

What is a pedestrian? (vocabulary)

What does a sign of this shape mean? (symbol identification)

What would be the best speed for driving on a rainy night on a road with this sign? (theory application)

The final task was to "marry" the strength to the need. Since checkers playing was an obvious strength and overlearning of material the goal, the obvious course was to incorporate the driver's education cards into a checkers format. The simplest solution was best; students could play checkers as much as they wished; but, before taking a turn, they had to draw an index card and answer the question correctly. I did prepare an answer booklet so that disputes could be solved by the players independently; since they'd go through all the cards at least once in an average game, it wasn't needed for long.

The goal of overlearning was achieved by simple repetition; boredom did not become a factor. Checkers are meant to be played fast, so the students became very adept at responding rapidly with the correct answer. And, of course, becoming knowledgeable in a subject which was important to them was very motivational.

Since an error in answering a question led to forfeiture of a turn, the students stayed alert and on-task while playing, hoping that their opponent would make a mistake. These cut-throat checkers players were so evenly matched in that skill that often the outcome of a game depended on who made an error on the driver's manual questions.

Plan Ahead
Organize Materials
Choose a Quiet Spot
Highlight the Main Idea
Concentrate
Communication-the exchange of

9 Comprehension Development

CHAPTER OUTLINE

ABOUT COMPREHENSION
INSTRUCTIONAL APPROACHES
INSTRUCTIONAL STRATEGIES
SPECIFIC REMEDIAL COMPREHENSION ACTIVITIES
EXTENDED REMEDIATION
REMEDIATION FOR THE CULTURALLY DIFFERENT

CHAPTER EMPHASES

- ☐ Comprehension should be taught as a personal process.
- ☐ Instructional approaches should reflect what teachers know about comprehension.
- ☐ Instructional strategies can be used with any approach.
- ☐ Materials for instruction should be interesting and relevant.

Note: All materials mentioned in this chapter are listed in appendix B, with characteristics specified.

To understand reading comprehension, it may be useful to start with a discussion of the skills needed for successful comprehension. The area of reading comprehension, however, is highly complex and a simple discussion of a set of selected subskills will not suffice. This chapter discusses some of the aspects of comprehension that teachers must understand in order to provide effective instruction. This discussion will be followed by a set of instructional approaches and some specific instructional strategies. Then each question raised in diagnosis will be treated with instructional suggestions.

ABOUT COMPREHENSION

Comprehension is so complex that very little is known about how each student processes information. In recent years many scholars have developed theories about how the process seems to work and researchers are now busy attempting to evaluate those theories. The following points about comprehension seem reasonable and have implications for instruction.

Comprehension Is Personal. Smith focuses on the personal nature of reading comprehension.[1] What the reader understands from reading a passage is related to the knowledge the reader brings to the passage. Prior knowledge on the assassination of President John F. Kennedy will have a large effect on how accurately a reader can process a passage on that subject.

Comprehension Requires Predicting. Students participate in comprehension through the active process of predicting. They must anticipate what is coming and then check to see if their predictions are correct. Risk taking is obviously involved in predicting. Frequent inaccurate predictions make the process risky. This, in part, explains why people enjoy reading about matter in which they have considerable prior information and shy away from matter in which they are not knowledgeable. Prior knowledge helps them make accurate predictions so less risk is involved in the activity.

Comprehension Must Be Practiced. Allington suggests that students need to read a lot to develop successful comprehension.[2] However, data indicate that readers experiencing difficulty in reading often have less time to practice reading, spending more time in skill-development activities.[3]

Comprehension Involves More than Answering Questions. Durkin reports that most classroom teachers stress comprehension assessment activities, such as question asking, to a greater extent than instructional activities.[4] Students do not learn during question-asking sessions—they either know or do not know the answers. Questioning strategies should be used to facilitate understanding in areas other than comprehension assessment.

Comprehension Needs Organization. Teachers should construct lessons so that students build on their previous knowledge. If students are expected to respond just to questions or to unrelated bits of information, comprehension will be negatively affected. Organizing information shows students how knowledge they already have filed away can be associated with new concepts to develop more accurate schemata about a subject. As students increase their understanding in this manner, reading becomes more meaningful.

Comprehension Requires Attention to Task. If readers are inattentive, comprehension becomes impossible. Boredom, difficult material, incorrect student expectations, and distractions can take students off task, creating a setting inconducive to comprehension. Everyone remembers reading a page only to realize that they haven't absorbed its content; they were thinking about something else when they should have been concentrating on what they were reading. In such cases, no comprehension takes place. Thus, classroom teachers should be sensitive to signs that a student's mind is wandering so that this problem can be quickly corrected.

Comprehension Involves Product and Process. The student's comprehension products may fail to provide us with useful insights into the processes that they used to produce them. Therefore, the comprehension process cannot be evaluated solely by examining products. For example, fluent, accurate oral reading does not necessarily indicate good comprehension, nor does answering all of a teacher's questions. While these types of products are encouraging indicators that comprehension has occurred, they do not give us full information about the readers' processes.

INSTRUCTIONAL APPROACHES

The selection of instructional approaches should reflect the information about reading comprehension just discussed. Instructional approaches that seem to fit this knowledge include the directed reading-thinking activity, the problem approach, the language-experience approach, and nonquestioning approaches.

The Directed Reading-Thinking Activity (D-R-T-A)

Stauffer has developed an instructional strategy that focuses on the teacher's role in directing reading as a thinking activity.[5] This strategy can be used with a large group of students or can be adapted to individualized instruction. The steps include the following:

1. Identify purposes for reading.
2. Guide students in adjusting reading rates with different purposes and materials.
3. Observe reading.
4. Develop comprehension.
5. Provide fundamental skill training activities.[6]

Stauffer's D-R-T-A emphasizes the student's place in the learning process. His rationale includes a list of assumptions about what students can do. The student is personally involved in each step of the lesson; the teacher is seen as a member of the group, not as the authoritarian figure. For example, in identifying purposes, the students are taught to make observations about the materials, set their purposes, then read to satisfy those purposes. The teacher is on hand to guide and assist, but not to dominate. When the students' purposes do not fit the information in the passages they are reading, the teacher helps them reset their purposes using what they have already read.

This approach is personal and draws on the prior knowledge of the students. It involves the act of reading and encourages attention to task. The students are continuously organizing and reorganizing new information so that it fits with their prior knowledge. Prediction and hypothesis setting take the place of direct teacher questions.

The Problem Approach

By making students responsible for the direction of their learning, the problem approach encourages student task-oriented behavior. Brigham lists the following essential steps to this approach.[7]

1. Ask students what they would most like to learn about. Then record responses on a chalkboard in the students' language. (Use silence and an expectant attitude to stimulate responses; try for at least one idea from each student.)
2. Ask students which ideas seem to go together, which ones include others, and which are different from the

rest. Record gradual organization processes of the group, while developing sets of general topics and individual questions.

3. Ask students what they wish to learn about first, second, etc., and the reasons for their choices. Take votes on their preferences and priorities.
4. Ask students if they have additional questions about their first choice topic, thereby breaking the main topic into several subtopics.
5. Copy the master plan from the board and have it typed and run off. Use this material for reading the next day. Ask questions such as "Is this what you decided to do?" "Is this the best way to do it?" "Are there ways in which you may wish to change it?" "How might these ideas be stated more clearly?"
6. Assign a committee of three to five students to explore each subtopic.
7. Have each committee elect a chairperson, a recorder, and perhaps a spokesperson for liaison with the rest of the class and the instructor. These positions may be rotated.
8. Chairpersons lead committees in developing resource plans. Questions are arranged in logical sequence. New questions are elicited and placed in sequence. Committees develop lists of resources to consult. Questions are assigned so that each student is responsible for exploring one or more questions individually, and perhaps one question with help from other students.
9. Each committee should have its own planning-record folder with copies of each item for each member. At the beginning of each meeting, work is reviewed by going over the notes of the preceding meeting. These notes have been taken by the recorders, typed exactly as they were written, and duplicated by the teacher. Included are the purposes, accomplishments, evaluation of the meeting, and any remaining questions.
10. Resource lists are expanded and resources tapped. Often this will require skills in letter writing, telephoning techniques, interview methods, and field trip planning.
11. Each committee decides what data it will use and in what form. Eventually it must decide on a format for presenting its findings to the class. This format may consist of a mock television news report, a videotape

production, a model or construction project, a role playing skit, or a slide and audiotape project. After a format is selected, the presentation is given.

12. The whole class evaluates each presentation after it is given, using these questions:
    - ☐ What have we learned?
    - ☐ Was it worth learning? Why?
    - ☐ How might we use what we learned?
    - ☐ What additional questions do we have?
    - ☐ What was the best thing about the way the ideas were presented?

These steps demonstrate to students the interdependence of purpose, planning, oral and written language communication, thinking, doing, and evaluation. All planning steps are recorded, as are all activity steps. Gradually, planning and implementation are integrated toward student-meaningful outcomes.

At each stage, thinking-language-organizational skills are developed *as* (and *only* as) students evidence a specific need for them. Skills are not developed at the instructor's convenience, but only as obvious student readiness occurs.

In all of these steps, students are asked to use and develop a wide range of thinking-language skills in an oral situation as a basis for their application in reading and writing activities. They are required to be active, responsible participants in the instructional situation.

With the problem approach the student is involved in a personal discovery of meaning. The student is the discussion maker, active learner, and organizer of information. The teacher serves as a resource for the students.

The Language-Experience Approach

The language-experience approach may be the most effective method of dealing with students with comprehension difficulties. After sharing a common experience (field trip, film strip, science experiment, etc.), the students develop a story that the teacher records. Comprehension of meaning is assured since the story is in students' words and concerns a recent experience. Stories can be collected and saved for future reading and comprehension skill extension. Some skill extension activities may include the following:

1. Developing suitable titles for the story.
2. Discussing the feelings of various persons in the story.

3. Adding a creative ending to the story.
4. Changing part of the story to alter the outcomes.
5. Checking to determine if the events as given by the students are in sequential order in terms of what actually happened.

As with the D-R-T-A and the problem approach, the language-experience approach is a personal approach to comprehension. It directly involves the students' prior knowledge and provides resource materials for successful reading practice.

Nonquestioning Approaches

The following approaches rely on instructional techniques other than teacher questioning to aid students with comprehension difficulties.

Communication with the Author. Students can write to the author of a story to obtain information such as why he or she wrote the book, what research was done to write the book, or details about his or her life.

Add or Change Endings. Stories may have surprise or expected endings. Students can write or dictate new endings and have fun sharing them.

Discussion or Debate. Controversial issues in a story or book can be discussed or debated. Students can attempt to determine the validity of a given action based on their prior knowledge or their research of the topic involved.

Communication with a Story Character. Various students can take the part of the story's characters. Other students can interview them, write them letters, question their activities in the story, or ask them to act out their part. These and other nonquestioning activities facilitate comprehension development without questioning. The students respond in a personal manner through a variety of organizational strategies. The teacher or reading specialist can pick one approach and follow it or combine approaches. This decision will probably be based on the student's age and interest, comfort with a given approach, and the materials available for instruction.

INSTRUCTIONAL STRATEGIES

Teachers may select from various instructional strategies when using each of the approaches discussed. These may be used with any approach, used some days and not others, and used with some students and not others. These should be used to help provide variety in instructional lessons.

Developing a Setting for Questioning

Students answer questions in two situations. One is a recall situation in which the reading materials are not available to the students. The other is a locate situation in which students can use the reading materials to locate answers to questions. Many regular classroom activities have stressed the recall situation, which involves not only reading comprehension, but also memory abilities.

However, remedial lessons should focus on locating skills. Students need to be allowed to use the reading material either to find or verify their answers. Students can answer about 30 percent more questions when locating than when recalling. Since remedial lessons should focus on strengths, locating is desirable. Students have probably read the materials if they can locate the answers. By stressing locating instead of recalling, students are encouraged to learn how to use reading materials. They begin to see books as resource materials that can be reexamined, and consequently develop mature reading skills.

Most people maintain some type of professional or personal library in their homes because they enjoy the privilege of rereading something that was of interest or because they need to locate information that has slipped from memory. After reading an interesting story in a book or the newspaper, people do not want to be expected to remember details. Similarly, in the establishment of mental set, recalling demands that the student remember as much as possible during the questioning period; locating calls for the student to be able to use the reading material during questioning.

Adjusting Materials

Materials for instruction are usually chosen by the teacher. If the materials are too difficult or uninteresting they should be replaced. Instead of trying to force students through such materials, the teacher should be aware of ways to adjust the materials or get different ones. Many students who are experiencing difficulty in comprehension are working in materials so difficult that they cannot possibly achieve success. By expecting them to practice reading in difficult materials teachers create a situation in which poor reading skills are encouraged. Inaccurate, nonfluent reading can be learned and reinforced when materials are too difficult. In such situations attention to meaning becomes difficult because too much attention is given to figuring out words. Read-along books, wordless books, and high-interest, low-vocabulary books should be acquired for these students. (A materials section is included in appendix B. Teachers should become familiar with these and other materials so that selections can be made for various students. Other materials may need to be rewritten to reduce either concept load or vocabulary difficulty.)

Providing Wait Time

Rowe's work discussing wait time should be considered by all teachers, but particularly by those working with handicapped readers.[8] Rowe found that teachers tend to give very little wait time, that is, the time between asking a question and calling for an answer. One second was the average wait time. By training teachers to wait for three seconds or longer, Rowe found that student responses increased and were more complete.

Rowe also found that the amount of time between the student's answer to a question and the teacher's response to the answer was very short. When teachers waited after a student responded, the student tended to expand the first response, and other students tended to interact without teacher interruption. By providing wait time after asking questions and before responding to answers, students are allowed time to think and form their responses as well as to elaborate on them.

Most teachers find applying wait time in their classroom difficult. Many are so accustomed to constant discussion and rapid-fire question-and-answer sessions that silence seems unnatural. Yet effective use of wait time can be learned if practiced. Students should know that they will be given more time than usual to answer a question. Teachers should allow three to five seconds and then note the increased quantity and quality of student responses.

Using Task Analysis

Task analysis has special application to reading comprehension. It can lead teachers to make appropriate adjustments when students become overwhelmed in a comprehension lesson and are unable to respond. Teachers should determine what the students do and what seems to be the difficulty. They hypothesize several adjustments that might improve the learning situation and check out each one through diagnostic teaching; then they alter their instructional plan.

Task analysis has been most useful when severe comprehension problems are encountered. The following example illustrates this.

Problem

Warren cannot recall literal details when reading in text material at an eighth-grade readability level.

Strengths

Warren can read orally with relative accuracy at eighth-grade level (IRI).

Warren can respond to about 20 percent of literal questions at eighth-grade level after silent reading (IRI).

Warren can respond to 90 percent of literal questions at sixth-grade level (IRI).

Warren appears to try hard to comprehend what he reads.

Hypotheses

Warren will:

H1. Respond if material is more interesting.
H2. Respond if permitted to locate the answers to literal questions at eighth-grade level.
H3. Respond if passages are shorter.
H4. Respond if made aware of purposes for reading.

Hypothesis Testing

H1. Obtain materials at the eighth-grade level with a variety of interests, let Warren select one to read, then check comprehension.
H2. Pick a passage that Warren can read aloud accurately and ask literal questions in a locate situation.
H3. Divide a passage into three parts, asking questions between each part.
H4. Prior to reading, discuss the purposes for reading with Warren.

Results

Hypothesis testing indicates that Warren responds successfully to situations 1 and 2, but that 3 and 4 seem to make no difference. An instructional plan is then drafted.

Instructional Plan

Instruction is adjusted by either allowing for self-selection or by encouraging the locating of answers, or both. If Warren responds successfully over time, then task analysis was useful in this setting. If he continues to have difficulties, the task analysis is repeated and new hypotheses developed.

Using Pupil Questions

When using questioning strategies teachers often do all of the work. They decide what is important, form a question, and make sure they have an answer. By using student questions, teachers involve students in those unimportant steps. Students come to the comprehension session prepared to ask, not answer, questions. They can ask questions of the teacher or other students. They should be able to justify their answers and locate them in the passage from which the questions are derived.

Students in the question-asking role increase their attentiveness and enthusiasm, while demonstrating that they comprehend the passage.

Interestingly, students tend to ask the types of questions that they hear from their teachers. And they tend to respond to the answers to their questions in the same manner in which their teachers respond when they ask questions. If a teacher does not like the type of question students are asking, his or her question-asking and answer-responding techniques should be reevaluated.

Developing Personal Outlines

Outlining is an effective way to organize a passage's important material. All too often, however, outlining activities are another of those "right" or "wrong" experiences that are so frustrating to students who are already having difficulty being "right." Personal outlining for a reading-comprehension lesson could involve steps like the following. Start by eliciting from the students which ideas they think are important or interesting. Such a start on a comprehension lesson tends to create a thinking atmosphere instead of a testing one. The teacher is encouraged to accept all suggestions, noting them on the chalkboard. Some may be quite divergent from the message in the passage, but it is important to know what the various students gather as the important message. Each idea is recorded without comment. After several ideas have been suggested, the students are encouraged to pick the one they think is really most important. The opportunity to change one's mind is likely to enhance the thinking process.

Next, pairs of students who agree about the important idea are formed. Their task is then to go back through the passage to find support statements or proof for their idea. A format sheet such as the following should be provided:

1. (Important idea)
   a. (Support)
   b. (Support)
   c. (Support)

Personal outlining helps the students elicit which ideas they think are important or interesting.

This procedure can be repeated in long passages of several paragraphs where there may be several important ideas. Students can then discuss or otherwise share their efforts. Aside from giving students practice in the important skill of outlining, this approach has several advantages:

1. The locating of literal facts has a purpose—the purpose selected by the students.
2. Students learn to locate swiftly and accurately since the location is specified.
3. On-task behavior is promoted since students are working in areas of their choice.
4. Poor choices for what is important are clearly illustrated to students since they have difficulty finding support for them.
5. Students accustomed to this approach perform well in literal comprehension activities that may follow.

Throughout this activity students are encouraged to paraphrase instead of using the exact words of the author. Those reading above the second-grade level can work effectively in this manner and learn to direct themselves after four or five lessons.

Personal outlining combines the notion that reading comprehension should be personal and that it should result in some type of organization of the material.

The transfer of this type of comprehension activity to a system of report development is clear. Now the students go to the library seeking certain information for a report. They read the materials, decide what is most important, go back to the material and seek support for their important ideas. When they come back to their classroom they can read their report, talk about it, and write paragraphs about each important idea.

Developing Think-Links

Another organization instructional strategy involves the use of think-links.[9] After reading a story, the teacher asks the students to think about what they have read. The teacher then uses the following strategy:

1. The teacher has students write the name of a character in the story with some words about how the character may have felt during certain parts of the story, such as the following:

2. The teacher then asks students when Andy was happy in the story. Various students will identify happy events and the teacher will record them:

3. Step 2 is repeated using other feeling words:

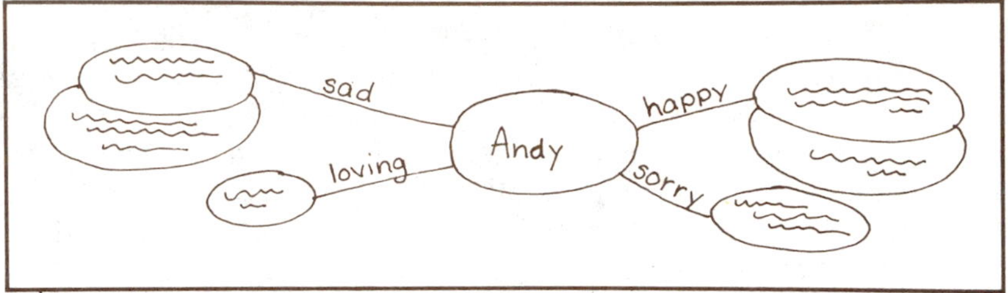

4. When all of the words have been used, the students see a reconstruction of the story they have read.

Think-links are not limited to character feelings. They may take any form and any content. For example, they could have a cause in the middle and events that relate to that cause on the outside. They could be used to summarize a science experiment or a geography unit. Once students have worked with their teacher developing several think-links, they can start to develop them independently.

Using Story Grammar Questions

Story grammar questioning helps students understand the organization of a story's basic elements. Instead of asking questions about unrelated story events, story grammar questions focus on text organization.[10] The questions help students realize the important organizational factors of the story: setting, initiating events, reaction, action, and consequences. Example questions might be:

- ☐ *Setting:* Where and when did this story take place?
- ☐ *Initiating events:* What caused the children to become startled?
- ☐ *Action:* What did the children do?
- ☐ *Reaction:* What did their parents do?
- ☐ *Consequences:* In what way were the children rewarded for their behavior?

The use of story grammar questions is an alternative to using questions which focus on mental processing. Instead, these questions focus on the story's major events and, as such, represent a holistic approach to story comprehension.[11]

Story grammar questions assist in the development of a schema for story structure. Using this schema while reading stories in the future can enhance comprehension.

Think-links allow students to actively think about what they have read.

Encouraging Retelling

This strategy involves retelling stories or portions of stories. Retelling is a personal reorganization of the parts of the story that made an impact on the students. One may ask students to retell parts of the story that were most interesting, parts that were most important, funny parts, or sad parts.

On short passages students may be encouraged to retell as much as they can. On long passages, chapters, or books, the retelling is usually centered on only part of the reading.

Retelling is open ended. The students do what they can do. Prompting can aid retelling. Such comments as "Who else was at the scene of the accident?" or "Why do you think she did that?" can help students recall the complete incident.

Retelling can be done in groups or on an individual basis. In groups, retelling has a sharing effect when each student retells his or her favorite part. Discussion can follow each retelling to make it more like a real-life sharing experience.

Encouraging Repeated Reading

Rereading passages can have positive effects on fluency and understanding. A history student will read and reread several times an account of a Civil War battle. Such rereading develops a permanent memory of the sequence of events. Educators are often reluctant to have students reread materials because they fear it will bore them. But, if the material is interesting and worth remembering, then rereading is not only advisable, it is essential. Repeated readings can be done orally or silently, depending on the purpose for the reading. Students often enjoy repeated readings and are proud to demonstrate their reading proficiencies to their teachers, parents, and peers.

Using Think Alouds

Think alouds offer students the opportunity to hear what a mature reader is thinking while reading. Davey details their process as follows.[12] As the teacher is reading a difficult passage aloud he or she thinks aloud about the strategies to be used in the difficult parts. For example, the teacher reads the title and makes a prediction or describes a picture made in the mind concerning an event. By modeling reading strategies, students see the thought processes involved and will do the same.

Mid-Chapter Summary

Four approaches have been detailed that can be used individually or in combination, each of which reflects what we know about comprehension. Then eleven instructional strategies were suggested for use with any of the approaches. Interest is sometimes maintained when a strategy is used for awhile, then set aside for the use of another, then used again. Each has its strengths and limitations, so it is not recommended that an entire remedial-comprehension program be developed through the use of only one strategy.

SPECIFIC REMEDIAL COMPREHENSION ACTIVITIES

As in other skill areas, specific remediation in reading comprehension will be discussed in terms of the questions asked as a result of a diagnosis:

1. Do larger units of material seem to interfere with comprehension more than smaller units?
2. Do difficulties occur with some types of comprehension and not others?
3. Does the student have difficulty using locating skills?
4. Does the student have difficulty reading content material? Why?
5. Does the student fail to comprehend most of what is read?

When a comprehension difficulty exists there will probably be no one answer. For example, the student having difficulty with locating skills will likely have difficulty in reading content materials also. Thus, teachers should continue to look at reading as a complex process, keeping in mind that single solutions are unlikely.

Units of Materials

Improving reading skills depends on the student's ability to respond to printed units of increasing length. In diagnosis teachers can easily note whether the reader's comprehension is limited basically to sentences, paragraphs, or larger units. In these cases the student is not able to recognize the relationship between units of varying sizes and the flow of ideas created by the author.

All remedial approaches must start at the instructional or independent level. When the difficulty lies in unit size, the instructional level should be geared to the largest unit each student can handle effectively. Using the D-R-T-A, teachers can help students set objectives for reasonable amounts of material. Students quickly become aware of the amounts of materials they can handle and learn to set objectives accordingly.

The paragraph appears to be a reasonable starting place, usually containing one major idea and some supporting details. Teachers should help students understand paragraph structure through identifying the topic sentence.

Materials such as *SRA Reading Laboratories* provide smaller units of materials at lower levels, but manage to maintain interest because each unit is complete in itself. Students can set purposes and read to answer these purposes, instead of just reading to answer the questions on the *SRA* card. Some materials have numbered paragraphs at easier levels. Locating skills can be taught by asking questions in relation to the paragraph number. Thus, the students can more easily locate the place in the reading where the answer can be found—a real time saver for beginning instruction.

Teachers can also adjust the amount of material included in experience stories. If a long story is dictated, the teacher can place it on two or three sheets, making parts 1, 2, and 3. Students can respond to each part and then finally to the entire story.

Using Newspapers. Teacher-made materials can be developed easily to help students handle large quantities of material. For example, a television guide from the Sunday newspaper can be used to help students handle varying amounts of printed material and to respond to tasks of varying difficulty. Students can be asked questions such as these:

- ☐ What show is offered on Channel 4 at seven o'clock on Tuesday evening?
- ☐ What sports programs are offered on Saturday?
- ☐ Select four movies you would like to watch during the week.
- ☐ What shows are featured at eight o'clock each day?
- ☐ Schedule your own television watching for the week for an hour each evening.

Learning Activities. Newspaper articles, classified advertisements, telephone yellow pages, cookbooks, shop manuals, catalogues, encyclopedias, and dictionaries can be developed into lessons similarly by starting with a specific activity requiring minimum reading and moving toward extended activities requiring considerable reading. Students in remedial programs can relate easily and enthusiastically to materials such as these, even though they may tend to be uninterested in reading. Some of these types of materials contain very small quantities of print and are therefore ideally suited for students who have difficulties with larger units.

Difficulties with Some Types of Comprehension

Teachers use questions to determine the student's ability to respond to comprehension activities. Teachers can gauge student strengths and needs by the type of questions they ask. The type of question and its response need careful consideration prior to discussion of remedial activities. All too often, the type of question asked in commercially prepared materials is designed to obtain specific facts from the story where students demonstrate only literal understanding. When working with groups of students, questions at the literal level can be asked of the entire group at one time. Using Durrell's idea of every-pupil-response cards, all can quickly respond to literal questions. Each reader, for example, has two cards, one stating *yes* and the other *no*. The teacher can select five or ten important details from the story and ask questions calling for a *yes* or *no* answer. Cards with names of story characters, dates, and numbers that indicate choices in multiple-choice questions can also be used. The teacher notes all of the responses; if answers to any questions are incorrect, reading is redirected or questions reformulated. Literal understanding can be checked in a short period of time, allowing more time for interpretive and problem-solving questions and activities. While literal comprehension is extremely important, the time normally allocated for it is disproportionally large.

When interpretive questions are asked, the reader is expected to respond by paraphrasing the ideas of the author. Such questions as the following may be asked:

- ☐ In your own words, state the most important idea of the story.
- ☐ How would you summarize the author's major point?
- ☐ Why did the major character lose his temper?

Interpretation requires the readers to draw on their experience to interpret the author's words. Although interested in accurate interpretation, the teacher must not have a preconceived statement of the answer. Readers interpret in the best way they can and their efforts must be accepted. If students' answers contain inaccuracies, they have either read incorrectly or have inappropriately applied their experiences. In either case, inaccuracy calls for reteaching rather than criticism.

When questioned at the problem-solving level, students are expected to think beyond the story's content and apply either critical- or creative-thinking skills to the author's ideas answering questions such as the following:

Creative

- ☐ What would you have done if you were Jim?
- ☐ Can you think of a better ending for the story?

Critical

- ☐ Did Jim make good decisions? Why?
- ☐ What reasons can you give for Father's actions?

Obviously, questioning at the critical- and creative-thinking levels calls for openness on the part of the teacher. When the teacher asks critical questions, the students must understand the author, must be able to interpret the author, and must apply their experiences in order to analyze what has happened. The students' answers may differ from the one that the teacher has in mind and still be accurate. If student reasoning is unclear, probing questions help students seek alternatives.

In creative thinking, any answer given is considered acceptable and correct. Students tend to enjoy creative activities and, when their answers are accepted, tend to become more creative. For example, a group of students is asked to think of a new title for a story with the idea of making the story into a television show. They are told that the title should attract attention. They usually start with rather traditional titles but soon open up as they see the teacher accepting all of their responses.

The teacher's responses to the student's efforts are perhaps even more important than his or her questions. Accepting, probing, reteaching, and making reading activities exciting for students depend on the teacher's attitude toward the responses they give. Students also will learn to accept and value varying peer responses as they see the teacher accepting them. For those in need of further explanation of the types of comprehension, *Programmed Reading for Teachers* may be a useful source of information.[13]

Three types of comprehension are considered in remediation: interpretive comprehension, literal comprehension, and problem solving.

Interpretive Comprehension. Strategies for developing interpretive comprehension skills can be developed through some of the following suggestions.

Closure activities can be used as excellent means of helping students develop awareness of interpretation. Given a cloze activity such as the following, groups of students can see how many words they can fit into the blank and still have the sentence make sense. Doing this calls for awareness of the meaning of the rest of the sentence.

Mike is a good football player.

Later, a full sentence can be provided, and students can add words that do not necessarily change the sentence's core meaning.

Pat is a tennis player.
Pat is a *tremendous* tennis player.

Using brainstorming, glossaries, or dictionaries, students add enhancing words to build many sentences without significantly changing the meaning of the sample sentence.

After experience stories are written, the teacher can write a paraphrased version of the same story. Students match the specific section of the teacher's story with their own. Once that skill is developed students can work in teams, paraphrasing their own stories.

Since interpretation involves the ability to relate one's thinking to the author's, the first step of the D-R-T-A, identifying purposes for reading, will need emphasis. Reading purposes will stress such activities as summarizing, reading between the lines, and determining the main idea instead of reading for details or facts. The first step of the D-R-T-A is also the place for building a background for the story. Pictures, discussions, film strips, and motion pictures may be used to assure that the students have experiences with the story's concepts. At other times, simply using several of the terms in the story and discussing situations using those terms assists the students when they encounter the terms in the story.

Building a story into a motion picture or play by identifying the three most important scenes and then formulating a selling title motivates students while subtly stressing the main idea. Several interested students can become involved in developing a play or a movie from the story. Then other students perform the roles without reading lines from their books. Interpretation using paraphrasing, inferring, and selecting the main idea will be essential. Many students demonstrate such skills in highly unique ways; for example, they may make a comic strip from a favorite story by creating both comic pictures and captions. Of course, a teacher's acceptance of such efforts is the key to encouraging students to continue trying.

Analysis of the topic sentence in a paragraph can also develop interpretation skills. The topic sentence contains the main idea. By stating the topic sentence in their own words, the students are exhibiting an understanding of the main idea and of paraphrasing. An independent activity can involve matching cut-out topic sentences with appropriate paragraphs.

Open-ended questions that ask students to summarize a written passage can be developed. Performances on these are acceptable at many levels of refinement. For example, a summary can be a word, phrase, sentence, paragraph, or several paragraphs. Summaries can be either written or oral and can be either drawn or acted out. By changing the activity, teachers can maintain student interest while continuing to develop the same skill.

Students can learn from their peers if they are grouped so that readers having difficulty paraphrasing can work with those who are good at it. They can work in teams of two or three to answer a teacher's question. By teaming students carefully, every student will be able to make contributions to the final product. Pairing students does not encourage independence, but it often helps students overcome frustration, hopelessness, or uncertainty. Teaming also assists in making students active, rather than passive, learners.

With older students, questions can be written (such as multiple-choice questions) relating to the story's content, but changing the author's wording. In such cases, teachers paraphrase the way they ask questions. The student's task then matches the paraphrased idea to the author's idea. Thus, students see that the same idea may be expressed in several different ways.

Sometimes a simple probing question can be helpful. For example, if a student answers with the precise words of the author, the teacher can respond, "Yes, that is correct. Now let's try to think of other ways to say the same thing." If the author has written, "The general led a successful charge," the teacher may suggest that the students attempt to say the same thing using another word for *successful* or *charge.*

When inferences are stressed as an interpretive skill, the teacher must be aware of two types of inferences: one the author provides intentionally and one the reader develops. For example, some authors lead the reader to a conclusion without actually stating it. Since inferring involves "reading between the lines," the teacher should talk with students about it in exactly those terms.

Elements such as mood, time, danger, and happiness are often only implied by the author. Questions such as "How do you think the player felt after the game?" "When in history did the story take place?" and "Would you consider the people to be in danger?" are examples of questions that stimulate students to infer. Each question can be followed by probing, "What did the author say to make you think that?" The probing activity helps students clarify their own thinking and understand how others have reacted to the same story they have read.

Cartoons can be used in activities designed to teach paraphrasing, obtaining the main ideas, and developing inference skills. For example, using three or four cartoons on the same subject, the teacher can have groups of students write captions for the cartoons and then let other groups try to match the captions with the pictures. Such an activity can be developed at many levels, all of which can be highly motivating.

When students have severe difficulty interpreting written material, the teacher should start with picture interpretation; this entails helping the student look at pictures that have story possibilities in terms of what appears in the picture and then moving to interpretation. For example, the teacher can ask, "How do you think the children feel?" "How is that street different from the street you live on?" and "Make up a title for the picture." Once students have skills in picture interpretation, these responses should be developed into experience stories.

When a reading specialist draws experience stories from pictures, both literal understanding and interpretation responses should be developed. To modify the language-experience approach in order to develop interpretation, students can be asked to change a sentence without changing the meaning, change a word without changing the meaning, identify the sentences that describe the picture and those that interpret the picture, and discuss the main ideas. By moving from pictures to language-experience stories, reading specialists can make a natural transition from vicarious experiences to reading.

The next step is interpreting stories written by others. Perhaps groups of students can write stories about the same picture. These stories can be compared using the same questions asked in individual picture interpretation. When students are successful with the stories of others, they indicate that they are ready to start with other printed material.

Literal Comprehension. Literal comprehension calls for the student to locate or recall specific facts or sequences from a passage. All literal comprehension should involve a situation where students are permitted to locate answers in the passage, not requiring recall from memory. Since a fact or sequence question has a right or wrong answer, the students have no options in a recall situation but to know or not to know the answer. However, when permitted to locate, if they do not remember the answer, they have a way to find it. The comprehension strategy suggested at the beginning of the interpretive section is also very useful in helping students become aware of how to find important facts in a story.

Pointing out the important information via italicized print, boldface type, information repeated for stress, and illustrated information highlights clues to important details to be remembered. Perhaps more subtle but equally useful are clues that words contain. Descriptive adjectives, proper nouns, action verbs, and the like all call attention to those types of details that should receive more careful attention, as in the following sentence:

The *large house burned* in the middle of the *night.*

Most basal material is designed to develop understanding skills. The classroom teacher using basal materials first must be certain that the student is working at the appropriate level and then select those lessons that appear to be most useful.

Understanding sequences causes considerable difficulty for many students. When this skill is deficient, students are limited in their ability to handle content-type materials and to fully appreciate reading of longer units. The thought processes needed involve perceiving groups of items that are related in time (i.e., one comes first, then the next, and so on). Initially, students must obtain sequencing practice from such activities as following oral directions, doing independent work from oral and written instruction, or discussing events from a story that has been read to them by another.

To help students develop sequencing ability, teachers normally start with a sequence of two events and advance to more involved sequences after this is understood. For example, teachers can begin with two events that are clearly representative of the beginning and ending of a story. When the students can sequence with two events (i.e., when they can tell which one came first), a third event, then a fourth, can be added. Starting with many events to sequence tends to smother readers with choices and does not lead to effective sequencing.

Placing comics taken from the Sunday newspaper in sequence is a motivating technique for teaching sequences. Teachers should start with obvious sequences and move toward more subtle ones. Comics that are cut apart and pasted to cards, are quite durable. Numbers on the backs of the cards indicating the sequence make the activity self-correcting. A teacher can build many sequence activities from comics in a short time and with little expenditure of school funds. Teachers can also develop sequence activities from newspaper headlines. Students can read the headlines and place the events in order. They can also match the headlines with newspaper pictures that they have placed in sequence.

Some experience stories can be cut into parts. When experience stories are stimulated by photographs taken during a trip, the photos can be arranged in sequence and topics can be written for each picture. Students can then arrange the parts to make a sequential story.

Directing the students' attention to sequencing words or clues that authors use for emphasis is usually valuable. Items that are numbered, steps in a process, dates, the mention of time, and the use of sequence words (e.g., *afterwards, before, during*) are all indications that the author feels the sequence of events is of particular importance.

Developing students' consciousness of sequence often is done best by more subtle means. Teachers may attempt to direct students to the idea of making a movie in which three or four scenes are to be produced by asking, "In what order should the scenes occur so that the audience will understand the story?" Many teachers have successfully used the technique of asking the students to retell the story. However, teachers should realize that the reader who is deficient in the sequencing skill may experience considerable difficulty in telling the story in sequence and may relate the details indiscriminately instead. In such cases locating sequential events is preferred.

Although initial instruction in this area should be conducted at easy reading levels, teachers should eventually move to the instructional level because the student is most likely to see the necessity for concentration in order to reach desired goals there.

The *Reading Skilltexts, Reading for Meaning, SRA Reading Laboratories, Working with Sounds, Reader's Digest Skill Builders, Standard Test Lessons in Reading,* and the *BFA Comprehension Kit* are the types of readily available materials assigned for literal understanding. Students should not be drilled in materials without immediate teacher follow up to evaluate and redirect, since continued failure causes materials to become burdensome and uninteresting. By correcting errors immediately, the teacher enhances the likelihood of reinforcing correct responses. Of course, it is usually better to provide answer keys so that students can check their own work. When they check their own answers, reinforcement possibilities increase. They are more involved in the appropriateness of their work; their responses are reinforced immediately; and they can look for the correct answer when they cannot figure it out from the question asked. Self-correction is a highly desirable activity for students and saves teachers considerable time.

Experience stories in which the student is asked to explain how to do something (such as build a model airplane) and then is directed to sequence the steps can serve as excellent starting points to teach sequencing. When possible, the teacher can obtain funds to purchase car, ship, or airplane models and help students see the importance of sequences by working with them in constructing models using the sequential directions on the box.

Problem Solving. Students usually are not thought to need remedial assistance if their only difficulty is in problem solving. However, problem-solving activities should be considered necessary and valuable in remedial situations. Such activities involve the reader in a reaction to the author's message. The reaction takes either a critical or creative form. A critical reaction calls for convergent-thinking activities where the author's ideas are challenged, defended, and evaluated. Creative reactions call for divergent-thinking activities where the author's ideas form a base from which new ideas can be developed.

When students set their own purposes, their choices frequently involve problem solving. They want to know how to use a piece of equipment, or they want to challenge the author's ideas. Such choices should be encouraged as a demonstration of mature thinking.

Newspaper reading is a natural activity for problem-solving lessons. Generally, the headlines are stated so that the students either wonder what the problem is or what the solution is. The articles also lend themselves to scanning, since they are generally written from the most important to the least important facts. Students can be encouraged to take sides on issues and find support for their sides in news articles and editorials. Students' views can be developed more fully if the teacher asks questions such as the following: "Do you agree with the author's position?" "Is the story true?" "Were the people justified in doing what they did?" Each of these questions can be followed by other questions such as "Why?" or "Why not?"

Problem solving can also be stimulated by allowing students to work in pairs or small groups. In groups, students get a chance to try out their thinking without committing themselves to a specific viewpoint. Problem-solving skills are often refined through give-and-take discussions.

Students often see problem-solving activities that are related to content subjects such as history as highly relevant. This gives the classroom teacher an opportunity to use content materials as reading instructional materials. Thus, the students are helped in two school subjects at once. This technique also prepares students for lessons focusing on materials that they have difficulty reading.

Myers and Torrance have developed a series of critical and creative activities for use at various classroom levels. Students enjoy working with these materials. For example, one activity involves asking, "What would happen if it always rained on Saturday?"[14]

With picture interpretation, problem-solving questions are asked about action pictures (e.g., "How would you feel if you were there?" or "What do you think will happen next?"). As students develop skill in responding to problem-solving questions concerning pictures, they can create language-experience stories. Once several groups of students have worked on the same picture, stories can be compared, read, and discussed. The use of materials such as *Tweedy Transparencies* (see appendix C) bring action and life to pictures. Even very young readers find these transparencies stimulating and thought provoking. Older students respond to them equally well, and the teacher can move from discussion to writing activities using the transparencies as a basis for instruction.

The teacher can use very easy reading material to help students develop problem-solving skills. With older students, newspaper advertisements and television commercials help stimulate problem-solving thinking. The teacher can ask students what the material is really saying with questions such as, "What words are used to influence the reader or listener?" "Is the ad truthful? Why or why not?" "How would a competitor rewrite this ad?"

Role playing ia also useful for students who have difficulty reacting to reading creatively. They can be encouraged to respond creatively through materials such as *Teaching Reading through Creative Movement,* which consists of records with voice, music, and stories, for students to act out. As students become freer in creative expression, they can react to many things that they read. After the creative expression, discussions about why they feel the way they do make a logical transition to creative discussions.

Difficulty Using Locating Skills

Locating information is a learned skill. It does not help handicapped readers much simply to allow them to use the book to answer questions. Instead, some systematic instruction is necessary, coupled with large amounts of practice.

If teachers start with materials that highly interest students and the objective of trying to obtain literal information, the chances of success are enhanced. Record club memberships, cooking instructions, and local map reading are the kinds of material that can get students accustomed to locating information before paragraph-size passages are introduced.

In longer passages, students should be encouraged to think first about whether the information needed is in the front, toward the middle, or at the end of the passage. Considerable time can be saved if students do not start searching in the beginning for information that occurs toward the end of the passage. The mental set for locating can be developed. Instead of trying to recall details, the student tries to get the flow and direction of the passage so it is easier to locate specific information.

Personal outlining provides an excellent means for teaching locating skills. With this strategy, students will be locating information that has already been deemed important. They can locate information for topics of interest in the library and in other types of resource materials.

Real-Life Reading File Folder materials have been developed to help students locate information using the types of materials they are likely to encounter in their daily lives. These materials stress the importance of using prediction strategies, critical reading, and vocabulary development, as well as locating strategies. Materials are classified according to the skills of following directions, obtaining information, and reading labels and forms. They are suited to students reading on the third-, fourth-, fifth-, and sixth-grade levels (see figure 9–1).

Newspaper activities are also useful in developing locating skills. A sports article about an important baseball game can be used to have students locate the reason for the high score. Obviously, every word in the article is not important to accomplish this objective. Students can be taught to skim through the article to get the important section or can locate the box score and determine which players were responsible for the scoring. In fact, all sections of the newspaper can require skimming to locate important information. The American Newspaper Publishers Association publishes and distributes (free of charge) a bibliography of the best materials available for using newspapers in an educational setting[15]. Wilson and Barnes present ideas for teachers to use local newspapers for the development of a variety of comprehension skills, including the locating of information.[16]

Difficulty Reading Content Material

Many students seem to read satisfactorily in reading classes but are not able to read content materials. One problem here may be that the content and readability of the materials are too difficult. Another may be that students find success when working under teacher direction and difficulty when working alone.

Teachers should first consider the readability of the material which the students cannot comprehend. Often extreme differences in readability exist between the books used in reading class and those used in content areas. Content-area books often are written at a level much higher than graded reading books. On an informal basis, the teacher should note the differences in the size of the print, the length of sentences, the number of difficult words, and the concept difficulty. If any of these factors varies noticeably from the reading class materials, the problem is probably in material difficulty. Yoakham,[17] Gunning,[18] Spache,[19] and Fry[20] present readability formulas that may be used to obtain a grade level of readability, although they do not evaluate the concept load of the material. The cloze procedure also has been developed to enable teachers to determine the ability of the student to handle materials; it will indicate the ability to handle concepts, as well as word and sentence structures. Taylor claims it is of value in determining readability.[21] This technique has been used at the University of Maryland reading clinic with the materials students are expected to read and has been found to be helpful. It involves these steps:

1. Select at random several passages containing about 100 words each.
2. Retype passages, leaving out every fifth word. (Authorities differ on which words to omit, but the fifth has been found to be effective.) As a rule, neither the first word in a sentence nor proper nouns should be omitted. An example of a clozure test on easy material would appear as follows:

   Nancy was anxious to ______ her birthday party this ______. She had invited some ______ from her room at school. She ______ that they would all ______ able to attend.

   Have the reader read the incomplete sentences, filling in the missing words. To "cloze" properly, the student must know the words and understand the concepts, thereby anticipating the author's ideas.

As teachers gain familiarity with the clozure technique, they will find it valuable in determining whether a book is appropriate for a given student.

Bormuth has found that a clozure test score of 38 percent right is approximately equal to a regular test score of 75 percent right.[22] Therefore, as a rule of thumb, clozure scores below 40 percent right should be regarded as danger signs for that student with that material. Either instructional adjustments are needed or easier material must be used for instruction. (For limitations of the 40 percent criteria, review chapter 4.)

Reading problems in understanding content materials usually do not become pronounced until the student has reached the fourth grade. It is at this point that content reading becomes a regular part of the school program and the student with study skill problems is clearly handicapped.

Strategies to Assist Students in Reading Content Material. The teacher should use the D-R-T-A with content area materials. Students who fail to see the need for attacking unfamiliar materials must be directed in the same manner used in reading class. Each step of the D-R-T-A must be used carefully in the development of skill in reading content materials, gradually permitting students to guide themselves through the steps.

Reading Forms and Labels 6-3

BIKE SHOP

Sometimes, when we can't repair things ourselves, we must take them to a repair shop. Most repair shops present the customer with an invoice when the work is done. An invoice is an itemized bill for goods and services.

Look at this invoice from Bill's Bicycle Shop.

INVOICE 5386

BILL'S BICYCLE SHOP

101 Main Street
Anderson, South Carolina
385-9360

Sales and Service

Name: Shirley Carter **Date:** 1/3/80
Address: 109 Edner Road
Anderson, S.C. **Phone:** 389-4290

Services Requested: Repair back fender and replace chain.

QUANTITY	MATERIALS USED	PRICE	AMOUNT
1	chain	3.50	3.50
1 sm. can	red paint - #303	2.50	2.50

DATE	WORK PERFORMED	HOURS	RATE	AMOUNT
1/5/80	Straighten fender & paint.	2	3.80/hr.	7.60
	Replace chain.	1/2 hr.	3.80/hr.	1.90

Work performed by: David Caley

Sales Tax .18

Total 15.68

X ______________________

Signature — The above work completed satisfactorily

All services guaranteed for 30 days after completion.

Use this page with duplicating pages Bike Shop 1 and Bike Shop 2

FIGURE 9–1
Sample of a locating skill lesson from *Real-Life Reading*. (Copyright © 1980 by Instructo/McGraw-Hill. Reproduced by permission; all right reserved.)

It looks like this bicycle needs some repair work. If you read and answer the following questions carefully, you will learn about invoices and repair expenses.

Write your answer in the space provided.

P 1. How do you think the bicycle might have been damaged?

Any reasonable answer is acceptable.

P 2. Can you list two advantages of taking a damaged bike to a shop instead of trying to fix it yourself?

It might look better afterwards.

It might last longer.

It might be safer to ride.

Or any reasonable answer.

L 3. Bill's Bicycle Shop is located at 101 Main St., Anderson, S.C.

L 4. The telephone number for Bill's Bicycle Shop is 385-9360.

L 5. Where was the bicycle taken for repairs?

Bill's Bicycle Shop

L 6. What services were requested?

Repair back fender and replace chain.

L 7. Who requested the repairs?

Shirley Carter

L 8. On what date were the repairs requested? 1/3/80

L 9. On what date were the repairs made?

1/5/80

C 10. Who made the repairs? David Caley

C 11. How much did it cost for 1 hour of labor?

$3.80

Older students may find it beneficial to follow a specific study technique in reading content materials. Several of these are available, the most prominent being SQ3R (survey, question, read, recite, review).[23] The effect of this type of technique is the same as a D-R-T-A except that students are to apply it to their studies without supervision. Independence in reading content material is the desired objective of this strategy.

Activities in which the students organize and classify ideas are useful in remediation. Students who cannot read in the content areas usually have difficulty with outlining skills. Beginning with completed outlines of material recently read, the teacher illustrates the method of following the author's train of thought. An outline format is then presented for students to complete, followed by simple outlining of clearly organized material with little or no direction from the teacher. The *Reading for Meaning* workbooks, designed for the intermediate and secondary grades, have practice exercises to develop students' abilities to organize material through a gradual exposure to outlining techniques. The *SRA Organizing and Reporting Skills Kit* has individualized exercises that gradually introduce the concepts of notetaking, reporting, and outlining.

When teaching notetaking skills, teachers might find it helpful to teach students to use the one-word note technique. After taking notes from a book or lecture, the students write a one-word note in the margin. That one word should denote the essential meaning of the section. When preparing for writing or examination, the location of the one-word note helps students quickly locate the section that needs to be reviewed in their notes.

The ability to follow directions has a direct relationship to the ability to perform in study situations. This skill depends on students' abilities to follow the sequence and organization of the author's thoughts, as well as their abilities to obtain the main idea. The *Specific Skills Series* (e.g., Using the Context, Locating the Answer) includes sets of intensive exercises in following directions at the various grade levels. Once the ability to follow directions is mastered, remedial sessions should provide opportunities to practice this concept at regular intervals.

Teachers can use many activities to help students develop mastery of following directions. As has been suggested, the use of model cars, ships, and airplanes helps a reader realize the importance of following directions carefully. Reading the directions on the box and following them step by step to completion can be a highly useful reading and learning experience. If students cannot read all of the instructions, they should work in pairs, helping each other. Learning centers can be developed to

Using newspapers, students can be instructed to follow directions ranging from simple to complex.

help students follow directions. Using pages from telephone books or newspapers, students can be instructed to follow directions ranging from the simple to the complex (e.g., find a phone number; find a phone number and address; find the phone numbers of three dentists and give their names, get their addresses, and determine which lives closest to your home).

Another SRA study aid, the *Graph and Picture Study Skills Kit,* is designed to be adapted to any subject area. These materials are useful in developing a type of reading often overlooked in remedial programs. The *Be a Better Reader* books provide specific suggestions for study in the major content areas, particularly for older students. The *Study Skills Library,* which provides specialized instruction in developing the same type of concepts, is useful with younger students. Individualized for clinical use, these materials can serve a highly useful function with students who are deficient in study skills.

Adaptation of the language-experience approach to content subjects has been very effective.[24] Four teachers agreed to work with students in the seventh grade who had serious reading problems. They taught mathematics, science, social studies, and English through the language-experience approach and were pleased to find that these students could learn the content when the materials were presented in a personalized, readable manner. Reading specialists can work with classroom teachers to develop skill in presenting material and information to the students without using texts (e.g., lecture, discussion, tapes, films, pictures, demonstrations, experiments); in drawing students' verbal expressions of what they have learned; in writing language-experience stories based on the students' contributions; and in developing reading and content skills from the written stories.

Reading specialists also can help content teachers rewrite materials that are too difficult. Basically rewriting involves cutting sentence length, eliminating complicated sentence structures, and reducing word difficulty through the use of synonyms.

Herber suggests several teaching strategies that are useful in helping students in the content areas.[25] He suggests that teachers use study guides to assist students in content reading. Study guides help students understand content objectives; guide students in using specific text materials to understand its organization; and assist them in using that material to meet the stated objectives. He suggests the use of small-group instruction to encourage risk-taking behavior, and suggests that such groups contain a range of achievement levels so that students can learn from one another.

Bruner and Campbell recommend studying book parts so that students can use the book organization to their advantage.[26] Lessons on the use of the table of contents, the index, the glossary, and the appendices are recommended. They also recommend lessons that help students use maps, graphs, pictures, and cartoons to assist comprehension.

When students have great difficulty with content reading, paired learning can prove helpful. Two students work together to accomplish the content objectives. This has a double effect. First, the student having the most difficulty feels that learning is possible and that help is available. Second, the helping student experiences the satisfaction of being able to help someone else and learns more in the process, since it is often through teaching that one gains a more thorough understanding of the material to be learned.

Failure to Comprehend Most Reading

For the student who does not respond to even the most simple comprehension checks, remedial techniques are difficult to apply because starting places are hard to determine. However, teachers must change any materials that cause the students difficulty; continued use of these materials cannot be defended. For these students, the level of the material must be easy, the interest of the material must be high, and the quantity small.

Intensified use of experience stories permits teachers to start with relatively easy, interesting material of as small a quantity as desired. Again, students are directed to demonstrate an understanding of the experience stories, which, because they contain their own concepts, can usually be done without difficulty. Once a feeling for this type of activity is developed, the student is exposed through the D-R-T-A or the problem approach to easy, interesting printed material.

Placing the student in reading situations that call for action and reaction is often successful. Signs, posters, and flash cards calling for reaction are developed from the opportunities that appear daily in and out of the classroom. One type of action material (involving a reaction from students at each step) is called *Programmed Reading*. As students read through the programmed books, they are expected to react to every sentence. Their reactions are immediately reinforced by the correct response. These materials place students in situations that demand thought about what they are reading.

Vocabulary exercises requiring students to respond nonverbally to printed symbols have considerable usefulness here. The *Nichols Slides* (or similar activities) can be used by starting with very simple, direct commands and progressing as students develop the skill (e.g., start with words such as *sit, stand,* and *jump,* and go to more complicated word combinations such as *stand and sing now* or *jump three times*). With these students, drill activities without contextual emphasis certainly should be discontinued.

Several techniques have been developed to encourage students to respond to reading in rather nontraditional ways. One involves the use of creative movement to display understanding of a story that has been read to or by the students. Materials entitled *Teaching Reading through Creative Movement* have been successful with seriously handicapped readers.

Another approach to eliciting student response is the use of popular music. A phonograph, records, and lyrics set the stage. Students listen to the music and sing along. When the music is over, the meaning of the lyrics is discussed. Rereading is done to verify opinions. Older students seem to respond well to remediation involving music as the motivator.

Reading which involves essential information for survival in society has also been used effectively. For example, students need to be able to read driver's manuals and job applications. *Real-Life Reading* materials are particularly useful because they are written at low readability levels but contain highly motivating content such as understanding skateboard rules, how to earn money, and using a television guide. These materials can be used in teacher-directed lessons until the students feel comfortable enough to work on them independently or in pairs.

EXTENDED REMEDIATION

The problems students encounter related to speed of reading and distractability can become instructional concerns.

Reading Speed

Slow reading speed often causes students to give inappropriate responses. In such cases, when students have been asked to read a selection (ample time must be allotted) and to answer several questions, their comprehension responses appear to be unsatisfactory because they have not completed the material. Upon careful examination, it is often found that they have responded properly to those questions related to the material that was read and have missed those concerned with material not read. Teachers must question why the students are reading slowly. If they are having difficulty breaking the written code, activities designed to increase reading speed are useless. The same is true if they are struggling with unfamiliar concepts. However, some students read slowly because they have applied oral reading speeds to silent reading, lack concentration, or do not know how to vary their reading speed. In these cases, some remedial instruction may be helpful.

Readers who have developed slow reading speeds should first be placed in reading material that is both easy and interesting. Unknown words should not be introduced because they slow or stop reading. The second step is to be certain that the students are reading for personally set purposes. Purposeless reading is bound to be slow. Teachers can use the first step in the D-R-T-A for purpose setting. Then they can help readers read for those purposes using skimming techniques. The newspaper can provide excellent material to teach skimming skills. Purposes are set according to what is known from the headlines, pictures, or prior information. Students will find the time needed for reading will vary with the type of purpose set. At times it will be useful for the teacher to set the purposes and permit a limited amount of time to find the answer. This is often best done after the material has been read silently. Readers can be asked a question and then asked where they remember seeing the answer in the passage. They quickly get the idea that one need not read all of the words in the passage to obtain a specific answer. As flexible rates are developed, students can begin to use those various rates in specific settings.

Prepared materials are available for students to use for practice exercises in reading within certain time limits. The *SRA Laboratories* have rate-building exercises in which the student must read and answer the question in three minutes. The student should be started with rate-building exercises at very easy levels. The emphasis here is on efficiency in relatively easy high-interest material. The *Standard Test Lessons in Reading* also have the three-minute time limitation. In the remedial session, the three-minute time limit will often need to be adjusted. Since there is no rationale for the three-minute limit, teachers should allow more time for those students who need it. Time should be monitored, however, and the students should be encouraged to complete the work accurately and swiftly as possible.

Other available exercises are designed to motivate improved time performance by emphasizing such reading-rate measures as number of words read per minute. In remediation none of this emphasis should be stressed without equal or greater emphasis on the quality of comprehension that accompanies the rate. The *Better Reading Books* are an example of this type of material to be used with older students, providing personalized charts for easy motivation to better speed and comprehension.

Charts and graphs that illustrate the students' progress are always helpful. These should be constructed so that each student can note small gains in improved rate, so that comprehension is charted as well as the reading rate, and so that the goals are realistically within reach. If students reach the graph's goal quickly, the teacher simply makes a new graph, again with easily reached goals. All such charts are maintained as private information.

Distractibility

A teacher must look for the reason why students become distracted. Perhaps students find the material so boring that everything else seems more interesting by comparison. In these cases, the purposes for reading may be adjusted or different materials can be used. However, some students are distracted by the classroom surroundings. Everything is asking for their attention—other students, learning centers, bulletin boards, artwork, and the teacher. In these cases, several suggestions are offered:

1. Distractible students should be placed so that other's actions are no more distracting than necessary. In the classroom, this would normally involve a front corner seat.

2. Remediation with distractible students should not be conducted in physical surroundings in which pictures and other distracting objects are prominent. In clinical situations, a plain room where a student's total efforts can be directed to the book should be used initially. In the classroom, distractible students should take their reading instruction in an area of the room that lacks extensive decoration.
3. When distractibility is recognized as a serious limitation, it is often helpful to use books that contain a minimum of pictures, thus permitting students to focus attention on the print and the skills necessary to read it.
4. Distractible students will need to have skill exercises in shorter duration periods. They should understand that their entire attention will be expected for a short time, after which they may move to another activity and return to reading skill activities later. In the clinic, varying activity as much as possible is helpful. Unfortunately, such adjustments are difficult and at times impossible in the classroom because they disrupt the activities of the other students. The classroom teacher, however, should provide a variety of activities and at least refrain from punishing students for distractibility over which they have no obvious control. In the more extreme cases, students should run, jump, and play actively in other ways between their periods of reading-skill activities. Opportunities should be used to get them to be active in as well as out of class. For example, the teacher could have them come to the chalkboard for some of their work and let them pass out materials to others, thus providing them with opportunities to release some of their energy. In this way, their tensions become relaxed, and they become more receptive to the required silent work at their seats.
5. Students who are easily distracted generally enjoy a program that has as much consistency as possible. When they can anticipate an interesting routine, they are more likely to be able to concentrate on it to its completion. In rare instances, continued distractible behavior, even after adjustments have been made, calls for medical referral. These students may be demonstrating symptoms of behavior that need medical attention.
6. Closed-captioned, prime-time television programs, where words appear on the screen to communicate the events being shown, can provide an excellent means for

Closed-captioned television provides an excellent means for reaching distracted students. (From "The Voyage of Mimi," PBS, Copyright 1984 by Bank Street College of Education. Used by permission; all rights reserved.)

reaching distracted students. This process, developed by the National Captioning Institute, requires a decoder which makes over forty hours of televison programming with captions available in a week. Although originally intended for use by the hearing impaired, hearing students who had been unable to concentrate on book reading are captivated by the captioned television. After two viewings of a show, they were able to read words from the captioning that they were not able to read prior to the viewing.

The Reluctant Reader

Most students experiencing reading difficulty are reluctant to engage in reading activities. However, the term *reluctant reader* as used in this section refers to those students who have the necessary skills for reading but are reluctant to use them. These students need to see reading as a rewarding experience. In every lesson, they should be reading for purposes that they feel are important. Drill-type activities should be held to a minimum, and purposeful reading should be increased.

Learning centers are excellent for providing students with independent learning activities.

First, these students need to see that free reading is an activity the teacher sees as worthwhile. Therefore, free-reading opportunities should occur periodically in all classrooms. *Free reading,* in this case, implies reading that is not followed by question-and-answer periods, and reading in which the students choose their own materials. As students develop the understanding that free reading can be fun and worthwhile enough to take school time, gradual attitude changes will likely be noted.

Developing a willing attitude toward reading obviously depends on the availability of books. The reluctant reader must have books available for free reading in the classroom and school libraries, and at home. There is little chance to develop attitudes and habits that favor reading when books are difficult or impossible to obtain. School administrators should note that attempts to be thrifty by cutting appropriations for classroom and school libraries make teachers unable to encourage the reading habit.

Learning centers that provide students with opportunities for selecting the materials they are going to use, for pacing themselves, and for correcting their own work have been used with considerable success with the reluctant reader.

Teachers should use every opportunity to promote free reading through the use of peer group recommendations. Students who have read interesting books and want to share them with others can often create more interest than the teacher can. Sharing may be done through brief, voluntary, oral reports;

through a classroom card file including the name of the book and the reasons that the student enjoyed it; or through a school book fair where interesting books are displayed.

The teacher can develop interest by reading to the students from books that contain stories and ideas of interest but would be too difficult for them to read themselves. Teachers who read children's books are able to provide book summaries to develop interest in new books as they appear in the library. Teachers can also influence attitude toward reading by showing enthusiastic interest in their own personal reading.

Teachers may find it useful to consult book lists prepared by authorities to facilitate the guidance of students. *A Teacher's Guide to Children's Books,*[28] *Children and Books,*[29] *Your Children Want to Read,*[30] *Good Reading for Poor Readers,*[31] *Creative Growth through Literature for Children and Adolescents,*[32] *Easy Reading,*[33] and *High Interest Easy Reading for Junior and Senior High School Students*[34] are seven examples. Through the use of such resources, the teacher can also recommend books to parents that would be appropriate gifts. Teachers should encourage parents to consider a book a valued, highly desirable gift.

Often reluctant readers are hesitant to select a book that is threatening in terms of volume. Perhaps due to pressure from adults, the readers have developed an attitude that taking a book from the library commits them to read the book from cover to cover. The teacher, of course, must discourage this attitude, for everyone has been in situations where, after starting a book, they feel no desire to finish it. Nevertheless, too many false starts tend to discourage students from sampling brief portions of books prior to selecting the books from the library. Two materials that let students sample books are *The Literature Sampler* and the *Pilot Library.* Both of these provide the teacher with a guide to a book's readability and the interest factors involved with it.

Extensive use should be made of book series that, while maintaining high interest, have low vocabulary levels and provide interesting reading. Without books to reinforce the skills that are being developed in remediation, the chance for transfer of these skills is seriously limited. Table 9–1 lists high-interest, low-vocabulary books that have been used effectively in classrooms and clinics. Books such as these are inexpensive and readily available.

Free reading may be permitted in materials such as the *SRA Reading Laboratories* and *The Reading Skill Builders.* When they are used for free reading, students should not be required to answer questions or to do the vocabulary exercises. Of course, selections should be at a recreational reading level.

TABLE 9–1
High-interest, low-vocabulary books.

Series	Vocabulary level	Publisher
About Books	2 to 4	Children's Press
All About Books	3 to 6	Random House
American Adventure Series	2 to 3	Wheeler
Bucky Buttons	1 to 3	Benefic Press
Cowboy Sam	1 to 3	Benefic Press
Dan Frontier	1 to 3	Benefic Press
Deep Sea Adventure Stories	1 to 3	Harr Wagner
Dolch First Readers	1 to 2	Garrard
Interesting Reading Series	2 to 3	Follett
I Want to be Books	1 to 3	Children's Press
Sailor Jack	1 to 3	Benefic Press
The Monster Books	2 to 4	Bowmar

Other types of material that can be used with reluctant readers are those classified as survival or functional reading materials. Throughout the discussions on remediation, attention has been called to the types of materials that students need to read in order to function and survive in our society. These materials have strong appeal, and are relevant and essential.

Survival materials include such items as medicine labels, danger signs, road signs, and warning notices. Students who cannot read these types of materials are in danger in day-to-day life. Their chances of survival in society are enhanced when remedial instruction includes these types of materials and the skills needed to read them. Functional reading materials include such items as newspapers, menus, employment forms, and phone books. If students are unable to read such materials, their ability to function in society is seriously limited.

Originally, survival and functional reading programs were being recommended for only the seriously handicapped reader. Today, however, these programs are recommended for all readers as an important part of the reading program. In many schools, they are developed in learning-center format, and students use them throughout the year.

In remedial programs, survival and functional reading materials are especially important. For seriously handicapped readers, the entire remedial program can be developed around such materials. Older students with serious reading problems especially profit from survival and functional reading programs. Sight vocabulary, word attack, and comprehension activities are drawn from the materials. Experience stories supplement the materials. Lists of words such as the Essential Driver's List and The Essential Vocabulary List are used.[35] Such programs encourage the readers, and they often ask for instruction beyond the survival and functional programs.

Students' interest and reading needs are surveyed. For example, a group of students may be about to obtain learner's permits for driving a car. All types of materials related to driving can be collected. The students can bring their driver's manuals and car maintenance manuals to the lessons, and instruction can be directed toward the understanding of such materials. Actual automobile trips can be planned during which students use their learned skills.

One elementary school developed boxes of actual materials needed to function or survive in society. One box included medicine bottles; another contained boxes, cans, and bottles from the grocery shelf; another held all types of maps. Students picked the area of concentration they wished to pursue and immersed themselves in the activities. A source of ideas about survival and functional reading activities can be found in the suggested readings at the end of this chapter.

The use of closed-captioned television is another motivating way to reach the reading needs of these students. As discussed earlier, closed-captioned television increases attention to task and provides students with a common experience with which to relate the drama on the television screen.

The work of Hancock, DeLorenzo, and Ben-Barka[36] provides numerous suggestions for teaching reading to refugee children. They suggest starting with the language experience approach. This source is rich with suggestions, commercial materials, references, and an important list of "do's and don'ts" for working with ESL students. This booklet is essential for teachers who work with refugee children.

REMEDIATION FOR THE CULTURALLY DIFFERENT

Some students come for reading instruction with experiential backgrounds that are quite different from other students and from their teachers. These students might come from foreign countries, and thus do not have adequate command of English since English is not their native language. Not only do these students have a problem with language, but they also might have trouble relating to the customs and values of American society. Another group of students have lived in our culture and speak English, but come from an environment that limits their ability to relate to the language and customs of our society. The approach to reading comprehension instruction with both of these types of students must start with language to which they can relate.

The language-experience approach is therefore a logical starting point. Using their own experiences as language for reading comprehension instruction eliminates most of the obstacles of learning for these students. Their skills with English and their personal experiences can be put into print and they will be able to relate to the printed message in a personal way. By providing common experiences through community field trips, science experiments, cooking activities, and games their language experiences can be extended and developed into additional printed experience stories. When moving from language experience stories to book reading the selection of reading materials is very important. Spache's book, *Good Reading for the Disadvantaged Reader,* can serve as a useful reference.[37]

Several programs are available for language skill development. The *Peabody Language Development Kits, the Visual-Lingual Reading Program,* and *Building Prereading Skills Kit-A-Language* can be used. The *Language Master* can also facilitate language and concept development. Written words and a picture representing those words can be placed on the cards. The teacher then orally records the word on the tape that appears on the bottom of the card. The students run these cards through the machine, seeing the word and the picture while hearing the word read.

SUMMARY

By selecting approaches for teaching comprehension that reflect what is known about comprehension, one can enhance the chances of a successful program. With these approaches, a variety of instructional techniques can be developed that will make the lessons interesting. Specific activities that are based on information that was obtained during the diagnosis are often needed. By using high interest materials with all instructional strategies, teachers can keep interest high, help students achieve success in large quantities, and assure positive student attitudes.

NOTES

1. Frank Smith, *Understanding Reading* (New York: Holt, Rinehart & Winston, 1978), 67.
2. Richard Allington, "If They Don't Read Much How They Ever Gonna Get Good?" *Journal of Reading* 21, no. 1 (October 1977): 57–61.

3. Linda Gambrell, Robert M. Wilson, and Walter N. Gantt, "Classroom Observations of Task-Attending Behaviors of Good and Poor Readers," *Journal of Educational Research* (July/August 1981): 400–404.
4. Dolores Durkin, "What Classroom Observations Reveal about Reading Comprehension Instruction," *Reading Research Quarterly* 14, no. 4 (1978–79): 481–522.
5. Russell G. Stauffer, *Teaching Reading as A Thinking Process* (New York: Harper & Row, 1969).
6. Ibid., 12.
7. Bruce W. Brigham, and Virginia H. Pilato, "A Heuropractice Strategy in Adults: A Psycho-Educational Procedure for Teaching Handicapped Adults," *Journal of Exceptional Adult Education* (Fall 1982): 7–11.
8. Mary Budd Rowe, *Teaching Science as Continuous Inquiry* (New York: McGraw-Hill, 1973), 242–66.
9. Frank Lyman, Chlene Lopez, and Arlene Mindus, *Elementary Language Arts Guide* (Clarksville, Md.: Howard County Board of Education, 1977), 47–69.
10. Marilyn W. Sadow, "The Use of Story Grammar in the Designing of Questions," *The Reading Teacher* (February 1982): 519.
11. Ibid., 521.
12. Beth Davey, "Think Aloud—Modeling the Cognitive Processes of Reading Comprehension," *Journal of Reading*, (October 1983): 44–47.
13. Robert M. Wilson, et. al, *Programmed Reading for Teachers*, Columbus, OH: Charles E. Merrill, 1980).
14. R. E. Myers and E. Paul Torrance, *For Those Who Wonder* (Boston: Ginn and Co., 1966), 1.
15. *Bibliography, Newspapers in Education*, ed. Merrill F. Hartsorn (Reston, Va: American Newspaper Publishers Association, 1983).
16. Robert M. Wilson and Marcia M. Barnes, *Using Newspapers to Teach Reading Skills* (Reston, Va.: American Newspaper Publishers Association, 1975).
17. Gerald A. Yoakham, *Basal Reading Instruction* (New York: Prentice-Hall, 1955), appendix I.
18. William A. Jenkins, ed., "The Educational Scene," *Elementary English* 37, no. 6 (October 1960): 411.
19. George Spache, *Good Reading for Poor Readers* (Champaign, Ill.: Garrard Press, 1968) chapter 4.
20. Edward B. Fry, "Fry's Readability Graph: Clarifications, Validity and Extensions to Level 17," *Journal of Reading* 21, no. 3 (November 1977): 242–51.
21. W. L. Taylor, "Cloze Procedure—A New Tool for Measuring Readability," *Journalism Quarterly* 30 (Fall 1953): 415–33.
22. John R. Bormuth. "Comparable Cloze and Multiple-Choice Test Comprehension Scores," *Journal of Reading* (February 1967): 295.

23. Francis P. Robinson, *Effective Study* (New York: Harper & Row, 1961).
24. Robert M. Wilson and Nancy Parkey, "A Modified Reading Program in a Middle School," *Journal of Reading* (March 1970): 447–52.
25. Harold L. Herber, *Teaching Reading in the Content Areas,* 2d ed. (Englewood Cliffs, N.J.: Prentice-Hall, 1978), chapter 4.
26. Joseph F. Bruner and John J. Campbell, *Participating in Secondary Reading* (Englewood Cliffs, N.J.: Prentice-Hall, 1978), 53–62.
27. National Captioning Institute Research Report 83–6, Falls Church, VA, 1983.
28. Nancy Larrick, *A Teacher's Guide to Children's Books* (Columbus, OH: Charles E. Merrill, 1969).
29. May Hill Arbuthnot and Zena Sutherland, *Children and Books* (Chicago: Scott, Foresman & Co., 1977).
30. Ruth Tooze, *Your Children Want to Read* (Englewood Cliffs, N.J.: Prentice-Hall, 1957).
31. George D. Spache, *Good Reading for Poor Readers* (Champaign, Ill.: Garrard Press, 1968).
32. Margaret Gillespie and John Conner, *Creative Growth through Literature for Children and Adolescents* (Columbus, OH: Charles E. Merrill, 1975).
33. Michael F. Graves, Judith A. Boettcher, and Randall A. Ryder, *Easy Reading* (Newark, Del.: IRA, 1979).
34. Marian White, *High Interest Easy Reading for Junior and Senior High School Students* (Urbana, Ill.: National Council of Teachers of English, 1979).
35. Corlett T. Wilson, "An Essential Vocabulary," *The Reading Teacher* 17 (November 1963): 94–96.
36. Charles Hancock, William DeLorenzo, and Alba Ben-Barka, *Teaching Pre- and Semi-Literate Laotian and Cambodian Adolescents to Read* (Maryland State Dept. of Education, 1983).
37. George D. Spache, *Good Reading for the Disadvantaged Reader* (Champaign, Ill,: Garrard Press, 1970).

SUGGESTED READINGS

Carin, Arthur A., and Sund, Robert B. *Creative Questioning and Sensitive Listening Techniques,* 2d ed. Columbus, OH: Charles E. Merrill Publishing Co., 1978. Carin and Sund illustrate how teacher's questions help and hinder learning and learners.

Cook, Jimmie E. and Earlley, Elsie C. *Remediating Reading Disabilities.* Germantown, Md.: Aspen Systems Corp., 1979. This book presents thousands of ideas for enriching instruction beyond the basal series. Chapter 9 focuses on numerous suggestions for making comprehension meaningful and interesting.

———. *Functional Reading*. Volumes 1 and 2. Baltimore, Md.: Maryland State Department of Education, 1975.

Robinson, Francis P. *Effective Study.* New York: Harper & Row, 1961. The teacher of older students who desires to stress study skills in remedial sessions will find the SQ3R technique well defined and explained in this book.

Rowe, Mary Budd. *Teaching Science as Continuous Inquiry.* New York: McGraw-Hill Book Co., 1973. Wait time is presented in detail. Every teacher working with handicapped readers should be familiar with Rowe's research and recommendations in relation to wait time.

Stauffer, Russell G. *Teaching Reading as a Thinking Process.* New York: Harper & Row, 1969. Stauffer provides rationales and procedures for use of the D-R-T-A. Any student not familiar with the D-R-T-A is referred to this source.

Wilson, Robert M., and Barnes, Marcia M. *Survival Learning Materials.* York, Pa.: College Reading Association, 1974. This book presents a rationale and many ideas for developing survival and functional learning materials.

Wilson, Robert M., *Programmed Reading for Teachers,* Columbus, OH: Charles E. Merrill, 1984. For those in need of fundamental information in the area of reading comprehension, this book will provide a quick overview of the process.

Editorial

Joetta Dayhoff
is a principal for the Washington County Public Schools in Maryland.

Andy, Bruce, Charlie, Danny, David, and Dwight were twelve-year-old seventh graders who were having difficulty reading material intended for their grade level. These students were very reluctant to engage in any type of reading activity. They possessed strengths in the areas of decoding, literal comprehension, and group participation. They exhibited weaknesses in the areas of higher-level comprehension skills, organizational skills, and study skills, as well as on-task behavior and self-concept as readers.

After examining and taking into consideration the strengths and weaknesses of the group, it was decided to employ the Problem Approach in order to involve the students actively in an instructional situation. The group decided they wanted to learn first about the various jobs and responsibilities involved in running a fast-food restaurant. Next it was decided that the best way to obtain the information was to contact a fast-food restaurant and arrange for a tour and a question and answer session with the manager. After the visit to the restaurant, the students summarized and demonstrated what they had learned by setting up their own fast-food restaurant. Various jobs with corresponding responsibilities were undertaken by each member of the group. Students from other classes were invited to visit the "restaurant," "purchase" food items, and ask questions pertaining to jobs, responsibilities, etc.

The students experienced successful instructional situations using this approach in that they were able to bring their experiential background and prior knowledge to the task in order to provide a resource of information. By being active participants involved in directing their learning, the group of originally very reluctant readers gained a new enthusiasm for reading through the Problem Approach. Their self-concepts as readers, on-task behavior, higher level comprehension skills, organizational skills, and study skills continually improved with each successive use of the approach.

A SMILE IS
STEELERS

10

Assessment and Planning for Handicapped Students

CHAPTER OUTLINE

HISTORICAL INJUSTICES TO HANDICAPPED STUDENTS
PROCEDURAL SAFEGUARDS
SPECIAL CONSIDERATIONS FOR DIAGNOSIS
SPECIAL CONSIDERATIONS IN REMEDIATION
AREAS OF POTENTIAL DIFFICULTY

CHAPTER EMPHASES

- ☐ Teachers should know about procedural safeguards which aid handicapped students.
- ☐ Working with handicapped students in both diagnostic and remedial capacities requires special consideration of their unique learning needs.
- ☐ Many of the same approaches and techniques that are used with students in the regular classroom may be adapted for use with handicapped students.
- ☐ Teachers should exhibit positive attitudes when working with handicapped students to aid them in achieving their fullest potentials.

The past decade has brought about sweeping changes in the ways handicapped students are viewed and educated. Handicapped individuals are being recognized as having the potential to make significant contributions to society if given the proper opportunities. These opportunities include the right to a free and appropriate public school education and the chance for many of the handicapped to be educated right beside their nonhandicapped peers. These important reforms have been brought about through the efforts of many individuals and advocacy groups who have encouraged far-reaching federal and state legislation aimed at serving handicapped students' educational needs.

These new and valuable rights have brought with them several attendant responsibilities which classroom teachers and reading specialists must share. Increasing numbers of handicapped students who previously were educated in self-contained special education classrooms are now being placed in regular elementary and secondary classrooms. This shift has required the regular classroom teacher to become increasingly involved in the education of many (although by no means all) handicapped students. Faced with this new challenge, the classroom teacher needs to acquire an added measure of knowledge and awareness of how to best meet the unique social, emotional, and learning needs of handicapped students.

Often the reading specialist is also asked to play an active role in designing and implementing an educational program for the handicapped student. Even if the reading specialist has minimal personal contact with the student, he or she may be called on to help with placement decisions and to serve as a resource person to the classroom teacher in selecting methods and materials to use with the student.

Teachers should have an awareness of the unique learning needs of individual students and understand the desirability of designing an instructional or remedial program which maximizes opportunities for personal success. For the handicapped student, however, such considerations take on even greater significance. Effort should be made to focus on these students' strengths to provide a viable means of highlighting what the students are able to do, rather than what they cannot do. This may, in turn, pay off in increased dividends to student self-esteem and academic attitudes. As students begin to feel better about themselves as learners, they often invest more effort in their remediation and become, in effect, partners with their teachers in their education.

In preparing to work with handicapped students professionals must be aware of pertinent legislational safeguards that have been enacted to protect handicapped students' rights. Although much legislation in the seventies and eighties has focused on the rights of the handicapped, perhaps the most far-reaching federal acts were Public Law 93-380 passed in 1974 and Public Law 94-142 passed in 1975. Although certain provisions of both laws have been widely debated, they have been generally praised as valuable advances in promoting educational opportunities for handicapped students between 3 and 21 years of age.

HISTORICAL INJUSTICES TO HANDICAPPED STUDENTS

Historically, the handicapped student has suffered from discriminatory treatment by the educational community. Although much of this discrimination was thought to be in the students' best educational interests, students were often placed in special programs using questionable criteria and kept in those programs even when their educational needs were not being met. The following specific injustices made legislative intervention necessary.

Exclusion from the Educational System

In the past many severely handicapped students in the community were excluded from an appropriate education due to a lack of facilities. Tragically, many of these students failed to reach their fullest potentials and were educated in the living rooms and bedrooms of their homes without benefit of the special methods and materials that a special class or school might have provided. Others were placed in private physical care institutions by their parents at great expense, yet they too often failed to receive an appropriate education because it was considered beyond the scope of a physical care facility.[1]

Placement without Parental Consent

Until recently students were placed in special classes and programs when the school officials determined that such a placement was in the students' best interests. Although on the surface this practice might appear to be well within the schools' proper expertise and province, an unbiased examination of the record indicates that certain special class placements in the past were made for administrative convenience. Not requiring parental consent allowed few opportunities to challenge the appropriateness of a student's special class placement.

Identification Based on a Single Assessment

Past inequities have resulted from a student being identified as handicapped by inadequate or inappropriate means. At times students were being identified as handicapped due to their poor performance on a single test. Perhaps the most prevalent and striking example of this practice was the use of a single intelligence score to justify placing a student in a class for the mentally retarded. When one examines the reliability and validity data for some intelligence tests, the injustice of single instrument assessment becomes obvious.[2]

Difficulty Returning to the Regular Classroom

Compounding the seriousness of special class or program placement based on a single test score, students, once identified handicapped, often never had the opportunity of "testing out" and returning to the regular classroom. Another factor which tended to retain students within the special education system was the decelerated pace of most classes for the handicapped and the different nature of the academic curriculum. Because of this slower pace and lack of opportunity to return to the regular classroom, many placements which should have been relatively short, such as some placements of emotionally disturbed children, became permanent instead.

Disproportionate Percentages of Minority Students

An examination of enrollment logs twenty-five years ago reveals that minority students were enrolled in special education programs at an unnaturally high percentage compared to the percentage of minority students in the general school population. This was due, in large part, to the testing instruments that were being used to identify students for special education services. Many of these tests contained items which were racially or culturally discriminatory. Furthermore, some of the standardization populations on which the test norms were based were not representative of the students in the schools in which the tests were being used.[3]

Classes Not Suited to Students' Needs

Sometimes students in the past were placed in classes that were inappropriate for them, such as the placement of cerebral palsied individuals who, despite average or above-average intelligence, were placed in programs for the mentally retarded. Such placements often sadly resulted in these students becoming educationally retarded by default.[4]

Segregation of the Handicapped

For many years self-contained special education classes and schools were the dominant and preferred system for educating handicapped students. A growing realization developed, however, that many handicapped students were much the same as their nonhandicapped peers. Routinely placing handicapped students in self-contained special classes denied handicapped students the social, emotional, and academic benefits of being educated along with their friends and neighbors.

PROCEDURAL SAFEGUARDS

Although some unjust practices of the past still remain, today the handicapped are protected by certain procedural safeguards through recent federal and state legislation. In assisting in the education of handicapped students, classroom teachers and reading specialists should be cognizant of the laws which have been designed to aid the handicapped. A brief overview of some of the requirements and procedures these laws mandate follows.

Free and Appropriate Public Education

A free, appropriate, public education that includes special education and related services must be provided for all students. This education should be designed to meet students' special needs, and provide safeguards for the rights of handicapped students and their parents. It should also provide for periodic evaluation of special programs to assure their effectiveness.

Categories of Handicapped Students

Children are considered handicapped if they have been identified as mentally retarded; hearing impaired or deaf; speech impaired; visually impaired; seriously emotionally disturbed; orthopedically or other health impaired; deaf-blind; multihandicapped; or specific learning disabled, and because of their impairments need special education and related services. The last category, specific learning disabled, will naturally include many students experiencing serious difficulties learning to read. Reading specialists, however, must be prepared to be involved with the assessment and instruction of all handicapped children.

Evaluation and Placement Procedures

Assessment of a student believed to be handicapped should be comprehensive and multidisciplinary. It should assure that diagnostic procedures are appropriate to the student's suspected impairment and that the student is subsequently correctly identified as being either handicapped or nonhandicapped. This provision has particular significance in the case of students believed to be specific learning disabled. Because the existence of a specific learning disability is difficult to establish with certainty, a wide variance has emerged in the number of students identified as being learning disabled in different school districts and states.[5] A clearer definition of specific learning disabilities is needed to assure that students are appropriately identified.

Assessment procedures should also be designed to be as fair as possible. Testing materials and procedures should be selected and administered so that they do not reflect cultural or racial discrimination. Multiple criteria and tests should be used so that no single instrument determines a student's placement or program.

At times, evaluation of a student suspected of having a disability will be undertaken by a multidisciplinary team. This is an excellent approach to evaluation since various professionals bring different perspectives to the decision-making process. If a team cannot be involved in the assessment, however, the diagnostician must take particular care to investigate varied causes, contributing factors, and approaches when considering student difficulties.

Parental Participation and Consent

The past ten years have witnessed tremendous gains in the rights afforded to parents of handicapped children. Parents now must be notified in advance of proposed changes in their child's educational placement. Such notification must be made in the parents' native language. If desired, parents may have access to records pertaining to their child's evaluation, performance, and placement.

When a local educational agency recommends that a student receive a change in his or her educational placement that requires special education or related services, the student's parents must consent to the placement. If the parents do not approve of the change, they may seek an independent evaluation or request an impartial due process hearing where they may challenge the proposed placement. Students who do not have parents to represent their interests in placement decisions (as in the case of students who are wards of the state) are entitled to have surrogate parents appointed to speak for them. The surrogate parents should not be members of the educational system that is recommending the change.

Individualized Education Program

An individualized education program (IEP) will be developed for each handicapped student. The IEP is developed from the results of the multidisciplinary assessment. It should reflect the cooperative efforts of a variety of persons including the following:

- ☐ The student (where appropriate).
- ☐ The student's teacher.
- ☐ One or both of the student's parents.
- ☐ A special education professional.
- ☐ Other individuals who can contribute to the process.

IEPs take many different forms in various educational agencies, but all IEPs must include the following:

- ☐ A statement of the student's present levels of educational performance.
- ☐ A statement of annual goals as well as short-term instructional objectives.
- ☐ A statement of special education or related services to be provided, as well as the extent to which the student will participate in regular education programs.
- ☐ The projected dates for initiation of services and the expected duration of those services.
- ☐ Appropriate objective criteria and evaluation procedures, and an annual evaluation to determine whether the objectives are being achieved.

An IEP must receive a review no less than once a year and must be in effect and approved by the parents before special education and related services can be provided (see figure 10–1).

Educational agencies and teachers must make good faith efforts to assist students in achieving the IEP's objectives and goals. However, neither school officials nor teachers may be held legally responsible if a student does not achieve the growth expected.

Least Restrictive Learning Environment

Many people mistakenly equate the terms *least restrictive environment* and *mainstreaming*. The least restrictive environment requires that handicapped students be taught along with their nonhandicapped same age peers as far as it is reasonably possible. For most handicapped students this will mean that they should be mainstreamed into the regular classroom for at least part of the school day. Clearly, however, mainstreaming is inap-

Individual Education Program

Child's Name *Margi Kraus*

School *12TH St.* **Grade** *5*

Date of Program Entry *Nov. 3, 1983*

Long-Term Goals:

1. *Develop comprehension in 2² reader.*
2. *Develop word attack system.*
3.

Summary of Present Levels of Performance

Comprehends well in 2¹ reader
Knows all initial consonants
Knows many rhyming syllables
Does not attack unknown words

Short-Term Objectives	Specific Ed. or Support Services	Person(s) Responsible	Percent of Time	Beginning and Ending Date	Review Date(s)
1. Margi will use non-questioning activities to further develop comprehension skills.	*classroom*	*classroom teacher*	*5*	*Nov. 3, 1983 - April 1, 1984*	*April 1, 1983*
2. Margi will substitute initial consonants to -AT, -IN, and -ING to form new words	*Title I Resource*	*Title I Resource Teacher*	*5*	*Nov. 3, 1983 - March 1, 1984*	*March 1, 1983*

Committee Members Present

Mrs. King - Principal
Mrs. Kraus - Parent
Mr. Fowler - Teacher
Mrs. Dayhoff - Title I Resource
Mr. Czarnecki - Vice Principal

Parent Approval ✓ **Yes** __ **No**

Louise Kraus
signature

Percent of Time in Regular Classroom ______

Placement Recommendation

Grade 5, Mr. Fowler

Committee recommendations for materials, techniques

use initial consonant substitution with Durrell Speech to Print Phonics. Use non-questioning strategies - Wilson, p312

Objective Evaluation Criteria:

1. Reading comprehension evaluation by vice principal
2. CRT now in use in school for initial consonant substitution.

CONFIDENTIAL INFORMATION:

FIGURE 10–1
An example of an Individualized Educational Program (IEP).

propriate for some handicapped students. When placement options exist for these students, they will be best served by the placement that is the least segregated from the regular school population.

Although acceptance of the least restrictive environment has brought about many positive social and emotional benefits for both handicapped and nonhandicapped students, the classroom teacher must remember that a handicapped child who has been mainstreamed will still need certain instructional adjustments in order to profit from regular classroom instruction. Success or failure in understanding this fundamental principle can often be the difference between success and failure for the mainstreamed student.

SPECIAL CONSIDERATIONS FOR DIAGNOSIS

Careful preparation and data interpretation are necessary in arriving at an accurate and comprehensive reading diagnosis. In the case of a handicapped student, however, the difficulties of diagnostic assessment are often complicated by the presence of the student's handicap. In undertaking the handicapped student's diagnostic reading assessment, attention should be given to the following special considerations.

The reading specialist should know details about the student's handicapping condition prior to assessing the student's reading performance. Diagnostic and remedial decisions may depend on the severity of the student's handicap. Clearly, certain instruments and procedures that may be used in assessing a student with moderate visual impairment will be inappropriate in assessing a legally blind student. For this reason the diagnostician would do well in many cases to request a medical or clinical summary of the student's handicapping condition. This may also spare the student from duplicating previous testing. By knowing about the student's handicap, the reading specialist will be in a better position to judge the effect of the handicap on the student's reading performance. For remedial purposes it will be useful to judge how much of a student's poor performance is attributable to the effects of a handicap (which is often not likely to change) and how much of that poor performance may be due to other factors such as inappropriate instruction or a negative attitude (which might be successfully overcome in a remedial setting). Prior to testing a handicapped student, reading specialists should explore the range and scope of remedial alternatives that will be available should the student be found to need remedial attention. Prior knowledge of available remedial alternatives may aid in diagnostic decision making about such things as which diagnostic lesson to try and the relative importance of the student's behaviors in both group and individual situations. Knowledge of the student's handicap will assist in making a thorough diagnosis.

At the outset of the actual evaluation the diagnostician should establish rapport with the student. Handicapped students, perhaps more than their nonhandicapped peers, need to feel relaxed and secure in the testing session. Depending on the nature and severity of the handicapping condition, the student may have undergone a great deal of prior assessment and feel frustrated, hostile, or embarrassed about the prospects of further testing. Therefore, so that accurate and effective diagnosis can take place, the reading specialist should conscientiously seek to relieve any apprehension that the student may bring to the diagnostic situation.

One novel method of establishing rapport with students is to begin assessment with a diagnostic lesson instead of ending it with one, as is commonly done. These diagnostic lessons can be aimed at the students' strengths or interests. This method may be best suited to handicapped students because of the large amount of diagnostic information that is available about them from previous assessment. When the reading specialist is confident that the handicapped student is at ease and is eager to perform to the best of his or her ability, the evaluation may proceed.

Reading assessment of the handicapped student, as with other students, should include formal and informal testing, direct observation in group and individual settings, and student self-assessment. The reading specialist should resist the natural temptation to rely on his or her favorite instruments. Such a practice can be especially misleading when working with handicapped students. Often such students perform poorly in certain conditions, but do well in other situations. (For example, a hearing-impaired child may perform poorly when questions are asked orally, but do well when responding to signed questions.) Reading specialists should limit the amount and duration of testing to that which is necessary to arrive at reliable hypotheses. Testing which goes beyond that point is superfluous and may only serve to fatigue and frustrate the student.

While administering a test the diagnostician must avoid giving subtle or overt hints. People often feel sympathy or pity for a handicapped student and, while such feelings may be natural, the reading specialist should be on the guard against conveying these feelings to the student or allowing them to taint the test's outcomes. Diagnosticians should remember that the student's interests are best served when the diagnostic findings are as accurate as possible.

Often placement decisions will be based on diagnostic assessment results. For the handicapped student, extremely important decisions, such as the likelihood of success after mainstreamed placement, may depend largely on the reading specialist's accuracy in evaluating the student. Diagnosticians should be able to defend the reliability and validity of the tests that they use. They should also have evidence that each test is a useful assessment instrument for students with specific handicaps. (For example, an auditory discrimination test would not be useful for assessing a deaf student.) Diagnosticians must also be able to demonstrate that a test is not culturally or racially biased. When data are derived from questionable testing instruments, misplacement may result. Correct placement is the responsibility of every individual who is involved in developing an IEP. These individuals share the further responsibility of making far-reaching goal-setting decisions based on their diagnostic recommendations. In order to make these recommendations the reading specialist must be knowledgeable, skillful, and well-prepared.

Subskill assessment is routinely used by some professionals, but it can lead to misplacement if all aspects of the reading process are not assessed. For example, it was once reported that a visually-impaired student had severe weakness in several of the visual discrimination skills. When the student's oral reading skills and silent reading comprehension were assessed, the student was found to be reading above grade level and up to potential. Upon further evaluation the student was found to be doing well in reading class where the teacher considered him a good student. Using a visual discrimination subtest to evaluate a student with visual impairment seems logical; however, in this case, the student had overcome those deficiencies despite an inability to perform on a given test. Had the total reading behavior not been assessed, this student would have been inappropriately placed in a program to improve visual perception.

Other subskill evaluation instruments can lead to similar misevaluation. For example, some readers cannot perform well on phonic subskill tests, yet they can read without difficulty. Others may not do well with auditory discrimination tests, yet also have no difficulty reading. Total reading performance must be assessed along with specific subskills.

Diagnostic assessment of the handicapped student should focus on strengths, although traditionally it tends to concentrate on weaknesses. Within the IEP, strengths can be reported within the section devoted to the student's present levels of functioning.

Looking at the handicapped students' strengths becomes even more important considering the fact that many teachers view handicapped students in a negative light. Teachers need to ask what reading skills a hearing-impaired student has developed, or be certain of how well a mentally retarded student reads. As strengths are identified and communicated to student, parents, and teachers, a new view of the student's capabilities emerges. In some cases this will be the first notation in school records regarding a handicapped student's strengths. When the IEP is developed, program adjustments for a student's strengths will be just as important as those adjustments made because of weaknesses. By emphasizing the student's capabilities, the student is granted a sense of self-worth and the parents are infused with a feeling of hope rather than despair.

Diagnosis of the handicapped student should be continuous. Again, although continuous diagnosis is important for all students, it has particular significance for the handicapped student for a number of reasons. First, some initial diagnostic findings may be incorrect. Without continuous reassessment, these erroneous findings can lead to misguided instructional efforts and unrealistic academic goals. Secondly, many handicapped students can be expected to make smaller and less dramatic gains than other students; continuous diagnostic assessment can aid the teacher not only in redirecting instruction, but also in demonstrating gains to the handicapped child. All students like to do well, and continuous diagnosis can provide a way of bolstering a student's self-concept. Finally, continuous diagnosis can help the reading specialist adopt a more prescriptive approach to remediation—something every handicapped student needs.

SPECIAL CONSIDERATIONS IN REMEDIATION

Not all handicapped students will require remedial work in reading. Many handicapped students have disabilities that do not affect reading growth (such as the orthopedically impaired). Other individuals may be performing at levels equal to their abilities despite having a handicapping condition which might be expected to inhibit reading (such as some visually-impaired students). When a remedial program is indicated, however, the following special considerations may help to guide the handicapped student's instructional program.

Beware of Labels

Because they are often identified for special services, handicapped students bear labels. Labels are an unfortunate by-product of federal and state funding systems which dispense monies to school districts based on the number of handicapped students (by category) that they report. While labels appear to exist out of administrative necessity, classroom teachers and reading specialists should exercise restraint in using labels. Research has shown that labels create anxiety and negative expectations on the part of teachers.[6]

When teachers are told that a given student is disabled, they tend to lessen their expectations for the student; the student, in turn, tends to achieve only up to those lowered expectations. Labels also tell little about a student's specific strengths and weaknesses and even less about instructional approaches that may prove successful with the student. This is primarily because labels are general and because students within labeling categories tend to be heterogeneous. For example, as much variation exists among the behaviors and abilities of learning disabled students as exists among so-called average students.

Reject Failed Methods and Materials

No single method can be expected to prove successful with all handicapped students or even with all students having the same disability. Nevertheless, teachers sometimes appear determined to defend the use of one specific method or material for handicapped students, even when it does not appear to be meeting with satisfactory results. Perhaps this tendency is due to the mistaken idea that because an approach has been developed and recommended for handicapped students, it will be universally successful. This can be a common outgrowth of labeling. If one method fails with a student, teachers should keep trying others until the student meets with success.

Set Realistic Goals

Realistic goal setting plays an integral part in any successful reading program. However, with handicapped students, effective goal setting takes on an even higher priority. If teachers set remedial goals too high and then fail to adjust them, the handicapped student will fall short of those goals, causing additional harm to his or her feelings of self-worth and ambition. On the other hand, if goals are set too low, some students will achieve up to those goals and no farther. One of the most difficult aspects of teaching is the ability to set goals that will challenge students to work to their highest capabilities, but which are not unattainable.

Adapt Instruction

Many of the same approaches and techniques that are used with nonhandicapped students in the regular classroom may be adapted for use with their handicapped counterparts. Frequently, the teacher will need only to make some special accommodation for the student's disability. For example, the language-experience approach might be used successfully with a blind child if the stimulus experience is one which can be perceived through the four senses he or she can use, and if the story is transcribed into Braille. Teachers must remember that their overall objective is to make program adjustments so that a disability does not handicap the student or that an existing handicap can be minimized.

Present Reading As "Making Sense"

Reading involves "making sense" of printed materials; yet a close examination of many remedial programs for handicapped students might lead one to conclude otherwise. In many programs for mildly mentally retarded students, for example, students spend the majority of instructional time attempting to read single words and parts of words. Many programs for the learning disabled emphasize word recognition drill to eliminate reversal difficulties even though attention to meaning might be a more prudent approach to reversal difficulties.[7] In reading, emphasis should be placed on obtaining meaning. Teachers should make every effort to help students see reading as a meaningful process.

Maximize Resource Efforts

A mainstreamed handicapped child often requires the resource services of two or three specialists. And, while such a multidisciplinary approach may be the best way to meet the student's educational needs, problems can arise when services are duplicated, approaches are counterproductive, and time is lost from the regular classroom. In an effort to minimize these difficulties, some schools have scheduled regular multidisciplinary staff meetings to discuss ways to coordinate the special services required by handicapped students. In these team meetings, diagnostic findings can be reviewed so that the group can determine how a student should be placed to minimize the time he or she must spend outside of the regular classroom. In many cases the resource person is asked to assist the student within the student's regular classroom. Team meetings can also be used to coordinate the student's remedial program so that all team members are kept informed of what each member is doing.

Unfortunately, personnel with little reading training often must provide reading instruction for students with multiple handicaps. Since such personnel may have limited understanding of the reading process, they may tend to rely on commercial materials that focus on subskill development. The reading specialist may want to offer suggestions for approaches and strategies that reflect a more complete understanding of the reading process.

It would be better, of course, if the reading specialist were assigned the responsibility of developing and implementing the reading portion of the IEP. The instructional program needs to be coordinated with the classroom teacher who is responsible for most of the other instruction. As in all instructional programs that remove students from the classroom, the IEP's effectiveness is related to the coordinated effort of all involved.

Use Support Systems

Placing one or more handicapped students in a regular classroom often creates additional demands on the time of an already busy classroom teacher. Fortunately, assistance for the classroom teacher is available in a variety of forms.

Resource personnel within the school provide one avenue of support for the classroom teacher. Special education teachers, adaptive physical education teachers, school counselors, reading specialists, and nursing personnel all have training with special students. These professionals are usually delighted to help and can aid the classroom teacher with useful suggestions and advice.

Within the classroom, the teacher can take advantage of student resources. Learning pairs and peer instruction provide two excellent ways of involving students in working with handicapped classmates. Allowing students to work on activities in pairs lets them help each other. Paired learning is especially important when students are working independently from the teacher. Peer instruction allows students who have mastery of a skill to help others learn it. Sometimes to learn a skill it takes an extra two or three times through a process. The student can be strong in one area and not in another, so that different students can be peer instructors at various times. Further, teachers should remember that handicapped students can serve as effective peer instructors just as well as nonhandicapped students. (For example, a deaf child can teach other students to sign.) By looking for handicapped students' strengths teachers will find areas in which they can be the helper.

Two final potential sources of support can be sought from community volunteers and parents. People with special skills or with extra time can help in the classroom for a portion of the day. They may assist a handicapped student who needs individual attention in order to complete some activities. Some communities have been very successful in organizing retired people to assist in neighborhood classrooms. Parents are another often untapped resource. Parents are usually eager to further their children's education and respond with enthusiasm when they are told how they can help.

AREAS OF POTENTIAL DIFFICULTY

Recent changes in the ways handicapped students are educated have created some situations that many teachers may find difficult. These difficulties can result in teacher frustration and discomfort. A discussion of a few of those areas follows.

Lack of Services While Awaiting IEP Approval

Since the IEP must be approved before special educational services can begin, a waiting period at the start of the school year may force the student to remain in an inappropriate placement. Although regulations exist to expedite the placement process, at times this waiting period can become quite extended. Teachers will need to provide instruction during the waiting time. They should assess strengths, help handicapped students feel comfortable in their classrooms, and plan programs that are practicable. They should also seek suggestions from reading specialists for materials and methods of instruction.

Lack of Teacher Training

Regular classroom teachers are usually not trained to work with specific types of handicapped students. Teachers should ask for in-service programs, resource assistance, and recommendations for materials and procedures. In these cases, teachers should not feel inadequate when asking for help. As teachers strengthen their teaching skills with the handicapped, their frustrations will diminish.

Lack of Time

Teachers have reported that they feel that they lack time to help their regular students when they must individualize programs for handicapped students who have been placed in their classroom for portions of the day. Teachers often feel pulled in many directions. Teachers should ask for additional help to relieve them of this time problem. They can use one or more of the resources mentioned earlier in this chapter so that they will have more time.

Distorted IEP

Teachers may be asked to implement an IEP in which the reading section is distorted. This usually occurs when the IEP lists objectives in terms of subskills. Teachers should make note of the difficulties in implementing the IEP and ask that it be reassessed. Observations can be made regarding the frustration that results when the student tries to complete the activities. These frustrations may relate to inappropriate materials or the lack of time to help the student feel success with the IEP's objectives. Once it is clear that the suggestions and goals in the IEP are inappropriate, a team meeting can be called to reassess the program.

Class Size

Special class sizes are sometimes controlled by national, state, or local rules and regulations, although most regular classroom sizes are not. As handicapped students find increasing opportunities to participate in these regular classes, some attention should be given to class size control. If this is not done, classroom teachers will likely come to resent the additional responsibilities placed on them without an adequate support system needed to make the delivery of those responsibilities a reality.

SUMMARY

Federal legislation has permitted sweeping changes in the ways which schools educate handicapped students. Legislation alone, however, cannot insure change. Sincere effort must be made by all who come in contact with handicapped students on a day-to-day basis to realize the potential which exists within the law. The two greatest obstacles to positive change in educating handicapped students appear to be money and attitude. Legislation can provide money, but the educators working with handicapped students must approach their task with desire to explore the limits of what each of these students *can* do.

Advances have already been made in the ways handicapped students are being educated. Increasing numbers of students who formerly were enrolled in self-contained special classes are now taught in classes with their peers. This serves to break down the barriers of fear and aversion that have plagued the handicapped student in the past. Furthermore, some handicapped students are discovering that they are not as handicapped as they once thought themselves.

Of course the picture is not all positive. Many students have handicapping conditions that make a regular classroom placement inappropriate. Misunderstanding and harassing of the handicapped still exist. The problems mentioned in this chapter are not yet solved. New priorities for the handicapped must be set and funding systems must be adjusted. But happily, handicapped students are now finding a new type of schooling waiting for them.

NOTES

1. Edward L. Meyen, *Exceptional Children and Youth* (Denver: Love Publishing Company, 1978), 12–18.
2. Ibid.
3. Sterling L. Ross, Henry G. DeYoung, and Julius S. Cohen, "Confrontation: Special Education Placement and the Law," in *Contemporary Issues in Special Education,* ed. Rex E. Schmid, Judee Moneypenny, and Ronald Johnston (New York: McGraw-Hill Book Company, 1977): 26–28.
4. Lloyd M. Dunn, "An Overview," in *Exceptional Children in the Schools,* ed. Lloyd M. Dunn (New York: Holt, Rinehart and Winston, Inc., 1973): 43–45.
5. Beatrice F. Birman, "Problems of Overlap Between Title I and P.L. 94–142: Implications for the Federal Role in Education," *Educational Evaluation and Policy Analysis* (May–June 1981): 5–19.
6. Bob Algozzine and Laura Stoller, "Effects of Labels and Competence on Teachers' Attributions for a Student," *The Journal of Experimental Education* (Spring 1981): 132–36.
7. Stanley L. Rosner, Jules C. Abrams, Paul R. Daniels, and Gilbert B. Schiffman, "Dealing With the Reading Needs of the Learning Disabled Child," *Journal of Learning Disabilities* (October 1981): 436–48.

———. *A Teacher's Guide to PL 95–142.* Washington, D.C.: National Educational Association, 1978. Uses a situation-response approach to explain some of the major implications of PL 94–142. Tackles controversial as well as legal implications. May be reproduced for teacher use.

Ballard, Joseph. *Public Law 94–142 and Section 504—Understanding What They Are and Are Not.* Reston, Va.: Council for Exceptional Children, 1977. Uses a question-answer approach to assist one in understanding PL 94–142 and Section 504. Provides detailed information and suggested additional references.

———. *Education for All Handicapped Children.* Washington, D.C.: National Educational Association, 1978. Uses a case-study approach to examine the impact of Section 504 and PL 94–142. Provides both positive and negative reactions of teachers, parents, and other school officials.

Gearheart, Bill R. and Willenberg, Ernest P. *Application of Pupil Assessment Information,* Third Edition. Denver: Love Publishing Company, 1980. This text provides useful explanations of technical aspects of testing instruments and short descriptions of many tests used by professionals who evaluate students with handicaps. It also suggests means by which diagnosis and remediation can be linked in an IEP.

Meyen, Edward L. *Exceptional Children and Youth.* Denver: Love Publishing Company, 1978. Chapter 1 presents an informative overview of recent changes in the field of special education. This text includes "Resource Guides" at the end of each chapter which suggest excellent source materials on a variety of topics.

Rosner, Stanley L.; Abrams, Jules C.; Daniels, Paul R.; and Schiffman, Gilbert B. "Dealing With the Reading Needs of the Learning Disabled Child." *Journal of Learning Disabilities* 14 (October 1981): 436–48. This interesting and provocative article presents the need for attending to the cognitive and affective needs of the learning disabled student when designing instruction. The authors question the use of several prevalent practices.

Wallace, Gerald and Larsen, Stephen C. *Educational Assessment of Learning Problems: Testing for Teaching.* Boston, Massachusetts: Allyn and Bacon, 1978. A well-researched book which presents informal and formal assessment techniques in a wide range of pertinent skill areas. The authors emphasize the need for active classroom assessment as a base for meaningful instruction.

Editorial

Karen Herrington
is a third-grade teacher for the Troupsberg Central School District in New York.

Julie, I was told by veteran teachers in my building, was a very slow learner with particular difficulties with reading. She had failed first grade, as had been predicted in kindergarten, struggled through second, and was now (at her parents' insistence) being transferred, not promoted, into my third grade classroom. Furthermore, Julie was an epileptic whose seizures had only recently been brought under control through medication. I thought Julie's records read somewhat like a poker hand upon which only a few people would dare place a substantial bet. However, after all I had read and heard about PL 94-142 and mainstreaming, I was resigned to being the one left holding the cards. It was my job to somehow change the odds in favor of Julie.

The outcome seemed rather bleak until one afternoon towards the end of the school year I found myself anxiously awaiting the arrival of Julie's parents. I leafed through my record-keeping papers, searching for the right words to put with my feelings. The decision had been made to retain Julie for another year in my third grade classroom. The test scores, report card grades, and samples of her daily work unmistakably confirmed what had to be said. Nonetheless, I didn't think that would make it any easier for them to take or for me to give.

I began the conference speaking of hopes, not despair, cans, rather than cannots; and chances to try again next year, rather than the failures of the past year. As I made references to Julie's strengths in reading, her mother interrupted with a sad recounting of the many teachers and physicians who had emphasized only what Julie could not do. Consequently, Julie's parents began to explain how they had become very bitter and unwilling to encourage their child's efforts to succeed. With this in mind, the remainder of the conference was spent on setting realistic goals for the next year and discussing what they could do to help Julie's reading progress, especially during the summer months. Although this conversation did not change plans to retain Julie, that meeting encouraged Julie's parents to accept their child, to realize she wasn't as handicapped as they had thought, and to at least give her the same chances as the brightest of her peers.

As I filed my report with the handicapped committee at the end of her second year in my classroom, I reflected on the gains Julie had made. In my mind, however unintentional it was, Julie had been dealt a great disservice by those who had concentrated only on what she could not do, believed it would always be that way, and imposed these attitudes upon her. Perhaps, they had failed her much more than she could have failed them. Admittedly, Julie may never become a top-notch student in reading, but she could feel good about herself and what she could do.

Two years have passed since Julie left my classroom, and although the current in the mainstream is often rough, I remain confident that she will stay afloat *if* her teachers give her and her parents (and many others like them) the positive support they so desperately need.

11

Evaluation of Diagnostic, Remedial, and Resource Programs

CHAPTER OUTLINE

CHAPTER EMPHASES

- ☐ The remedial program must be continuously evaluated.
- ☐ Evaluation of remedial programs should be made on the basis of student change.
- ☐ Educator evaluation should be included in the remedial program's evaluation.

Instruction that has been determined effective to diagnose the strengths and needs of students stands a good chance of succeeding. Upon completion of such a remedial program, students are likely to be improved readers. The educator must determine what changes have taken place and assess the extent of those changes. Many questions need to be answered in an effective evaluation of a remedial program, such as the following:

1. Has performance in reading improved?
2. Has attitude toward reading changed?
3. Has reading become a chosen free-time activity?
4. Could more have been accomplished with more efficient diagnosis?
5. Was observed progress attributable to the remedial program?
6. Have parents noticed behavior changes?
7. Did observed changes occur in areas stressed in the remedial program?
8. If the program was conducted outside of the classroom, has the classroom teacher been able to build on the progress made there?

These and other questions should be studied and answered. Naturally, not all of them apply to every situation, and some are more difficult to answer than others. For example, if a student made great gains during a remedial program that was designed to supplement what the teacher was doing in the classroom, to what does one attribute the progress? Maybe the teacher made important adjustments in instruction and is responsible for the student's improvement, or maybe it was from an effective remedial program; more than likely, it was some combination of the two.

GUIDELINES FOR EVALUATION

The following guidelines, applicable to all education, have particular application when evaluating the effectiveness of remedial reading programs.

Evaluation Should Have a Broad Base

Ample allowance must be made for factors such as improved medical attention, relaxed home pressures, and reaction to both negative and positive diagnosis. If a student has been provided with glasses as a result of physical screening, a proper evaluation of the tutoring program must give consideration to the effect of the glasses as well as to the instruction. In an examination of clinic cases at the University of Maryland, for example, it was found that students referred for inadequate visual screening performance made better progress (as a group) if the parents followed the referral advice than students whose parents did not follow referral advice. Apparently, attention to the visual needs of these students had an effect on the progress they made. The appropriate importance to be attributed to each factor in evaluation is extremely difficult and, at times, impossible to determine.

Evaluation Should Be Continuous

Continuous evaluation is crucial to effective instruction. It involves many of the same processes as diagnosis (i.e., an evaluation of the student's skill development and reading effectiveness). Evaluation of past performance should be considered diagnosis for future instruction, therefore evaluation should be continuous.

Evaluation Should Be Objective

Objective measures of performance should be used in an effort to control bias. One often reads evaluation reports that state that "the teachers and students were enthusiastic about the progress that had been made." Although enthusiasm is a highly desirable factor, it cannot be the sole basis for evaluation of program effectiveness. However, nonobjective evaluation techniques are certainly valuable and are not to be precluded by this guideline.

Evaluation Should Be In Terms of Established Goals

It is sometimes desirable and natural for considerable progress to be noticed in areas for which instruction had not been planned. Such progress, however desirable, must be considered secondary to the program's goals. Teachers must be cautious about claiming credit for attitude change, for example, unless the program included attitude change in its objectives.

Student Self-Evaluation

Student evaluation of remedial progress and remedial programs should not be overlooked. Students often render insights toward remediation that elude educators. Teachers should seek student self-evaluation and program evaluation, and they should use these in evaluating remedial programs.

Pupil–teacher conferences can be used for self-evaluation. If students feel that they will not be penalized for their honesty, many can provide accurate, useful statements concerning their feelings about how they have done in their remedial sessions, or about their reactions to specific materials and techniques. Questionnaires also can be used in student evaluation. Questions concerning how they feel they have performed in terms of specific objectives, the portions of the program they enjoyed most and least, and the changes they would recommend may be included. Finally, contract evaluation can be used for self-evaluation. Such evaluation occurs immediately after the contract is completed so students can evaluate their own work honestly.

CHANGE IN STUDENT BEHAVIOR

The teacher's first concern is the program's effect on student behavior. Basically, four areas of changes are open for observation in student behavior; attitude, reading behavior, test results, and school performance.

Attitude Changes

If students enter remedial programs with poor attitudes toward reading, school, and themselves, one of the remedial program's major goals would be to improve those attitudes. Data for justi-

A major goal of the remedial program is to strengthen good attitudes toward reading, school, and self.

fication of attitude change are readily available. Behavior in class, willingness to attend to reading tasks, choice of reading for free-time activities, willingness to discuss ideas obtained from reading, and willingness to be helpful to others (perhaps as a tutor) are all useful indicators of attitude changes.

Following remedial sessions at the University of Maryland reading clinic, parents are petitioned for information on changes they have noticed. The most frequent change noted is that the student is now reading. "He picks up the newspaper and actually reads it." "She reads road signs and billboards now as we drive down the road." Such comments show that the students are happy to display their reading skills and see themselves as readers. Information can be obtained from students as well as parents to assure the reliability of the responses. The inherent danger of interviews and questionnaires is the tendency for respondents to maintain a "halo" effect. Therefore, the interview or questionnaire should be structured to avoid pointing to obviously expected responses.

Classroom behaviors provide readily observable indications of students' attitudes. Observation in the classroom, when systematically approached, gives teachers the advantage of examining student behavior in real-life reading situations rather than having to make judgments about students based solely on paper-and-pencil tests. Miccinati and Pine suggest the use of running commentaries; shadow studies which note student behavior at 15 minute intervals; checklists; and anecdotal records.[1] One way to assess reading attitudes with any of these methods would be to note how a given student uses Sustained Silent Reading (SSR) time in the classroom. What is the student reading? What percent of the time is the student engaged in on-task behavior? How long does it take the student to settle down and begin reading? The systematic observation of the answers to these and other questions may shed some light on the nature of the student's reading attitudes.

Reading attitudes may also be assessed with an attitude scale. A paired scale requires a student to express a preference between two stimulus objects, activities, words, phrases, or pictures. A pairing instrument which uses pictures to assess the reading attitudes of primary-age children is Askov's Primary Pupil Reading Attitude Inventory.[2] A summated rating scale requires a student to respond to a statement along a five point continuum which ranges from *Strongly Agree* to *Strongly Disagree.* The Heathington Primary Attitude Scale and the Heathington Intermediate Attitude Scale are examples of summated rating scales.[3]

Reading Behavior Changes

During remedial activities teachers should keep records of reading behavior changes which indicate what skills in reading the students display that they could not display when the program started. These data will be available if teachers collect them as instruction proceeds. Evaluated contracts can be a source of such data. Informal, teacher-made check tests can be administered when the teacher feels that some students have developed a new skill. Teachers are more receptive to a discussion of reading behavior changes of their students than to a discussion of test score improvement. The changes in reading behavior can be readily used in the daily classroom reading program.

Behavior changes can be noted and recorded best through some type of systematic observation procedure. By establishing a list of kinds of behavior desired and by observing students periodically with the use of a checklist, the frequency of that behavior can be recorded. If such behavior were observed two times in twenty observations at the beginning of a program and eighteen times out of twenty observations later in the program, then one can start to talk specifically about that behavior change. Casual observations, however, are very difficult to quantify.

One useful means for teachers to gain insights into a student's reading behavior change is to keep a record of the nature and amount of a student's independent reading. It might be expected that, if significant changes are occurring in a student's skills and attitudes, those changes will be reflected in the student's independent reading habits. The teacher should be cautioned, however, to not merely look for the student to select more difficult books to read. In many cases with remedial reading students a positive step is reflected when they select *easier* reading material. This is because so many poor readers self-select books on the basis of pictures, covers, topics, and so on, and end up selecting books that are too difficult for them to read independently.

Test Results

By diagnosing from test answers, posttesting can provide some information about student progress in a remedial program. But the problems are almost great enough to discourage much reliance on pre-posttest results.

First, the results that report gains in reading levels are impossible to interpret in terms of reading behavior. For example, a report indicating that a student gained four years in reading comprehension tells nothing about the student's actual reading behavior. Second, gain scores are notoriously unreliable. On many tests, a difference of one or two items can make a large gain score. Third, it is difficult to obtain two forms that are truly equivalent of any test. When different forms are used, it is difficult to determine whether noticed gains are the result of the remedial program or the test form that was used.

When educators use test results to evaluate remedial programs, they should use teacher-made criterion-referenced tests (CRTs), containing numerous items for each objective, to assure maximum reliability. Some examples are:

1. Word lists taken from reading materials at various levels can be used to measure gains in word recognition.
2. Paragraphs followed by carefully constructed questions taken from materials of varying reading levels can assist in measuring gains in reading accuracy (when reading orally) and in comprehension (when reading silently). By structuring the reading tasks, insights can also be gained into both recall and locating abilities.
3. Skill quizzes constructed by teachers to assess students' abilities to perform in the areas of given instruction can be used to measure skill development. Such information is useful for the teachers who will work with the students next. The information is reported in terms of reading behavior and can be interpreted further if desirable.

Table 11–1 illustrates how CRT pre-post evaluation can be used to evaluate one aspect of comprehension performance. Each student made impressive gains.

TABLE 11–1
Use of criterion-referenced tests for pre-test and post-test evaluation of comprehension

Response to Interpretive Questions				
Student	**Passage Level**			
	Grade 5		**Grade 6**	
	Pre	Post	Pre	Post
Brook	70%	100%	50%	80%
Jennifer	80%	100%	60%	90%
Andrea	60%	90%	40%	70%

Performance in School

For those students who have been removed from the classroom for remedial assistance, the ultimate evaluation of the success of the program is in terms of how well they do when they return to the classroom. Feedback from the classroom teacher is one source of information; grades earned are another.

Teachers can be interviewed or polled through a questionnaire to discuss observed changes in classroom behavior. If the students improve behavior in small groups out of the classroom, the teacher must be certain that those changes carry over into the classroom setting. If not, then the program should be adjusted either in the classroom or for more extended remediation out of the classroom.

Grades are another way of looking at classroom performance; however, many variables that influence grades cannot be evaluated by grades alone. Over a long period of time, the grades in table 11–2 seem to tell us that Nancy was doing poorly prior to remediation and has done much better since remediation.

These changes, however, cannot necessarily be attributed to the remedial program. Perhaps fourth grade represents the year in which a difficult personal situation was resolved in Nancy's life. Or, perhaps Nancy experienced a positive change in attitude related to school. In the case of an individual's grade improvement, teachers cannot attribute the change directly to the remedial program. However, if most of the students enrolled in the program showed similar gains, this might indicate that the program was having a positive effect.

WAYS TO INTERPRET GAIN SCORES

Bleismer suggests methods of using gain scores regardless of the severe limitations they have for interpretation.[4] These interpretations of gain scores create some interesting problems when

TABLE 11–2
Earned grade record over time

Student's Name Nancy					
Subject	**Remediation**				
	Grade 2	**Grade 3**	**Grade 4**	**Grade 5**	**Grade 6**
Reading	D	D	C	B	B
Language	C	C	C	B	B
Spelling	D	F	D	C	C

one is attempting to evaluate a remedial program through gain scores.

Grade-Level Improvement

Bleismer, in citing three basic post-remediation evaluation techniques, calls this a simple pretest and posttest comparison. If a student enters a remedial program reading at 4.5 grade level and leaves the reading program at 5.5 grade level, a teacher can conclude that the student has gained 1.0 years in grade level. Obviously, the adequacy of the test instrument used to determine grade-level performance limits this aspect of evaluation. It does not account for the student's chronological or mental age increase or for changes that would have occurred without remediation.

Reading skill performance as compared to grade level is of particular interest to both the classroom teacher and the principal because it has much to do with the student's placement in a particular room and within a class.

Reading Potential

Evaluation of reading potential attempts to determine whether students are working up to expected levels. Bleismer calls attention to the fact that potential (mental age) will change with age and that estimates must be adjusted for effective evaluation.[5] Regardless of a student's grade-level performance and ability to perform in an assigned classroom, growth up to potential is generally considered a desirable goal of remediation. In table 11–3, if Jim has an estimated potential of 5.0 and a reading level of 3.0, his working development is lagging behind his mental development by 2.0 years. If, after a semester of work, this reading level rises to 4.2, his potential will have to be reestimated before growth can be measured.

Note that in table 11–3 Jim's reading potential increased as he grew older, thereby lessening the apparent effect of the dif-

TABLE 11–3
Comparison of potential and achievement

Student's Name Jim		
	January	May
Potential	5.0	5.8
Reading	3.0	4.2
Difference	2.0	1.6

ference in reading grade-level changes. Remedial sessions accelerated his growth over his potential by .4 years (found by subtracting the differences). Reading potential techniques will be of more interest to the reading specialist than to the classroom teacher or the parent. One major problem with using potential as a standard occurs when remedial efforts are being made to improve skills related to these measures of potential. In those cases, potential will be misleading if used as a standard. For example, if a remedial program includes opportunities for language development, opportunities of potential improvement are also included. Such programs actually have resulted in considerable improvement on language-related tests of intelligence.

Past Performance

Evaluation of skill improvement in terms of students' previous performance rates is of some advantage with older students. Bleismer recommends that the identifiable variables be controlled.[6] Suppose that Judy (see table 11–4) has completed six years of school and has scored at a grade level 4.6 before remediation is begun. This indicates an average gain of .6 years of reading skill for each year in school (4.6 − 1.0 ÷ 6). (Note that 1.0 must be subtracted, as all children start with a reading level of 1.0 [the zero month of first grade]). If she obtained a reading level of 5.5 by the end of one year in remediation, the gain would be .9 years of skill in one year (5.5 − 4.6 = .9). Yet she is not reading up to grade level and may not be reading up to expectations. She has not progressed even one full year under intensive remediation. Nevertheless, improvement is greater than it has been in the past, thus indicating that the remedial program is profitable to her.

Note that the gain of .9 years is greater by .3 years than could have been expected from the average of previous efforts. While of interest to the reading specialist and the classroom teacher, the rate of improvement during remediation is little

TABLE 11–4
Comparison of current achievement with past achievement

Student's Name *Judy*			
Years in School	**Average Yearly Gain Before Tutoring**	**Gain During Year of Tutoring**	**Growth Attributed to Tutoring**
6	(4.6 − 1.0 ÷ 6) = .6	.9	.3

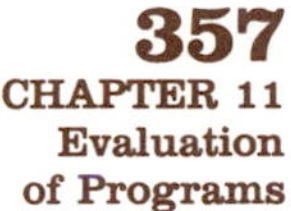

Evaluating students' previous performance rates is particularly useful with older students.

consolation to the student or the parent, especially if the student remains limited in classroom performance.

Evaluation of past performance is limited by the unlikely assumption that the past performance was evenly distributed. However, with older students who have significant reading deficiencies, this method of evaluation may provide the most useful indication of student progress.

Limitations

All of the evaluation techniques suggested here are limited by the instruments being used to make comparisons. Standardized tests are inherently unreliable and cause notable gains to be suspect due to the error factor of the measuring instrument. Grade-equivalent scores on these tests are not equal units for measuring gains. Misinterpretation of grade-equivalent scores on standardized tests has become so widespread that the Delegates' Assembly of the International Reading Association has adopted a resolution urging test publishers to eliminate grade-equivalent scores from their tests.[7] If such tests are used at all, standard scores should be used. In addition, the test selected may not measure the skills that were remedial objectives, and the standardization population may be mismatched with the remedial group. Thus, standardized tests should usually only be used to indicate gains with groups of students; informal tests can be used to measure the gains of individual students.

Two other problems occur when evaluating with standardized tests. First, all standardized tests contain error in their measurement; the amount of error makes score changes possible by chance. Therefore, small gains in standardized test scores over short periods of time cannot be considered highly accurate. Second, students may *regress*. If a group of students were given a standardized test today and then readministered the same test a week later, low-scoring students would, by chance, tend to improve their scores (scores would tend to move toward the mean), while high-scoring students would decrease their scores (scores would tend to move toward the mean). This phenomenon has obvious implications in evaluating the reading performance of students who have been initially referred for special programs in reading due to their low performance on a standardized test.

EDUCATOR EFFICIENCY

The educator's efficiency is difficult to evaluate and is, therefore, less likely to receive the evaluation efforts that student growth receives. Educator efficiency in programs should be evaluated in the following areas.

Adequacy of Diagnosis

Because of emphasis placed on the proper use of diagnosis and the time spent in accomplishing it, it can validly be included in evaluation. Educators must determine whether diagnosis has uncovered a student's remedial strengths and needs effectively and precisely. Furthermore, they must decide that the diagnosis, while not overextended, is complete enough to cover the areas of the students' skill development. When there is a failure to evaluate in all areas, inefficiency will likely develop in remedial sessions. At times, teachers use tests that, for them, appear to supply essential information for a diagnosis; however, upon closer examination, these tests do not provide any information that could not be determined more readily by other diagnostic techniques.

Adequacy of Remedial Approach

As educators become accustomed to working in remediation, specific approaches often develop into standard procedures with all students. The resulting error here, unless there are constant attempts at evaluation, is that diagnosis is disregarded, since a given remedial approach is used with all students. For example, if all students were to be tutored through the use of the language-experience approach, diagnostic conclusions are not used to determine the remedial approach. Through evaluation of remedial approaches the educator is led to develop the variety of effective approaches prescribed by the students' diagnostic strengths and needs.

Adequacy of Remedial Techniques

Similar to the difficulty of not selecting adequate remedial approaches, using a prescribed technique with all students regardless of the remedial approach is equally limiting and should be avoided through careful evaluation of remedial techniques. For example, a graph to illustrate progress will not motivate all students in all remedial techniques. The evaluation of techniques will save time in remediation and lead the educator to those techniques best suited to the students' strengths and needs.

Adequacy of Remedial Materials

As educators become familiar with the manuals and contents of the variety of materials available in remediation, they are likely to select and use those that appeal most to them. This action is appropriate when these materials are selected after an evaluation of their effectiveness; however, if they are selected on the basis of familiarity alone, their adequacy should be evaluated. As the flood of materials continues, the educator will need to be involved with more material evaluation.

In addition to the materials' appeal, educators need to consider the appropriateness of the level of materials. As stated throughout this text, students experiencing difficulties in reading must be placed in materials which they can handle with ease. The single indicator of a successful remedial program is when students are reading fluently and with ease. The press to move these students to more difficult materials usually only results in frustration for students and teachers alike.

A variety of techniques is available to assist the educator in the various aspects of evaluation discussed here. The teacher can and should consult with other teachers; ask for help from a reading resource person in the school or district; read evaluations of materials in the professional literature; talk with students about books they like and dislike; conduct studies using certain materials with one group of students and other materials with another group; examine the activities required by the materials and compare them to objectives for the remedial program; and give students choices of materials to use, observing their consistent selection of one over another.

Single-subject experiments have a long history in psychology and psychiatry, but have been used infrequently in education. The appeal of studying the effects of an intervention on one subject over a period of time holds considerable merit in evaluating educational innovation.

Recently, considerable attention has been given to using single-subject research ($N = 1$) to evaluate the effects of schooling on individual students.[8] Adapted from case study research, single-subject research is an acceptable, maybe even preferred, way to study individuals.

In $N = 1$ research, subjects serve as the controls, and baseline data is collected over a period of time. Once a pattern of behavior is observed and that behavior stabilizes, an intervention is introduced. The effects of that intervention are also observed over time in the same manner that baseline behaviors were observed.

The advantages of $N = 1$ studies are:

1. Data are collected over time. One unusual behavior is not compared to one intervention behavior, but many data points are used.
2. The subject becomes the control in the experiment.
3. Specific interventions can be isolated and studied in detail.
4. These studies, when replicated, provide convincing evidence of the effects of an intervention.

As with other types of evaluation, much rests on the validity of the dependent variable. Therefore, natural school evaluation techniques should be used (e.g., the number of sight words learned in a lesson).

Adequacy of Total School Efforts

If requested, the reading specialist should be able to conduct an evaluation of the total school efforts in the area of diagnostic and remedial reading. Assuming that the reading specialist is acquainted with research design and controlled experimentation techniques and has the ability to interpret research data, there is little reason for not using such techniques. Burg, Kaufman, Korngold, and Kovner present an evaluation model that consists of the following four major stages: (1) Needs assessment; (2) Program planning based on the needs assessment; (3) Formative evaluation, including implementation evaluation and progress evaluation of students in the program; (4) Outcome evaluation, both in terms of skills and attitude.[9] To be effective, evaluation must be as broadly based as possible and involve students, parents, classroom teachers, reading specialists, support staff, and administrators. The evaluation should also be based on the stated goals of the reading program and not on the evaluation team's subjective impressions. Some schools involve college or university consultants in chairing the evaluation effort because of the particular expertise of these people and because evaluation conducted by people from outside the school is less likely to reflect bias.

Adequacy of the Resource Role

If the reading specialist functions in a resource role, that role deserves careful evaluation also. How one functions on screening committees, in teaming situations, in helping teachers try new ideas or materials, and when conducting staff development sessions are examples of areas that may be included.

Reading specialist self-evaluation, classroom teacher evaluation, and supervisor evaluation can all be included. Questionnaires, observations, and teacher requests for assistance can be used to compile an evaluation report.

The resource role is of major importance (see chapter 13) and therefore should receive a most objective and careful evaluation. If ignored, a real possibility exists that one may go on performing functions that are not valued by others and are thereby ineffective. For example, a reading specialist may develop a newsletter each month that highlights new materials that have arrived in the school. If, upon evaluation, the reading specialist finds that no one reads the newsletter, then another form of communication about new materials should be developed. To continue with the newsletter would be a waste of effort because it has proven an ineffective way for informing teachers of new materials.

If teachers do not value the resource role and would prefer that the reading specialist work more with students, a reevaluation of the activities in that resource role need to be undertaken. Discussions with staff and supervisors may facilitate a better use of the reading specialist's time and efforts. For example, one may find that classroom teachers really appreciate the efforts to facilitate the use of new materials by way of demonstrations but they do not value the half-hour-per-week staff development sessions on classroom management. Reevaluating the staff development sessions would then be in order and a possible increase in the demonstration of new materials may be useful.

Adequacy of District-Wide Reading Programs and Personnel

While evaluating individual teachers and school-wide reading programs is highly desirable, district-wide reading programs and personnel should also be evaluated. This type of evaluation is usually initiated by supervisory personnel on central office staffs. Various school personnel can be surveyed with a questionnaire that lists the program objectives or with sampling interviews. The questionnaires or interviews can provide data regarding the number of teachers or students serviced and an indication of their perceived effectiveness. By obtaining that information from teachers, reading specialists, and school-based administrators, the central office staff has data that can be used for school board decision making, public relations, and for central office staff meetings.

SUMMARY

Evaluation should be carefully planned for all remedial programs. To make valid comparisons, pretesting and noting behavior prior to remediation are essential. To evaluate the student success in a remedial program, teachers should be expected to use assessments of attitudes, reading skills, test performance, and classroom performance. To assure professional growth, teachers should continuously evaluate their own effectiveness in both diagnosis and remediation.

NOTES

1. Jeannette L. Miccinati and Mary A. Pine, *Observing Students' Reading Skills* (York, Pennsylvania: The College Reading Association, 1979), 11–34.
2. Eunice N. Askov, *Primary Pupil Reading Attitude Inventory* (Dubuque, Iowa: Kendall/Hunt Publishers, 1982), 6.
3. Betty S. Heathington, *Heathington Primary Attitude Scale* and *Heathington Intermediate Attitude Scale* in *Teaching Reading*, ed. J. Estill Alexander (Boston: Little, Brown and Company, 1983), 365–68.
4. Emery P. Bleismer, "Evaluating Progress in Remedial Reading Programs," *The Reading Teacher* (March 1962): 344–50.
5. Ibid.
6. Ibid.
7. Delegates' Assembly of the International Reading Association, "Misuse of Grade Equivalents," *The Reading Teacher* (January 1982): 464.
8. Alan E. Kazdin, *Single-Case Research Designs* (New York: Oxford University Press, 1982), chapter 1.

9. Leslie A. Burg, Maurice Kaufman, Blanche Korngold, and Albert Kovner, *The Complete Reading Supervisor: Tasks and Roles* (Columbus, OH.: Charles E. Merrill Publishing Company, 1978), 101–11.

SUGGESTED READINGS

Anderson, Scarvia and Ball, Samuel. *The Profession and Practice of Program Evaluation.* San Francisco: Jossey-Bass Publishers, 1980. The authors present educational evaluation as a foundation for program improvement. This comprehensive book examines the match between evaluation purposes and evaluation methods. Chapter eight discusses ethical responsibilities in evaluation.

Burg, Leslie A.; Kaufman, Maurice; Korngold, Blanche; and Kovner, Albert. *The Complete Reading Supervisor: Tasks and Roles.* Columbus, OH: Charles E. Merrill Publishing Company, 1978. Several of the chapters of this book are of interest from an evaluation perspective. In chapter six, a model for evaluation is discussed. Chapter eight surveys observational techniques for measuring teacher performance, pupil-teacher interaction, and pupil behaviors. The book closes with a discussion of evaluation as it applies to in-service staff development.

Farr, Roger. *Reading: What Can Be Measured?* Newark, Delaware: International Reading Association, 1969. Farr takes an objective but critical look at evaluation instruments used by reading personnel in the schools and in clinics. He provides guidelines for the application of research to work in reading. Farr has made a significant contribution that should be considered required reading.

Kazdin, Alan E. *Single-Case Research Designs.* New York: Oxford University Press, 1982. A thorough discussion of methods for using single-case research. Techniques for conducting such research, an argument in favor of these types of designs, and a discussion of the advantages and limitations of single-case research are included. If teachers want to conduct this type of evaluation they should study a book such as this.

Maginnis, George. "Evaluating Remedial Reading Gains." *Journal of Reading* (April 1970): 523–28. This article discusses several of the inherent problems involved in evaluating remedial reading. Maginnis presents several positive suggestions for avoiding those problems.

Miccinati, Jeanette L. and Pine, Mary A. *Observing Students' Reading Skills.* York, Pennsylvania: The College Reading Association, 1979. In a 52 page monograph the authors present a rationale for classroom observation, suggest methods for employing observation in a systematic manner, and give illustrations of practical applications of observational techniques in classroom settings. A very useful and informative guide to observational techniques.

Smith, Richard J.; Otto, Wayne; and Hansen, Lee. *The School Reading Program: A Handbook for Teachers, Supervisors, and Specialists.* Boston: Houghton Mifflin Company, 1978. Evaluation is discussed as an integral part of effective program development in chapter seven of this text. The authors make the point that educational decision making is most sound when based on objective and reliable evaluation.

Editorial

Marianne Pfeiffer
is a reading specialist for the Howard County Public Schools in Maryland.

Edith was a second-grade student. Informal diagnostic testing done by her classroom teacher at the beginning of the school year indicated that she had not retained many of the reading skills she had been taught during first grade. The classroom teacher asked me as the school reading specialist to conduct further assessment of Edith's reading.

Word recognition and silent reading comprehension scores from an Informal Reading Inventory suggested that she would probably be most successful in a basal of a lower readability level than the basal she had apparently "finished" in the spring of first grade. Further assessment showed that Edith had strengths in word meaning and use of context clues, but showed weaknesses in word recognition, word attack, and silent reading comprehension.

A review of Edith's cumulative folder showed that Edith had progressed steadily through all of the first-grade readers, but that skill testing conducted at the end of each reader showed "fragile" growth with progressively more skill deficiencies.

A conference was held with Edith's mother, Mrs. Hensley, to discuss starting Edith in a corrective reading program. Mrs. Hensley shared great concern about Edith's progress in reading and feelings about school. Mrs. Hensley stated that during her preschool years Edith had been a happy, relaxed child who greatly enjoyed singing or putting on skits for an audience. Now she was shy and withdrawn around adults. Mrs. Hensley also shared that during her preschool years Edith had enjoyed being read to or looking at books, but that she no longer was interested in either.

Edith began receiving corrective reading help in addition to her classroom reading instruction. The classroom teacher and I tried to build on Edith's strengths using reading material we were sure Edith could successfully read. Each time we conferenced with Mrs. Hensley we shared careful documentation of Edith's reading "successes." Mrs. Hensley often requested reinforcement activities to use at home, and we supplied her with many games and activities which we hoped would be enjoyable as well as reinforcing.

In March at a report card conference Mrs. Hensley, the classroom teacher, and I all agreed that Edith had made substantial progress in reading since the fall. We discussed Edith's strengths in the areas of word recognition, word attack, literal and interpretive comprehension, and study skills. We were all obviously pleased with the conference, but before Mrs. Hensley left she shared one "problem." It seemed that at home in the evenings Edith didn't want to leave the books she was reading to do reading games and activities with her mother.

Mrs. Hensley probably didn't anticipate the look of shock that was on my face. Had we really failed to communicate to Edith's mother that the overall goal of the year's classroom and corrective reading instruction had been to help Edith become a "reader"? As flashes of previous conferences went through my mind I sought evidence that we had not forgotten to verbalize our goal. I felt relieved as I remembered fragments of conversations in which we had discussed Edith's attitude toward reading as well as how we planned to help her realize and use her reading strengths. Possibly our failure came in not clearly defining the term "reader." I then remembered suggested book lists and discussion concerning allowing Edith to read books of her own choice. As I concluded that at no one point had we lost sight of our goal, I also realized once again the importance of continuous evaluation which keeps not only the day's objective, but the overall goal in our minds and in our verbalizations. Parents and students can only assume that what we verbalize is what we consider important.

Later I reflected on one more lesson I had been retaught during this conference—the importance of student self-evaluation. Mrs. Hensley, the classroom teacher, and I had been concerned about Edith's initial negative attitude toward reading. As we saw the change in Edith's attitude and reading ability we should have been more sensitive to and supportive of Edith's image of herself as a "reader." If we had been more attuned we might have realized that Edith had a more efficient and possibly clearer perception of the situation than we did. She recognized her reading strengths and she was enjoying putting these into use. It seemed that she realized the goal of the year's activities had been for her to become a reader and, when not encumbered by adults, a reader was precisely what she was.

12
Parental Roles

CHAPTER OUTLINE

PARENTS CAN HELP

CHAPTER EMPHASES

- ☐ Parents can help.
- ☐ Parent involvement is increasing.
- ☐ Parent training programs are helpful.

Don't worry, we'll handle it" is quite often the only suggestion that some teachers offer parents who are seeking ways to help their children with reading difficulties. Today, such advice is inappropriate and will likely fall on deaf ears because parents increasingly are involving themselves in their children's education. As the educational level of our adult population rises, as the emphasis on education for success in life continues, as education continues to be examined in the public press, and as commercial exploitations of parental concerns expand, teachers must help parents assist their children with reading. It is imperative that educators seek the ways parents can be most helpful in terms of the educational goals that they have established.

On the other hand, without proper guidance, parents may "help" their children in inappropriate or harmful ways. For example, uninformed parents often attempt to motivate their children through comparisons with brothers, sisters, or playmates. More often than not, undirected parental activity merely compounds the child's dislike of reading and actually interferes with progress in a remedial program.

Parental anxiety is likely to mount as a child's progress in reading declines.[1] When children sense parental anxiety reading difficulties can become compounded. Parents must have their concern and anxiety channeled into useful, helpful educational activities. Teachers should not just tell parents not to worry, but establish a role for them through which they can be most helpful.

Parental anxiety can easily be increased when parents read articles about dyslexia and believe their children to be its victim. The term *dyslexia* is commonly misused and only excites parents without cause. Teachers should discuss specific reading difficulties and avoid using terms that carry little meaning and serve only to excite parents.

Clinical and classroom diagnostic and remediation situations inherently demand that the parental role vary. The difference in roles is generally one of degree; the very nature of clinical situations demands that parents become more actively engaged in their child's remediation. In this chapter, as parental roles in diagnosis, remediation, and prevention of reading difficulties are discussed, suggestions are given to both the classroom teacher and reading specialist for directing parents toward useful activities. However, teachers and specialists should remember that all parents may not be able to perform all of these roles.

PARENTS CAN HELP

Parents teach their children to walk, talk, and do numerous other activities required to survive in society. Educators rely heavily on the ability of the parents to teach their children these skills. When they do not fulfill this responsibility, parents leave their children ill-equipped for progress in school. As the children develop difficulties in reading, educators logically call on their first teachers, their parents, to assist in any way that will be useful. The suggestions that follow, then, are based on the following beliefs:

1. Parents can help.
2. Parents often know best what makes their children react most effectively.
3. Children want parental support and assistance and strive to please their parents through school success.
4. Without parent-teacher teamwork, success with readers experiencing severe difficulties will be unnecessarily limited.
5. When directed toward useful roles, parents are usually willing to follow the advice of educators.

Parental Roles in Diagnosis

Except for the classroom teacher, parents most likely will be the first to recognize that their children are not making satisfactory progress in developing reading skills. Although the classroom teacher may fail to observe signs of frustration in a student, one can be certain that such awareness will not escape parents for long. The responsibility for the initial identification of the reader's difficulties, in such cases, often falls to the parents. Parents should be directed to observe their children in reading and call to the educator's attention any of the following symptoms of frustrated reading:

1. Avoidance of reading.
2. Inability to complete classroom assignments or homework.
3. Inability to discuss with parents material that he or she has just read.
4. Habitual difficulty in attacking unknown words, especially if the difficulty is noticed after two or three years of schooling.
5. Word-by-word, nonfluent oral reading, especially when he or she has practiced this reading silently before reading it orally.

6. Complaints from the child of visual discomfort in reading periods of fifteen minutes or more.
7. Inability to complete real-life reading activities that should be understandable for a child of that age.

By directing the educator's attention to specific symptoms such as these, parents may identify reading difficulties before they become serious enough to necessitate the more formal types of reading diagnosis and remediation. Upon receiving observations such as these from parents, the educator should conduct as much diagnosis as necessary to find the nature of the difficulty.

Parents may become overly anxious while observing their children for these symptoms. Parents whose children do not have reading difficulties should be aware of this, just as other parents need to know the nature of their children's reading difficulties. In this way, needless anxieties can be relaxed, thus creating better learning situations.

Many schools involve parents in each step of the diagnosis. Permission is requested before assessing the student's reading achievement. Results are discussed with parents, and parents are involved with screening committees that seek the most appropriate resource assistance for the student. In cases involving handicapped students, parent signatures must be obtained to place the student in an optimum learning environment. Public Law 94-142 requires parent signature and provides for parental appeals when they disagree with the placement of their handicapped child.

Another important role of parents in diagnosis is to supply information in support of or in conflict with the tentative hypotheses that have been established in classroom diagnosis or initial screening techniques. The parents' role in clinical diagnosis, then, is to supply supporting observations concerning their children's work in school, attitudes toward reading, and physical wellbeing. Without this information, which is frequently obtainable through either questionnaires or interviews, the reading specialist is likely to err in making judgments based on relatively short exposure to the children. It is generally more effective to obtain information from parents after tentative hypotheses have been reached, lest the parents' opinions tend to bias the examiner.

Parents have complete responsibility for the follow-up in areas in which referral has been made. Parents have the right and responsibility to attend to the physical and emotional needs of their children, and teachers usually expect the parents to take children to vision specialists, neurologists, psychiatrists, and other specialists.

As parents become involved in the diagnosis, they should also be consulted concerning the findings. Perhaps nothing is more frustrating to parents than to know that their child has undergone extensive study, yet they have not been consulted about the findings. However, making diagnostic conclusions available to parents is far more than a courtesy because quite often parents must enact the suggestions alleviating the problem. At times, when parents become involved in the process, their child will make almost immediate progress and no longer need remedial intervention from the school.

Any time a diagnosis of a student has been conducted, the parents should be informed in detail of the results. In the past, parents didn't receive a full report with test scores because it was thought they could not interpret those scores and might misuse them. Consequently, parents were making inferences from vague descriptions that were far more serious than were indicated by the case. Today educators suggest that parents get a full report of any diagnosis, including test scores. In this way, parents are not left with vague descriptions of their child's performance. Parents are today sent the same report sent to the schools, discussing every aspect of diagnosis, including test scores, their interpretations, and the recommendations for remediation.

Parents appreciate this openness. They feel fully informed, and they know what information is going to the school. They can follow up on the report with a parent-teacher conference. Naturally, instances will occur when a parent may abuse such information and go to the school with an "I told you so" type of comment. In general, however, far less abuse occurs when parents are fully informed than when they are partially informed.

Parental Roles in Remediation

For parents to have any role at all in remediation, they must have a general understanding of the educational goals set by the person conducting the remediation. This is not only ethically appropriate but reaching the goals is far more feasible when the parents are effectively involved. The first task, therefore, is to inform parents of realistic goals and of the general approaches to be used in attaining these goals. These goals should be short range and easily attainable so that the child, the parent, and the educator all can see clearly that progress is being made. Of course, this will necessitate contacting the parent as the goals are readjusted and as progress in reading skills is made. Again, contacts with parents are most effective when they occur in consultation sessions.

The most appropriate role for parents after they understand the program is to provide situations in the home whereby the skills learned in remediation can be reinforced. Although reinforcement activities may be time consuming, parents should recognize the necessity for providing reinforcement opportunities. Specifically, this work involves parents in the following actions:

1. Providing a quiet, comfortable, and relaxing place for reading in the home.
2. Providing a planned time during the day when the household becomes suitable for reading: the television is turned off; other members of the family pursue reading interests; and a pleasant attitude regarding this time is created.
3. Assisting the child with material that is difficult in either word pronunciation or sentence and paragraph meaning. One of the parents should always be available to help the student, but must not "breathe down the child's neck." The parent (while reading something of personal interest) simply may be in the same room and available to the child, if needed.
4. Assisting the child with follow-up exercises that are sent home after a remedial session. The parent must understand that the child is learning a skill and will probably not be perfect in these attempts. Neither the classroom teacher nor the reading specialist will send material home for practice unless there is relative assurance that it can be completed with some satisfaction. However, instances will arise when, regardless of the care taken, the child will take home materials that are too difficult to read without assistance.
5. Being available when the child needs an audience or when a discussion is desired following either oral or silent reading. Parents should display interest in what the child has read, thus permitting a sense of having done something that pleases the parents.
6. Providing the praise and reward for demonstrations of skill development. Since the materials sent home for practice should allow the child to demonstrate reading strengths, positive reactions from parents can do much to help the child feel good about being a reader.

These activities should be conducted in cooperation with the reading specialist or the classroom teacher; specific activities should be developed by these educators in terms of the goals that already have been explained to the parent. Furthermore, teachers should demonstrate these techniques to parents. Illustrating how effectively the recommended suggestions actually work with their child builds the parents' confidence in the recommendations.

Parents should understand what *not* to do as well as what to do. Depending on the educational goals, the educator should anticipate the types of problems likely to arise and direct the parents away from them. One way in which the educator can avoid a potential problem is to assist parents in channeling their natural desire to help their child into constructive activities. If a parent feels his or her child has a great deficiency in phonics skills, for example, the educator should be informed and the parent provided with an explanation of when that skill will become a part of the program. Furthermore, it should be made clear that no matter how great the temptation to have the child "sound out" the word, it is the parents' job to tell the child unknown words until the sounding skill is approached remedially. These examples relate to phonics. Although it is in this area that most parents feel most anxious, it is the area in which they generally do the poorest job of assisting educators. As a general rule, therefore, parental attention should be directed away from instruction in phonics, while opportunities are provided for the parents to notice their child's development in reading through carefully prepared home assignments. Once again, children demonstrate their strengths to parents through such activities as reading orally an experience story that they have mastered, drilling for five minutes on the word cards they have mastered, and discussing exciting problem-solving activities that they worked on in school.

Another parental role in remediation is obtaining books for the children to read. Normally, the educator will supply the first books from materials available in the remedial program; however, since the supply of books is often limited, parents can be encouraged to assume responsibility for obtaining books. The educator, in this case, will supply the parent with a list of appropriate books for the child to read at home, asking the parents to obtain these books from libraries, friends, bookstores, and the like. Consideration for the level and the interest factors of available books should be evaluated in the recommendations made to parents. Teachers may want to recommend books to parents near the child's birthday or at holidays so that books can be included on gift lists. More than simply supplying the child with a book, such activity develops the attitude that a book is something of considerable worth because it is given as a special gift.

Parents should also take the responsibility for taking their children to the library on a regular basis, where children experience book self-selection and develop the library habit.

Parents commonly want to supplement the efforts of the remedial program with commercially available materials. Unless these materials are in accordance with the educational goals that have been established and unless the educator knows of the materials and can recommend their appropriateness for this child, they should be avoided. By placing parents in the teacher's role, unsuitable commercial materials may involve the parents to a degree that is unprofitable for them, the child, and the educational goals for which they all are striving.

Parents can become involved in two more ways. First, seminars that are designed to help parents understand the nature of their children's reading difficulties and to help them understand the approach in remediation can be conducted. These seminars often include the involvement of public school personnel such as principals, reading specialists, and supervisors so that parents can obtain answers to their concerns about all areas of their child's schooling. The seminars can reduce a lot of unnecessary anxiety.

Further, parents can become instructional material constructors. Many parents bring their children to the reading clinic and wait for them instead of going home and coming back. Teachers can ask them if they would like to help. Clinicians can leave plans and materials for the construction of games, centers, or posters, and the parents can develop the materials. The parents can personally deliver the materials to the clinician and stay to observe them in use. This process will increase parental understanding of the remedial program.

While parents need to know their role in helping to correct their children's reading difficulties, it is even more desirable for them to know what they can do to head off reading difficulties before they have a chance to develop. Next to the classroom teacher, parents can do more to prevent the development of difficulties than anyone else. Sometimes teachers will face parents who are not anxious about their children's lack of success in reading. When unconcerned, parents are less likely to seek assistance even if it becomes necessary, thus implying to the children that they do not care. Each school and each teacher should take every opportunity to present preventive information to parents. Programs during Education Week, PTA meetings, individual conferences with parents, and notes sent to the home may be used to help parents prevent the occurrence of reading difficulties.

Next to the classroom teacher, parents can do more to prevent difficulties from arising than anyone else.

The following suggestions are designed to inform parents of activities that diminish the possibility that their child will develop poor reading habits and skills. They should be recommended by educators only when appropriate. No attempt is made here to supply a formula that will work with equal effectiveness with all parents.

Physical Care. Parents who desire to avoid the complications involved with failure in school (in reading, particularly) should examine their children's physical needs. A visual examination prior to entering school and every other year thereafter is excellent insurance of proper vision. An annual physical examination with follow-ups that are recommended by the family doctor eliminates the necessity of waiting until symptoms of physical disability become so apparent that they interfere with school success. Many physical difficulties go unnoticed until failure in school is so acute that remedial programs are inadequate to handle them. For example, if children have refused to read for years because of visual discomfort, they have a void of reading experiences for which, at times, it is impossible to compensate.

A quick look around any classroom makes it apparent that many children come to school without proper rest. Since most teachers consider the first period of the morning the most effective instructional time, children need to be awake and alert. Parents who need suggestions concerning the amount of sleep their children require should consult the family doctor.

Along with adequate rest, children need a substantial breakfast. Children who go without breakfast, fighting hunger long before lunchtime, are incapable of efficient use of school time. Recommendations for minimum breakfast requirements are readily available; however, when in doubt, parents should consult the family doctor. If parents send children who are physically sound to school, they have a greater chance to succeed.

Emotional Climate. Children who are secure, loved at home, and understood will experience little interference with school success. Parents can implant an attitude that learning will be fun and, though difficult at times, always worthwhile. They can develop such an attitude by incorporating (1) no threats for failures in school (e.g., withdrawing television privileges); (2) no promises for success in school (e.g., paying for good grades); (3) respect and confidence in the teachers; and (4) interest and enthusiasm for what is being accomplished in school. Parents should avoid criticizing the school and its teachers in front of their children. As parents, they have a right to voice their objections, but they should do so to the school authorities and teachers rather than to the children. When children have the attitude that the school is weak and the teachers are incompetent, learning difficulties are compounded. Furthermore, parents can be directed to avoid as much as possible directly or subtly comparing their children to peers and siblings. The reaction of a child who is striving to do as well as another student is seldom positive or desirable. More concern should be demonstrated over each child's ability to perform as well as possible; performance that matches a sibling's should not be the goal adopted to satisfy parents.

Setting an Example. All parents usually strive to set a good example for their children. In reading, that example can be one of reading for enjoyment. Children who from their earliest years notice that both parents seem to enjoy spending portions of their leisure time reading can develop a favorable attitude toward reading before entering school. Some leisure reading may be done orally for the children or for the family. All oral reading should be accomplished with as much skill as possible; therefore, parents should first read silently all materials that they plan to read orally. Often parents are inclined to discontinue oral reading as soon as their children develop skills in reading; however, oral reading by parents should continue. Parents should take every opportunity to read to children the books that are of interest to the children but that are too difficult for their present reading skills. Children who come to school with family leisure reading experiences have definite advantages in learning to read because they realize the wonders that reading can unlock for them.

Some parents have found success with a daily silent reading time. All family members read for ten to twenty minutes. They read materials of their choice for their own enjoyment. Such sessions provide additional models of reading for fun.

Providing Language Experiences. Parents are to be encouraged to use every opportunity to widen their children's language experiences. Through such activities as reading to children, taking them on trips, and discussing events with them, situations are created in which language can be developed through experiences. Parents should be encouraged to lead children into discussions that will add listening and speaking vocabulary words to the experiences. It is, of course, the listening and speaking vocabularies upon which the reading vocabularies hinge. Parents miss opportunities to help their children by failing to discuss trips and experiences with them. Trips about which little is said are not necessarily useless, but all parents should be encouraged to reinforce experiences with language experiences relating to them. For example, during a trip, parents can let children help read maps, menus, and road signs; they can take photographs and discuss them later; and they can help children write captions to be placed on the backs of photographs. Alerted to the potential of structuring language experiences, parents can learn to use them more effectively.

Regulating Out-of-School Activities. Parents who permit their children to do as they wish with all out-of-school time indicate their lack of concern for their children's wellbeing. First, parents must understand that a full school day takes a good bit of concentration and is mentally fatiguing. Therefore, children should be exposed to opportunities after school for active, expressive free play. Outdoor play, which physically releases children, is desirable when possible. Secondly, the school program relies on the interest and excitement that can be developed by the teacher and the materials from which the children are learning. Therefore, unusually large amounts of television viewing may interfere with the school program. After five hours of murder, passionate love, dancing girls, and comedies, children are not likely to fully appreciate a program that features the elementary school band or a story in the first-grade reader that must be geared to a limited reading vocabulary. Although no formula is prescribed, teachers might suggest limiting children to an hour of television viewing an evening. Of course, parents cannot expect children to sit in the living room and not watch the shows that the parents are watching. This suggestion, then implies that television viewing for the family should be restricted, especially during school days. Parents should also be encouraged to understand the need for children to accomplish home assignments and have some quiet time. Quiet time, of necessity, involves the entire family.

Following Advice. Parents must be encouraged to follow the suggestions of school personnel in matters concerning the education of their children. The greatest difficulty in this respect is when parents consider the age at which children should enter first grade and the decision to have students remain another year in a given grade. Each school system has its own method for determining whether children are ready to profit from first-grade instruction. When, after careful consideration, the school advises parents to withhold a child from first grade for one year, parents should carefully review the reasons behind such a recommendation and abide by the school's decision unless they have some compelling evidence that the school is in error. Parents should remember that educators have the best interests of students in mind, too, and that the school often has a more objective perspective of the child's level of skills and maturity. Confrontations between parents and the school often create needless student anxiety and result in some students being placed in school programs for which they are not ready. Scores of children with reading difficulties are victims of early entrance against school advice.

School advice in connection with the retention of children generally receives parental concern that is passed directly to the children. Educators not only want the parents to comply with this advice but to embrace it with enthusiasm so that children feel they have not let their parents down. Unfortunately, in our pass-or-fail system, other children pick up the connotation of failure that will, unwittingly, create some disturbance within the children. Failure need not be compounded in the home by parental anxiety. To start with, parents can refer to retentions as "repeating a year" instead of "failing a year." Perhaps the time is near when retention in school will not be marked by failure to be promoted at the end of the year. All children should be on a program of continuous progress, making it realistically impossible for each failure to occur. Continuous progress involves an educational program in which each learner starts each year in terms of the points that instruction ended the preceding year. In the final analysis, it is the present system, not children, that creates the failures. Many schools have instituted continuous progress programs, much to the satisfaction of parents, children, and teachers.

Reinforcing Learned Skills. As discussed under "Parental Roles in Remediation," skills learned in school can be reinforced by understanding parents in the home. Home reading situations should always end pleasantly with children feeling satisfied. Parents who cannot control their anxieties and tempers should avoid working with their children at home. When children read orally to anxious parents, difficulty frequently arises regardless of the care teachers have taken to make sure that the children can read the books that have been sent home.

In practical terms, when children come to unknown words, parents should tell the children the words. If they miss them again, they should be told again and again. Words missed with regularity should be noted and sent to the teacher for analysis of the type of error and the necessary instruction. However, parents are seldom satisfied with this limited role; thus, the following course of action is suggested. When children miss words time after time, the parent should print the words carefully on cards. When the reading is finished and the story has been discussed, a few minutes can be spent glancing over these cards. As the words are pronounced, the children should be asked to use them in sentences, which should be written on the back of the cards with the target words underlined. Preceding the next reading session at home, a little game-like drill can take place in which the children read the sentences and the unknown words.

Pitfalls in Parental Cooperation

Obviously, numerous attempts at parental cooperation go astray, creating more harm than good. Educators must be alert to these pitfalls and, when signs of their appearance occur, use alternate approaches to parental participation.

Lack of Contact. Perhaps the worst pitfall teachers make is not contacting parents. Since parents will assume roles, they will best be taken in terms of the school's program. Parental contacts should be periodic, calling for follow-up sessions to reinforce parental behavior. All too often, one parental conference is considered sufficient to meet the need for parental involvement. However, this is untrue. In a six-week summer program, for example, three formal parental conferences and numerous informal conferences are needed to assist parents in becoming effective helpers.

Underestimating Parental Love. Even those parents who appear to be unconcerned love their children. However, parental love easily can be misdirected. For example, some parents criticize the school in attempts to make their children feel more comfortable. When schools ignore parental love, this can result in a lack of cooperation between parents and educators. As has been suggested, sending the children home with activities that will permit them to demonstrate their strengths to the parents gives parents opportunities to demonstrate their love for their children with positive reinforcement.

Needless Anxiety. Many parents confront educators with considerable anxiety. They are afraid, frustrated, and upset. To make such parents useful partners, educators need to work with them to overcome these feelings of anxiety; overanxious parents find it extremely difficult to work with their own children in any activity. When conversing with parents, the educator should listen to what they have to say—really listening and postponing judgments. Extra care should be taken to make activities for such parents as positive as possible. As parents start to relax and gain confidence in the school's program, they can become more helpful partners.

One Parent. Educators often are forced to settle for the reactions and opinions of only one of the child's parents. Teachers must avoid this pitfall, for children act to please both parents. Therefore, every opportunity should be made to involve both parents, even if a home visit is required to attain this end. Often after talking with the other parent, teachers have reversed their opinions of the home and the learning climate. Due to the large number of single parent homes, involving both parents in school programs may be impossible. Teachers should be alert to these situations to avoid causing embarrassment to one-parent families.

Failure to Follow Up. When a remedial program is finished, the parents deserve a summary of the results. Unless parents receive a final report, they may continue with remedial activities that

Numerous informal conferences are needed to help parents become effective helpers.

are no longer appropriate. The summary, therefore, should include specific recommendations for future parental roles concerning the children's changing needs.

Assuming the Teacher's Role. Sending workbooks home so that parents are placed in a teacher's role is seldom useful and often harmful. Educators must clearly see the difference between the parents' role as reinforcer of learned skills and the educator's job of developing new skills. Workbook activities provide too many teaching situations for most parents to handle well. However, if children have worked in a skill activity successfully in school, allowing them to demonstrate that success to their parents should be encouraged.

Overreaction to Information in the Press. Newspapers and magazines often carry articles about some aspect of reading: "Scores are down"; "Be sure your school is using this approach"; "Your child's diet can affect learning." These and other such topics build anxiety. Teachers should help parents obtain as much information as possible before reacting to such articles. The information in the article may be true but inapplicable to a certain school or to their child. The information in the article may be a distortion that needs clarification. And, at times, the information may be inaccurate, requiring that correct information be supplied.

Training for Parents. Today's parents likely will have training sessions available to them. These sessions are usually designed to inform parents about reading and offer suggestions on how they can help their children at home.

Many administrators are inviting parents to teacher inservice sessions. Those administrators feel that parents should know what training teachers are getting and what innovations are being suggested. By informing them in this manner, educators avoid misinterpretations.

Some reading clinics offer classes for parents of children who are attending the clinic. They inform the parents about their objectives, their procedures, and the anticipated outcomes of the clinic experience. They talk about how reading difficulties get started and how they can be corrected. They offer strategies for parents to use when they need to contact school personnel about their children, and offer ideas that parents can use at home. Attendance at such classes is excellent, and responses are enthusiastic.

Parents serve as aides and volunteers in many schools. As such, they get two types of training. They attend workshops and seminars designed to instruct them in their role in the school, and they get on-the-job training from the teacher with whom they are working. Frequently, parents are enrolled in graduate classes, not working for a degree, but simply becoming better informed.

Many colleges now offer courses designed for parents who are interested in helping their children. Parents are interested in knowing about the reading process, about how reading is taught in school, and about how they can help at home. In almost every instance parents state that they have been working with their children and that they intend to continue to do so. An educators' best action is to provide parents with enough information so that what they do at home can be as helpful as possible.

SUMMARY

Educators must evaluate the student's home situation and make specific recommendations as to which roles are most appropriate for parents to enable them and educators to work as a team. All parental roles should be in keeping with the educational goals that the remedial program is attempting to accomplish. When parents are not actively involved, needless limitations are placed on the educator's effectiveness. Assuming that most parents are going to help their children with reading, educators must direct their efforts toward the most useful purposes.

NOTES

1. Robert M. Wilson and Donald W. Pfau, "Parents Can Help!" *The Reading Teacher* 21 (May 1968): 758–61.

SUGGESTED READINGS

Burmeister, Lou E. *Foundations and Strategies for Teaching Children to Read.* Reading, Massachusetts: Addison-Wesley Publishing Company, 1983. Chapter five focuses on ways in which the community, the school, and individual teachers can get parents involved in developing the reading abilities of their children. Included are examples of activities, letters, and fliers that have met with success in promoting parental involvement.

Gambrell, Linda B. and Wilson, Robert M. *28 Ways to Help Your Child Be a Better Reader.* Paoli, Pa.: Instructo/McGraw-Hill Book Co., 1980. Practical suggestions are offered to parents so that they can work with their children. Suggestions take little time and do not interfere with school curricular activities.

Landau, Elliott D. *Creative Parent-Teacher Conferences.* Salt Lake City, Utah: E. D. Landau, 1968. This work presents guidelines for various types of conferences with which educators are confronted. It offers specific suggestions to make conferences effective.

Oliastro, Louis A. *Parents Teach Your Child to Read.* Uniontown, Pa.: LIZ Publications, 1979. This seven-page booklet provides information for parents about how to use photographs of their children's experiences as a basis for language development. As the children talk about the pictures, the parents record the story. These personal stories with pictures are then used for reading instruction.

———. *The Reading Teacher* (May 1970). Through twelve articles featuring the role of parents in reading activites, this entire issue of the *Reading Teacher* focuses on parental roles in reading education.

———. *The Reading Teacher* (November 1980). Three articles by Joan Raim, Nicholas Criscuolo, and Anne Auten, respectively, provide interesting ideas about involving parents in school reading programs.

Trelase, Jim. *The Read-Aloud Handbook.* New York: Penguin Books, 1982. The author urges parents to encourage the reading development of their children by reading aloud to them on a regular basis. Suggestions are given for effective reading aloud and an annotated bibiliography of more than 300 titles offers a wealth of excellent read aloud books.

Wilson, Robert M., and Pfau, Donald W. "Parents Can Help!" *The Reading Teacher* (May 1968): 758–61. This article summarizes a study in which parents were asked how they helped their children at home. Children were grouped as below-average readers and above-average readers. Those children receiving most parental assistance at home were the below-average readers.

Editorial

Patricia M. Russavage
is the principal for Lettie Marshall Dent Elementary School in Mechanicsville, Maryland.

Parents want to help their children learn to read. In our elementary school we feel very strongly that parents should be actively involved in their child's reading program.

In our Corrective-Remedial Reading Program, we use games to teach reading because they're individualized and adaptable. They give the necessary practice and repetition without the dullness and monotony characteristic of drills, worksheets, or workbooks. Children like games and coaxing is rarely needed. By basing each game on a popular format such as Bingo, directions are kept to a minimum. Children know these game formats and can even play many of them independently once they have been explained.

We discovered that reading games were very effective in improving specific reading skills, but we also noticed a slight problem. Children were highly motivated to play them and often wished to continue playing even when we had run out of time. To solve this problem, we decided to talk to the parents at PTA about continuing games at home.

When the parents arrived, we explained how games were being used to reinforce reading skills. We described some games being used and mentioned some of the reading skills that were featured.

Parents were then invited to the reading room, where their own children taught them how to play the games. Having the children teach their parents how to play the games did much to enhance the self-concepts of the children. Proud parents thoroughly enjoyed themselves.

We distributed a booklet to the parents containing complete directions for constructing reading games using inexpensive and easily available materials (magic markers, index cards, file folders, etc.). At the request of several parents, we scheduled a time each week when able and interested parents could come to school to construct reading games along with us. We later arranged a loan system so that the teacher-constructed games in the reading room could be signed out by the parents and used at home at the suggestion of the child's classroom teacher.

The enthusiasm, response, and follow-through of the parents was tremendous. One dad commented several weeks later, "This sure beats the two-hour battles I used to have trying to get my son to practice reading at home. It's fun. And it really works!"

Communication between home and school has improved as a result of this game sharing. We have observed considerable improvement in reading for many of the children who have been using the reading games at home with their parents. Probably the best thing that has happened has been the strengthening of the bond between parent and teacher and the cooperative efforts of both to help children achieve their educational goals. Parents truly feel a part of their child's educational program and this positive parent-teacher relationship is clearly evident to the child.

13 Professional Roles

CHAPTER OUTLINE

CHAPTER EMPHASES

- ☐ The classroom teacher and reading specialist should work together to decide a student's reading placement.
- ☐ Reading specialists should plan their time to be able to work with all types of students.
- ☐ Teachers must know the legal ramifications of their actions.
- ☐ Teachers should model desirable reading habits to influence students.

Public concern over school reading programs continues to grow. Newspapers, magazines, radio, and television focus public attention on the strengths and weaknesses of reading programs. Professional concern about reading is reflected in the large number of reading journals being published and the extensive amount of reading research published each year. Public and professional concern has resulted in pressures on school systems to produce better readers and to supply more reading support programs. Unfortunately, such pressures occasionally create more problems than they solve. Hastily developed programs may emerge, inappropriate materials may be incorporated, personnel with questionable qualifications may be hired, and too many duties may be placed on personnel already employed. Therefore, consideration of professonal responsibilites and roles may help both the teachers and the administrators who are planning reading programs.

PROFESSIONAL RESPONSIBILITIES

"Am I qualified to help students having difficulties with reading?" "How will I be able to start a program in my classroom?" "To whom should I look for help?" These are questions educators ask when they realize that many students with reading difficulties could be helped by establishing special reading services. Prior to implementing programs, however, teachers must understand their professional responsibilities in establishing remedial programs.

The Student

Regardless of the type of program or the competency of the person conducting it, consideration first must be given to the student who is to benefit from the program. Educators are professionally responsible for directing students toward those programs that seem to be best designed for their needs. Referral need not reflect negatively on educators if they decide that they cannot assist the student as well as another can; rather, this action credits them. Clearly, many educators feel threatened when they become aware that they cannot help certain students. To call for outside help may seem to indicate a lack of competency. However, the diagnosis and correction of many reading difficulties cannot possibly be handled by any one person. Consequently, to call for assistance when it is needed is a sign of professional maturity.

Cooperation

As mentioned in previous chapters, diagnosis and remediation are programs that cannot be conducted without full cooperation from all persons involved with the student. Programs that are conducted in isolation limit the ability to offer the student a complete program. Therefore, programs should not be instituted without thorough communication with the student's parents, classroom teacher, and other resource personnel.

Referral

When possible, all referrals—medical, psychological, and psychiatric—should be made prior to remediation and formation of program procedures. It is inefficient to start a remedial program without consultation when a student demonstrates symptoms of difficulties in these areas. All conclusions should be considered tentative until verified by appropriate professional assessment. Even then the final effectiveness of a diagnosis is only confirmed during instruction. The educator does not refrain from working with these students; however, the full efficiency of remedial programs normally will not be realized without referral reports.

When considering the role of the reading specialist, the school screening committee becomes important. As discussed previously, the screening committee consists of teachers, administrators, specialists, and sometimes parents or students. The committee works to bring the most appropriate school resources to assist the teacher with students who are experiencing difficulty with their learning activities.

Qualification

In an attempt to avoid confusion, the term *reading specialist* has been used throughout this book to describe any reading professional who is not currently teaching within the regular classroom and who has responsibility for the developmental or remedial reading program within a school. There exists, nevertheless, considerable confusion within the field regarding the terms used to designate reading professionals. The terms "reading specialist," "reading consultant," "reading supervisor," "reading teacher," and "reading tutor" appear to be defined differently within various states and school districts. Nowhere does this confusion appear to be greater than in the case of the "reading specialist." A study undertaken by the Evaluation Committee of the International Reading Association reveals that the term "reading specialist" appears to have become both a generic and a specific term. In some cases, reading professionals are designated as "reading specialists" after completing a certificate program which bears that name. In other cases, teachers refer to themselves as reading specialists due to the nature of the job that they hold in the schools.[1] It is the professional responsibility of the school administration to assure that reading specialists who are engaged in remedial and resource roles within their schools have the necessary training and state certification to do their jobs properly.

Code of Ethics

When remediation is conducted outside the classroom, the educator is professionally responsible for avoiding casting unwarranted reflections of inadequacy on the school program, particularly to parents. However, if the school program is suspect, the educator is professionally obligated to consult appropriate school personnel in an effort to remedy the deficiency. (See the Code of Ethics approved by the International Reading Association in appendix D of this book.)

Guarantees

An educator can seldom guarantee specific outcomes of specialized reading services. Many variables may influence a student's performance in reading. To offer guarantees to parents or school officials is clearly unethical. What can be offered, however, are the best services of the personnel who willingly perform carefully conducted evaluations.

THE READING SPECIALIST IN THE SCHOOL PROGRAM

Program Suggestions

The following suggestions are designed to assist reading specialists assume the role that will best suit the needs of the schools for which they are responsible and the students within those schools. A reading specialist may assume responsibility for more than one of these program suggestions, for they are frequently related.

Diagnosis. As discussed in chapters 2, 3, 4, and 5, clinical diagnosis is a major responsibility of most reading specialists. The reading specialist conducts the diagnosis and prepares the recommendations with directions for remediation. Many reading specialists feel that they can be very useful to the classroom teacher through diagnostic services, because it may be difficult for the classroom teacher to find the time that clinical diagnosis requires.

Remediation. Often the job responsibility of reading specialists involves working instructionally with students. The following strategies have been used effectively in working with students.

1. Some reading specialists find working with students in the classroom to be advantageous. The classroom teacher works with some students and the reading specialist with others. Communication problems are diminished as both the teacher and the specialist have opportunities to learn from one another. By working in the classroom, the reading specialist has the opportunity to work with all types of readers. Such a strategy can also be a means for training a classroom teacher to use a new technique. For example, one principal places the reading specialist in first grade for an hour every morning. The specialist works with students, referred by the classroom teacher, using the V-A-K-T technique with students having difficulty developing sight vocabulary. Working one to one, the reading specialist reinforces the words the students select to learn from their language-experience stories.
2. Other reading specialists prefer to work with the students outside of their regular classrooms. They establish a learning environment that is different from that which the students are accustomed. Distractions are lessened, and students feel honored by such attention. This strategy usually calls for the reading specialist to work with small groups of students who have similar strengths and needs. One reading specialist has set up a rich learning environment and accepts students referred by classroom teachers on a contract basis. The students may come one day for a little reinforcement, or they may come on a regular basis.
3. In order to serve as many students as possible, some reading specialists establish miniclinics.[2] A small group of students comes for a short time period to develop a specific skill. For example, a teacher may have seven third graders who are having difficulty locating information. A miniclinic can be set up for two weeks, one hour a day, for these third graders. At the end of the clinic, the students are evaluated; the evaluations are shared with the teacher; and a new miniclinic can be developed for other needs.

Most reading specialists will find it useful to use some combination of these three strategies with students in remedial situations. One reading specialist works during the morning with students who have been identified as having serious difficulties with reading, while afternoons are composed of the following activities:

1. She conducts miniclinics. All types of readers attend these various miniclinics, including some gifted and talented students.
2. She conducts diagnosis when it is needed.
3. She meets with each team in the school during its planning time at least once a week.
4. She schedules time when she will be available to work in classrooms with teachers. At times she works with students and at other times she works with the teachers.

This type of scheduling allows maximum use of various skills. It also keeps the reading specialist from getting bogged down with one type of activity all day long. All students view the reading specialist as a helpful person in the school, not just those who are experiencing difficulty with reading.

Planning Planning with teachers so that students' educational programs are coordinated can be an important part of the reading specialist's responsibilities. In schools where teachers work and plan in teams, the reading specialist should make efforts to be a part of every planning session. If a unit on space is being planned, then that unit can be incorporated into the instruction being conducted by the reading specialist. The reading specialist may also take the initiative of coordinating the schoolwide reading program.

Clinic Director. In larger school districts, a particularly skilled reading specialist may direct a reading clinic in an attempt to serve severely handicapped readers. Clinics usually are established in buildings to which the students can be brought for help. As director of the clinic, the reading specialist may assume all of the roles discussed in this chapter, as well as the administrative functions of the clinic, supervision of staff, and the communication between clinic and classroom.

In-service Education. Occasionally, the reading specialist will find it worthwhile to conduct in-service programs with classroom teachers. Through demonstration, discussion, and consultation with authorities, teachers gain insights into effective methods of working with readers experiencing difficulties. In these situations, the specialist's responsibility is to inform teachers who have a common lack of understanding in certain areas. Reading specialists do not need to view in-service programs as

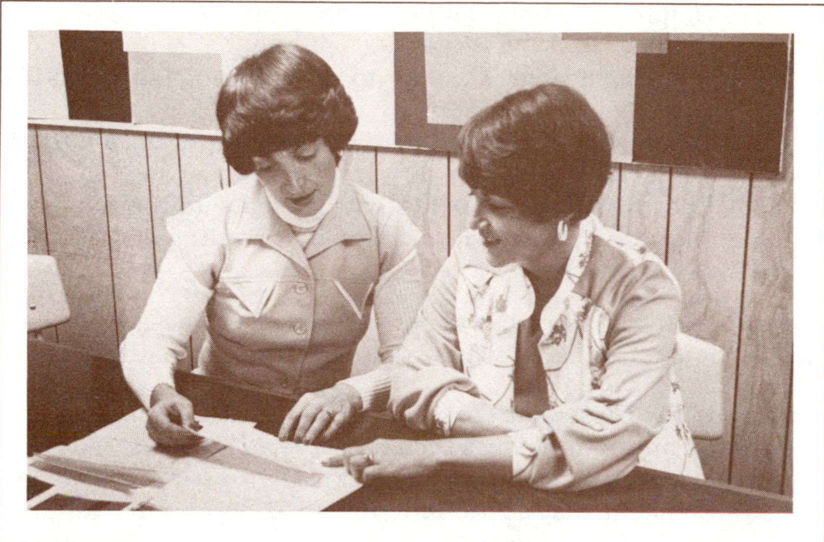

Teachers and reading specialists should coordinate educational programs for students.

formal, day-long training sessions. In addition, while releasing teachers from classroom time for in-service programs is desirable, it is not always necessary.

Reading specialists can form many successful strategies involving small amounts of time. They can prepare informational notes on recent developments in reading and pass them on to teachers. Any teacher interested in more details can contact the reading specialist. For example the reading specialist reads an article on wait time and shares the idea in a note to the staff, or the specialist receives some new information about oral reading diagnosis and shares it with the staff. At times, one seemingly insignificant idea has a better chance of being implemented than do ideas that require major changes and considerable training of the teachers.

Some reading specialists have developed fifteen-minute modules for in-service programs. These modules deal with a single concept and include handouts, transparencies, and materials for implementation. The specialist announces which modules are available, and interested teachers sign up for the modules of their choice. At a designated time, the teachers meet and the module is presented. Discussion follows, and the teachers decide whether they want to try the new idea. They also may decide they would like to try it but would need some help from the reading specialist during the initiation of the idea. Examples of some of these short modules are:

1. Helping teachers develop maze tests from one of their books.
2. Showing teachers a way to develop notetaking skills with their students.
3. Discussion of the meaning of test results from a diagnostic session.
4. Sharing a new material that has come to the school.
5. Discussion of a position taken by a reading authority in a recent article.

At times enough interest is generated in one of these short sessions that teachers ask for more information on that topic.

Resources for Classroom Teachers. Many reading specialists find their training best suits them to serve as resource people to the classroom teacher. Instead of working with students outside the classroom in diagnostic and remedial activities, resource teachers can aid the classroom teachers in various ways:

- ☐ *By helping with diagnosis.* Test administration, scoring, and interpretation can be conducted as a team, thus permitting the classroom teacher to learn diagnostic skills.
- ☐ *By helping in the classroom with students who are experiencing difficulty.* Planning and team teaching special lessions as well as offering continued support to help the teacher better handle students with reading difficulties allows for teacher development as well as providing service to students.
- ☐ *By obtaining materials for the teacher.* Instead of keeping reading materials in a reading room, the reading specialist can bring needed materials to classroom teachers and help them use them effectively. The resource specialist may obtain materials that the teacher requests and may recommend new materials for certain situations. Resource specialists can also suggest professional materials such as books, pamphlets, and articles.
- ☐ *By planning with the teacher to develop effective instructional goals.* The classroom teacher, using the knowledge and skills of the reading specialist, can develop better plans for instruction.
- ☐ *By evaluating program effectiveness.* By applying research and evaluation skills, the resource specialist can assist classroom teachers in looking objectively at their reading programs, modifying portions of the programs

that appear to be weak, and assisting them in emphasizing portions of the programs that appear to be strong.

- ☐ *By interpreting for teachers the reading research that may have application for the classroom.* As a result of their own reading, attendance at conferences, formal course work, and discussions with their colleagues, resource specialists should stay alert to the most recent trends, research, methods, and materials in reading remediation.

Generally, resource personnel should be assigned duties that will allow them freedom to work effectively with teachers. They should not be assigned to evaluate teachers. They should not set policies that teachers must follow, nor should they force themselves into situations where the teachers do not want their assistance. In effect, resource people should be assigned duties in which they can practice the philosophy of acceptance and challenge with teachers.

Summer School. An increasingly large number of schools are establishing summer programs for students who have not made adequate progress during the school year. Reading specialists often will be responsible for such programs, with particular emphasis being placed on screening and selecting students who are to be assisted. In addition, they may be responsible for selecting teachers who will be involved. The financing of these programs, while normally assumed by the school, may to a small extent be supplemented by a nominal fee paid by the parents. Such a fee stimulates a more serious attitude toward the work required in the program. Summer programs may make it possible for students to remain in the classroom during the year, thereby providing them the fullest opportunity to benefit from the classroom program. Of course, students with serious reading deficits cannot always profit from summer programs alone. To avoid the stigma of failure that is often attached to such programs, summer facilities can be developed for good readers as well. All types of readers can then be involved, making it no disgrace to attend a summer reading program.

Public Relations. Public relations duties, which include PTA meetings, conferences with parents, and home visits, may fall to the reading specialist. At such meetings, the school's reading program can be explained, questions answered, and misinterpretations corrected. The reading specialist can take advantage of the suggestions mentioned in chapter 12 when provided with opportunities to meet the public. Public relations opportunities such as conferences with parents and home visits as well as public speaking engagements may be available to reading specialists.

Supervising Tutoring. Many schools conduct tutoring programs to facilitate the learning of certain children. Tutors can be volunteers from the community, older students, teacher aides, and peers. To be effective, these programs need careful organization and supervision. These tasks often fall on the reading specialist since much of the tutoring is done in the area of reading.

A tutor handbook has been developed to help teachers plan, organize, and implement a tutoring program (see the Suggested Readings at the end of this chapter). It includes suggested instructional activities which are appropriate for tutors.

Training Paraprofessionals. As paraprofessionals become more available for reading assistance, the job of training those persons will fall on reading specialists. The better paraprofessionals are trained, the more useful they will be. A model program for such training has been developed in Prince Georges County, Maryland. Hundreds of paraprofessionals are trained and supervised by reading specialists as they work with classroom teachers to help individual students.

All schools are being encouraged to consider the maximum use of such personnel to assist overburdened teachers. Reading specialists will need to consider the many duties that paraprofessionals can perform, and develop training programs to make their work as effective as possible.

Pitfalls for Reading Specialists

Programs developed by reading specialists are not without potential difficulties, especially for those with little experience. Certain pitfalls can be encountered in establishing reading programs. Anticipating these before beginning such a program may relieve reading specialists of frustrating situations that can ultimately cause considerable difficulty.

Overloading. Reading specialists often assume responsibilities that overload them to a point of ineffectiveness. First, they should not be expected to assume all the roles that have been suggested in this chapter; rather, they should start where they can be most effective and slowly expand as they see opportunities. Second, in the diagnostic and remedial role, they cannot be expected to carry the same student load as a classroom teacher. The very nature of the clinical situation precludes large groups. When overloaded, the reading specialists' effectiveness will be limited unnecessarily.

Inadequate Housing. Teacher's rooms, damp basements, and even worse locations have been relegated to the reading specialist to conduct diagnostic and remedial programs. Assuming that a program is worthwhile, the school administrator must make provisions for a well-lighted, comfortable, nondistracting environment for the students and the teacher. To be most effective, housing considerations should be built into the basic plans for the program's development.

Screening. Final responsibility for determining which students can be helped most effectively must be left to the reading specialist. Without diagnosis, a given classroom teacher is likely to select the least intellectually able student for remedial attention, when intellectual ability alone is not a sufficient criterion for program enrollment. Reading specialists should provide for the screening of all referred students, yet retain the right to reject any student who they feel cannot profit effectively from the established program. They will have to reject temporarily those students who add to the tutoring load, creating class sizes that cannot be taught effectively. Interschool relations may be strained unless clear-cut procedures are established concerning the final responsibilities for identifying students to be accepted in the reading specialist's programs.

One such procedure involves the screening committee that contains all of the resource personnel available in the school, as well as the principal. The reading specialist makes recommendations regarding reading placements to the committee. Others provide their input and a decision is made.

The Image. Specific efforts should be made to avoid the reading specialist's image as the educator who works with failures. As previously suggested, reading specialists should work in the classroom, participating in all types of programs for readers. Such adjustment will help the students assigned to them relax their anxiety about their failures. It will also prevent specialists from getting a distorted opinion of the school's reading program. (This occurs easily when one works hour after hour, day after day, with only the shortcomings that a given system has produced.) Working with teachers in the classroom also aids reading specialists in maintaining perspective, especially concerning the difficulties teachers may have working with specific students in large groups.

Another aspect of image is related to the way teachers view reading specialists. Reading specialists should be treated as part of the teaching staff, assuming their share of teacher special chores such as bus duty or playground duty. They should attend all teachers' meetings and, in general, do what teachers do. If the image is developed that the reading specialist gets special treatment, rapport with the teaching staff will suffer.

Demonstrations. Normally, demonstrations are requested when teachers are uncertain of how to use a new technique or material. Traditionally, the demonstrator replaces the teacher and thereby becomes ineffective. Demonstrations should be conducted with the classroom teacher as a participant. Specifically, the classroom teacher plans the lesson with the reading specialist; the classroom teacher teaches portions of the lesson; the classroom teacher remains in charge of the class; and the reading specialist assists in planning and executing the lesson. As soon as is practical after completing such lessons, the classroom teacher and the reading specialist should discuss what happened and how it can be applied to an everyday situation.

Using techniques such as these removes teachers from the passive, observing role and places them in an active, participating role. Teacher behavior is more likely to be modified with such an approach.

This procedure does not rule out the use of a demonstration when it is appropriate. For example, if a new material is provided and no one knows how to use it, it would be appropriate for the reading specialist to prepare a lesson for others to observe.

THE CLASSROOM TEACHER IN THE SCHOOL PROGRAM

Program Participation

Classroom teachers participate in school programs with readers in several ways. An understanding of the possibilities may assist each teacher to serve most effectively.

Classroom Diagnosis. As teachers develop skill in the techniques of classroom diagnosis, they are likely to find themselves assigned to students who are in need of this service. The best teachers will perform this type of function as an ongoing part of their teaching program. The administrator should not overload teachers since excessive numbers of weak students obviously will hamper their efforts with all students assigned to them. Classroom teachers will provide additional input to screening committees when sharing the information from a classroom diagnosis.

Classroom Remediation. Teachers should work to develop successful readers using their remediation skills. The following strategies are useful for teachers working with readers experiencing difficulties in the classroom setting.

1. With flexible skills grouping teachers can establish skills groups for specific purposes; when the purpose is accomplished, the group is disbanded and a new group is formed. If ten students need instruction on the use of initial consonant substitution, then a skill group is formed. As students gain the skill they leave the group.
2. Using small bits of time when all other students are occupied, teachers can provide the reinforcement necessary for practice sessions to be successful. For example, such time can be used to review a lesson taught the day before or to go over the student's sight words.
3. Some administrators arrange for released time for teachers with skill in remediation. This time is set aside so that small group instruction can take place without distracting the entire class. The benefit of such arrangements on student progress has been well worth the administrative inconvenience.
4. Some teachers find a few moments before and after school useful for that little bit of extra instruction and attention that makes so much difference to students.
5. Most of what has been discussed under remediation can be incorporated into the regular reading lessons being taught. For example, the regular lessons can focus on locational skills and strategies if students need practice locating information.

Classroom teachers will find combinations of these strategies effective in conducting classroom remediation.

Tutoring. Having developed skills in diagnosis and remediation through either in-service programs or formal course work, many teachers serve as tutors in school-established programs. The teachers' activities in these programs are usually supervised by the reading specialist and are directed toward the instruction of individuals or small groups.

Demonstration. When teachers are particularly skillful in either classroom diagnosis or remediation, other teachers should observe them. Observations may be made during after-school programs or through released time. To foster positive feelings about their teaching competencies, teachers should be permitted to evaluate their own strengths and to offer their rooms for observations. Reading specialists can assist classroom teachers in identifying their strengths and urge them to offer their talents for the benefit of their colleagues.

Public Relations. All teachers have the responsibility of interpreting the school's program to parents. Those who have studied the program more thoroughly may assist in events such as the PTA in order to illustrate the program's features clearly to parents. Parents may accept the classroom teacher in this role better than they do the reading specialist because they know that the classroom teacher works with their children each day.

Pitfalls for the Classroom Teacher

Like reading specialists, classroom teachers also must be alert to several pitfalls in their roles.

Overloading. Teachers who are skilled in diagnosis and remediation may become overloaded with poor readers. Ultimately, overloading is detrimental to effectiveness with these children. Even when using free periods, short sessions before and after school, Saturdays, and summers, many good teachers need more time to do an efficient job. In addition, teachers must regulate their time so that relaxation and recreation are part of their daily schedule. Their major responsibility continues to lie with the whole class and the education of all students assigned to them. Thus, overloading should be avoided.

Replacement. Some teachers contend that they do not need to work with students in reading if the students are working with the reading specialist. This position is difficult to defend. The reading specialist should only supplement and reinforce what the classroom teacher does during regular instruction. The students who need extra help should be learning from both the classroom teacher and the reading specialist in a planned cooperative program.

Shortcutting. Attempting to diagnose without using the suggestions in chapters 2, 3, and 4 leads to inadequate classroom diagnosis. However, after limited experience, classroom teachers can start to modify and refine these suggestions to use in classrooms and to suit the needs of their students. After several diagnostic efforts, teachers will realize that their students are all proficient in some areas and that study in those areas is not essential in classroom diagnosis. However, this does not justify excluding major portions of classroom diagnosis.

Cooperation. Regardless of negative feelings toward the total school reading program, all teachers should work as team members to help students. Gross distortions of the school program in an effort to satisfy personal philosophies of teaching reading must be avoided when they interfere with the overall school objectives. By cooperating and attempting to convince the school of the need for basic changes, teachers will better serve their students. Needless to say, discord within the school should remain within the school and not become a topic for community gossip.

Continued Study. As changes occur in the field of reading, teachers must continue to study. Some find studying educational periodicals useful. Specific reference can be made to the journals of the International Reading Association,[3] the National Council of Teachers of English,[4] the College Reading Association,[5] and the National Reading Conference.[6] These organizations are striving to keep teachers informed of developments in the reading field. Other teachers prefer in-service workshops and institutes; still others prefer formal course work in the colleges and universities. Of course, most teachers seek a suitable combination of methods.

Many teachers lack important contemporary knowledge in the ever-changing field of children's literature. As stressed throughout this book, reading skills and reading attitudes go hand-in-hand. Teachers need to have current knowledge of children's books; yet, a study by Wendelin, Zinck, and Carter notes that many pre-service and in-service teachers are woefully outdated in their knowledge of current children's literature.[7] Teachers should establish a personal reading plan that will keep them informed of changing developments in this field.

OUT-OF-SCHOOL PROGRAMS

Many educators take part in out-of-school programs designed to assist readers that are experiencing difficulties. Some find themselves teaching in these programs; others have parents asking them for their opinions of the programs; and still others find these programs to be interfering with the school's educational objectives. A brief look at the nature of some of these programs may assist the educator in making decisions concerning them.

Examples of Programs

Teacher-Education Clinics. Many teacher-education institutions operate reading clinics to educate teachers. Students who are brought into these clinics for assistance are generally diagnosed and tutored by teachers doing advanced work in the reading field. Normally the costs for services in teacher-education clinics is small since the programs are not expected to pay for themselves. These programs' effectiveness generally relates to the effectiveness of the clinical supervision that the teachers receive and the prerequisites for entrance of college students into clinical courses.

Some teacher-education clinics limit themselves to diagnosis, while others include remediation. Although the thoroughness of each program varies, they generally follow the guidelines of clinical diagnosis and remediation presented in this text, and can be considered reliable.

Privately Operated Clinics. A variety of privately operated clinics are usually available in large population centers. Designed for financial profit, these clinics generally charge fees much higher than those charged at teacher-education clinics. The effectiveness of these clinics is clearly limited by the personnel and materials available for diagnosis and remediation. Referrals to this type of clinic should be made only after acquaintance with the personnel and the philosophy of the clinic. Private clinics should work with the schools. Unless cooperation is achieved, the effects of privately operated clinics are limited.

Private Tutoring. Programs designed by private tutors are generally restricted by the proficiency of the tutor and by the materials available for precise diagnosis and remediation. These private tutoring programs are most effective with readers who are experiencing mild difficulties in reading. Students with severe problems seldom benefit. However, many excellent, well-qualified private tutors perform highly satisfactory services; unfortunately, others cause more harm than good. Private tutors are obligated to work closely with the school, which involves the students in an instructional program every day. No justification can be found for programs that do less. Referral should be based only on a personal evaluation of effectiveness.

Commercial Programs for Parents. Often advertised as panaceas, programs that place parents in teachers' roles assume that all teachers have a common deficiency and that instruction with a given technique can be done without diagnosis. Unless the educator is familiar with the program's contents and unless a diagnosis has been conducted to pinpoint the remedial area, these programs are not recommended. All such programs are not inherently bad; some of them are well designed and have been used with considerable success. The educator must study them closely. An assessment should also be made of each parent's suitability as a teacher.

Temporary Programs. Several private companies have organized short, intensive programs designed to send materials and instructors into schools and industry to improve general reading skills. Many of these are well designed and taught excellently; others are not. The long-term gains of such programs must be questioned, and these companies should be willing to answer questions and submit research concerning these programs so the educator can evaluate their relative worth.

Out-Patient Parental Instruction. Several clinics have been established to diagnose children and train parents to conduct remediation. Amazing results have been reported with this technique; however, the long-term gains need evaluation. Out-patient clinics usually handle large numbers of children and usually request periodic return for reevaluation and retraining for the parents. Since the programs are out-patient in nature, their overall costs are not great, although the per-hour cost may be high. These programs are generally designed for children with specific disabilities and usually should follow referral from medical personnel, psychologists, psychiatrists, or reading professionals.

Pitfalls of Out-of-School Programs

The basic limitations of each out-of-school program have already been mentioned. Specifically, however, the pitfalls of such programs include the following points.

Goals. Do these programs assist teachers toward the most desirable educational goals or do they, in reality, interfere with these goals? Once this question is answered, referral may be made on a more informed basis. When the programs are found to conflict with the school's goals, attempts should be made to reconcile the differences. When reconciliation is not possible, educators should strongly recommend nonparticipation by the parents of their students.

Personnel. The effectiveness of all of these programs depends on the supervisory as well as the instructional personnel involved. Weakness in personnel means weakness in the program. No compromise can be made by educators in demanding that out-of-school programs meet certain quality standards.

Intention. Since each of these programs has aims beyond simply assisting students, it must be determined if assisting students is even included in their aims. Naturally, all programs claim to help readers having difficulties, but money or teacher education may become so important that the student does not seem to matter. When alternate aims prevail, the worth of the program is suspect.

ACCOUNTABILITY

Teachers should be accountable for providing efficient instruction based on diagnostic techniques. If they lockstep students through one commercial program or are indifferent to students' individual learning styles they should be held accountable for student failure. The teacher who knows the strengths and needs of children and who provides the best possible instruction is truly teaching with accountability.

Accountability has nothing to do with obtaining the same results with all students. It has nothing to do with helping each student read on some mythical grade level. It refers to helping each student learn successfully—a task that can only be done with a diagnostic teaching approach.

Of necessity, accountability requires careful record keeping. Careful record keeping does not need to be a time-consuming activity. In some school districts and states, however, mandatory record keeping interferes with quality instructional programs. At times different agencies request the same type of information but use different forms. Administrators at all levels should try to consolidate information needed and minimize record keeping while remaining able to account for student progress.

LEGAL RESPONSIBILITIES

Teachers have always had to act within the law. Today, however, considerable attention has been directed to the rights of students under the law. Many school districts have developed student handbooks that identify particular student rights. Some entail

A diagnostic teaching approach can help each student learn more successfully.

using common sense, while others involve following special procedures under the law. Every teacher should be well informed about the laws in their state, as well as local school district policies.

Some particular legal responsibilities need attention when working with test results. McClung discusses them at length.[8] Educators should be able to defend the validity and reliability of any tests used for making decisions about placing students. If the tests used in instructional planning cannot be defended, the decisions cannot very well be defended. Yet students continue to be labeled and grouped by the data obtained from tests of questionable reliability and validity. If such practices continue, educators are placing themselves in legal jeopardy.

Other matters also deserve attention. Students have the right to privacy, due process, and fair treatment. They should also be allowed to view their personal records. The technical discussion of these rights is beyond the scope of this text, but several suggested readings at the end of this chapter should be studied in order to obtain detailed information on student rights.

BE A READER

Teachers must be readers. If they are to nurture students to value reading, they must set the example. How can one develop a love of reading in students when there is no love of reading within oneself?

Teaching to strengths can make learning to read enjoyable and successful.

Duffey found that 34 percent of the teachers surveyed in his study were not reading a book and that 50 percent had no plans to read a book.[9] Twenty percent reported that they were not reading any professional literature. Duffey states that the trend he reported is continuing as he collects data on teacher reading habits.

A determined effort can change the sorry picture painted by Duffey's data. Teachers should read to their students every day. They can go to a book store and pick a good book for their own reading enjoyment and provide time in school for student reading of personally enjoyable material. As the student reads, so should the teacher. Teachers should also subscribe to professional journals. They should talk with students about what they are reading, showing enjoyment and enthusiasm. A teacher's desire to be a reader can often make a difference to students' desire to be readers. They should not let this opportunity slip by them.

SUMMARY

Once the professional roles of the classroom teacher and reading specialist are understood, programs can be developed to incorporate them appropriately. An awareness of the types of programs available within the realms of the school permits educators to strive to develop those that the needs of their community demand. All facilities—local school, county, state, college, and university—should be incorporated when it is felt that they can be helpful.

Out-of-school programs for children must be evaluated, and cooperation should be encouraged when possible. In areas where out-of-school programs proliferate, more concentrated efforts will be needed to assure educational programs of the greatest effectiveness for students.

Teachers should be aware of the legal ramifications of their actions in decision making. They should also model the reading habit for their students.

NOTES

1. International Reading Association, "What's In A Name: Reading Specialist?" *Journal of Reading* (April 1979): 623–28.
2. Barbara Kapinus, "Miniclinics," *Journal of Reading* (March 1981): 516–18.
3. *The Reading Teacher* and *Journal of Reading* (Newark, Delaware: International Reading Association).
4. *Language Arts* and *The English Journal* (Champaign, Illinois: National Council of Teachers of English.)
5. *Reading World* (Shippensburg, Pennsylvania: Shippensburg University, College Reading Association).
6. *Journal of Reading Behavior* (Clemson, South Carolina: National Reading Conference).
7. Karla Hawkins Wendelin, R. Ann Zinck, and Sylvia M. Carter, "Teacher's Memories and Opinions of Children's Books: A Research Update," *Language Arts* (April 1981): 416–24.
8. Merle S. McClung, "Competency Testing: Potential for Discrimination," *Clearinghouse Review* (September 1977): 439–48.
9. Robert V. Duffey, "What to Do?" *The Reading Teacher* (November 1973): 132–33.

SUGGESTED READINGS

Bean, Rita M. and Wilson, Robert M. *Effecting Change in School Reading Programs.* Newark, Delaware: International Reading Association, 1981. A thorough discussion of the reading resource role is presented in this book, with practical suggestions for making this role a successful one.

Clague, Monique W. "Competency Testing and Potential Constitutional Challenges of Every Student." *Catholic University Law Review* 28, no. 3 (Summer 1979): 469–509. Clague cites court cases relating to competency testing and discusses their implications.

Cohn, Stella M., and Cohn, Jack. *Teaching the Retarded Reader.* New York: Odyssey Press, 1967. The authors discuss in detail the roles and responsibilities of reading personnel in establishing and administering reading programs. Based on experience in the New York city schools, this book offers many practical suggestions.

Combs, Arthur; Avila, Donald L.; and Purkey, William W. *Helping Relationships.* Boston: Allyn & Bacon, 1971. This book provides an interesting discussion of the ways people relate to one another. It also provides specific suggestions for developing successful strategies when working as a resource to others.

Harper, Robert J., and Kilarr, Gary, eds. *Reading and the Law.* Newark, Del.: IRA, 1978. Seven articles regarding the law and the reader are presented. Written for lay persons, this book should be a must reading for all educational decision makers.

Koskinen, Patricia S. and Wilson, Robert M. *Developing a Successful Tutoring Program.* New York: Teachers College Press, 1982. Provides information for getting a tutoring program started and keeping it going, with general as well as specific teaching strategies. Two companion booklets, one for adults and one for student tutors, are also available.

McClung, Merle S. "Competency Testing: Potential for Discrimination." *Clearinghouse Review* (September 1977): 439–48. McClung discusses six potential areas of legal difficulty in the use and interpretation of competency testing as a criterion for high school graduation.

Robinson, H. Alan, and Rauch, Sidney J. *Guiding the Reading Program.* Chicago: SRA, 1965. The reader will find this entire book an excellent source of information. Subtitled *A Reading Consultant's Handbook,* the emphasis is on developing reader insights into all aspects of the reading program from the specialist's viewpoint. This, it would seem, is required reading for the reading specialist.

Roserand, Nancy and Frith, Margaret eds. *Teaching with Books Children Like.* Newark, Del.: IRA, 1983. Practical suggestions for using trade books in the classroom to stimulate the desire to read. Includes a very interesting chapter on writing by children for children.

Editorial

Suzanne Clewell
is an educational specialist for the Montgomery County Public Schools in Maryland.

The resource role of the reading specialist in providing in-service education for teachers is an essential function that is often misunderstood by classroom teachers. Classroom teachers may view the reading specialist, their peer, as suspect in this role. However, in a leadership role, the reading specialist is often asked by the principal to provide in-service sessions for a variety of purposes.

Since time is precious in the instructional day, in-service sessions should be planned with a clear focus as efficiently as possible. Providing teachers with a written agenda stating objectives of the session helps to establish this purpose. One purpose may be to inform teachers of new curriculum materials adopted by the school district. In this case, modeling a specific lesson with teachers as learners is most effective. For example, if characterization is an instructional objective, the reading teacher could teach the lesson showing how to compare character traits from two folk tales. The teachers would be actively involved as the audience. In this way, teachers can take the demonstrated lesson and adapt it to their materials and student groups. It is important that interesting material be used and that the reading specialist does not "talk down" to the audience. Occasionally, adult reading material can be used as the source for a specific activity. A creative and enthusiastic idea which involves the audience as participants is more likely to be accepted than a lecture format with presentation of information.

Long-range planning of instructional units is a school-wide purpose which the reading specialist can begin to address in an in-service session. Teachers welcome a format to use and appreciate a "sample plan" using their materials by grade level. From this sample, teachers can identify specific objectives and units to be taught and plot out their own plan. Individual follow-up sessions may be necessary to complete the task. If reading specialists are involved, they have a clear picture of how they might team with teachers in assisting students with remedial needs.

Another school-wide in-service need may be to assist teachers with appropriate diagnostic strategies using their basal materials. The reading specialist can provide the guidelines for developing the informal assessment and establish the in-service time as a work session for teachers to prepare questions for passages. During the session, the reading specialist can assist individual teachers. Classroom teachers value productive time in making an assessment measure they understand and can use.

A final school-wide purpose for in-service sessions is to share new instructional strategies or new ideas from conferences and journal articles that may have an impact on the school-wide reading program. Both primary and intermediate levels of students should be addressed in this effort. For example, if the reading specialist shares a vocabulary strategy, it is useful to show its application with both easy and more difficult materials. A way to assess appropriateness for total staff is to survey teachers in their needs and provide the information which is most widely requested.

Glossary

The number that appears in parenthesis following the definition denotes the chapter in which the term first appears.

acuity The sharpness of vision or hearing. (3)

aliteracy A lack of desire to read despite possessing average or above-average reading ability. (1)

amblyopia Visual difficulty resulting from suppression of the vision in one eye (sometimes called lazy eye). (3)

articulation The ability to speak clearly and distinctly. (7)

auding The ability to listen to and comprehend oral language. (3)

audiometer A screening device used to test ability to hear at various pitches and levels of loudness. (3)

baseline In single subject research, the observed behavior of a student prior to an intervention (11)

binocular fusion The ability of the brain to construct a single image from the sensory input of both eyes. (3)

cloze test A test constructed by deleting selected words from a passage. (4)

comprehension The ability to make sense of spoken or written language. (1)

concurrent validity Establishing test validity by comparing a given test to another well-regarded test of similar abilities. (3)

content validity Establishing test validity by an expert examination of test items. (3)

context Skill in identifying unknown words through use of meaning cues in the test. (4)

criterion-referenced test (CRT) A test comprised of items matched to specific educational objectives (sometimes called a mastery test). (4)

dialect A language variation that is common to a region or group and that has certain identifiable characteristics. (1)

dialect transfer The ability of a language user to adapt the dialect used to the demands of a social situation. (7)

discrimination The ability to either see or hear likenesses and differences. (3)

dominance preference Study of the consistent use of the muscles on one side of the body as governed by the brain. (5)

dyslexic A label often used by medical professionals to describe a reader who is experiencing severe reading difficulties. (1)

free reading Reading sessions in materials of the reader's choice which is not followed by questioning. (9)

frustration level The level at which materials may be considered too difficult for a student to read successfully, even when given assistance. (4)

functional literacy A term used to describe a person who lacks minimal reading and writing skills necessary for everyday living. (1)

gain scores Differences in student performance between pretest and post-test results. (11)

grapheme A printed symbol. (4)

halo effect The tendency of respondents on self-report instruments to attempt to cast themselves in favorable light. (11)

independent level The level at which a reader can successfully read without assistance. (4)

independent variable The factor in an experimental research study that is manipulated by the researcher. (11)

Individualized Education Program (IEP) A written plan required by law which details the current levels of performance, special services, and educational goals and objectives for each student who has been identified as requiring special education. (1)

informal reading inventory (IRI) A test developed from materials used for reading instruction. (4)

instructional level The level at which a reader can successfully read if given necessary assistance. (4)

intelligence quotient (IQ) An estimate of a person's intellectual potential which is derived by dividing a person's mental age by that person's chronological age and multiplying by one hundred. (3)

intervention In an educational research study, the action on the part of the researcher that is intended to produce learning. (11)

language disabled A label used to identify a person who experiences difficulty in comprehending or using language. (1)

learning disabled A label used to identify persons of average or above-average intellectual ability who demonstrate difficulties in acquiring specific academic skills. (1)

learning modalities Those sensory systems through which a student evidences the greatest strengths. (5)

lockstepping The tendency for students who are placed in groups or materials to remain in those groups or materials despite evidence that such placement may be inappropriate. (13)

mainstreaming The educational practice of placing a handicapped student in a regular classroom for all or part of the school day. (10)

maze test A variation on cloze testing in which three alternatives are presented in place of the deleted word. (4)

mental age (MA) An estimate of a person's intellectual potential which is derived by multiplying a person's intelligence quotient by that person's chronological age and dividing by one hundred. (3)

minimal brain dysfunction A label used to identify students who experience learning difficulties which are attributed to presumed brain damage. (1)

neurological disorders Difficulties associated with malfunctions of the central nervous system. (3)

ocular motility Movements of the eye encompassing such abilities as fixations, pursuit, saccadic movement, accommodation, and convergence. (3)

orientation The ability of the eyes to maintain proper spatial relationships on a page. (5)

paired scale A forced choice test which requires a student to express a preference between pairs of words, activities, etc. (11)

percentile A statistical means of reporting test performance which designates the point on the normal curve at or below which a given percentage of students scored on the test. (4)

phonics Use of sound–symbol relationships in identifying unknown words. (1)

predictive validity The degree to which a score on a given test can be used to forecast future performance. (3)

Public Law 94–142 A federal law enacted to provide protective safeguards for handicapped students. (1)

readability The relative difficulty of a given piece of reading material for a student. (4)

reading expectancy level An estimate of a student's reading potential which may be useful in helping to set realistic goals for that student. (3)

regression Those portions of student scores that are obtained by chance will tend to move toward the mean on subsequent testing. (11)

reliability A statistical term used to designate the ability of a test to measure consistently. (3)

reliability coefficient A decimal measurement of test consistency. (3)

reluctant reader A person who possesses reading skills but who is not inclined to read. (9)

semantic The system of language which governs meaning. (4)

sight vocabulary Words that are recognized instantly and accurately regardless of the context in which they are encountered. (4)

Snellen Chart A screening device for visual acuity at a distance of twenty feet. (3)

specific reading disability A term used to identify difficulty in reading which is attributable to poor perceptual processing. (1)

standard error of measurement An estimate of test reliability which represents the relationship between a student's obtained score and that student's hypothetical "true" score. (3)

standardized test A test, often of achievement, in which standards of performance have been determined by the average performances of large groups of students. (4)

stanine A statistical means of reporting test performance which divides the normal curve into nine parts. (4)

stereopsis Visual ability to judge relative distances and depth. (3)

strabismus Vision disorder resulting from poor eye muscle coordination. (3)

structural analysis Skill in identifying unknown words through use of meaningful parts of words (such as prefixes, suffixes, etc.). (4)

summated rating scale A test which requires responses to be made to statements on a continuum (usually a five point scale). (11)

Sustained Silent Reading (SSR) Time set aside in the school day for students and the teacher to read silently from materials of their choice. (11)

syntactic The system of language which governs the arrangement of words into meaningful patterns. (4)

telebinocular A screening device for a wide variety of vision abilities. (3)

validity The ability of a test to measure what it purports to measure. (3)

validity coefficient A decimal measurement of a test's ability to measure what it claims to measure. (3)

word attack skills Those skills that a reader brings to bear in identifying an unknown word. (1)

Appendix A
Diagnostic Instruments

Appendix A, provided for the reader's reference, is based on the tests that were cited in this book. No effort has been made to include all known reading tests, nor have evaluations of the tests' merits been included. For that type of information the reader should refer to Buros's *Reading Tests and Review*.

The age range of each test is approximated. In diagnosis the use of a test will depend on the instructional level, not the age, of the child. The educator must determine this instructional level and then select the appropriate test.

Administration time for tests often varies with a child's age. The reader should accept these times as approximate—a factor that may determine whether a test is used in a particular situation.

Publishers are coded. The key to the codes is in appendix C. The reader is referred to the publisher for the tests' costs, specific directions, and other useful information.

Name of Test	No. of Forms	Type	Age Range	Approximate Administration Time, Reading Section	Evaluates: Speed	Comprehension	Vocabulary	Word Attack	Spelling	Auding	Other	Publisher's Code
DIAGNOSTIC												
Woodcock Reading Mastery	2	Individual	7–11	10–30 min.		X	X	X				AGS
California Phonics Survey	2	Group	13–20	40 min.				X				CAL
Diagnostic Reading Scales	1	Individual	6–14	1 hr.	X	X	X	X		X		CAL
Diagnostic Reading Tests	2–4	Group and Individual	5–13	Varies	X	X	X	X				CDRT
Diagnostic Reading Test (Bond-Balow-Hoyt)	1	Group	8–14	90 min.				X		X		LC
Doren Diagnostic Reading Test	1	Group	8–12	3 hrs.			X	X				ETB
Durrell Analysis of Reading Difficulties	1	Individual	6–12	40–60 min.	X	X	X	X	X			HBJ
Gates-McKillop Reading Diagnostic Test	2	Individual	6–12	1 hr.	X		X	X	X	X		TC
Gilmore Oral Reading Test	2	Individual	6–14	15 min.	X	X	X	X				HBJ
Gray Oral Reading Test	4	Individual	6–18	15 min.	X	X	X	X				BM

Monroe-Sherman Group Diagnostic Reading Aptitude and Achievement Tests	1	Group	8–14	90 min.	X	X	X	X	X		Arithmetic	NEV
Reading Versatility Test	2	Group	11–15 16–Adult	25 min.	X	X						EDL
The Roswell-Chall Diagnostic Reading Test of Word Analysis Skills	2		7–12	5–10 min.				X				EP
Standard Reading Inventory	1	Individual	6–14	40–50 min.	X	X	X					PP
Woodcock-Johnson Psycho-Educational Battery	1	Individual	6–Adult	2 hrs.	X	X	X	X	X	X		DTR
INTELLIGENCE												
California Test of Mental Maturity	1	Group	5–6 6–8 9–13 12–14 14–19 15–21	50 min.							Language and non-language	CAL
ACHIEVEMENT												
Botel Reading Inventory Revised	2	Individual and Group	6–18	15–30 min.			X	X	X			FOL
California Achievement Tests	2	Group	6.5–7 7–9 9–11 11–14 14–17	2 hrs. 2 hrs. 2½ hrs. 2½ hrs.		X	X	X	X		Language, Math, Reference skills	CAL
Dolch Basic Sight Words	1	Individual	6–8	15 min.			X					GP

Name of Test	No. of Forms	Type	Age Range	Approximate Administration Time, Reading Section	Evaluates:							Publisher's Code
					Speed	Comprehension	Vocabulary	Word Attack	Spelling	Auding	Other	
ACHIEVEMENT												
Durrell Listening Reading Series	1	Group	Prim. 6–8 Inter. 9–12	80 min.		X	X			X	Compares listening ability with reading achievement	HBJ
Gates MacGinitie Reading Tests	2*	Group	6–7 7–8 8–9 9–11 11–14 14–17	40 min. 40 min. 50 min. 45 min. 44 min. 44 min.	 X X X			X X X X X X		X X X X X X		TC
Iowa Test of Basic Skills	2	Group	8–14	70 min.		X	X				Language, Work-Study, Arithmetic	HMC
Metropolitan Achievement Tests	4	Group	6–8 9–12 12–18	50 min.		X	X			X	Science, Language, Arithmetic, Social Studies	HBJ
Stanford Achievement Tests	4	Group	6–8 8–9 10–12 12–15	45 min.		X	X				Arithmetic, Study, Science, Social Studies	HBJ

*There are three forms for age levels 9–11 and 11–14.

The Test of Reading Comprehension	1	Group	7–14			X	X				Syntactic similarities, Content area vocabularies, Reading directions	PE
INTELLIGENCE												
Durrell Listening Series	1	Group	5–7 8–11 12–14	25 min.						X	Part of Durrell Listening-Reading Series	HBJ
Full Range Picture Vocabulary	2	Individual	2–Adult	10–15 min.						X		PTS
Illinois Test of Psycholinguistic Abilities	1	Individual	2–10	1 hr.							Language development	UIP
Kaufman Assessment Battery for Children	1	Individual	2.5–12	30–50 min.							Sequential processing, Simultaneous processing, Achievement	AGS
Peabody Picture Vocabulary Test	2	Individual	2.5–18	15 min.						X		AGS
Slosson Intelligence Test	1	Individual	2–Adult	10–30 min.							General mental maturity	SEP
Stanford-Binet Intelligence Scale	1	Individual	2–Adult	1 hr.							General mental maturity	HMC
Wechsler Intelligence Scale for Children—Revised	1	Individual	5–15	1 hr.							Verbal performance	PSY

Name of Test	No. of Forms	Type	Age Range	Approximate Administration Time, Reading Section	Evaluates: Speed	Comprehension	Vocabulary	Word Attack	Spelling	Auding	Other	Publisher's Code
SCREENING TESTS												
Keystone Visual Survey Telebinocular	1	Individual	5–Adult	15 min.							Far and near point visual skills	KEY
Reading Eye Camera	1	Individual	6–20	10 min.							Photo-graph eye motion	EDL
Spache-Binocular Reading Tests	1	Individual	5–Adult	5 min.							Binocular reading efficiency	KEY
Vision: Concepts about Print	1	Individual	5–7	5–10 min.								HP
Auditory: Audiometer	1	Individual or Group	3–Adult	15 min.							Auditory acuity	MAI
Test of Auditory Discrimination	1	Individual	5–8	20 min.							Auditory discrimina-tion	AGS
Wepman Auditory Discrimination Test	2	Individual	5–10	10 min.							Auditory discrimina-tion	JMW
Personality: The Cal-ifornia Test of Per-sonality	2	Group	5–8 9–13 13–15 14–21	50 min.							Personal and social adjustment	CAL

Dominance: Harris Test of Lateral Dominance	1	Individual	5–Adult	5 min.							Hand, eye and foot dominance	PSY
STUDY SKILLS												
California Study Method Survey	1	Group	12–18	40 min.							Study habits	CAL
ATTITUDE												
Heathington Attitude Scale	2	Group	6–8 9–11								Attitude	IRA
Survey of Study Habits and Attitudes—Brown Holtzman	1	Group	14–21	20 min.							Study habits	PSY
PERCEPTION												
Frostig Developmental Test of Visual Perception	1	Group and Individual	3–8	30–45 min. (Ind.) 40–60 min. (Gr.)							5 aspects of visual perception	CPP
Purdue Perceptual Motor Survey	1	Individual		1 hr.							Perceptual motor abilities	CEM

Appendix B
Remedial Materials

Appendix B provides a reference for reading aids. Specific information concerning these materials may be found in publishers' catalogues and brochures. The publishers' key may be used by checking appendix C.

Many of the cited materials may be used in a variety of ways to help problem readers. The use cited is based upon experience but in no way is intended to suggest that the material should be limited to these functions.

The suggested age level must be considered flexible and regarded as the most advanced level. The educator will find many of these materials used with children of older age and interest levels.

Teacher-made materials are often more suitable to meet the needs of children experiencing severe difficulty with reading. Teachers should take opportunities to update their knowledge concerning materials for instruction continuously. Most journals carry reviews of materials periodically. *Reading Teacher* carries a section on new material each year [e.g., "New Materials On the Market," *Reading Teacher* 32, no. 5 (Feb. 1979): 548–79].

Primarily Designed to Assist in Instruction of	Name of Material	Reading Level	Interest Level	Format	Publisher
ALL SKILLS	1. Action Reading System	E	S	Kit	SBS
	2. Addison-Wesley Reading Program	E	E	Basal	AD
	3. Audio Reading Kits	E	E	Kit	EPC
	4. Be A Better Reader	S	S	Workbook	PH
	5. Breaking the Code	E	E/S	Workbook	OP
	6. Breakthrough to Literacy	E	E	Kit	BOW
	7. Careers	E/S	E/S	Kit	HBJ
	8. Clues to Reading Progress	E	E/S	Kit	EPC
	9. Comics Reading Libraries	E	E/S	Kit	KIN
	10. Controlled Reader	E/S	E/S	Machine	EDL
	11. DISTAR Reading Activity Kit	E	E	Kit	SRA
	12. F.A.C.T.	E/S	E	Kit	RAI
	13. GO	E/S	E/S	Workbook	SBS
	14. The Hilltop Series	E	E	Books	AB
	15. Language Master	E/S	E/S	Machine	BHC
	16. Leavell Language Development Service	E	E	Machine	CLB
	17. Let's Read	E	E	Basal	CLB
	18. Merrill Linguistic Readers	E	E	Basal	CEM
	19. Merrill Reading Skill Text	E	E	Books	CEM
	20. The New Kaleidoscope Readers	E/S	S	Books	AD
	21. Newslab	E/S	E/S	Kit	SRA
	22. Open Highways	E/S	E/S	Basal	SF
	23. Palo Alto Sequential Steps	E	E	Basals	HBJ
	24. Peabody Rebus Reading Program	E	E	Kit	AGS
	25. Phoenix Reading Series	E	E/S	Workbook	PH
	26. Phonetic Keys to Reading	E	E	Basal	EC
	27. Plays for Reading Progress	E/S	E/S	Kit	EPC
	28. Point 31	E	E/S	Kit	RDS
	29. Quick Skills	E	E	Kit	COR
	30. RD 2000	E	S	Kit	RDS
	31. Read Alongs	E	E	Books	SP
	32. Read Better Learn More	E/S	E/S	Workbook	Ginn
	33. Reading Accelerator	E/S	E/S	Machine	SRA
	34. Reading Attainment System	E/S	E/S	Kit	AAP
	35. The Reading Box	E/S	E/S	Act. Cards	EI
	36. Reading Laboratory	E/S	E/S	Kit	SRA
	37. Reading Response Cards	E	E/S	Act. Cards	CTP
	38. Reading Skill Builders	S	S	Kit	RDS
	39. Reading Tactics	S	S	Workbooks	SF
	40. Reading Work-A-Text	E	E	Workbook	CAM
	41. Scope Skills Book	E	E/S	Workbook	SBS
	42. Signals	S	S	Basals	SF
	43. Spotlight on Reading	E/S	E/S	Workbook	RH

	44. Sprint Reading Skills Program	E	E	Kit	SBS
	45. SRA Basic Reading Series	E	E	Basal	SRA
	46. Super Kits	E	E/S	Basal	SF
	47. Tachistoscope	E/S	E/S	Machine	KEY
	48. Taskmaster Cards	E	E	Cards	RA
	49. Teaching Reading Through Creative Movements	E	E	Kit	KIM
	50. Text Extenders	E	E	Kit	SBS
	51. The Thinking Box	E/S	E/S	Act. Cards	BP
	52. Top-Pick Readers	E/S	E/S	Books	RDS
	53. Troll Talking Dictionary	E	E	Book	TA
	54. Troll Read Alongs	E	E	Books	TA
	55. Troll I Can Read Series	E	E	Books	TA
	56. Websters Reading Centers	E/S	E/S	Kit	WMcH
COMPREHENSION	1. Adventures in Mystery	E	E	Kit	EI
	2. Adventures in Reading	E	E	Workbook	SCH
	3. Amazing Adventures	E	E	Kit	NY
	4. Best in Children's Literature	E	E	Kit	BOW
	5. Better Reading Books	E/S	E/S	Books	SRA
	6. Bill Martin Instant Readers	E	E	Books	HRW
	7. Bookshop	E	E	Kit	DCH
	8. Breakthrough	S	S	Kit	AB
	9. Camera Patterns	E	E	Books	SAD
	10. Comprehension Games Kits	E	E	Games	CGC
	11. Comprehension Skills Laboratory	E/S	E/S	Kit	BFA
	12. Comprehension We Use	E	E	Workbook	RM
	13. Counterpoint Skill Power Builder	E	E	Kit	COR
	14. Detecting the Sequence	E	E	Workbook	BL
	15. Developing Reading Comprehension Skills	E/S	E/S	Workbook	OC
	16. Drawing Conclusions	E	E	Workbook	BL
	17. Following Directions	E	E	Workbook	BL
	18. Getting the Facts	E	E	Workbook	BL
	19. Getting the Main Idea	E	E	Workbook	BL
	20. Guinness Book of World Records	E	E/S	Kit	SIN
	21. Incentive Language Program	E/S	E/S	Kit	BOW
	22. Invitations to Personal Reading	E	E	Kit	SF
	23. Listen and Think Series	E	E/S	Kit	EDL
	24. The Literature Sampler	S	S	Kit	LM
	25. Locating the Answer	E	E	Workbook	BL
	26. The Monster Books	E	E	Books	BOW
	27. Narrative Writing	E/S	E/S	Kit	PPP
	28. National Football League Kit	E	E/S	Kit	BOW
	29. New Practice Readers	E	E/S	Workbook	WMcH
	30. Nichols Slides	E/S	E/S	Tachistoscope Materials	KEY

Key: E = elementary, S = secondary, E/S = elementary/secondary.

Primarily Designed to Assist in Instruction of	Name of Material	Reading Level	Interest Level	Format	Publisher
COMPREHENSION	31. The Owl Books	E	E	Books	HRW
	32. Pilot Library	E/S	E/S	Kit	SRA
	33. Practicing Reading	E/S	E/S	Workbook	RH
	34. Reader's Workshop	E/S	E/S	Kit	RDS
	35. Reading Comprehension Basic Skills Centers	E	E	Kit	SCH
	36. Reading Comprehension Kits	E	E	Kit	EI
	37. Reading for Concepts	E	E/S	Workbook	WMcH
	38. Reading for Understanding	E/S	E/S	Kit	SRA
	39. Reading Incentive Program	E/S	E/S	Kit	BOW
	40. Reading Skilltexts	E/S	E/S	Books	CEM
	41. Reading, Thinking and Reasoning	E/S	E/S	Workbook	SV
	42. Scholastic Literature Kits	S	S	Kit	SBS
	43. Scholastic Pleasure Reading Library	E/S	E/S	Kit	SBS
	44. Short Stories Around the World	E	E	Kit	EI
	45. Six-Way Paragraphs	S	S	Workbook	JAM
	46. Spotlight on Reading	E/S	E/S	Workbook	RH
	47. Spotlight on Writing	E/S	E/S	Workbook	RH
	48. Sprint Libraries	E	E	Books	SBS
	49. Standard Test Lessons in Reading	E/S	E/S	Workbooks	TC
	50. Star Wars Attack on Reading	E	E/S	Workbook	RH
	51. The Superstars Series	E/S	S	Workbook	SV
	52. Target Copper—Reading Comprehension Kit	E	E/S	Kit	AD
	53. Top Flight Readers	E	E/S	Books	AD
	54. Triple Action Unit	E	S	Kit	SBS
	55. Triple Takes	E/S	E/S	Workbook	RDS
	56. Understanding Questions	E	E	Workbook	DW
	57. Understanding What We Read	E	E	Kit	NY
	58. Using the Context	E	E	Workbook	BL
	59. Visual-Lingual Reading Program	E	E	Transparencies	TT
FUNCTIONAL READING	1. Following Directions	S	S	Visuals	SBS
	2. Getting Applications Right	S	S	Visuals	SBS
	3. I Can Make It On My Own	E	E	Resource Book	GO
	4. The Job Ahead	E	S	Workbook	SRA
	5. Reading Contracts and Forms	S	S	Visuals	SBS
	6. Reading for Survival	E	S	Workbook	CAM
	7. Reading for the Real World	E/S	S	Workbook	CEM
	8. Reading Skills for the Real World	E	S	Kit	BFA
	9. Real Life Reading Skills	E	S	Kit	SBS
	10. Real Life Reading	E	E/S	Kit	INST
	11. Scoring High in Survival Reading	S	S	Workbook	RH
	12. Survival Guides	E	S	Workbook	JAN
	13. What's Cooking	E	E	Kit	BOW

STUDY SKILLS	1. Dictionary Skills	E	E/S	Workbook	CA
	2. EDL Study Skills Library	E/S	E/S	Kit	EDL
	3. Graph and Picture Study Skills Kit	E	E/S	Kit	SRA
	4. Life Skills Reading Books	E/S	E/S	Books	CP
	5. Map and Globe Skills Kit	E/S	E/S	Kit	SRA
	6. Organizational Skills	E	E/S	Workbook	CA
	7. Organizing and Reporting Skills Kit	E	E	Kit	SRA
	8. Outline Building	E/S	E/S	Kit	CA
	9. Reading for Meaning	E/S	E/S	Workbook	JBL
	10. Reading, Researching & Reporting in Science	E	E/S	Kit	BFA
	11. Reading, Researching & Reporting in Social Studies	E	E/S	Kit	BFA
	12. Reading without Words: How to Interpret Graphic Material	E/S	E/S	Workbook	SBS
	13. Research & Study Skills Centers	E/S	E/S	Kit	CA
	14. Research Lab	E	E/S	Kit	SRA
	15. Skimming & Scanning	S	S	Workbook	JAM
	16. Study Skills for Information Retrieval	E/S	E/S	Workbook	AB
	17. Super Syllabo	E/S	E/S	Game	CA
	18. Syllabo	E/S	E/S	Game	CA
	19. Target Purple—Study Skills Kit	E/S	E/S	Kit	AD
	20. Thirty Lessons in Outlining	E	E/S	Workbook	CA
READINESS	1. Adventures in Living	E	E	Books	WP
	2. Alpha Time	E	E	Kit	AR
	3. Auditory Discrimination Kit	E	E	Kit	DLM
	4. Auditory Discrimination in Depth	E	E	Kit	TR
	5. Beaded Alphabet Cards	E	E	Cards	ID
	6. Boehm Kit	E	E	Kit	DLM
	7. Building Pre-reading Skills Kit-A-Language	E	E	Kit	Ginn
	8. Concepts for Communication	E	E	Kit	DLM
	9. Developing Pre-reading Skills	E	E	Kit	HRW
	10. Follow the Path	E	E	Act. Cards	TE
	11. Goal	E	E	Kit	MB
	12. Goldman-Lynch Sound & Symbols—Development Program	E	E	Kit	AD
	13. Happily Ever After	E	E	Kit	AD
	14. Invitations to Story Time	E	E	Books	SF
	15. Kindergarten Basic Skills Center	E	E	Kit	SCH
	16. Language Activity Cards	E	E	Kit	SAD
	17. Learning Basic Skills Through Music	E	E	Record	EA
	18. Listening	E	E	Kit	DLM
	19. Listening to the World	E	E	Kit	AR
	20. Peabody Language Development Kit	E	E	Kit	AGS
	21. Peg Board with Designs	E	E	Act. Cards	DLM
	22. Pick Pairs	E	E	Game	GP
	23. Picture Readiness Game	E	E	Game	GP

Primarily Designed to Assist in Instruction of	Name of Material	Reading Level	Interest Level	Format	Publisher
READINESS	24. Read and Tell (Level 3)	E	E	Pictures	MAC
	25. The Reading Bridge	E	E	Kit	BFA
	26. Reading Visuals & Manipulatives	E	E	Kit	CAM
	27. Ready Steps	E	E	Kit	HMC
	28. Sequential Cards	E	E	Cards	INC
	29. Sesame Street Pre-reading Kit	E	E	Kit	AD
	30. Sound, Order, Sense	E	E	Kit	FOL
	31. Sweet Pickles—Early Childhood Program	E	E	Kit	BFA
	32. Sweet Pickles—Readiness Program	E	E	Kit	BFA
	33. Target Red: Auditory-Visual Discrimination Kit	E	E	Kit	AD
	34. Teaching Reading Through Creative Movements	E	E	Record	KIM
	35. Visual Discrimination	E	E	Ditto	CPP
	36. Visual Motor	E	E	Ditto	CPP
VOCABULARY	1. Basic Sight Cards	E	E	Cards	GP
	2. Compound Words	E	E	Game	DLM
	3. Developing Your Vocabulary	S	S	Workbook	SRA
	4. Gold Cup Games	E	E	Game	BOW
	5. Homonyms	E	E	Workbook	DW
	6. Homophone Cards	E	E	Game	DLM
	7. In Other Words	E	E	Book	SF
	8. Lessons for Self-Instruction	E	E/S	Kit	CAL
	9. Linguistic Block Series	E	E	Blocks	SF
	10. Match	E	E	Game	GP
	11. Non-Oral Reading Series	E	E	Books	PES
	12. Pictocabulary Series	E	E	Workbook	BL
	13. Picture Word Cards	E	E	Cards	GP
	14. Practical Vocabulary	E	S	Workbook	SBS
	15. Practicing Vocabulary in Context	E/S	E/S	Workbook	RH
	16. Sight Phrase Cards	E	E	Game	GP
	17. Spello Word Game	E	E	Game	ID
	18. Target Green—Vocabulary Development Kit 1	E/S	E/S	Kit	AD
	19. Target Orange—Vocabulary Development Kit 2	S	S	Kit	AD
	20. Understanding Word Groups	E	E	Workbook	DW
	21. Vocabulary Builder Series	E	E	Game	CA
	22. Vocabulary Improvement	E	S	Workbook	SBS
	23. Vocabulary Laboratories	E/S	E/S	Kit	BFA
	24. Words to Use	E	E	Book	SAD
WORD ATTACK	1. All About Reading Box	E	E	Kit	INC
	2. Alpha One	E	E	Kit	AR
	3. Basic Phonics Review Workbook	E	E	Workbook	JBL
	4. Consonant Lotto	E	E	Game	GP

5. Context-Phonetic Clues	E	E	Kit	CA
6. Durrell-Murphy Phonics Practice Program	E	E	Kit	HBJ
7. Get Set	E	E	Games	CA
8. Merrill Phonics Skill Text	E	E	Workbook	CEM
9. Patterns, Sounds and Meaning	E	E	Workbook	AB
10. Phonics for Fun	E	E	Kit	AR
11. Phonics Rummy	E	E	Game	KEN
12. Phonics Skilltexts	E	E	Workbook	CEM
13. Phonics We Use	E	E	Workbook	MCP
14. Phonics We Use	E	E	Game Kit	RM
15. Prescription Games	E	E	Game	INN
16. Reading Lab 1—Word Games	E	E	Game Kit	SRA
17. Road Race	E	E	Game	CA
18. Schoolhouse Kits	E	E	Kits	SRA
19. Sea of Vowels	E	E	Game	ID
20. Sound Hunt	E	E	Game	APA
21. Sounds Floor Games	E	E	Game	SIN
22. Speech to Print Phonics	E	E	Kit	HBJ
23. Spelling Learning Games Kits	E	E	Game Kit	RM
24. Sweet Pickles Phonics Program	E	E	Kit	BFA
25. Syllabication	E	E	Workbook	DW
26. The Syllable Game	E	E	Game	GP
27. Take	E	E	Game	GP
28. Target Blue: Structural Analysis Kit	E	E/S	Kit	AD
29. Target Yellow: Phonetic Analysis Kit	E	E	Kit	AD
30. Vowel Lotto	E	E	Game	GP
31. What the Letters Say	E	E	Game	GP
32. Word Analysis Kit	E	E	Kit	CA
33. Word Game Safari	E	E	Game	BFA
34. Working with Sounds	E	E	Workbook	BL
35. Working with Words	E	E	Workbook	Ginn
36. Webster Classroom Reading Clinic	E	E	Kit	WMcH

Appendix C
Key to Publisher's Code

AAP Ann Arbor Publishers
611 Church Street
Ann Arbor, Michigan
48104

AB Allyn & Bacon Inc.
470 Atlantic Avenue
Boston, Massachusetts
02210

AD Addison-Wesley
Publishing Company
Sand Hill Road
Menlo Park, California
94025

AGS American Guidance
Service
Publishers' Building
Circle Pines, Minnesota
55014

APA American Publishing
Aids
Covina, California
91722

AR Artista Corporation
P.O. Box 6146
Concord, California
94524

AVR Audio-Visual Research
1509 Eighth Street,
S.E.
Waseca, Minnesota
56093

BFA BFA Educational
Media
2211 Michigan
Avenue,
Dept. 3064
Santa Monica,
California 90406

BHC Bell & Howell Company
7100 McCormick Road
Chicago, Illinois 60645

BL Barnell Loft, Ltd.
111 S. Centre Avenue
Rockville Centre, New York 11571

BM The Bobbs Merrill Company
P.O. Box 558
4300 West 62 Street
Indianapolis, Indiana 46206

BOW Bowmar/Noble Publishers, Inc.
4563 Colorado Boulevard
Los Angeles, California 90039

BP Benefic Press
1250 Sixth Ave.
San Diego, California 92101

CA Curriculum Associates
94 Bridge Street
Chapel Bridge Park
Newton, Massachusetts 12158

CAL California Test Bureau
CTB/McGraw-Hill
Del Monte Research Park
Monterey, California 93940

CAM Cambridge Book Company
888 Seventh Ave.
New York, N.Y. 10106

CDRT The Committee on Diagnostic Reading Tests
Mountain Home, North Carolina 28758

CEM Charles E. Merrill Publishing Company
1300 Alum Creek Drive
Columbus, Ohio 43216

CLB Clarence L. Barnhart Reference Books
Box 359
Bronxville, New York 10708

CGC Comprehension Games Corp.
63-110 Woodhaven Blvd.
Rego Park, N.Y. 11374

COR Coronet Learning Programs
68 East South Water Street
Chicago, Illinois 60601

CP Creative Publications
P.O. Box 10328
Palo Alto, California 94303

CPP Consulting Psychologists Press
Palo Alto, California 94306

CTP Creative Teaching Press
514 Hermosa Vistas Avenue
Monterey Park, California 91754

DCH DC Heath & Company
125 Spring Street
Lexington, Massachusetts 02173

DLM Developmental Learning Materials
7440 Natchey Avenue
Niles, Illinois 60648

DTR Diagnostic Teaching Resources Corp.
50 Pond Park Road
Hingham, Massachusetts 02043

DW Dexter & Westbrook Ltd.
958 Church Street
Baldwin, New York 11510

EA Educational Activities
P.O. Box 392
Freeport, New York 11520

EC The Economy Company
1901 N. Walnut Street
Oklahoma City, Oklahoma 73125

EDL Educational Development Laboratories
Huntington, New York 11746

EI Educational Insights
150 West Carob
Compton, California 90220

ENC Encyclopedia Britannica Educational Corporation
425 N. Michigan Avenue
Chicago, Illinois 60611

EP Essay Press
P.O. Box 5
New York, New York 10024

EPC Educational Progress Corporation
P.O. Box 45663
Tulsa, Oklahoma 74145

ETB Educational Test Bureau
720 Washington Avenue, S.E.
Minneapolis, Minnesota 55414

FOL Follett Publishing Company
1010 W. Washington Boulevard
Chicago, Illinois 60607

Ginn Ginn & Company
191 Spring Street
Lexington, Massachusetts 02173

GO Goodyear Publishing Company
1640 Fifth Street
Santa Monica, California 90401

GP The Garrard Press
1607 North Market Street
Champaign, Illinois, 61820

HBJ Harcourt Brace Jovanovich Inc.
757 Third Avenue
New York, New York 10017

HM Heinemann Publishers
4 Front Street
Exeter, New Hampshire 03833

HMC Houghton Mifflin Company
One Beacon Street
Boston, Massachusetts 02108

HRW Holt, Rinehart and Winston
521 Fifth Ave.
6th Floor
New York, N.Y. 10175

ID Ideal
Oak Lawn, Illinois 60453

INC Incentives for Learning
600 West Van Buren Street
Chicago, Illinois 60607

INN Innovations for Individualizing Instruction
P.O. Box 4361
Washington, D.C. 20012

INST Instructo Corp.
A Division of McGraw-Hill
Paoli, Pennsylvania 19301

IOWA The State University of Iowa
Bureau of Audio-Visual Instruction
Iowa City, Iowa 52240

IRA IRA
800 Barksdale Road
Newark, Delaware 19711

JAM Jamestown Publishers
P.O. Box 6743
Providence, Rhode Island 02940

JAN Janus Book Publishers
2501 Industrial Parkway West
Hayward, California 94545

JBL J B Lippincott Company
East Washington Square
Philadelphia, Pennsylvania 19105

JMW Joseph M. Wepman, Ph.D.
950 East 59th Street
Chicago, Illinois 60637

KEN Kenworthy Education Service
P.O. Box 3031
Buffalo, New York 14205

KEY Keystone View Company
2212 East 12th Street
Davenport, Iowa 52803

KIM Kimbo Educational Records
Box 55
Deal, New Jersey 07723

KIN King Features
Department 1198
235 East 45th Street
New York, New York 10017

LC Lyons & Carnahan
407 E. 25th Street
Chicago, Illinois 60616

LM Learning Materials
100 East Ohio Street
Chicago, Illinois 60611

MAC The Macmillan Company
866 Third Avenue
New York, N.Y. 10022

MAI MAICO Hearing Instruments, Inc.
7375 Bush Lake Road
Minneapolis, Minnesota 55435

MB Milton Bradley Co.
Springfield, Massachusetts 01101

MCP Modern Curriculum Press Inc.
13900 Prospect Road
Cleveland, Ohio 44136

NEV Nevins Publishing Company
810 North Avenue West
Pittsburgh, Pennsylvania 15233

NY Nystrom
3333 Elston Avenue
Chicago, Illinois 60615

OC Oceana Educational Communications
P.O. Box 396
Chappaqua, New York 10514

OP Open Court Publishing Company
Box 599
1058 Eighth Street
Lasalle, Illinois 61301

PAR Programs for Achievement in Reading
Abbott Park Place
Providence, Rhode Island 02903

PE PRO-ED
5341 Industrial Oak Blvd.
Austin, Texas 78735

PES Primary Educational Service
1243 West 79th Street
Chicago, Illinois 60649

PH Prentice-Hall
Englewood Cliffs, New Jersey 07632

PP Pioneer Printing Co.
Bellingham, Washington 98225

PPP Pied Piper Productions
P.O. Box 320
Verdugo City, California 91046

PSP Popular Science Publishing Co.
McGraw-Hill Text Film Dept.
1221 Avenue of the Americas
New York, New York 10020

PSY Psychological Corporation
757 Third Avenue
New York, New York 10017

PTS Psychological Test Specialist
Box 1441
Missoula, Montana 59801

RA Rodmar Associates
P.O. Box 354
Horsham, Pennsylvania 19044

RAI Raintree Publishers Group
205 W. Highland Avenue
Milwaukee, Wisconsin 53203

RDS Reader's Digest Services
Pleasantville, New York 10570

RE Reading Education
14506 Perrywood Drive
Burtonsville, Maryland 20730

RH Random House
201 East 50 Street
New York, N.Y. 10022

RM Rand McNally & Company
8255 Central Park Avenue
Skokie, Illinois 60676

SAD William H. Sadlier Inc.
11 Park Place
New York, New York 10007

SBS Scholastic Book Service
Sylvan Avenue
Englewood Cliffs, New Jersey 07018

SCH Frank Schaffer Publications
26616 Indian Park Road
Palos Verdes, California 90274

SEP Slosson Educational Publications Press
140 Pine Street
New York, New York 14052

SF Scott, Foresman & Company
1900 East Lake Ave.
Glenview, Illinois 60625

SIN Singer Education Division
1345 Diversey Parkway
Chicago, Illinois 60614

SP Sundance Paperbacks
Newton Road
Littleton, Massachusetts 01460

SRA Science Research Associates, Inc.
155 N. Wacker Drive
Chicago, Illinois 60606

SV Steck-Vaughn Company
P.O. Box 2028
Austin, Texas 78768

TA Troll Associates
320 Route 17
Mahwah, New Jersey 07430

TC Teachers College Press
Teachers College
Columbia University
1234 Amsterdam Avenue
New York, New York 10027

TE Trend Enterprises
P.O. Box 8623
White Bear Lake, Minnesota 55110

TR Teaching Resources
100 Boylston Street
Boston, Massachusetts 02116

TT Tweedy Transparencies
207 Hollywood Avenue
East Orange, New Jersey 17018

UIP University of Illinois Press
Box 5081
Station A
54 E. Gregory Drive
Champaign, Illinois 61820

WMcH Webster Division
McGraw-Hill Book Company
1154 Roco Avenue
St. Louis, Missouri 63126

WP Western Publishing Co. Inc.
1220 Mound Avenue
Racine, Wisconsin 53404

WWS Weston Woods Studios
Weston, Connecticut 06880

Appendix D

IRA Code of Ethics*

INTRODUCTION

The members of the International Reading Association who are concerned with the teaching of reading form a group of professional persons obligated to society and devoted to the service and welfare of individuals through teaching, clinical services, research, and publication. The members of this group are committed to values which are the foundation of a democratic society—freedom to teach, write, and study in an atmosphere conducive to the best interests of the profession. The welfare of the public, the profession, and the individuals concerned should be of primary consideration in recommending candidates for degrees, positions, advancements, the recognition of professional activity, and for certification in those areas where certification exists.

**Code of Ethics,* International Reading Association, Newark, Delaware. Reprinted by permission.

Ethical Standards in Professional Relationships

1. It is the obligation of all members of the International Reading Association to observe the Code of Ethics of the organization and to act accordingly so as to advance the status and prestige of the association and of the profession as a whole. Members should assist in establishing the highest professional standards for reading programs and services, and should enlist support for these through dissemination of pertinent information to the public.
2. It is the obligation of all members to maintain relationships with other professional persons, striving for harmony, avoiding personal controversy, encouraging cooperative effort, and making known the obligations and services rendered by the reading specialist.
3. It is the obligation of members to report results of research and other developments in reading.
4. Members should not claim nor advertise affiliation with the International Reading Association as evidence of their competence in reading.

Ethical Standards in Reading Services

1. Reading specialists must possess suitable qualifications . . . for engaging in consulting, clinical, or remedial work. Unqualified persons should not engage in such activities except under the direct supervision of one who is properly qualified. Professional intent and the welfare of the person seeking the services of the reading specialist should govern counseling, all consulting or clinical activities such as administering diagnostic tests, or providing remediation. It is the duty of the reading specialist to keep relationships with clients and interested persons on a professional level.
2. Information derived from consulting and/or clinical services should be regarded as confidential. Expressed consent of persons involved should be secured before releasing information to outside agencies.
3. Reading specialists should recognize the boundaries of their competence and should not offer services which fail to meet professional standards established by other disciplines. They should be free, however, to give assistance in other areas in which they are qualified.
4. Referral should be made to specialists in allied fields as needed. When such referral is made, pertinent information should be made available to consulting specialists.

5. Reading clinics and/or reading specialists offering professional services should refrain from guaranteeing easy solutions or favorable outcomes as a result of their work, and their advertising should be consistent with that of allied professions. They should not accept for remediation any persons who are unlikely to benefit from their instruction, and they should work to accomplish the greatest possible improvement in the shortest time. Fees, if charged, should be agreed on in advance and should be charged in accordance with an established set of rates commensurate with that of other professions.

Name Index

Subject Index

Robert M. Wilson

Bob Wilson is currently Professor of Education and Director of the Reading Center at the University of Maryland. He is the author or coauthor of numerous books and articles. His current research interests center upon the various aspects of reading comprehension. His writing reflects his public school teaching experiences as well as his work with students in the University of Maryland Reading Clinic and in the public schools of Maryland.

He is a Past President of the College Reading Association and has been honored by his undergraduate and graduate institutions for his work in the field of reading.

Craig Cleland

Craig Cleland is currently an Assistant Professor of Education at Mansfield University in Pennsylvania. His teaching responsibilities include undergraduate and graduate courses in reading education and children's literature. He has been widely published in professional journals and was a contributing author to a major elementary developmental reading series. A popular inservice speaker and consultant, he combines a dual background in elementary and special education with a practical approach to teacher education. In addition to teaching, speaking and writing, he serves on a wide variety of professional committees at university, local, state, and national levels.